FRONTIERS OF
FAMILY LAW

FRONTIERS OF FAMILY LAW

Editors

Part I – 1993

Andrew Bainham, LLB (Wales), LLM, PhD (Cantab), Solicitor
University Lecturer in Law,
University of Cambridge

and

Judge David Pearl, MA, LLM, PhD (Cantab)
Chief Adjudicator, Office of Immigration Appeals,
Honorary Professor, University of East Anglia, Norwich

Part II – 1995

Judge David Pearl, MA, LLM, PhD (Cantab)
Chief Adjudicator, Office of Immigration Appeals,
Honorary Professor, University of East Anglia, Norwich

and

Ros Pickford, MA (Cantab)
Centre for Family Research, University of Cambridge

**Centre for Family Law and Family Policy,
University of East Anglia, Norwich**

John Wiley & Sons
Chichester · New York · Brisbane · Toronto · Singapore

First edition published 1993

This second edition published in the United Kingdom in 1995 by

John Wiley & Sons Ltd,
Baffins Lane,
Chichester,
West Sussex,
PO19 1UD

National 01243 779777

International (+44) 1243 779777

On page 75

Two lines from "The Parent" by Ogden Nash
reprinted by permission of Curtis Brown Ltd
Copyright © 1933 Ogden Nash

Four lines from "This be the Verse" by Philip Larkin
reprinted by permission of Faber & Faber Ltd

Other Wiley Editorial Offices

John Wiley & Sons Inc., 605 Third Avenue,
New York, NY 10158-0012, USA

John Wiley & Sons Inc., Editorial, Administration & Marketing,
7222 Commerce Center Drive, Suite 240,
Colorado Springs, CO 80919

Jacaranda Wiley Ltd, 33 Park Road, Milton,
Queensland 4064, Australia

John Wiley & Sons (Canada) Ltd, 22 Worcester Road,
Rexdale, Ontario M9W 1L1, Canada

John Wiley & Sons (SEA) Pte Ltd, 37 Jalan Pemimpin #05-04,
Block B, Union Industrial Building, Singapore 2057

British Library Cataloguing Publication Data

A catalogue record for this book is available from the British Library

ISBN 0471 95730 5

Typeset in 10½/12pt Baskerville by The Setting Studio, Newcastle upon Tyne
Printed and bound in Great Britain by Bookcraft (Bath) Ltd
This book is printed on acid-free paper responsibly manufactured from sustainable forestation,
for which at least two trees are planted for each one used for paper production.

Contents

Preface

The Centre for Family Law and Family Policy at the University of East Anglia was established in 1990. The first series of seminars given by visitors to the centre gave rise to the essays published in 1993 under the title *Frontiers of Family Law*. A second collection of essays has resulted from the second series of seminars and it was decided to publish both collections of essays in one volume. The work of arranging the second series of seminars and editing the resulting essays has been undertaken by my former colleagues Ros Pickford and David Pearl, who was formerly Director of the Centre. It gives me great pleasure to acknowledge their valuable efforts in the work of the Centre in general and the preparation of this volume in particular. I am pleased to say that Judge Pearl, as he now is, will remain associated with the School and the Centre as an Honorary Professor.

Gareth Miller,
Director of the Centre for Family Law
and Policy and Dean of the School of
Law at the University of East Anglia,
Norwich

Part I

1993

Introduction

The papers in this volume derive from a series of seminars in the Centre for Family Law and Family Policy at the University of East Anglia, Norwich. The seminars were led by visiting scholars from Africa, America, Asia and Europe. The common theme of the papers is the law's response to critical policy issues affecting the family ranging from the legal and moral dilemmas of assisted conception at one end of the family cycle, to the devolution of family property on intestacy at the other.

The first two contributions by Richards and Schäfer are concerned with the interests, public and private, which arise where children are caught up in the process of divorce. Martin Richards questions directly whether there is a public or state interest in the well-being of children going beyond the private concerns of divorcing parents. The Children Act 1989 has diluted the supervisory role of the courts in scrutinising the arrangements for children and places much emphasis on private ordering and parental agreement. But should we, asks Richards, simply "let parents get on with it" or is there a more proactive function for the law than simply to provide a mechanism for dispute resolution? Richards reviews the extensive empirical evidence on the adverse effects of parental divorce on children and delineates a set of policy goals for alleviating these. He sees the best hope in a process of mediation which pays proper attention to the psychological needs of divorcing adults. At the heart of Richards' thesis is the desirability of creating a "culture of expectation" that dual parenting will continue in the post-divorce situation. He rejects the "very persistent prejudice that children should never have more than two parents" and with it the feminist "primary caretaker" model. In their place he puts forward his own radical alternative presumption for the allocation of child care following divorce.

The creation of the office of Family Advocate in South Africa in 1990 provides a striking contrast with the contemporaneous English reforms. While in England one effect of the Children Act is arguably to marginalise the public interest and the role of the courts, the South African legislation reasserts the importance of public scrutiny of private arrangements for children on divorce. Ivan Schäfer's account of the jurisdiction and functions of the Family Advocate, and the complementary role of the Family Counsellors appointed to assist him or her, clearly shows the acceptance in South Africa of the principle of mandatory investigation of children's interests which looks behind parental agreements. The Family Advocate is in effect a "watchdog" with investigatory powers whose prime function is to represent the independent interests of children on divorce. Whereas in

England the Children Act has effectively abolished the so-called "declaration of satisfaction", an essentially similar requirement has been preserved in South Africa. At the same time the increase in the independent representation of children in England by guardians *ad litem* in "public" family proceedings has not been extended to "private" family proceedings, most notably divorce. Schäfer's paper provokes a reconsideration of these sharp divisions between the public and private spheres regarding representation. The South African development also illustrates an alternative approach to the near abandonment of judicial investigative procedures which are not perceived to be working well – to reform them so that such interventions as do occur may be meaningful and not perfunctory. We may well ask how those cases which *are* suitable for intervention in England will come to light at all in the absence of an office comparable to that of the Family Advocate. The Centre for Family Law and Family Policy is currently conducting empirical research into this question.

The papers by Duncan and Bruch highlight what are probably two of the most urgent international problems facing families – intercountry adoption and child abduction. William Duncan's paper focuses on the fundamental issues raised by intercountry adoption and the current international efforts to address them at the Hague Conference on Private International Law. Duncan notes the historical shift in thinking from "parent-centred" to "child-centred" adoption and sees the current debate about "exclusivity" versus "openness" as an aspect of this. He notes the considerable variation in domestic conceptions of adoption in different parts of the world and finds it ironic that, at a time when several countries are moving towards "open" adoption, there is widespread support at the Hague for the "clean-break" model for intercountry adoption. The tension between international concerns and individual national interests is an important theme in Duncan's paper. Thus, while an avowed objective of the Hague Convention will be to secure international co-operation between states of origin and receiving states, fundamentally different national attitudes to such matters as non-agency adoptions or the need for a probationary period represent significant obstacles. Yet greater problems are posed by the practical difficulties of giving effect to the child-centred approach in a world in which the supply of children for intercountry adoption vastly exceeds the demand. Duncan concludes that the Convention's success may ultimately be measured more by its contribution to the fostering of child care services in countries of origin than by the number of adoptions effected under it.

Carol Bruch's contribution is concerned with another Hague Convention – that on the Civil Aspects of International Child Abduction 1980. She calls on her extensive research into the operation of the Convention in nine countries to give an evaluation of the experience under it particularly, but not exclusively, in England. Bruch provides a practical account of the workings of the Convention where children are snatched to or from England. It is the latter situation which may well expose some unintended consequences of the reforms in the Children Act 1989. The operation of the Convention requires a wrongful taking or retention but what precisely is wrongful for these purposes? Bruch exposes the inherent ambiguities in the concept of parental responsibility, especially those arising from its continuation after divorce, and the consequential importance of obtaining residence or other orders where there is any hint that one parent might seek to remove a child permanently from the country. It is by no means clear that, in the absence of an order, such a removal would be contrary to the Convention. Here Bruch makes reference to the so-called "custodial interference statutes" in the United States which can provide a solution but which have no counterpart in England. She highlights the vulnerability of the unmarried father who will usually possess no rights capable of violation under the Convention. She also touches upon what, with the growing legal autonomy of children, may in future years be one of the most difficult questions of all – ought a return to be ordered where a "mature" child is resisting it?

The contributions of Shifman and Morgan look at modern reproductive technologies and their implications for our existing conceptions of the family. Pinhas Shifman's discussion of surrogate motherhood in Jewish and Israeli law reminds us that the practice of surrogacy is not really a modern phenomenon at all but one with ancient antecedents. While the arguments about modern surrogacy usually revolve around adults' alleged *rights to* a child versus the *rights of* a child, in biblical times and traditionally in Jewish law the emphasis has been on the religious *duty* to procreate. Shifman argues that the modern version of surrogacy is not likely to be regarded as contrary to public policy in Israel because of the coincidence of this religious duty and civil rights to privacy in family decision-making. But this is subject to the overriding criterion of the welfare principle in determining the care of a child born under such an arrangement.

Derek Morgan, in his analysis of the regulation of medically assisted reproduction, takes up a theme of earlier chapters. Should the matter be left to private ordering or does the state have a legitimate interest in regulating new technological developments? Morgan considers a range of possible responses and describes the widely divergent approaches in England, Denmark, Austria and Canada. In particular he contrasts the polar extremes of the English *laissez-faire* policy and the repressive "prohibitive licensing regime" recently established in Austria. The central challenge, for Morgan, is "to obtain all the benefits and advantages of these developments in reproductive technology but to control these developments and guide them in the directions that we want". Yet Morgan reveals that what is "wanted" will differ markedly between societies depending on the official interpretation of what is an acceptable "family" or what is "natural" and he offers some observations on what he sees as the manipulation of laws, customs and values to this end. The crux of the matter, as pointed out by the Law Reform Commission of Canada, is whether a society wishes to place greater weight on protecting the traditional family than on other significant values such as equality, personal autonomy and non-discrimination in the reproductive arena.

Norio Higuchi also discusses assisted reproduction in the context of a wider examination of the acquisition of legal parenthood in Japan. Higuchi demonstrates the traditional significance of the blood tie in Japanese society but shows how legal and biological parenthood have not always coincided. For Higuchi the most significant determinant of parentage in modern Japan is "agreement among the interested parties consistent with social mores". Thus, despite evidence that a large majority of Japanese disapprove of the practice of AID, it has nonetheless existed without legal challenge or legislative intervention for the last 40 years. Higuchi explains this as the harmonisation of two inconsistent ideas – the value of the blood link and the need to have a child within marriage. As long as confidentiality is preserved and the appearance is maintained of a child conceived within marriage, this "delicate harmony" is preserved. It is thus the agreement of the various parties not to reveal the true circumstances of conception which is of paramount importance in determining parentage and not the biological truth of the situation. But Higuchi notes that such an apparently happy compromise will be much more difficult, if not impossible, to achieve where biological truth is palpably obvious as in the case of surrogacy. Higuchi's paper raises profound issues for any society about the comparative worth of genetic truth and family stability. Does the child, for example, have an inalienable right to know the truth or should the legal system perpetuate what amounts to mass deception, however altruistically grounded?

The final three chapters all deal with issues of family property and finance. While Oldham and Masson focus particularly on the "new property" in career assets and pension rights respectively, Miller analyses more generally the various familial claims arising on intestacy.

Thomas Oldham's aim is to suggest ways in which the dialogue towards fair rules for the economic consequences of divorce in the United States may be advanced. He identifies the failure to take into account the respective economic *prospects* of divorcing spouses, when dividing assets and awarding income support, as a major cause of dissatisfaction. But to what extent is it "fair" to regard career assets as "property" available for distribution? Oldham has some sympathy with the suggestion that a spouse suffering career damage arising from family responsibilities should be compensated by the other on divorce. He does, however, have a number of reservations, particularly about the cause of the career damage and the complex questions of valuation which might arise. The unpredictability and inconsistency of awards on divorce is the central theme of Oldham's thesis. In his view it is the attempt to provide one set of rules for all divorces, and the failure to distinguish between different kinds of divorce, which have led to vague and contradictory results. His proposed solution is a post-divorce income-sharing model which would differentiate between long and short marriages and childless and "childful" marriages. Although directly concerned only with the United States, Oldham's paper tackles some universal issues about policy goals on divorce. Thus, it reopens the perennial questions about the nature of marital commitments and the respective merits of judicial discretion versus presumptive guidelines for property and financial reallocation.

Judith Masson also concentrates on the standard of living following divorce – specifically that of former wives in later life. She refers to recent studies both in the United States and in England quantifying the rising incidence of poverty among this group. She identifies as the causes of the problem a combination of limited pension rights (especially the inadequate level of the state pension) and the failure of divorce law to provide an effective mechanism for the redistribution of assets from pension funds. Masson castigates previous official responses to the problem which have either pretended that it does not exist or that it is too complex to solve. She sees the solution, in part, as a question of better pension design and she advocates a power of pension-splitting on divorce. Here she encounters, in common with Oldham, problems of what constitutes property, problems of valuation and choices between discretionary or rule-based judicial powers. She also touches on the extent of marital obligations and the influence of the "clean-break" doctrine. As Masson's title suggests, the essence of the problem is to locate the responsibility for supporting ex-wives in an increasingly ageing population. It is clear from her conclusion that the best solution lies in ensuring the adequacy of state pension provision, that she at least sees this as the primary responsibility of society as a whole.

Gareth Miller discusses the reform of intestacy laws and offers an evaluation of the English Law Commission's recommendations. In particular he takes issue with the Commission's central recommendation that in all cases of intestacy the surviving spouse should take the whole of the estate. Just as Oldham emphasises in his paper the different kinds of divorce and the difficulty of establishing a uniform regime to govern them all, so Miller draws attention to the very different circumstances of intestacy. He identifies the striking feature of post-1925 reforms as the extension of the rights of the surviving spouse at the expense of children and other family members. The current proposal of the Law Commission can be seen as the culmination of this process. Even so, the existing rules can work hardship on the surviving spouse in cases in which there is insufficient capital in the estate to provide for old age and we are reminded here of Masson's concern at the incidence of poverty among elderly women. In most cases, however, the surviving spouse will be well placed on intestacy at least when compared with the situation of cohabitants or stepchildren who fall wholly outside the rules and whose only hope of support from the estate is the discretionary jurisdiction governing family provision. Children of the deceased's former marriage are a particularly significant group given the high incidence of divorce and remarriage. The crucial question on intestacy is the proper weight to be attached to the competing interests of family members often from more than one "family" and how to devise appropriate techniques for achieving the correct balance in a host of individual circumstances. This is, as Miller reveals, no easy matter involving as it does the hallowed principle of testamentary freedom (which underlies the intestacy laws) and the familiar question of the nature and extent of family obligations.

Acknowledgement

The editors wish to express their thanks to Sue Sargant of the School of Law, University of East Anglia, Norwich for all her efforts in producing the manuscript for publication.

Contributors

MARTIN RICHARDS is Reader in Human Development in the University of Cambridge. He carries out research there in the Centre for Family Research which he leads. His research interests cover a number of areas of family life, marriage and the development of children. A particular concern has been the effects of parental divorce on children. His books include *Divorce Matters* (with Jackie Burgoyne and Roger Ormrod) (Penguin, 1987), *Infancy* (Harper and Row, 1980), *Children in Social Worlds* (editor with Paul Light) (Polity Press/ Harvard Press, 1986) and *Sexual Arrangements: Marriage and Affairs* (with Janet Reibstein) (Heinemann, 1992).

IVAN SCHÄFER is Professor and Head of Department of Law at Rhodes University, Grahamstown, South Africa, Advocate of Supreme Court of South Africa. He is a Family Advocate, a member of SA Law Commission (Family Law) and is General Editor of Butterworth *Family Law Service.*

WILLIAM DUNCAN is a member of the Irish Law Reform Commission and an Associate Professor of Law at the University of Dublin, Trinity College. He has represented Ireland at the Special Commission of the Hague Conference on Private International Law on Intercountry Adoption, and is a member of its drafting committee. He is a member of the Executive Council of the International Society of Family Law.

CAROL BRUCH is a Professor of Law at the University of California, Davis, who teaches and writes in the fields of family law, family property law and the conflict of laws. A 1960 graduate of Shimer College, Illinois, she received her law degree with honours in 1972 from Boalt Hall, the University of California, Berkeley and served as a law clerk to the late Associate Justice Wm O Douglas of the United States Supreme Court. She has been a visiting professor at Boalt Hall, Columbia University, Munich, Cologne, Cambridge and the London School of Economics.

PINHAS SHIFMAN has been a Professor of Law at the Hebrew University since 1988. He has held a number of visiting positions in the United States, in particular at Yeshiva University, New York University and University of Miami. He is a member of the Israeli Bar and has published extensively in family law and medical law in both English and Hebrew.

DEREK MORGAN is a Lecturer in Law at Cardiff Law School, University of Wales. A graduate of the University of Kent, he has taught at the Universities of Brunel, East Anglia, Newcastle upon Tyne, University College Swansea and, as visiting Professor, at Osgoode Hall Law School, Toronto. He is co-author of *Blackstone's Guide to the Human Fertilisation and Embryology Act* and co-editor of *Birthrights: Law and Ethics at the Beginnings of Life*, Routledge. He has written in the areas of medical and health care law, torts, intellectual property, banking and commercial law and the law of procedure.

NORIO HIGUCHI is Professor of Law at the University of Tokyo. He was formerly Professor of Law at Gakushiun University. His specialisms include Anglo-American law, contract, tort and family law. He has written extensively on legal issues affecting children and parenthood. His recent publications include *Oyako to Ho* (Laws of Parent and Child: A Comparison of Japan and the United States) (Kobundo,1988) and *The Patient's Right to Know of a Cancer Diagnosis: A Comparison of Japanese Paternalism and American Self Determination* (1992), 31 Washburn LJ. 455-473.

THOMAS OLDHAM is a graduate of the University of California at Los Angeles. After practising law in Los Angeles for six years he became a law foundation scholar and is currently Professor of Law at the University of Houston Law School. He has had visiting professorships at the University of Colorado and the George Washington National Law Center. More recently, he was visiting scholar at Wolfson College, Cambridge. He has been President of the Family Law Section of the American Association of Law Schools. He is author of a number of books and journal articles including a book entitled *Divorce, Separation and the Distribution of Property*.

JUDITH MASSON has lectured and researched in family law since 1975, first at Leicester University and, since 1991, as Professor of Law at Warwick University. She was Harkness Fellow at the University of Michigan in 1991-92. She has also participated in the Institute of Fiscal Studies project to examine the development of a community property system for England; *Property and Marriage an Integrated Approach* (1988). She is a member of the Working Party established by the Pensions Management Institute to develop a system for reallocating pension rights on divorce. She is co-author (with Professor Stephen Cretney) of *Principles of Family Law*, 5th ed (1990).

GARETH MILLER has been a Professor of Law at UEA since 1979. He was Dean of the School of Law 1979-1985 and Pro-Vice-Chancellor from 1989-1992. He has also been Adjunct Professor of Law at the London Law Centre of the University of Notre Dame, Indiana. His main interests are family law, property law, succession and taxation. His published works include *Family Property and Financial Provision*, 3rd ed (1993) and *The Machinery of Succession* (1977). He is also the author of the section on "The Taxation of Husband, Wife and Children" in the *Personal Tax Volume of the Taxation Service* sponsored by the Institute of Chartered Accountants in England and Wales.

Chapter 1

Private Worlds and Public Intentions – the Role of the State at Divorce

Martin P M Richards
Centre for Family Research, University of Cambridge

Introduction

When divorce in England and Wales first became a matter for the civil law in 1857, the main concern of the government was to restrict the exit from marriage. Divorce was then a rarity – the annual number did not exceed a thousand a year until 1918. Today numbers run at about 150, 000 a year and now the (present) government's chief pre-occupation is to control public expenditure, both the legal aid bill and the welfare benefits subsequently paid to divorced women and their children.

It was only after about a century of civil divorce that there was legislative concern for the well-being of children and provision was made for the courts to scrutinise the post-divorce arrangements made for child care. Current proposals for divorce law reform (Law Commission, 1990), though couched in a general framework which pays due attention to the interests of children, seeks to remove this particular legislative provision. Indeed, the general approach, like that of the Children Act 1989, is to let parents get on with it without surveillance or control unless there are particular reasons for intervention. But in what ways can, or should, the law be used to protect the well-being of children at divorce? Should there be any role beyond that of adjudicating disputes that cannot be settled privately (within or outside the shadow of the law)? Since the Divorce Reform Act of 1969, divorce has been available, effectively, on demand, so the state no longer attempts to restrict the exit from marriage (a situation made more explicit in the Law Commission reform proposals). Should a similar approach be taken to the well-being of children; that parents should be free to make whatever post-divorce arrangements they wish, constrained only by the child protection legislation?[1] Or, is there a more positive and useful role the law could play?

---

1   Their freedom of course may be significantly restricted by such crucial matters as the employment possibilities open to women and men, provision of child care facilities of various kinds and assumptions about the roles that men and women may play in child care. My point here is focused on the much narrower issue of legislation directly concerned with divorce.

In this paper I will first briefly outline what research has established about the consequences of parental divorce for children and then I will go on to consider ways in which the divorce process might be modified to reduce some of the ill effects that have been found. I shall consider two broad areas: (a) whether action could or should be taken to reduce the number of divorces, and (b) the maintenance of relationships between children and parents and other family members after divorce and financial consequences of divorce for children and their caretakers. My intention is to stimulate debate and to suggest that a better understanding of divorce and its social and psychological consequences may lead to a reappraisal of the role of the state in its regulation.

Consequences of parental divorce for children

Children of divorcing parents tend to show a period of disturbed behaviour – either acting-out disruptive behaviour or depressive and anxious patterns. This may last through the whole process of divorce beginning months or years before a separation and continuing some time after this. School work often shows some falling off around the time of separation and, as effects for educational attainment may be cumulative, children are likely to leave school with fewer qualifications and have a reduced chance of going on to a university (*e.g.* Hetherington, Cox and Cox, 1978; Maclean and Wadsworth, 1988; Kuh and Maclean, 1990; Elliott and Richards, 1991; Wallerstein, 1991; Amato and Keith, 1991).

Some effects may persist into adulthood and studies in Britain and the United States have found lower occupational status and earnings, earlier marriage and divorce and increased frequency of psychological and psychiatric problems (Amato and Keith, 1991). In short, parental divorce may be associated with downward social mobility for the children.

Of course, effects of divorce are very variable depending on many aspects of the particular circumstances and such things as the age of the children, the social position of the family and the living arrangements after the separation. Not all children show significant persistent effects. However, these are sufficiently common and of such importance – we are talking of effects which in some cases influence the life-long chances for adults – that it seems reasonable that we should regard these as the prime concern which we need to consider when discussing interventions at divorce (Richards, 1991).

Why should parental divorce have these long-term effects? Clearly, this is a very complex question and there are no simple answers. But we may point to a number of key interrelated factors which play a crucial role in a young person's journey from their childhood home into their independent life as a young adult. My approach is to consider the ways in which parental divorce may influence these. These factors are educational attainment and vocational training, leaving home and setting up an independent life elsewhere, forming a cohabitation or a marriage and the beginning of reproduction. Parental divorce has been shown to influence all these factors. It is through varying combinations of these factors that divorce is likely to have its effect on social mobility (Richards, 1991). But the significance of the divorce effect is variable depending on both individual and social factors.

The analysis of the follow-up study of the cohort of children born in 1958, for example, suggests that girls from middle-class homes show the strongest effects in early adulthood while boys from working-class backgrounds are least affected (Richards and Elliott, 1992). Moreover, the links are certainly complex. Nevertheless we can point to a number of crucial effects of parental divorce. So, for instance, a child that does badly at school is more likely to leave at the minimum age with few or no qualifications and is less likely to proceed to further education or training and so has reduced job prospects. Children who have left education are more likely to leave home and live independently.

Marriage and cohabitation are more probable for those living independently and, associated with these, are earlier reproduction, which in turn may further reduce employment possibilities, especially for women. The association between leaving home and marriage and cohabitation, is probably the end result of two different processes; leaving home because a decision has been taken to get married and, because those living independently may be more likely to form relationships that develop more rapidly into cohabitation or marriage. Where relationships are difficult or strained at home a young person may choose to leave earlier than otherwise.

A poor relationship with a step-parent is a significant factor for some. Social class differences may be very important here, not least because of the need for financial resources to find independent accommodation. We should also note that matters which are controlled by government action such as rules for job training allowances, welfare benefits and council tax may have a direct bearing on the financial consequences for parents and young people of the latter staying or leaving home. Availability of jobs and housing are also of obvious significance.

Divorce is associated with a sharp drop in income for homes with children. In Britain, a majority of households containing divorced women and their children become dependent on state benefits for at least a period of time (*e.g.* Maclean, 1991) and some remain caught in the poverty trap. Inadequate income reduces children's educational attainment and in many other ways has adverse effects on their life chances. While parental remarriage, and probably cohabitation, may improve incomes, the levels are seldom restored to those preceding the divorce. And even if these events have beneficial effects for household income, they may lead to further psychological and social disruptions for children. Follow-up studies (*e.g.* Kiernan, 1992) tend to show small but consistently negative effects for

15

children from remarriage homes as compared with those where a mother remained on her own after the divorce.

After divorce most children live with their mothers and fathers become, at best, occasional visitors in their lives. Research in Britain and the United States suggests that within a short time of separation many children cease to have a relationship with their father (*e.g.* Seltzer, 1991). The breaking of established relationships with fathers and other family members may have significant effects on a child's social development and their capacity to form and sustain relationships with others. When a father disappears from a child's life that child often feels a persistent sense of abandonment and loss which damages their self-esteem and sense of worth. Lack of self-esteem, in turn, has many psychological and social consequences. The loss of a parent and kin may also have economic and social effects for children which may continue into adult life. Fathers who are in contact with their children are more likely to be contributing towards their support and, though there seems to be no direct evidence to make the point, other transfers of money and practical support are likely to be reduced or cease where divorce ends effective contact (see Finch, 1990).

Conflict between parents before and after divorce is associated with poorer outcome for children (Emery 1982, 1988). Where parents are living together, if the conflict is conducted in such a way that children are not directly involved, they seem to be protected from some of its consequences (see Rutter, 1988). An important point here is that the effects of inter-parent conflict for children may be relatively benign if the children are able to see their parents settle their differences and restore good relationships. Conflict in the closing stages of a marriage or after separation may be more serious because it is less likely that this happens and because children, and the arrangements for their care, are more likely to be the subject of disputes. Conflict between parents will often erode parent–child relationships or end them.

Separating and divorced adults tend to have higher rates of psychological and physical illness (Elliott, 1991). Parents who are ill, depressed, preoccupied and generally under stress, are less effective as parents and their children may lack sustained support and emotional engagement. Such parental difficulties may further exacerbate the psychological problems of the children of divorce.

These problems may also be increased by moves which may mean a change of school and loss of friends and familiar peers. Changes of school tend to be associated with poorer educational attainment.

The analysis I have sketched out provides a set of clear issues which could become goals for policies related to divorce and children. Such policies should aim to encourage the maintenance of a child's existing relationships with parents and the wider family and kin, ensure an adequate income to post-divorce households with children, to reduce as far as possible conflict between divorcing parents or, at least, encourage its expression in areas that do not involve children, encourage the provision of emotional and practical support for divorcing parents who have the care of children and, finally, avoid as far as possible moves of house or school. On this latter point we should note that the availability of reasonably priced housing, whether to rent or buy, is of particular importance to divorcing couples and their children. I have necessarily stated the policy objectives in broad terms. It will not always be desirable to strive to maintain relationships with both parents. The evidence suggests that it is the breaking of already existing relationships which has ill effects for children. In rare cases, existing relationships may be detrimental to children if they continue. However, I suspect that such cases are much less common than many professionals working in the field choose to believe. It is also important to realise that the loss of a parent usually means the permanent loss of half of a child's kin relationships which may have profound emotional, social and financial consequences.

Can we reduce the number of divorces?

There is a belief, especially among some of those associated with the law, that if divorce was made harder to obtain, the numbers would be reduced and some of the attendant consequences for children would therefore be avoided (see Mears, 1991 for a recent example of this line of argument). While it would not seem a sensible policy for a state to provide incentives for couples to divorce, making the legal process of divorce more difficult seems unlikely to have the desired outcome. Those who argue for harder divorce seem to have an exaggerated view of the power of the law to control people's domestic living arrangements. Their model seems to be that of a sluice gate which stands between the married and the divorced. The wider this sluice is opened, the more of the married that will become divorced. Such a view suggests that it is only the difficulty of getting out that keeps people married. It also presupposes that the difficulty of divorce is governed by the complexity or otherwise of the legal hurdles. Divorce is always difficult in a social and emotional sense for adults and children and there is no reason to think that, except in a few odd instances, people do not think hard and struggle with alternatives before taking legal action (Burgoyne et al, 1987).

There has been a steady increase in the rate of divorce since civil divorce became possible (Phillips, 1988) but the evidence suggests that changes in divorce law have followed rather than created, the increase. As we also know from the example of countries where divorce is not permitted, people are well practised in finding ways of reordering their domestic life, whatever the law says.

To these arguments, we might add the point made already that the difficulties for the children of divorce may begin long before their parents separate, so that their lot may not be improved by trying to force their parents to stay together. By the time parents decide to separate some of the damaging processes may already have started.

Are there other ways of reducing the divorce rate? Many suggestions are made. One currently fashionable is to suggest that we should make marriage more difficult and perhaps demand some training or preparation of some kind. Quite what this might consist of is unclear. Others have argued that because early marriage is associated with divorce we should try to delay the age of marriage. But how?

All these kinds of arguments seem to miss two basic points. The first is that marriage rates are now dropping and cohabitation is increasing. It is probable that cohabitation is being transformed from a prelude to marriage to its alternative. Perhaps we are moving towards the Scandinavian model which is approaching a situation where only a minority of the population marries. In Britain approaching a third of all children are born outside marriage and in two thirds of these cases the birth registration is made jointly. It seems reasonable to assume that many of these are cohabiting couples. As yet we lack any information about the consequences of the ending of a cohabitation for children but there seem to be few reasons to believe that they will be any more benign than the ending of a marriage. Given the relative lack of institutionalised processes for dispute resolution at the ending of cohabitation, outcomes could be worse. Attempts to regulate marriage – either at entry or exit – seem likely to increase cohabitation. If we provide legal processes for regulating the exit from marriage partly on the grounds that they may serve to protect the welfare of children, should we not do the same for the ending of cohabitation?

The second point concerns the reason for the increased rates of divorce. The rise in divorce is associated with the development of companionate marriage (Phillips, 1988; Reibstein and Richards, 1992). Expectations for marriage have risen as have the range of functions it is expected to fulfil. Spouses are now seen as friends, lovers, helpmates and companions for leisure time as well as lifelong marital partners. These extended functions, the high ideals of what marriage should provide, have made marriage relationships both more exclusive and more vulnerable. This vulnerability is further increased by the growing extent to which close relationships among the unmarried are now sexual and most spouses enter marriage with the experience of several earlier sexual relationships. This changing nature of marriage has meant that increasing numbers of spouses, especially women, find that their satisfaction with their marriages may fall quite steeply after the early years. This is particularly true after the arrival of children. I suggest that reasons for divorce in many cases are different for men and women. I believe that if men initiate a divorce it is more often because they have another partner to go to, while women are more likely to be motivated by a desire to leave an unsatisfactory marriage. The great majority of divorces are now initiated by women, a point to which I will return. (These arguments are spelt out more fully in Reibstein and Richards, 1992).

The influences that have led to the present day style of marriage have a long history and may be traced back to developing ideals of domestic life early in the nineteenth century (Richards and Elliott, 1991; Reibstein and Richards, 1992). They have been shaped by complex social and economic forces and seem most unlikely to be directly controllable by the action of any government. Leaving aside the effects of world wars which produced marked peaks in the marriage and divorce rates, there are a number of other factors which in the short-term do seem to influence divorce rates and probably lie behind some of the fluctuations in recent years. The following all seem likely to depress divorce rates: high house prices and a shortage of state housing, low rates of welfare support for poor single parent households, lack of availability of both part-time and full-time jobs for women, lack of child care facilities and high cost of child care in relation to the earning abilities of women. It seems undesirable to try and manipulate any of these factors in order to try to influence the divorce rate, not least because all of them are damaging to the welfare of children.

The final point I want to make concerns the "marriage savers". Do their activities influence divorce rates? Clearly, many who work in this field believe they have some impact and the government subsidy for the various marriage guidance organisations is justified partly on these grounds. However, I am unaware of any evidence about their effectiveness in preventing divorce and, given the relatively small number of couples who use these services, even if their effectiveness was high the impact would be relatively small. However, this is not to suggest that these agencies do not perform a number of useful functions. They may well be effective in helping some couples to renegotiate the nature of their marriages and thereby increase their marital satisfaction. Such a function may have become more important as the idealism of marriage has increased and its contradictions have grown.

Public attitudes towards divorce and knowledge of its consequences may well have changed over the last couple of decades. The main theme of much of what is presented about divorce in the media concerns the difficulties for children and the financial hardship it often brings. It seems reasonable to suggest that awareness of the complications of divorce may encourage people to seek alternatives. Certainly things have moved on since the 1960s and 1970s when it was often suggested that divorce was an obvious and straightforward solution to an unsatisfactory marriage. It seems plausible to suggest that the growing awareness of the difficulties and complications of divorce, coupled with economic factors and the housing crisis, have held divorce rates more or less constant since the late 1970s.

In conclusion, I would suggest that very little can be done by public policy to reduce the divorce rate and, therefore, we need to accept the situation and turn attention to the ways divorce is handled by the legal and associated institutions.

Parental and kin relationships and maintaining children

Earlier in this paper I argued that children are likely to do better in the long-term if they maintain relationships with both their parents and the kin network on both sides of their family after a parental divorce. We know that in practice, in Britain, the United States and elsewhere, the usual pattern is for children to live with their mother after divorce and for around half of fathers (at best) to remain in regular contact. As far as mothers are concerned, we should expect the post-divorce pattern we see, as it is simply the same situation as is found within marriage. The bulk of child care is provided by women in marriage, as it is afterwards. In only very few cases is the mother's position of the primary caretaker challenged at divorce. What had been the mother's role as principal caretaker in the joint household becomes that of residential parent in a single parent household. While she may be faced with all sorts of increased difficulties in this new situation – juggling child care and employment, housing and financial difficulties etc the basic role remains the same.

The complications arise in trying to see how a father can fit into the post-divorce pattern when the mother's primary role within one household is translated into that of a single parent (or one with a new partner). Within a typical marriage the father is out at work each day while the mother is either at home as a full-time carer of children, or combines work, and, importantly, the organisation of substitute child care while she is working, with child care and domestic work. A father fits what care-taking he does, and his other time with the children, into the basic pattern set up and maintained by the mother. In most households fathers engage with their children when the mother is present too. This is unlike the typical pattern for a mother who will spend a lot of time on her own with her children. Or to put it in other terms, if a father is to maintain a relationship with his children his role *vis à vis* children is likely to change at separation much more radically than that of a mother. He has to become a sole care-taker for the times he is with his children, unless he simply passes on the care to a new partner or a relative.

A change for a mother is that there may be times when she is *not* with her children, if they are visiting their father. For some women this can pose a significant psychological threat to their role as a mother and it is frequently experienced as a loss. So at many separations a mother may not wish her children to go to see their father, and a father may be unable or unwilling to change his life to become a part-time sole carer. Control over visiting, and more generally over contact with a father, may be one of the few areas in which a mother may feel she has some power so it is not surprising that so many disputes get focused on these issues. Where a divorce has been initiated by a mother and the father feels he is losing his marriage, his wife and his home, he may push for as much time with his children as possible as a way of retaining some element of his past life. Again, this may help to add emotional fuel to conflicts over children which stand in practical and symbolic ways as the bones for contention.

New partners may further complicate the picture. Father involvement tends to fall off if either he or his ex-spouse acquires a new partner. This is likely to be for somewhat different reasons on each side. The residential mother may have fantasies about creating a new family for which ties with the "old" father may seem a threat best met by keeping the children around and denying them visits to the other parent. While for the non-residential parent, a relationship with a new partner may feel threatened by the occasional presence of children who are reminders of the old marriage and intimacy with another. Running through these situations is a very persistent prejudice that children should never have more than two parents and when a new one arrives, an old one has to go. I suggest that children have a much greater tolerance for non-standard family forms than adults (see Funder, 1991). Indeed discomfort about such arrangements seems particularly strong among professionals who deal with children who often seem to regard such arrangements as "confusing" for children. I suspect this is a matter of projection and the potential confusion lies more with the adults than the children.[2]

It is usual to regard children as conservatives in their views of family life. Certainly they may resent change and can be very sensitive about the ways others may regard their living arrangements. However, children may have few presuppositions about the roles various adults in their lives should play. One can cite cases of children who see nothing but gain in the addition of further adult figures who can come to occupy quasi-parental roles in their lives. But we know too little about how children experience arrangements in non-traditional family structures and we should be very wary about assuming on their behalf the existence of strong views in favour of idealised family forms.

There is also the issue of conflict between parents which may lead to a reduction in contact between parents and can erode parent-child relationships. I shall have more to say about this below.

Given the pervasiveness of a pattern which places little emphasis on the need for continuing relationships between children and non residential parents, and the strength of the beliefs and institutions that support this, change is not going to be easy. The evidence suggests that very little has occurred over recent decades in the United States (Seltzer, 1991) and the situation seems similar here. A first step which we have begun to take in the Children Act 1989 is to make the legal change so that at least we do not take parental responsibility from most fathers at divorce. At present, according to the judicial statistics (before the new Act) sole custody orders are made in 78% of cases (71% to the mother and 7% to the father) and only 21% are orders for joint custody. However, the situation illustrates the whims of the English judicial system with some courts granting joint custody in over

---

2   A parallel argument could be mounted here about the concept of adoption and the great adult fantasy that it is possible to create and end kinship relationships at the stroke of a court order.

80% of cases while in other courts, especially in the north of England, any joint custody orders are an extreme rarity. The law has important symbolic power and the least we should do is to provide a legal and public expectation that both mother and father will continue to retain a parental role after divorce.

But can we do more? Certainly if there are better ways of settling disputes between parents and conflict were reduced and some of the emotional tensions that so often continue between past spouses were addressed more directly, we might expect more fathers to stay in the picture. I will discuss this further below. Apart from this it seems a matter of creating a culture of expectation so that we accept, as the slogan goes, "Divorce is for adults, not children". We need small changes on many fronts. Schools, for instance, should be encouraged (required?) to send information to both parents if they do not share the same address. Divorcing parents should receive written information about the post-divorce needs of children and the range of workable residence and visiting patterns.

"Making fathers pay" might help. At least, it seems reasonable that all fathers (at least those who have lived in a household with their children)[3] should maintain the duties of fatherhood or indeed this should be so for all non-residential parents. I have heard therapists argue that if their clients do not pay for their therapy they will not take it seriously; could not the same principle apply to those who voluntarily enter parenthood and have the means to pay? We take it for granted that our standard of living will fall when we have children within marriage. Why should divorce end that expectation? However, the difficulty here is devising a scheme that is effective in achieving these ends. Most such schemes share the limitation that they cannot do any more than reallocate needs in the all too common situation where the total resources of the couple is not enough to support two post-divorce households. It seems unlikely that the Child Support Act 1991 will overcome these difficulties (Eekelaar, 1991).

A difficulty we should not duck here is the difference between his and her divorce. He is likely either to have been left or to be leaving for someone else. If the former, he may feel a strong sense of injustice at losing his marriage, children, house and having to pay for continuing support – or at least that is a way that a vocal minority will put it. If he is moving into a new relationship, guilt may provide some motive to pay, but a new partner may increasingly resent supporting another woman's children. Of course, not everyone is driven by such motives. However, the coming of legal "no fault" divorce has perhaps allowed us to believe that couples separate with a similar detached view of divorce. They do not. Blame, accusation, and strong feelings of injustice are the norm at divorce and they get in the way of couples making reasonable arrangements about children and money. Neither the legal fiction of the lack of fault or imposed orders do anything to relieve the situation, rather the reverse.

---

3   Defining who is a father is not always simple. Pre DNA profiling we muddled by with a workable definition of social fatherhood (see Deech, 1992). Perhaps we should be hesitant to let molecular biology make social policy for us.

Indeed, neither the public ordering of the court, nor most private ordering provide an adequate arena for expressing the feelings that accompany marital separation. Studies of the legal process of divorce (*e.g.* Davis and Murch, 1988) show that many of the participants feel that the legal procedures do not engage what they see as the "real" issues. Affidavits take instances from a private reality and present them in a context where they lose most of their meaning. There is always a deep sense of betrayal when events from a private and once shared reality are forced into public in the provocative legal prose of an affidavit. People are not allowed their say in a manner that fits their own sense of justice. They are told to look forward at a time when their prime concern is history and its rewriting. The wounds go very deep but they feel that the doctor is not even interested in seeing them.

Most conciliation (mediation) takes the same stance. Agendas are strictly controlled and anyone who tries to talk about how the present situation came about is wrapped over the knuckles and told – directly or indirectly – to attend to the business at hand and look to the future (Dingwall and Greatbach, 1990).

Marriage, as Berger and Kellner (1964) argued in a perceptive paper that has deservedly become a classic, involves the joint construction of a private shared and exclusive reality. Identities are anchored in the shared meaning of the relationship (Askham, 1984). Maybe legally we do not become one anymore, but we aspire to a social and psychological fusion. It follows, therefore, that the process of uncoupling is very painful and provokes powerful irrational feelings (Vaughan, 1987; Weiss, 1975). Yet we try to get people to divide their lives, children and property without even acknowledging the deep sense of anger, love, betrayal and hate that most are feeling.

At separation many people are literally out of their minds. They will do things and treat people in ways they never have before and never will again. Any family lawyer can provide numerous examples of what has to be regarded as typical behaviour: he broke into her house and tipped the contents of the dustbin into the double bed where she and her new partner sleep; she went through the family photograph album cutting him out of each photo; he slashed the tyres of her, once their, car; she burnt the postcard he sent to the children while he was away on a business trip. We expect them both to be calm and rational, yet we present them with a system that allows them to take their irrational behaviour into the public arena of the court where it may be validated by the professionals who become drawn into their warring world. Court contests seem to be designed to allow the trivia of every day life to become elevated to a point where it becomes the basis of long-term decision-making. The result is adults and children who may feel damaged and bruised by their experience, a great deal poorer and not necessarily with any sensible solutions to their problems. I suggest that until we begin to address the feelings of the participants at divorce we cannot expect people to make sensible decisions about the long-term interests of their children.

My noting of the restrictiveness of some styles of conciliation and mediation may have seemed rather dismissive. A major problem is that under both of these two terms are gathered together a very wide range of activities. It is not simply that there are many variants in practice, but there is dispute about some of the basic techniques. A common model is of a kind of public school debating contest with each team represented by one of the spouses and the neutral chair seeing that everyone keeps to the point and to time. There tends to be a polarisation between those who come from the pragmatic dispute resolution tradition, often with a background of labour disputes work, and those who draw on more therapeutic frameworks. There is little thought about how the two might be combined in the very special circumstances of a dispute between two parties who were once intimate and emotionally interdependent and whose union may have represented a bridge between two kinship networks.

Some of the influence from family therapy has been less than helpful as it puts little stress on the ambivalence of loss and love that may dominate the feelings of each warring spouse. Not surprisingly, the evaluation of mediation has had a somewhat mixed press (see Bruch, 1988). But not all evaluation has been negative (Kelly, 1991). My guess, and it can be no more on present evidence, is that mediation can be effective if (a) it is comprehensive and we get rid of the silly British fiction that we can sort out issues to do with children without discussing where they will live or how they are to be supported; (b) it does allow clients to express something of their feelings and so engage the private reality that was their marriage (drawing here on appropriate psycho-dynamic traditions); (c) it provides some help and encouragement to couples to see that their quarrels can be conducted in ways that are more or less damaging for them and/or their children; (d) it is offered in context where other services such as counselling and direct support for children are also available; and finally (e) deals in realistic and practical solutions for individual cases rather than idealised and generalised arrangements.

I think mediation is the best hope we have, but it needs more money, more experimental schemes, and more hard thinking about its dynamics and how they may relate to the psychology of uncoupling. When it is done in the spirit I am proposing it does have some interesting effects (see for example Johnston and Campbell, 1991). Children receive more financial support, agreements are likely to be kept and there is more contact between non-residential parents and their children (Kelly, 1991). But we need to be careful to judge post-divorce arrangements by appropriate criteria. Increased contact between children and non-residential parents may mean that there is more scope for continuing conflict between parents. Some continuing conflict may be a reasonable price that has to be paid for the better contact (Masheter, 1991) but good mediation can help to ensure that it does not stand in the way of necessary discussions about children (Kelly, 1991).

One other very important point needs to be made about the ways in which couples end their marriages. Most go on to further marriages or cohabitations after divorce and recoupling often stimulates fertility. Sadly, however, second and subsequent relationships are more prone to divorce than first time marriages. It seems reasonable to assume that the unfinished business of the first marriage – emotional as well as financial – is an important determinant of the stability of the second. Addressing the psychological issues of divorce and providing couples with a forum in which to do this might have significant benefits for any subsequent relationships and children that might be born in these.

I am sure it is right for the Law Commission to recommend that divorce is available on demand with a suitable delay in which to sort out arrangements about children and money and without the need to provide a fictional historical account of the marriage in a legal format. Courts are not the place in which to argue about the private world of intimate relationships. The present system seems to have the worst combination of offering opportunities through affidavits to rehearse all sorts of marital quarrels which break faith with an erstwhile partner but then to ignore these issues and give the divorce the nod.

It is much more difficult to see how the courts might be used to settle those cases of disputes about children that mediation cannot shift. Perhaps we should try to follow the same kind of system and we should define the areas of acceptable dispute in litigation over children. Perhaps the easier cases are the few where there is a straight dispute about residence (custody), about where the children should live. The vast majority of such disputes concern parents who are as fit and able to care for children as any other; *i.e.* they are what Winnicott might have called "good enough" parents – who have both played some part in the care of the children before the separation.

Relying on evidence of who did most during the marriage is usually not very relevant as the divorce changes most things. Also the needs of children change through development and with the roles that the two partners may take. Perhaps all that is required is for each parent to establish that they have practical plans for how they would look after children under whatever scheme they are proposing for their future care. In these disputes parents often try to suggest, directly or indirectly, that their partner is unfit to have the care of children. I suggest that such evidence should be inadmissible. If there are such concerns, these should be dealt with by the appropriate child protection procedures and only when any such issues have been resolved should a custody hearing take place.

The principle of the primacy of the welfare of the children should still obtain in such situations but I suggest it should be given a single simple definition, that the children should reside with whichever parent is able to convince the court that they are the parent most likely to foster and maintain the children's links with the other parent. Such a criterion has a long history (Solomon, 1 Kings 3.16-28) and should ensure that attention is focused on the welfare of the children rather than the supposed moral worth of each parent. Here my argument directly contradicts that of those feminists who have argued for a system based exclusively on who was the primary caretaker within marriage (Smart and Sevenhuijsen, 1989). While such a system is attractive in its simplicity, it fails to take account of the changes in living arrangements and employment that divorce may bring and seems likely to reinforce further the expectation that child care should remain a mother's duty.

We need to make the court hearing truly a last resort. I do not intend, yet again, to rehearse all the arguments in favour of family courts. It is sufficient to say, that in the New Zealand family courts there is an important step between the mediation phase and the formal court hearing. This is a conference with the judge. The indications are that such hearings – in which the judge controls the agenda – lead to a substantial reduction in contested hearings, at least when they are coupled with an effective provision of mediation and counselling. Another advantage of these hearings is that the judge can speak with the authority of the court and there are certainly cases where parents pursue their disputes until somebody with authority tells them what to do. These meetings avoid the situation in which each side simply maintains their position, concedes nothing and piles up ammunition for the last stand.

Disputes around contact, and matters such as the removal of children from the jurisdiction are much harder to resolve, not least because they are so often an arena in which the conflicting emotions of the once intimate are played out. It seems unlikely that there are any simple principles to guide solutions. What about the father who consistently fails to turn up on agreed access days or the mother who refuses to let a father see his children despite access orders? In the latter case do we put the mother in prison as the occasional exasperated judge has tried to do or transfer the children to the father? Nothing is gained by the former and in the latter situation perhaps the father is unable or unwilling to take them. Similarly, heavy handed treatment is unlikely to encourage a father to take his responsibilities more seriously. I think the best we can suggest is mediation, compulsory if necessary, and a court hearing as the very last resort where appropriate. The problem is, of course, that in the end, we cannot impose arrangements on parents who are determined to thwart an order. Such cases are rare but if everything has been exhausted, mediation with due attention to the psychodynamic agenda, a determined attempt to discover the reasons for the refusal, an informal meeting with a judge and a court hearing – there is nothing for it but an occasional supervised access visit until such time as children are old enough to make their own choices.

I will finish with a few words about money. I leave this to last not because it is unimportant but because all the points have been made before (Maclean, 1991). Divorce leads to poverty and poverty stunts the development of children and blights the lives of their mothers. We can try to make fathers pay but we need to ensure that the exercise is one to benefit children and their carers and not simply the exchequer. But any such scheme must be coupled with a much better safety net than we have at present, so that where fathers can't pay the state must provide.

Making fathers pay might have some interesting consequences for second families. At present a father can effectively wipe the slate clean and start again with a second family. Ensuring transfers to existing children and giving them some preference over subsequent ones might depress fertility in second marriages. Would that be an unreasonable consequence?

Acknowledgements

Some of our research on the consequences of divorce has been supported by a grant from the Health Promotion Research Trust. I would like to thank Jane Elliott, Nanci Griffith, Shelley Day Sclater and Christina Sinclair for help in the preparation of this paper but I must point out that none of them necessarily agree with the views I have expressed here. Jill Brown and Sally Roberts, as always, have provided excellent administrative and secretarial services.

References

Amato and Keith, "Parental divorce and adult well-being. A meta-analysis" (1991) 53 *J Marriage and the Family* 43-58.

Askham, *Identity and Stability in Marriage* (Cambridge University Press, 1984).

Berger and Kellner, "Marriage and the construction of reality" (1964) 46 *Diogenes* 1-25.

Bruch, "And how are the children? The effects of ideology and mediation on child custody law and children's well-being in the United States" (1988) 2 *Int J Law & The Family* 106-126.

Burgoyne, Ormrod and Richards, *Divorce Matters* (Penguin Books, 1987).

Davis and Murch, *Grounds for Divorce* (Clarendon Press, 1988) .

Deech, Paper presented at the Seventh World Conference of the International Society on Family Law, Opatija, Yugoslavia, 1991, now published as "The Unmarried Father and Human Rights" (1992) 4 *J of Child Law* 3-10.

Dingwall and Greenbatch, *Divorce Conciliation A Report to the Wates Foundation* (Centre for Socio-Legal Studies, Oxford, 1990).

Eekelaar, "Child support – an evaluation" (1991) 21 *Family Law* 511-517.

Elliott and Richards, "Children and divorce: educational performance and behaviour, before and after parental separation" (1991) 5 *Int J Law & The Family* 258-276.

Elliott, "Divorce and adult health: the mediating effects of gender", Unpublished paper. (Child Care and Development Group, University of Cambridge, 1991).

Emery, "Interparental conflict and the children of discord and divorce" (1982) 2 *Psychological Bull* 310-330.

Finch, *Family Obligation and Social Change* (Polity Press, Cambridge, 1990).

Funder, "Children's construction of their post-divorce families: a family sculpture approach", in Funder (ed), *Images of Australian Families* (Longman, 1991).

Hetherington, Cox and Cox, "Play and social interaction in children following divorce" (1978) 4 *J Social Issues* 26-49.

Johnston and Campbell, *The Impasses of Divorce* (The Free Press, New York, 1991).

Kiernan, "The impact of family disruption in childhood and transitions made in young adult life" (1992) *Population Studies* in press.

Kuh and Maclean, "Women's childhood experience of parental separation and their subsequent health and socioeconomic status in adulthood" (1990) 22 *J Biosocial Science* 1-15.

Kelly, "Mediated and adversarial divorce resolution processes: A comparison of post-divorce outcomes" (1991) 21 *Family Law* 382-388.

Law Commission, *The Grounds for Divorce*, Law Com. Report No 192 (HMSO, 1990).

Maclean and Wadsworth, "The interests of children after parental divorce: a long term perspective" (1988) 2 *Int J of Law and the Family* 155-166.

Maclean, *Surviving Divorce: Women's Resource after Separation* (Macmillan, 1991).

Masheter, "Post divorce relationships between ex-spouses: the role of attachment and interpersonal conflict" (1991) 53 *J Marriage and the Family* 103-110.

Mears, "Getting it wrong again? Divorce and the Law Commission" (1991) 21 *Family Law* 231-233.

Phillips, *Putting Asunder. A History of Divorce in Western Society* (Cambridge University Press, 1988).

Reibstein and Richards, *Sexual Arrangements* (Heinemann, 1992).

Richards, "Divorce Cambridge Style: New Developments in Conciliation" (1990) 20 *Family Law* 436-438.

Richards, "Children and Parents after Divorce", paper presented at the Seventh World Conference of the International Society on Family Law, Opatija, Yugoslavia, 1991 and to be published in the proceedings of the meeting.

Richards and Elliott, "Sex and Marriage in the 1960s and 1970s", in Clark (ed), *Marriage, Domestic Life and Social Change, Writings for Jacqueline Burgoyne* (Routledge, 1991) .

Richards and Elliott, "*Economic and social consequences of divorce*", in preparation (1992).

Rutter, "Functions and consequences of relationships: some psycho-pathological considerations", in Hinde, Stevenson and Hinde (eds), *Relationships within Families* (Clarendon Press, 1988) .

Seltzer, "Relationship between fathers and children who live apart: The father's role after separation" (1991) 53 *J Marriage and the Family* 79-102.

Smart and Sevenhuijsen (eds), *Child Custody and the Politics of Gender* (Routledge, 1989).

Vaughan, *Uncoupling: Turning Points in Intimate Relationships* (Methuen, 1987).

Wallerstein, "The long-term effects of divorce on children: a review" *J Amer Acad Child and Adolescent Psychiatry* (in press, 1991).

Weiss, *Marital Separation* (Basic Books, New York, 1975).

Chapter 2

The Family Advocate in South Africa

Ivan Schäfer

Professor of Law, Rhodes University, South Africa,
Visiting Fellow, Centre for Family Law and Family Policy,
University of East Anglia, 1990-91

Introduction

The Office of Family Advocate has its roots in the monumental work of the Commission of Inquiry into the Structure and Functioning of the Courts in South Africa which was appointed in 1979 under the chairmanship of Appellate Division Judge GG Hoexter.[1] The fifth and final report of the commission, which was submitted in 1983[2], drew attention[3] to the negative effect of the adversary divorce procedure which:

> "hampers the process of adjudication in divorce. The adversary system often results in crucial differences within the family in respect of which the court ought to give a decision being artificially withheld from the court's adjudication."[4]

Moreover, the commission was concerned about:

> "the unsatisfactory manner in which many undefended divorce actions are disposed of [which] is partly due to the fact that both the question whether the marriage has irretrievably broken down[5] and the investigation into the suitability of the proposed provision for minor children are considered by the court purely in the light of the plaintiff's one-sided testimony."

---

1 See Government Gazette 6761 of 1979, GN 286 of 1979.
2 Report No RP 78 of 1983.
3 At para 8.9.5.
4 See Schäfer, *The Concept of Family Courts in South Africa*, unpublished doctoral thesis (University of Natal, 1981) 287.
5 The Divorce Act of 1979 provides for one principal ground of divorce; namely, for the irretrievable breakdown of the marriage provided the court "is satisfied that the marriage relationship between the parties to the marriage has reached such a state of disintegration that there is no reasonable prospect of the restoration of a normal marriage relationship between them" (s 4(1)). The Divorce Act also makes provision for a Divorce to be granted on the grounds of the defendant's mental illness or continuous unconsciousness while the Dissolution of Marriages on Presumption of Death Act 1979 effectively creates a further, albeit rare, ground of divorce; namely, where the Supreme Court, on the application of a married person who seeks leave to presume the death of his missing spouse, may order that the marriage between the parties shall be dissolved from the date of the presumed death of the missing spouse.

Consequently, divorce settlements often turned out to be unsatisfactory so that ill-considered decisions regarding the children of divorce resulted, sooner or later, in welfare agencies having to step in to try and resolve a continuing family problem.

Amongst the many far-reaching recommendations of the commission was that an Office of the Children's Friend be created[6] "to see to the proper protection of the rights of minor or dependent children."[7] In making this recommendation the commission had in mind as a model the family advocate system in operation in the Canadian Province of British Columbia.[8] Reacting to this recommendation the legislature passed the Mediation in Certain Divorce Matters Act 24 of 1987.

Prior to this Act coming into force on 1 October 1990[9], it was widely circulated among all interested persons and bodies for their comments. This included judges of the various divisions of the Supreme Court, representative bodies of the attorneys and advocates profession and also various welfare organizations with an interest in the welfare of children.

In order to gauge the various responses of such persons and bodies[10], and to advise the Minister of Justice on the drafting of the regulations to give effect to the provisions of the Act, an Implementation Committee was appointed in May 1990.[11] This committee felt that the acid test for the success or otherwise of the Office of Family Advocate in South Africa was for it to "commence business" as soon as possible on a pilot project basis, initially in the Transvaal Provincial Division at Pretoria (but excluding the Witwatersrand Local Division at Johannesburg).

---

6   At para 8.11.4.
7   Other recommendations were for the divorce procedure to be amended whereby, *inter alia*, no summons for divorce could be issued until such time as an investigation into the welfare of the children of the parties had been carried out. It was also proposed that no order for divorce should be granted until both parties to the divorce had testified in court (unless there were good and sufficient reasons for the absence of the defendant): see para 8.10.3. This particular proposal was not well received and although a Bill was published to give expression to this recommendation no further action has been taken: see *e.g.* Hahlo, *The South African Law of Husband and Wife* 5th ed (1985) ix who described it as a "Do-Gooders Bill, well intentioned but impracticable and unnecessary." The other proposal of note was the recommendation for the establishment of a family court system in South Africa: see para 7.8 and Chapter 8.
8   See para 8.11.5 where this official is described as follows: "the family advocate is always available to intervene on behalf of a child, to give legal advice, to provide legal assistance in a family crisis situation, and to attempt to resolve issues in the best interests of the child and the family.... If the matter is to be heard, the family advocate will investigate investigatory reports so that the hearing can proceed expeditiously with an independent body of evidence and due note of all relevant material."
9   In terms of Proclamation R181 of 1 October 1990.
10 Which were by no means unanimous. Some serious misgivings, especially by members of the Bar, the Side-Bar and the Bench, were expressed about the practicability of the Act.
11 This committee still continues to sit from time to time under the chairmanship of Mr Justice D H Van Zyl. The committee is comprised of a member of the attorneys' profession, a legal academic, members of the social work profession and members of the Department of Justice.

The Family Advocate: appointment, jurisdiction and powers

It is a requirement of the Act that any person appointed as a Family Advocate must be "suitable for appointment ... by reason of his involvement in or experience of the adjudication or settlement of family matters."[12] The first Family Advocate[13] was appointed on 1 September 1990. Her progress was closely monitored and it soon became obvious that further appointments would have to be made. A second Family Advocate was appointed for Johannesburg with effect from 1 April 1991. The demand for the establishment of the Office of Family Advocate in the rest of the provincial divisions of the Supreme Court became so great that it could no longer be ignored. Family Advocates have since been appointed in Bloemfontein, Cape Town, Port Elizabeth, Grahamstown and Durban. Further appointments can be expected.[14]

The main function of the Family Advocate is to safeguard the interests of the minor or dependent children of divorce and to assist the court to discharge its duty in terms of section 6(1) (a) of the Divorce Act of 1979 which requires the court, before granting a divorce, to be satisfied that the arrangements "made or contemplated with regard to the welfare of any minor or dependent child of the marriage are satisfactory or are the best that can be effected in the circumstances." Accordingly, in terms of section 4(1) of the Mediation in Certain Divorce Matters Act the Family Advocate shall have jurisdiction to institute enquiries in respect of:

(i) divorce actions where minor or dependent children are involved[15]; and
(ii) applications made for the variation, rescission or suspension of an order with regard to the custody or guardianship of, or access to, a child previously made in terms of the Divorce Act.[16]

If the court so orders, or if any party to the above proceedings requests it, the Family Advocate shall hold an enquiry. In addition, the Family Advocate is given the discretionary power to apply to court at any stage of the above

---

12 S 2(2) Mediation in Certain Divorce Matters Act.
13 Professor FJ Bosman, formerly of the University of South Africa.
14 Apart from some minor exceptions, the overall reaction to the Office of Family Advocate has been most enthusiastic and positive. This is in direct contrast with the erstwhile lukewarm reception. The present positive reaction can be contrasted with the Australian experience when family courts were first established in 1975: resistance was particularly noticeable amongst the practising members of the legal profession. This resistance changed to general enthusiasm after family courts had become a *fait accompli.*
15 A divorce action includes an application for an interdict or the interim custody of, or interim access to, a child *pendente lite* made in terms of Rule 43 of the Uniform Rules of the Supreme Court: *Terblanche* 1992 1 SA 501 (W).
16 The power to institute enquiries is only exercisable *after* a divorce action has been instituted, or *after* an application for variation etc has been made. Thus the Family Advocate has no power to institute an enquiry, for example, before an application for variation etc is made and no party can compel a Family Advocate to institute such an enquiry with a view to determining whether to launch an application.

proceedings, where he deems it in the interests of any minor or dependent child, for permission to hold an enquiry.

Where the parties to an action for divorce or an application which has been launched after the commencement of the Mediation in Certain Divorce Matters Act[17] have arrived at a settlement, further steps to have the settlement made an order of court cannot be taken until such time as the Family Advocate is furnished with a copy "of all particulars in relation to such settlement, in so far as such settlement relates to any minor or dependent child of the marriage concerned."[18] The aim of this provision is to enable the Family Advocate to indicate whether or not an enquiry is contemplated in respect of the settlement. Such an enquiry may become necessary where the consent paper contains clauses regarding the children which are substantially at variance with information already collected by the Family Advocate[19], and which might indicate that one or other of the parties in an unequal bargaining position has been pressurised into an agreement which is not in the best interests of the children. Even if there is such a discrepancy an enquiry might not necessarily be justified and all that the Family Advocate need do is to draw the attention of the court to this fact so that some explanation can be elicited from the parties as to its justification; that is, before the consent paper is made an order of court.

To enable the Family Advocate to give proper expression to his powers and duties the regulations in terms of the Act require a completed prescribed form to be filed with the summons for divorce or the application for a variation, rescission or suspension of an order regarding the custody or guardianship of, or access to, any child previously made in terms of the Divorce Act.[20] A copy of the summons or application, together with the completed prescribed form is routinely passed on to the Family Advocate by the registrar of the Supreme Court. The defendant or the respondent may, if they wish, also complete, and file with the registrar, the prescribed form[21] and this will also be passed on to the Family Advocate.

The prescribed form[22] requires the person completing it to disclose the minimum information one would reasonably expect a judge or Family Advocate to have in order to decide whether an enquiry in terms of the Act is required or not. Apart from the usual personal particulars, the prescribed form requires the person completing it to disclose where the children are presently living, who is looking after them, and what the arrangements are that have been made or proposed regarding the custody of, access to, and

---

17 The Act came into operation on 1 October 1990: Proclamation No R181 of 1990.
18 Reg 3(3).
19 Either from the prescribed forms completed by the parties or as a result of enquiries made by the family counsellors at the request of the Family Advocate.
20 The prescribed form is referred to as Annexure "A" in the regulations. Annexure "B" is the form prescribed for completion by the defendant or respondent.
21 Reg 2(2).
22 The prescribed form is similar to the "statement of arrangements" that petitioners in undefended divorce actions complete to assist the court to discharge its duties in terms of s 41 Matrimonial Causes Act 1973: see *Undefended Divorce* (Lord Chancellor's Office, 1977).

guardianship of, the children. Any details regarding their learning problems, or physical or mental disabilities have to be disclosed and also whether any of the children have been convicted of any criminal offence or whether they are subject to any "care or supervision order". If the children or the family are known to, or have had dealings with, any welfare organisation this fact must also be disclosed.

The enquiry itself is characterised by its informality and the Family Advocate is given the power to institute an enquiry "in any manner he deems expedient or desirable."[23] He may call for the submission to him of "such affidavits or other statements in writing or reports or documents or things"[24] as he deems necessary and he may appoint anyone to assist him in the enquiry.[25] Such persons need not necessarily be formally qualified social workers. In South Africa there are many private and voluntary welfare organisations, particularly among the Black communities, who have over the years performed a very valuable service. Although many of their members have no formal social work qualifications, they have gained immensely in practical experience and the indications are that their services will be readily made available to the Office of the Family Advocate.

Within 15 days of the completion of his enquiry the Family Advocate must submit his report and recommendations to the court.[26] At the same time, he "shall deliver or cause to be delivered to the plaintiff or the defendant, or the applicant or respondent, as the case may be, copies of such report and recommendation."[27]

Recommendations of the Family Advocate

There is nothing in the Mediation in Certain Divorce Matters Act, or the regulations, that make it obligatory for the court to follow the recommendations of the Family Advocate.[28] Therefore, it cannot be said that the Family Advocate will usurp the traditional role and function of the Supreme Court as upper guardian of all minors within the area of its jurisdiction.

With the passage of time, it is anticipated that the parties concerned, and the Supreme Court, will generally follow the recommendations. Thus, the Transvaal Provincial Division of the Supreme Court, where the Family Advocate has been in existence the longest, usually endorses the Family Advocate's recommendations.

---

23 Reg 5(1).
24 Reg 5(2).
25 Reg 6.
26 Reg 5(3).
27 *Ibid.*
28 *e.g.* in *Martens* 1991 4 SA 287(T), the court declined to follow the Family Advocate's recommendation that 11-year old twin girls be returned to their mother's custody. The twins had been "snatched" from their mother in Germany and it was three and a half years before they were traced to South Africa.

Interestingly, the Office of Family Advocate has the capacity to make a valuable contribution to the development of the law. For example, in *Van Erk*[29] it was on the strength of the convincing and persuasive report and recommendations of the Family Advocate that Van Zyl J was persuaded to depart from well-established precedents to the contrary that the time had now arrived to recognise the inherent right of access by a natural father to his illegitimate child.[30]

Assuming that the court favours the recommendations of the Family Advocate, but one (or both) of the parties objects to them, then there is no reason why the onus should not be placed on such party to show that the recommendations should not be followed.[31] However, the experience thus far has been that the parties are generally inclined to support the recommendations of the Family Advocate because he is not perceived as representing either of them. For this reason, it is important for the Family Advocate and family counsellors to make clear to parties that their sole interest is the welfare of the children.

Family counsellors

Family counsellors may be appointed to assist the Family Advocate.[32] They have a "bridging" role to play enabling the legal and social work disciplines to interact in a practical and meaningful way in the divorce scene. Both the Mediation in Certain Divorce Matters Act and the regulations are silent on the powers and functions of family counsellors. Section 3(1) merely states that the family counsellor is "to assist the Family Advocate with an enquiry." However, it can confidently be stated that the family counsellor will have at least the following functions to perform; namely:

(i) to write and collect reports for, and to make recommendations to, the Family Advocate. This means that family counsellors might have to interview the parties to the action or the application and, in appropriate circumstances, the children as well. It may also be necessary, for example, to interview the teachers of the children concerned, or anyone else who has had dealings with the children or the family;

(ii) to act as a link between the Family Advocate and the helping profession.[33] In this way the specific requirements of the Family Advocate can be made known to those who are called upon to assist the Family Advocate so that there can be a proper focus on the relevant issues;

---

29 Unreported judgment: case no 20690/1991 dated 5.2.1992.

30 See also *Terblanche* 1992 1 SA 501 (W) at 504 where the Family Advocate was complimented for an "outstanding report and extremely helpful recommendations."

31 It is arguable that where opposition to the Family Advocate's recommendations is vexatious and without foundation there is no reason why the opposing party should not be penalised by an order for costs.

32 S 3(1) Mediation in Certain Divorce Matters Act.

33 *e.g.* social workers, clinical psychologists, medical practitioners and even ministers of religion.

(iii) to participate in the mediation process in so far as it concerns the children. In this regard, marriage counselling could be recommended if it should appear that the marriage has not really broken down; and

(iv) to assist the Family Advocate generally with the enquiry, to guide the Family Advocate with regard to any recommendations to be made and to perform such tasks and duties as the Family Advocate may require.

It is conceivable that family counsellors could be called upon to appear in court at the trial to justify any of the recommendations they make to the Family Advocate. The Family Advocate, who may appear at the trial of any divorce action or hearing and who may lead any evidence and cross-examine witnesses, must therefore be careful not to place himself in the position of a witness.

A matter still to be resolved is the extent of the privilege, if any, of communications made to the Family Advocate or the family counsellors during the course of an enquiry. The present indications are that such communications are not privileged and this may well cause some difficulties in the future.[34]

Some observations

A question that comes to mind is the extent to which the Mediation in Certain Divorce Matters Act will affect the traditional interventionist approach of our judges who have always regarded themselves as the upper guardians of all minor children within the area of their jurisdiction.[35]

The following aspects of the interventionist approach need to be noted; namely:

(i) the interventionist approach is nothing more than a symbolic expression of concern for the welfare of children – an empty and meaningless ritual[36];

(ii) but where intervention is clearly called for, it sometimes happens that a judge fails to rise to the occasion[37]; and

---

34 *Cf* McCrory, "Confidentiality in Mediation of Matrimonial Disputes" (1988) 51 MLR 442.

35 See, *inter alia*, *Calitz* 1939 AD 56 at 63; *Ex Parte Simpson* 1953 1 SA565 (A) at 579; *Botes v Daley* 1976 2 SA 215 (N).

36 This is not to suggest an attitude of indifference on the part of our judges but, rather, this is due to the nature of the divorce procedure which makes it impossible for our judges to discharge their duty in terms of s 6 of the Divorce Act, especially when confronted with a long roll of divorce cases each motion court day.

37 An example of this is the unreported case of *L v L* presided over by Rein AJ in East London in 1988 (Case No 85 of 1988). This was an unopposed divorce where the father asked for the custody of two minor children aged 6 and 2 years. The judge correctly commented that it was most "unusual for two youngsters like that to be with their father" but then continued, without further ado, to accept the father's untested response that the defendant wife was happy for him to have the custody of the children because "her boyfriend's children were enough for her to cope with." *(cont. overleaf)*

(iii) on the other hand, some judges appear to take an over-robust view of their interventionist role.[38]

Despite the above ambivalence, the Supreme Court is generally very jealous of its role as upper guardian of all children within the area of its jurisdiction. But what will undoubtedly change is the extent of the court's active intervention. Thus, the court will now be able to rely on the Family Advocate to perform a useful "watchdog" function. The Family Advocate is able to intervene in a manner that the court cannot. Active intervention on the part of the court itself may well decrease since any intervention will normally take place at the instance of the Family Advocate acting on his own initiative, or where ordered to do so by the court, or at the request of either of the parties, and will, therefore, be much more meaningful than before.[39] Intervention will no longer be an empty symbolic exercise. Furthermore, the power of intervention will not go by default and will occur only where this is necessary.

(cont.) Custody was granted to the father. No consideration appears to have been given to the arrangements (if any) made for the welfare, care and upbringing of the 2-year old child. The fact that the 6-year old child was attending a primary school appeared to satisfy the learned judge that the child would be properly cared for. No mention was made of who was to look after the 2-year old child while the husband was at work and no arrangements appear to have been made to look after the 6-year old child during the school holidays or the afternoons when the father would still be at work. One should not be surprised to learn that subsequent to the granting of the divorce order an application had to be made to the Childrens' Court to have the children removed from the father and placed in care. It then transpired that the father had changed his employment over 20 times in the previous 8 years. Furthermore, the home and personal circumstances concerning this particular family were already well-known to local welfare officials.

38 An example is the case of *Schlebusch* 1988 4 SA 548(E) where the judge saw fit to intervene to refuse an order for joint custody despite the fact that both parents had asked for it. Mullins J's refusal to grant the order for joint custody was, on his own admission, influenced by the "traditional viewpoint in regard to the placing of children in the custody of a single parent or individual" :(at 550). He was also concerned about the possibility of the parents, one of whom lived on a farm and the other in a nearby town, disagreeing with each other in the future over the upbringing of their children, despite the fact that there was no indication that this was going to happen. The evidence was that the parents were still on good terms with each other at the time of the divorce and one wonders whether the judge was correct to assume that any future differences between them were necessarily going to be of the nature to make joint custody unworkable. After all, even in intact families, differences inevitably occur over the upbringing of children and these do not necessarily result in an "irretrievable breakdown" of the joint parenting relationship: see Schäfer "Joint custody" (1987) 104 SALJ 149. The court's unnecessary intervention was based purely on speculation of what might happen if the parents should disagree with one another over the upbringing of their children. Joint custody should have been granted in this case for it to have a chance to work in practice, as the parents obviously hoped it would, but the judge was not convinced of the beneficial effects of a joint custody order.

39 It would seem this is also the motivation behind the introduction of the philosophy of non-intervention contained in s 1 (5) of the English Children Act 1989 which came into force on 14 October 1991. S 1 (5) states that "Where the court is considering whether or not to make one or more orders under this Act with respect to a child, it shall not make the order or any of the orders unless it considers that doing so would be better for the child than making no order at all." The apparent advantages of this new section are cited by the English Law Commission in its Report No 172 of 1988 at para 3.4: see also Bainham, *Children. The New Law. The Children Act 1989* (1990) 15-16. As Bainham (1990) 20 *Family Law at* 145 points out: "The non-intervention principle is likely to result in a changed perception of the public interest in private family proceedings. It will have the greatest impact on divorce. The intention is that the new s 8 orders (*i.e.* "contact"; "prohibited steps"; "residence" and "specific issue" orders) should not be granted routinely in the way in which custody and access orders were made under the old law. They should be made only where the court can see some positive benefit to the child."

Moreover, it is confidently anticipated that the effect of the report and recommendations of the Family Advocate will be to curb the judicial instinct to be bound by precedent which may sometimes be out of step with modern developments.[40] Alternatively, where the common law or judicial precedent is silent on a particular matter then the report and recommendations of the Family Advocate could have an important impact on the court's decision to adopt a bold and innovative approach to such matter.[41]

It has also been noted that since the establishment of the Office of Family Advocate some judges are only too happy to refer matters to the Family Advocate for an enquiry to be conducted.[42] This can be construed as meaning:

(i) that the judges are now willing to acknowledge their inability under the former divorce procedure to discharge in a meaningful way their duty in terms of section 6 of the Divorce Act; and

(ii) that the judges are beginning to recognise the value and importance of the role of the Family Advocate in actions or applications where the interests of children are concerned.

This welcome development is undoubtedly attributable to the fact that judges no longer regard the Family Advocate as a threat to their jealously guarded role as upper guardian of all children within the area of their jurisdiction. Indeed, Family Advocates have an important complementary role to play. It is, after all, the court and not the Family Advocate that makes the final order.

Finally, mention should be made of the apparently contradictory procedures under which the Family Advocate operates. Thus, any enquiry the Family Advocate conducts is characterised by its lack of formality, while his appearance in court in terms of the Act is governed by the traditional adversary procedure. This contradiction can be explained on the basis that if the Family Advocate is unable to make a recommendation because it is impossible to do so[43], or where the recommendation is not accepted by the court, or the parties, and the matter proceeds to trial in the ordinary way,

---

40 As was, it is submitted, the case in *Schlebusch* above (see n.38 above).

41 As, for example, in *Van Erk, supra* n 29 where Van Zyl J thought that the recognition of the natural father's right to access was "amply justified by the precepts of justice, equity and reasonableness and by the demands of public policy." See p 42 of the unreported judgment.

42 An obvious reason for this is that the judges just do not have the time (or inclination) to conduct the type of investigation that the Family Advocate has the power to conduct: *cf* Davis, MacLeod and Murch "Undefended divorce: should section 41 of the Matrimonial Causes Act 1973 be repealed?" (1983) 46 MLR 121 at 146 where it was pointed out that judges, in any event, seemed "ill at ease in a role which required direct communication with the parents." Some of the criticisms of the "Children's Appointment" are considered by Schäfer "Alternative divorce procedures in the interests of children: some comparative aspects" (1988) 51 *Tydskrif vir Hedendaagse Romeins-Hollandse Reg* (*Journal of Contemporary Roman-Dutch law*) 297 at 300-305.

43 *e.g.* where, notwithstanding the Family Advocate's power in terms of reg 5(2) to call for the production of any statements, reports, affidavits etc the Family Advocate is confronted with a total lack of co-operation either from the parties themselves or on the part of those who have had dealings with the family and who are unprepared to disclose essential information, reports, or documents.

the court will at least have the benefit of the Family Advocate's report and the annexures upon which the recommendations have been made. These documents, together with the prescribed form[44], will help to crystallise the issues that are in contention between the parties. In the final analysis, the court will be in a better position than before to give proper expression to the best interests of the children involved.

---

44 Which both parties to the action or the application have the right to complete.

Chapter 3

Regulating Intercountry Adoption – an International Perspective

William Duncan*

Professor of Law, Trinity College, Dublin

Introduction

The paper will begin with an attempt to outline some of the trends in adoption which are apparent in different countries. My account will be brief and selective and it will be offered as a prelude to the second and major theme of the paper which will be a discussion of some of the issues raised by intercountry adoption, and of the current efforts by the Hague Conference on Private International Law to achieve international agreement on the regulation of intercountry adoption.

The functions of adoption: parental needs, children's interests

Like all human institutions, that of adoption had tended to adapt itself to changing social needs. It is well known that in many countries the adoption of children began as a means of ensuring the continuation of a family line, especially for the purposes of passing on property.[1] Generally speaking, early systems of adoption appear as devices intended primarily to satisfy parental needs, whether this be, for example, the need for an heir or, as in the Hindu tradition, the need for a child to perform certain spiritual tasks for the parent. The introduction of adoption into the laws particularly of some common law countries (including Ireland) in the twentieth century, was seen as a convenient way of resolving two social problems. It offered unmarried mothers a means of avoiding the stigma and economic hardship associated with birth outside marriage, and it offered childless couples the opportunity to rear children.

---

* Professor Duncan is a member of the Irish Law Reform Commission. He is also a member of the Drafting Committee for the International Convention on InterCountry Adoption currently being formulated by a Special Commission of the Hague Conference on Private International Law.

1 For example, Roman Law and the Code Napoleon of 1804.

The modern approach to adoption tends to be more child-centred and to emphasise the child's right to live, in love and security, within a family. Thus Article 20 of the United Nations Convention on the Rights of the Child views adoption as a means of providing alternative care for a child who is deprived of his or her family environment, and places an obligation on States Parties who allow adoption to "ensure that the best interests of the child should be the paramount consideration." The process of adoption, in theory at least, is now seen as one of seeking a family for a child whose biological family has ceased to function, rather than that of seeking a child for the benefit of the prospective adopters.[2]

There are three comments which I would like to make about this modern child-centred approach to adoption. The first is the obvious one that if adoption is a means of finding parents for children with needs it is important that the law be flexible enough, first to allow all children with such needs to be adopted, and second to enable the most appropriate parents to be selected to meet the needs of the child. There has consequently been a tendency in some countries gradually to liberalise their rules relating to the adoptability of children and eligibility to adopt. (For example, rules limiting the adoption of children by reason of their age, status or health, and rules forbidding adoption by single parents.) However, tradition continues to exercise constraints on this development, particularly in countries where religion or superstition support an ideology of the family which does not place children's needs uppermost.

The second point is that this child-centred approach may sometimes be more of an aspiration than a reality. The ideal of adoption as a process of seeking suitable parents for children-in-need requires, for its practical implementation, a degree of control over the processes of selection and matching which some countries have not yet achieved. This is still a serious problem in the context of intercountry adoption, especially where independent adoptions are concerned (see below).

A third point is that the principle that the child's interests should always be paramount in adoption is not reflected in every aspect of adoption law, even in those countries which accept the general principle. For example, in several countries[3] rules which provide for dispensing with the consent of biological parents do not allow this to occur simply on proof that adoption would on balance appear more likely to improve the child's prospects. In other words, some weighting is given to parental rights. Also, in intercountry adoption, the principle that priority should be given to placement of the child in his/her country of origin, though based

---

2   The justification for the modern institution of adoption may be found in the principle, recognised in the preamble to the UN Convention on the Rights of the Child, "that the child, for the full and harmonious development of his or her personality, should grow up in a family environment, in an atmosphere of happiness, love and understanding."

3   For example the United Kingdom, Ireland, Israel.

principally on considerations of the child's interests, is sometimes given broader political and economic justifications. In short, both in national and in intercountry adoptions, there is concern lest the principle of giving priority to the child's interests be used as an excuse for social engineering, that is to justify a more generalised transfer of children from poor to wealthy parents, or from developing to rich economies.[4]

Some questions of supply and demand

There has been a quite dramatic reduction in the number of children available for adoption domestically in many of the developed countries over the last 25 years.[5] (In Ireland, for example, the number of domestic adoptions fell from 1, 443 in 1975 to 649 in 1988.) There are a variety of reasons for this. Overall birth rates have been falling in these countries, and while out-of-wedlock birth rates have risen in many countries, the social supports now given to single mothers, combined with a lessening in the disadvantages and stigma attached to "illegitimacy", have meant that fewer children born outside marriage are made available for adoption.

One of the effects of this phenomenon is that more attention can be paid to children with special needs, for example to older and handicapped children. Another effect has been that the demand for children domestically in these countries far exceeds the number of children available for adoption. In some countries this has led to the imposition by agencies of selection criteria which go beyond the statutory minimum. But, more important, is the fact that it has led to the upsurge in applications for intercountry adoption.

By contrast, the figures for abandoned children in developing countries remain staggering. It is estimated by UNICEF that about 155 million children under five in the developing countries live in absolute poverty.[6] There are about 100 million abandoned children who "subsist only by back-breaking work, or turn to petty crime, prostitution or begging."[7] Every war or civil upheaval seems to add to this tragic picture. In Europe, much attention has been paid in the recent past to Romania where the official estimate of abandoned children is 67, 339.[8] But the scale of the problem is far greater in Latin America, Asia and Africa, where the fundamental

---

4   Nor will the welfare of the child necessarily be the paramount consideration in determining custody of a child in circumstances where an adoption order is found to be invalid. See, *e.g.* the judgment of the Supreme Court of Israel *Re Return of Adopted Child to Brazil,* 16 June 1988, and the Irish case of *M* v *An Bord Uchtala* [1977] IR 287.
5   In the United States adoptions fell from an all-time high of 175, 000 in 1970 to 104, 088 in 1986. *Adoption Factbook* (National Committee for Adoption, 1989).
6   UNICEF, *State of the World's Children* (1991).
7   Damien Ngabonziza, Secretary General of International Social Service. "Moral and Political Issues facing Relinquishing Countries" (1991) 15 *Adoption and Fostering* 75.
8   Statement by Mme. Zugravescu, Chairperson of the Romanian Committee for Adoption, 30 January 1992.

causes remain poverty and, in some countries, continuing economic deterioration.[9] The same economic conditions hinder the development of child care (including adoption) services in the developing countries, despite the widely accepted view that priority should always be given to placement of abandoned children in families in their own communities – a view eloquently expressed by the Indian Supreme Court in 1984 in *Laxshmi Kant Pandey* v *Union of India*. The development of adoption services in developing countries will no doubt continue to be a principal theme. It is obviously of great importance for those who come from the wealthier countries to appreciate the problems involved, and to avoid developments, especially in the context of intercountry adoption, which may frustrate efforts to build up local services and encourage domestic placements of children. For example, it is noteworthy that in Romania (the country which accounted for about one third of intercountry adoptions worldwide in 1991), the number of Romanian families wishing to adopt has been on the increase.[10] Yet there has been some concern that the efforts of some Romanian families may have been frustrated by their inability to match the large sums of money at the disposal of foreign adopters.

The international situation of a ready supply of children from the poorer counties, and a strong demand for adoption especially from childless couples in developed countries, as has been pointed out by Hans van Loon, has acquired a structural dimension[11] to which the language of economics has been applied. One of the problems created by this situation, in which supply exceeds demand, is that a child-centred approach to placement is difficult. While adoption should be a process of seeking families for children, "one ends up looking for children to satisfy the needs of the couples or families wishing to adopt."[12] Even worse, pressure from economically favoured adopters, combined with the guilt that biological parents may feel at depriving a child of a future free from poverty, may further contribute to the family rupture. "Not even local official or private child welfare agencies are exempt from this pressure, when the sending of a child to a distant and idealised country is portrayed as an easy and more promising alternative to the creation and administration of family support programmes, an arduous task whose success will not always be evident in the short run."[13]

Different concepts of adoption: exclusivity v openness

Being brought up in the West, the concept of adoption which formed my first mental image of the institution was a rigid one which emphasised the

---

9   See Hans van Loon, *Report on Intercountry Adoption* (Hague Conference, 1990) 62.
10 About 25% of adoptions in Romania in 1991 were national.
11 Above, at 58.
12 Becker, "The Pressure to Abandon" (1988) 5 Nos 2/3 *International Child Rights Monitor*, Defence for Children International, speaking of the situation in Brazil.
13 *Ibid.*

idea of the clean-break – the complete integration of the child into the adoptive family and the severance of ties with the biological family. This exclusivist concept of adoption is in part based on considerations of the child's welfare – the need for continuity and permanence in the child's life, and the importance for the child of being accepted as a full member of his/her new family. But, in retrospect, it can also be seen how this idea of the cleanbreak coincided with adult interests in the adoption process. It provided a neat solution to the problems of birth outside marriage by offering the biological mother a confidential mechanism by which she could avoid the social disgrace and hardship which her condition attracted and build a new life for herself. In short, the concept of clean-break adoption may be as much the product of the social stigma attaching to out-of-wedlock birth, as of considerations of the child's interests. It is, therefore, fascinating to observe the reappraisal of the clean-break doctrine which has been apparent for some time, and the attempts to introduce, not necessarily a completely new paradigm, but greater flexibility and openness in adoption arrangements geared to meet the needs of specific children.

Greater recognition is being given to the importance for the child of his/her biological ties. In some countries this began with changes in legislation or practice enabling adopted children to gain easier access to birth records with a view in some cases to contacting birth parents. More recently it has been evidenced by a willingness to contemplate open adoption, or adoption with contact, particularly for non-infants. What began as a recognition of the need to provide maximum information on birth parentage to adoptive children and their adoptive parents, has now moved on to an exploration of the circumstances and ways in which continuing contact with biological parents may benefit adopted children. This is now a concern, for example, in the United Kingdom where it is felt that the clean-break approach, particularly when applied to children adopted after infancy, may have done damage.

As John Triseliotis has said: "The significance of the emotional links between especially an older child and a mother or father or a grandparent were often underestimated and some children were cut off from emotional life lines before they had established new ones." Furthermore, "A range of studies suggests that contact does not threaten the stability of the placement, provided the new family have agreed to it. On the contrary, contact seems to help stabilise the arrangements."[14]

This is one of the many areas in which international comparisons are instructive. The clean-break model of adoption is not universal. In many countries an adoption order does not have the effect of completely severing the child's relationship with the biological family. For example, this is the position under systems of simple adoption which are common in South America, but which also exist in other countries such as France. However, there is a need for caution in making such comparisons. The maintenance

---

14 Triselioitis, "Permanency Planning" (1991) 15 *Adoption and Fostering* 6.

of legal ties with biological parents often has more to do with retaining inheritance rights than social links. Nevertheless, examples do exist, even in the context of intercountry adoption, of open adoption. For example, under Nepalese law an intercountry adoption will only be permitted under conditions which permit the child to have direct correspondence or contact with his/her biological parents, and which allow the child the opportunity of returning to his/her country of origin on coming of age, if he/she so wishes.

The idea of open adoption does pose obvious practical difficulties in the intercountry context.[15] Indeed, there seems to be a widely held view among delegates at the Hague Conference that adoption which completely severs the ties with the biological family is the most appropriate model for intercountry adoption. There is a certain irony in this at a time when on the domestic front a number of countries are reassessing the value for the adopted child of retaining links with biological parents.

The adoption process: two issues

In discussions at The Hague, two major issues concerning the adoption process, and the safeguards surrounding it, have emerged. The first concerns the question of so-called "independent" or "private" adoptions. The second relates to the desirability of having a "waiting" or "probation" period after placement of the child and before the adoption is made.

Independent adoptions

An independent adoption may be defined as one which occurs without the involvement of an authorised professional adoption agency. Such adoptions are still permitted in many countries both in the domestic and intercountry contexts, despite the fact that the United Nations Convention on the Rights of the Child, in Article 21 (e), clearly favours placement of children for intercountry adoption by "competent authorities or organs". One of the reasons why prospective adopters prefer to use independent, rather than agency, channels is that "the demand for children (usually babies) is larger than the number of available children through adoption agencies." Other reasons include the avoidance of delays and waiting lists.[16]

While there is evidence associating independent adoption with a variety of bad practices, abuses and illicit activities (for example poor selection and matching of adoptive parents, pressure on biological parents, failure

---

15 These difficulties relate to the physical problems of continued contact over large distances. Problems relating to consent also arise, where, in the country of origin, the biological parents have agreed to a simple adoption while in the receiving country simple adoption is not recognised.

16 See generally Defence for Children International et al, *Preliminary Findings of a Joint Investigation on Independent Intercountry Adoptions* (March 1991).

to explore alternatives in the child's country of origin, failure to determine a child's adoptability, falsification of documents, improper financial gain, trafficking and sale of children), agreement on this is not universal among countries of origin, some of which associate these practices also with agency adoptions. Nevertheless, a number of countries of origin have clearly viewed the elimination of independent adoptions as a crucial element in combating bad or illicit practices. One of the first was India which insists that "every application from a foreigner desiring to adopt a child must be sponsored by a social or child welfare agency recognised or licensed by the government of the country in which the foreigner is resident."[17] Other countries such as the Philippines and Columbia have a similar rule. And most recently Romania, following advice tendered by a group of independent experts who visited the country in March 1991[18], has barred private adoptions and insists on the use of agencies approved by the Romanian Committee for Adoption and governments in the respective receiving states.

Despite this general trend in favour of agency adoptions, there remains a strong lobby, particularly in the United States, to allow individual professionals, such as lawyers and doctors, a continuing role in arranging intercountry adoptions. The arguments are that such persons are subject to professional standards and controls, that they can sometimes operate more efficiently, flexibly and swiftly than agencies, and that where they need to call upon other experts (for example, in preparing home studies) they do so.

Whatever the merits of the opposing arguments, it appears unlikely that the United States, which receives far more children through intercountry adoption than any other state[19], would ratify a Convention which insists on agency adoption as an exclusive principle. The compromise that appears likely to be struck is one whereby individual countries will be able, if they so wish, to insist on agency adoption in their own cases, but as between countries which do not insist on agency adoption, individual professionals may still be allowed to act subject to control and supervision by central authorities. The matter is, however, still not resolved, and many states and international bodies remain convinced that one of the principal objects of international co-operation – the elimination of the abuses associated with intercountry adoption, especially the sale of and trafficking in children – will not be achieved unless there is strict adherence to the principle embodied in the United Nations Convention on the Rights of the Child.

---

17 See *Laxshmi Kant Pandey* v *Union of India*, above.
18 Defence for Children International and International Social Service, Romania, *The Adoption of Romanian Children by Foreigners* (April 1991)
19 The estimated number of intercountry adoptions world-wide per annum is 20, 000. In 1987, the foreign adoption count was 10, 097, though by 1989 it fell to just below 8, 000.

The waiting or probation period

There continues to be a strong difference of opinion internationally over the value or need for a post-placement and pre-adoption probation period, especially in intercountry adoptions. Many South American countries continue to doubt the value of probation, and view with alarm the idea of allowing a child to leave their borders without his/her status as an adopted child already fully secure.[20] On the other hand, the period of probation is seen in a number of European countries (especially the United Kingdom and Switzerland) as an indispensable stage in the process of securing the integration of the child in the adoptive family.

From the point of view of international co-operation, this conflict in opinion about how best to secure the welfare of the child within the adoption process poses extreme problems. Some countries which insist on a probation period in domestic adoption are prepared to compromise in the international context by recognising adoption orders granted abroad to their own residents despite the absence of probation.[21] Other states, such as the United Kingdom, appear unprepared to accept the compromise, and argue that safeguards for the child in intercountry adoption should not be any less than those which apply to domestic adoptions. How this impasse will be resolved is not yet clear. One possibility is a form of conditional recognition by the receiving state which would become final after a successful probationary period.[22]

Towards international co-operation in the regulation of intercountry adoption: a proposed Convention

I should like to turn now to the work being done at the Hague Conference on Private International Law, the object of which is the drafting of an international Convention on Intercountry Adoption which should be finalised in 1993, the year in which the Conference happens to celebrate its 100th birthday. More than 50 countries, and about a dozen non-governmental organizations, have been taking part in this important venture which began with a first meeting of the Special Commission in June 1990. From its conception, the project has benefited greatly from the wisdom and commitment of Mr Hans van Loon, a member of the Hague

---

20 See, for example, the Inter-American Children's Institute Report on the Meeting of Experts on the Adoption of Minors, which preceded the approval of the *Inter-American Convention on Conflict of Laws Concerning the Adoption of Minors*, in La Paz in 1984.
21 See, for example, Ireland's Adoption Act 1991.
22 This solution presents several problems. The child's status would, during the probationary period, be different in the sending and receiving states. This would lead to legal complications in the event of the placement breaking down. Also the child's status in other Contracting States would have to be clarified.

Conference's Permanent Bureau. His initial research provided a crucial foundation for subsequent discussions.

Objects of the Convention[23]

The objects of the Convention will be threefold:
(i)   to establish safeguards to ensure that intercountry adoptions take place in the best interests of the child and with respect for his or her fundamental rights;
(ii) to establish a system of co-operation amongst states to ensure respect for those safeguards and thereby to prevent the abduction, the sale of, or traffic in children;
(iii) to secure recognition in Contracting States of adoptions made in accordance with the Convention.

Fundamental provisions

The form which the Convention is likely to take is broadly as follows.

There will first be a number of fundamental provisions. These include some basic conditions which must be satisfied before an intercountry adoption may take place. Prominent among them is the requirement that the state of origin must have given due consideration to possibilities for the child's placement in that state[24], combined with the general requirement that intercountry adoption be in the child's best interests. There are rules relating to consents to adoption (including, where appropriate, the child's consent), which emphasise the need for counselling and full information and that the consent should be free, unconditional, and not induced by payment or compensation. The responsibility for ensuring that these conditions are met lies with the state of origin, as does the duty to establish that the child is adoptable.

The receiving state, on the other hand, must determine whether the prospective adopters are eligible and suited to adopt, and that the child will be authorised to enter and reside permanently in that state.

There is likely to be a fundamental provision forbidding unsupervised contact between prospective adopters and biological parents, the object of which is to reduce pressure on biological parents and to help ensure that the adoption process focuses less on the search for children and more on the search for suitable parents. Another basic provision will prohibit the transfer of a child to a receiving state until the child's placement has been agreed and it is clear that no legal bars to adoption exist. This is to avoid the all too common situation in which a child, for whom adoption is legally

---

23 Comments refer to the *Preliminary Draft Convention on International Co-operation and Protection of Children in Respect of Intercountry Adoption*, drawn up by the Special Commission of February 1992.
24 Reflecting the important principle of subsidiarity contained in Art 21 (d) of the UN Convention on the Rights of the Child.

impossible, enters into a legal limbo following transfer to the receiving state.

Central authorities and accredited bodies

The Convention will establish a system of State Central Authorities in each contracting state. Their function will include co-operation with one another through the exchange of general information relevant to intercountry adoption. The Central Authorities will also have functions in respect of specific intercountry adoptions which may be delegated to "accredited bodies". These will no doubt normally be approved adoption agencies. Standards are set for accreditation but, as has already been mentioned, there will possibly be a provision enabling individuals, such as lawyers, to continue to act where the states concerned permit them to do so, but subject to supervision.

Procedures

A chapter on procedures will spell out in greater detail the respective steps to be taken by the Central Authorities (or accredited bodies) of the receiving state and the state of origin, in relation to such matters as the preparation of reports on the prospective adopters and the child, the transmission of such reports, the placement process, obtaining consents, obtaining permission for the child to enter the receiving state, and co-operation in making the arrangements for the transfer of the child. Provision is also made for safeguarding the child in the rare cases where the placement breaks down. The Central Authority in the receiving state will be obliged to take the measures necessary to protect the child and to arrange for the placement of the child in another family; only as a last resort will the child be returned to the state of origin.

Recognition

The Convention will provide for automatic recognition of adoptions made in accordance with the provisions of the Convention. Grounds for refusing recognition will be very narrow. As already mentioned, there may be a system of conditional recognition in exceptional cases, as a response to the concerns of states who insist on a period of probation; but there remains a good deal of opposition to this. There will also hopefully be a provision relating to the effects of adoption on the status and rights of the child, which again is proving difficult to formulate.

General comments on the proposed Convention

Regulation based on co-operation

The fundamental provisions as well as the procedures in the Convention make it clear that the Convention is based on a model of co-operation, and a sharing of responsibilities between the authorities of the receiving state and the state of origin. The underlying assumption is that effective regulation of intercountry adoption, including the elimination of abuses, cannot be fully achieved by unilateral state action. This theme of co-operation will also be reflected in a provision for the calling of regular meetings at The Hague at which Contracting States and their Central Authorities will be able to review the practical operation of the Convention.

Flexibility of jurisdiction and choice of law

Apart from its fundamental provisions, the Convention adopts a flexible approach to a number of matters which in the past have given rise to conflict. This is particularly apparent in the Convention's *laissez-faire* approach to some of the classic problems of private international law. Thus the Convention takes no position on the question of which is the more appropriate jurisdiction in which to make the adoption order – the receiving state or the state of origin. The view taken is that, as long as there is agreement between states on the appropriate division of responsibilities and functions leading up to the adoption, and agreement on the fundamental conditions for the making of the adoption, it matters not in which state at the end of the day the adoption order is made. The Convention, in its various drafts, has also maintained a conspicuous silence on choice of law rules relating to such matters as capacity (to adopt or to be adopted) and consent. It seems to be accepted that there should be maximum flexibility on these matters. There is no point in insisting, for example, that the laws of a particular receiving state be applied to the issue of consent if that state does not insist upon the application of its own rules. On the other hand, there remains some concern that silence on choice of law matters could lead to misunderstanding or confusion in particular cases, and may, therefore, inhibit co-operation.

A vital role for states of origin

The fundamental provisions, combined with the procedural rules, confer major responsibilities on states of origin. It is the state of origin which will have the major responsibility in regulating the process of "matching", in ensuring that the rights of the child and the biological family are protected, in exploring alternative placements for the child in the country of origin and in combating illicit practices. The effective discharge of these responsibilities will require a level of supervision, a degree of administrative control and a range of services, which for many countries of origin – with their scarce resources and sometimes vast geographical areas – will be difficult to achieve. There will also naturally be a desire in many such countries to concentrate limited resources on the development of domestic family support and child placement services. If the Convention is to operate successfully, these basic facts of life will have to be recognised, especially by the wealthier receiving states, who may have to consider whether they are contributing sufficiently to the development of such services in the poorer countries.

Minimum rules which may be supplemented

It is important, particularly for states like India which have already developed sophisticated controls on intercountry adoptions, to point out that the Convention will establish a set of *minimum* standards and procedures, which may be supplemented by additional safeguards thought appropriate or necessary by individual states. For example, whatever is the outcome of the discussions concerning the place of "independent" adoptions within the Convention, it will undoubtedly be open to individual states to insist upon "approved-agency" adoptions in their own cases.

"Regulation": the hallmark of the Convention

It is important, finally, to remember that the principal purpose of the Convention is not so much to "facilitate" intercountry adoption as to "regulate" it in a manner which best protects and promotes the interests of children. Certainly the Convention may improve and clarify procedures in those cases where intercountry adoption is in the best interest of the child; but equally it should help to avoid intercountry adoption in those cases where it is inappropriate. The Convention will represent a beginning. Its success may well be measured as much by what it does to encourage and stimulate the growth of child care services in countries of origin as by the number of intercountry adoptions effected under it.

Chapter 4
Child Abduction and the English Courts[1]

Carol S Bruch
Professor of Law, University of California, Davis

This paper concerns recent English experience with child abduction, particularly under the Hague Convention on the Civil Aspects of International Child Abduction of 25 October 1980. This Convention returns children to their homes so that custody litigation will take place there, not in their new location. By restoring the *status quo ante*, the abductor will be denied any tactical benefit from the abduction, and other abductions will be discouraged.

The Hague Convention is one of three international conventions devoted to this problem, two of which are operative in Britain. The European Convention, which emphasises the enforcement of custody judgments[2], and the Hague Convention, which operates whether or not a judgment has been entered, are found in Schedules to the Child Abduction and Custody Act 1985. The third international document, the Inter-American Convention on the International Return of Children of 15 July 1989, has not yet been ratified by any country and is not, so far as I know, currently under consideration in the United Kingdom. Twenty-four countries, in contrast, already belong to the Hague Convention[3], the focus of my remarks

---

1   I have added a few citations for the reader's benefit. More complete documentation is available in my related publications, cited in n 5 *infra*. Other relevant recent publications concerning the topic include the written materials prepared for the Legal Action Group (LAG) /Law Society Seminar, International Child Abduction, 10 July 1991, a booklet produced by the Lord Chancellor's Department, *Child Abduction* (Feb 1992) and *Clarke Hall and Morrison on Children*, Division 1, para 932 *et seq.*

2   European Convention on Recognition and Enforcement of Decisions Concerning Custody of Children and on Restoration of Custody of Children of 20 May 1980.

3   As of 28 April 1992, the Convention was ratified by Argentina, Australia (only for the Australian States and mainland Territories), Austria, Canada, Denmark (except the Faroe Islands and Greenland), France (for the whole of the territory of the French Republic), Germany, Ireland, Israel, Luxembourg, the Netherlands (for the Kingdom in Europe), Norway, Portugal, Spain, Sweden, Switzerland, the United Kingdom of Great Britain and Northern Ireland (also extended to the Isle of Man), the United States of America and Yugoslavia.Letter from Adair Dyer, Esq., First Secretary, Permanent Bureau, Hague Conference on Private International Law to Professor Carol Bruch (28 Apr 1992) ("no new ratifications or accessions since Ecuador in January"); Hague Conference on Private International Law, Circular No 2(92), No 155 (92) DY/M (Feb 28 1992). As of 16 April 1992, the following countries had acceded to the Convention and had had their accessions accepted by the indicated number of other parties to the Convention. Belize (accepted by 13 countries); Ecuador (accepted by 5 countries); *(cont. overleaf)*

here, and ratifications are accelerating.[4] Accordingly, the Hague Convention now reaches into Europe, the Western Hemisphere, Australasia and, with Israel's ratification, the Middle East.

This popularity has been gained by a creative and effective mechanism that I wish to highlight here in remarks that draw upon my research in nine countries on the Hague Convention in operation.[5]

Although the title of this paper emphasises the role of English courts in child abduction cases, my remarks go further. Children who are snatched to this country are the subjects of most British judicial opinions on abduction, of course. But children who are taken *from* England are of equal concern, and I will address the implications of the Children Act 1989 for local parents who are left behind when their children are abducted internationally.

Let me begin by examining how English courts deal with children who are brought here. This will help us understand how courts abroad can be expected to treat cases involving children who have been taken from England.

Where does a case seeking to return a child from England begin? The best place, quite literally, is at the governmental office in the child's home country that is responsible for cases under the Hague Convention (that country's Central Authority). This foreign Central Authority will forward the request for the child's return, together with necessary information, to the Central Authority for England and Wales, located in the Lord Chancellor's Department.[6] If the request arguably falls within the

---

(cont.) Hungary (accepted by 15 countries); Mexico (accepted by 13 countries); New Zealand (accepted by 12 countries); the list of acceding countries remains valid as of 28 April 1992.Letter from Adair Dyer, *supra* & enclosure. Accessions in lieu of ratifications are made by countries that are not members of the Hague Conference on Private International Law. An accession is effective only between the acceding country and those contracting states that have accepted the accession. Art 38. Although Mexico is now a member of the Hague Conference, accession rather than ratification was required because it was not a member on the date the Convention was opened for signature.

4   Belgium, Greece and Italy have signed but not yet ratified the Convention, which is also under consideration in other states.

5   A preliminary report of this study will appear as a chapter entitled "International Child Abduction Cases: Experience Under the 1980 Hague Convention" in John Eekelaar and Petar Sarcevic, editors, *Parenthood in Modern Society: Legal and Social Issues for the Twenty First Century* (forthcoming), Martinus Nijhoff (hereafter cited as Bruch, *International Child Abduction Cases*). A more complete publication is in preparation (hereafter cited as Bruch, *in preparation*). In addition to library research, the English aspects of my research, which are reflected in this chapter, have included meetings with the Lord Chancellor's Department, solicitors and barristers handling Hague cases, members of Re Unite, concerned academics, and members of the House of Commons Working Party on Child Abduction.

6   The Child Abduction Unit, Lord Chancellor's Department, Trevelyan House, Great Peter Street, London SW1P 2BY, tel 0171-2108837/ 8704/8746/8530, fax 0171-210-8559. Scotland has its own Central Authority for Scotland, located in the Scottish Courts Administration, 26/27 Royal Terrace, Edinburgh EH7 5AH, tel 0131 556-0755, fax 0131 556-3604, and its own procedures. Although it is possible for the requesting party to approach a foreign Central Authority directly or, indeed, to go directly to court in that country, requesting assistance through the British Central Authority has distinct advantages. In addition to obtaining access to the expertise of its staff, claimants whose cases are forwarded by the Central Authority receive legal aid without regard to the usual means and merits test. This is an aspect of British law that is not required by the terms of the United Kingdom's treaty obligations. Although the Convention ordinarily requires free legal representation for claimants, countries are permitted to enter a reservation restricting their obligation to absorb costs to cases for which legal aid would be available to local *(cont. overleaf)*

Convention, the Department will instruct a solicitor to act on the petitioner's behalf, and a request for the child's return will be filed in the High Court in London.[7]

The court, in turn, will order the child's immediate return to its place of habitual residence if it concludes that the child's removal or retention (for example, following an authorised visit) violated the custody rights of the petitioner.[8]

The first and most important question, then, is whether there was indeed a wrongful taking or retention. "Wrongfulness" for this purpose is determined according to the law of the place that was the child's habitual residence immediately prior to the challenged event.

Pre-event custody order exists

Assume, for example, a case in which the child's mother had custody under an Australian order that was violated when the father took the child from its home in Sydney to London. This is an easy case, since the wrongfulness of his removal is readily shown, and the court will order that the child be returned at once unless an authorised defence applies.[9]

Is the outcome the same if the child and its mother live in London and it is an English order that is violated when the child's father removes the child to Sydney? Indeed, if the mother's custody rights are sufficiently established by an order under section 8 of the Children Act 1989, the answer is yes, subject once again to any authorised defence. This follows since section 2(8) of the Children Act and provides that even if the father has parental responsibility under section 2, he may not act inconsistently with an order entered under the Act. This result is echoed by the Child Abduction Act 1984, which imposes criminal sanctions for the unconsented removal.[10] The father's removal of the child is, therefore, wrongful under English law, and the Convention directs the child's immediate return.

Although residence orders will clearly be available less frequently under the Children Act 1989 than were custody orders, it can be hoped that courts will understand that they are appropriately granted whenever there is any identifiable likelihood of a future international custody dispute.[11] So, for

---

7   *(cont.)* residents. The United Kingdom has entered that reservation, but nevertheless has chosen to absorb all legal costs for requests from abroad for the return of children that the UK Central Authority concludes present arguable cases under the Convention. For parties whose cases are not handled by the Central Authority (including those whose children are removed from England), the normal requirements for legal aid apply.

7   Jurisdiction for cases initiated abroad that seek relief under the Convention lies in the High Court; venue lies in London. See Child Abduction and Custody Act 1985, ss 4, 24. In Scotland, the Court of Session has jurisdiction. *Ibid.*

8   Art 3. Citations are to the Convention.

9   See *infra* notes 38-44 and accompanying text.

10   Child Abduction Act 1984 s 1(1), (2) (a)-(b), (3) (a) (i). The exceptions of s 1(5) do not apply when the child's removal would breach a court order. *Ibid* s 1 (5A).

11   See Hegar and Greif, "Parental Kidnapping Across International Borders" (1991) 34 *International Social Work* 353.

example, a section 8(1) residence order should be entered if there have been threats of abduction, or if the parents come from different countries or either has strong foreign connections (such as lengthy vacations, a second residence, extended family or employment opportunities abroad).

Precisely how this order is worded is unimportant, so long as it is possible for a foreign court to identify the custody rights of the parent who has been left behind and to ascertain when the child's removal or retention abroad violates them.

In the English context, there is an unusual "holiday" provision that requires special attention. The Children Act 1989 and the Child Abduction Act 1984 normally permit the holder of a residence order to take a child abroad for up to one month without the other parent's consent.[12] A stay that is intended to be indefinite but in fact terminates before one month does not appear to be proscribed. It is, therefore, possible that even if a parent in whose favour a residence order has been entered moves abroad lock, stock and barrel, clearly indicating no intention to return, the removal may not be wrongful at the time of departure for Convention purposes.[13] Such difficulties can be avoided by an appropriately-worded residence order, since the one-month rule does not override contrary provisions in orders entered under Part II of the Children Act.[14]

A section 8 order might accordingly provide specified periods of contact or might prohibit the child's removal by one or either parent unless specified consent requirements, court approval, or other conditions are satisfied.[15] Similar concerns and a similar cure exist for cases in which the residence order runs in favour of both parents under section 11(4). Here wrongfulness can be established, *inter alia*, by acts that are inconsistent with the periods in which the order provides that the child is to live in the respective households.

---

12 Children Act 1989 s 13(2); Child Abduction Act 1984 s 1(4).

13 The difficulty may not be cured once a month has been exceeded, since the original removal was authorised although the retention beyond one month was not. In a Convention case involving a non-marital child, the House of Lords reasoned that when a parent who is entitled to remove a child does so with an intention not to return, the parent's action effects a change in the child's habitual residence. *In re J (A Minor) (Abduction: Custody Rights)* [1990] 3 WLR 492 (House of Lords). For my criticism of this analysis, see Bruch, *International Child Abduction Cases, supra* n 5. Nevertheless, to the extent that *In re J* controls, it is possible that the child's habitual residence would be abroad, rather than in England, a month after its removal. If so, the law of the new habitual residence, not English law, would determine whether retention beyond one month was wrongful. See Children Act 1989s 13(1) (b)-(2). Surely this should not be the rule. Instead, *In re J* should be distinguished on the ground that this parent's right to remove the child is for temporary purposes only and does not encompass a right to effectuate a change in the child's habitual residence. This reasoning is consistent with the legislative history and Children Act s 13. See Parliamentary Debates, House of Commons, Standing Committee B, Children Bill [*Lords*], Third Sitting, 16 May 1989 (Morning) cl 12 at 70–74 (indicating a desire to prevent child abduction without discouraging "normal and reasonable" behaviour).

14 Child Abduction Act 1984, ss 4, 4A.

15 S 11(7) provides that a s 8 order may impose conditions.

This discussion applies equally, of course, to any custody order, whether it is entered before or after a divorce, or between parents who were never married.[16]

No pre-event custody order

But in many cases, no custody order is in place when the child is taken or retained. Whether or not the child's parents were married, snatches may occur at or after the moment of parental separation, either before custody proceedings have been commenced or during litigation but prior to judgment. How, then, does the Hague Convention operate if a child is removed (or retained) for whom no custody order exists?

The rule is precisely the same. If the taking or retention was wrongful under the law of the child's habitual residence, a person whose custody rights were violated may request the child's return, whether or not an order was in place.

In re J[17] was such a "no-order" case. Here, however, the person requesting the child's return to Australia was an unwed father. Under the law of Western Australia, he had no custody rights unless or until they were granted by court order. As a result, the mother's departure with their child was not wrongful, as it did not "breach ... rights of custody attributed to [him] under the law of the State in which the child was habitually resident immediately before the removal."[18]

In the converse fact pattern, if my London neighbour carries out her plan to move to Australia next month with her non-marital child, and the child's English father thereafter employs the Convention to seek the child's return, the Australian courts will be equally correct in denying his application. For, absent a court order granting parental responsibility or an appropriate parental responsibility agreement, an English unwed father, like his Western Australian counterpart, has no rights that might be

---

16 It is, of course, significantly less likely that pre-event orders will be in place in cases involving a non-marital child. See Children Act s 4(1).

17 *In re J* (*A Minor*) (*Abduction: Custody Rights*) [1990] 3 WLR 492 (House of Lords).

18 The quoted language is included in the definition of "wrongful" in Art 3(a). After her departure, the father in *In re J* obtained a Western Australian order declaring that the mother's taking was wrongful. But the House of Lords reasoned, correctly in my view, that it was free to decide the question of wrongfulness under the Convention for itself. The Australian court, which seems to have considered the mother's behaviour morally improper, did not substantiate the legal basis for its decision. Rather its opinion was inconsistent with the local law that provides custody rights to non-marital fathers only by court order. Under the Convention, the mother's actions are tested by conditions on the date they occurred, making the father's subsequent order irrelevant to the question of the child's taking. A more difficult question is raised by the possibility that the subsequent order, which also granted the father custody, might have rendered the mother's retention of their child in England after the order was entered wrongful. The House of Lords concluded not, since it held that the child's habitual residence was in England on that date. For my criticism of this aspect of the House of Lords' decision, see Bruch, *International Child Abduction Cases, supra* n5.

breached by the removal of his child.[19] If there is a problem in these cases, it lies with the fathers', domestic custody laws, not with the Convention which honours whatever rights they have.

How then does the Convention operate if the "no order" case does involve someone with existing rights – for example, a married parent or an unwed father from a place that accords him pre-decree custodial rights?

Once again, wrongfulness is determined by reference to the statutes or case law of the child's habitual residence.[20] (To avoid delay and expense, the Convention dispenses with evidentiary formalities concerning the proof of foreign law[21], and Central Authorities are authorised to provide information on the custody law of the child's habitual residence.[22])

Although the question is usually quickly resolved to the benefit of the parent who has been left behind, the question is not always open and shut. What is the result, for example, if the parents have equal, co-existing custody rights during their marriage (often called "joint custody rights") ? May one parent nevertheless make and implement a unilateral plan to move abroad with the child without breaching the custody rights of the other parent?

This question may well arise in the American context, for unless some other legal rule provides to the contrary, custody exercised during an ongoing marriage (or during separation) is joint and several.[23] That is, as a matter of custody law, absent a court order there is no requirement that the parents spend equal amounts of time with their children or that either parent make that option or any particular variation on it available to the other parent. Indeed, I am unaware of cases even asserting such an obligation on one parent's part or such a right on the other's. Instead, although custodial rights certainly may be exercised together, each parent also has the power to act alone, whether to give consent to an operation or to send a child to summer camp, or to decide more generally where the child will travel or live. The remedy for a disagreement that cannot be resolved informally is a child custody proceeding, and courts are empowered to grant custody orders appropriate to the child's best interests, even within an intact marriage. Rarely, of course, do matters proceed to litigation during marriage unless there is a disagreement over medical care

---

19 See Children Act 1989 ss 2(2) (b), 3, 4(1) (a)-(b); Child Abduction Act 1984 s 1(5), (7)(b).

20 Art 3.

21 Art 14.

22 Arts 7(e), 8(f). Although the Convention always requires that courts act expeditiously (Art 11), it recognises that wrongfulness may be more difficult to ascertain if no existing order was violated. Accordingly, a court considering the return request is permitted to ask that the applicant obtain a decision or determination from authorities in the place of the child's habitual residence that the taking or retention was wrongful before entering its decision. Art 15. The Central Authorities are, to the extent practicable, directed to help the applicant in this exercise. *Ibid.* In fact, this procedure is rarely employed, and courts normally rely on the source materials made available to them.

23 This may also be the rule in non-marital relationships. In California, for example, an unwed father obtains the same custody rights as a married father in defined situations. See Cal. Civ. Code ss 197, 47004(a) (4) (West Supp. 1992). The same rule may apply to an unmarried father under an English parental responsibility agreement or order for parental responsibility. See Children Act 1989 ss 2(2) (b), 4.

or, perhaps, parochial school attendance. But the theory is in place, and it requires a parent who wishes to prevent the other parent from exercising custody decisions unilaterally to seek a court order limiting that person's behaviour, not the converse. In other words, generally the acting person does not need to go to court to seek authorisation to do something alone, even if the planned behaviour will upset or inconvenience the other parent or is contrary to that person's known wishes.[24]

Does this mean, then, that there are no wrongful pre-decree removals from the United States? Hardly – in most (perhaps all) states, laws now circumscribe one parent's right to diminish the other parent's access to their child. Generally these are criminal laws, and often they prohibit behaviour only if it is *intended* to interfere with the second parent's relationship with the child. Accordingly, even where such statutes exist, a removal may be lawful despite its negative impact on the left-behind parent's interactions with the child if, for example, it is prompted by a parent's genuine desire to escape domestic violence, to live with members of the extended family or, perhaps, to find suitable employment. Nevertheless, where "custodial interference" statutes or other laws restrict unilateral removals, it may be relatively easy to establish that a taking was wrongful within the meaning of the Convention. And, as time goes on and courts become increasingly concerned about child snatching, one can expect case law developments to cut back on a parent's ability to act unilaterally in cases of relocation.

English courts often send children back to the United States in pre–decree situations. But the courts sometimes have not been as careful as they might have been in ascertaining wrongfulness under state law. Instead, they sometimes assume that the English doctrine that the acting parent is damaging the other parent's equivalent right to exercise custody applies whenever joint custody rules are involved. As I have explained, this reasoning may well be incorrect when applied to another legal system. It is the law of the child's habitual residence that controls this question under the Convention, not the law of the court hearing the return petition.

What of the converse situation? What should happen when a child is removed from England by one parent at a time when joint parental responsibility exists as a matter of law because no court order has been entered? Until recently, this possibility existed only for married couples prior to divorce. It may well become the usual case under the Children Act 1989, even following divorce.[25]

The question, of course, is whether a left-behind parent without a court order will be able to demonstrate that the child's removal from England was a breach of his or her rights under English law. The matter has been a topic of recent debate. Ian Karsten QC has expressed concern that the new

---

24 In other words, the view of the Convention's Reporter, set forth in n.27 *infra*, has not been a part of American custody law. Whether United States courts will accept her view as a matter of Convention interpretation is not yet known.

25 See Children Act 1989 s 2(1).

Children Act, by discouraging the entry of court orders, may disadvantage the recovery efforts of parents whose children have been snatched. He has recommended that solicitors seek residence or prohibited steps orders to ensure quick relief in case of an abduction. The Lord Chancellor, considering this fear unfounded, has pointed out that before the 1989 Act, "either parent [might] exercise parental rights or discharge duties unilaterally."[26] Asserting that this same rule continues under the new Children Act, he reasons that there should be no change in the auspicious results previously achieved under the Convention. The custody breach in either event, according to his view, consists of disregarding a person's rights or interfering with the exercise of those rights.[27]

The very fact that the Lord Chancellor has made this statement renders it more likely that foreign courts will adopt his view. For the Convention authorises a petition to include relevant documents, including materials "emanating from a Central Authority, or other competent authority of the state of the child's habitual residence, or from a qualified person, concerning the relevant law of that state[28]", and the Lord Chancellor's remarks, if set forth in the correct form, will certainly qualify.

There is, however, a problem of uncertain dimensions with his contention that the law continues unabated in its protection of the non-abducting parent. Section 85(3) of the Children Act 1975 authorised any person with a joint parental right to exercise that right unilaterally only if no joint holder had "signified disapproval of its exercise or performance in [the given] manner." This provision was not carried forward into the Children Act 1989. Although the Child Abduction Act 1984, which was then, and remains, in force, usually requires consent for a child's move abroad from each person having parental responsibility, its requirements are less inclusive.[29] Whether these differences prove unimportant remains to be seen.

---

26 The Lord Chancellor cited the Guardianship of Minors Act 1973 s 1 for this proposition. Excerpts from a speech given by the Lord Chancellor on 12 October 1991 (provided by Peter G Harris of the Lord Chancellor's Department) .

27 *Ibid.* (citing Elisa Perez-Vera, Explanatory Report para 71 at 447-48 in *Hague Conference on Private International Law, III Actes et documents de la Quatorziäme session*, Child Abduction). Perez-Vera states, "[F]rom the Convention's standpoint, the removal of a child by one of the joint holders without the consent of the other, is equally wrongful, and this wrongfulness derives in this particular case, not from some action in breach of a particular law, but from the fact that such action has disregarded the rights of the other parent, which are also protected by law, and has interfered with their normal exercise." In the Lord Chancellor's view the Children Act has made no substantive change in the law and therefore should not be thought to have altered the situation under the Convention. Lord Chancellor's speech, *supra* n.26.

28 Art 8(f), (g) (information must be in the form of a "certificate or affidavit"); see also Art 7(e) (authorising the Central Authority to supply information of a general nature concerning the laws of its country).

29 No consent is needed if a person would consent, or the person removing the child tried to reach the other person but could not, or (in some circumstances) the second person unreasonably refused to consent. Child Abduction Act 1984 s 1(5). Even an unreasonable refusal to consent is controlling if the person refusing has a residence order in his favour, or has custody, or if the taking breaches a domestic court order. See *ibid* s 1 (5A) , (7) (b).

In an effort to "lay to rest any concerns about the absence of court orders as a result of the Act's injunction against making them unnecessarily", the Lord Chancellor also stated that "any parent who has reason to believe a child may be removed will no doubt seek a residence or even a prohibited steps order, and I see no reason why a court would feel discouraged by the Children Act from granting one in those circumstances."[30] It is certainly to be hoped that English courts will heed his words, since, as the "holiday" exception and the differences just mentioned indicate, some questions persist concerning the sufficiency of the new law.[31]

Order obtained after event

Often, following an abduction, the parent left behind initiates legal action at home. The request may be for a declaration that the child's taking was wrongful.[32] It may instead be an effort either to establish or modify a custody order – almost invariably to provide for sole custody by the petitioner. Or it may be for both a declaration and a custody order. Because the hearing is generally *ex parte* and because the court will look on the abduction with displeasure, it is extremely likely that the requested order will be granted.

What impact do these orders have when they are presented in an English action requesting the child's return? A declaration that the taking was wrongful is likely to be very influential if (i) it comes from the place that was the child's habitual residence immediately before the taking or retention, (ii) it sets forth that place's relevant law, and (iii) it explains what custody rights were violated, how and when. Although, as demonstrated by *In Re J*[33], this declaration is not binding on the court hearing the return petition, it will be received with great deference.

Post-hoc custody decrees are more problematical. Although courts often treat such orders as though they establish wrongfulness, that is not necessarily the case, witness again *In Re J*.[34] What a grant of custody to the left-behind parent does demonstrate is that the place that was the child's

---

30 Lord Chancellor's remarks, *supra* n.26.

31 See *supra* n 12-16, 29 and accompanying text ("holiday" provisions and repeal of Children Act 1975 s 85(3)).

32 Such declarations are often obtained in the High Court, then used successfully abroad in cases seeking the return of children to England. Interview with Gillian Noury, Ralph Haring & Co, London, November 1991.

33 [1990] 3 WLR 492 (House of Lords).

34 *Ibid.* Post-event orders have also occupied the English courts in another context. Parties whose children were abducted before the effective date of the Convention have argued that subsequent orders have rendered what was originally a permissible taking into a wrongful retention. In other words, they have asserted that the former custodian's refusal to return a child, as directed by an order that was entered after their departure, constitutes a wrongful retention. The courts have not been persuaded. Instead they have emphasised that the Convention was not intended to apply retroactively. See *Re H; Re S (Abduction: Custody Rights)* [1991] 2 FLR 262 (House of Lords).

habitual residence continues to assert jurisdiction over the case even after the child's departure. That is not the same thing as determining that the removal was wrongful when it occurred. Instead, if the original removal was lawful and the child's habitual residence is thereby shifted to England, the subsequent custody decree from the child's former home is relevant only if English law recognises it, *i.e.* considers the local parent bound by it.[35] The parent's refusal to return the child to the left-behind parent, now the legal custodian, would then constitute a wrongful retention under local law for Convention purposes, albeit by reference to obligations imposed by the foreign judgment.

Consider the converse situation, then, when a court in the United States is presented with a return request accompanied by an English order entered after the child's departure.[36] Indeed, since *In Re J* does not control, I think it is likely that the court would conclude that England continues to be the child's habitual residence and would apply English law on that basis. Even if it concluded that the child's habitual residence had shifted to the United States, however, I would expect the English order to be honoured because the parent who ignores it is wrongfully retaining the child as a matter of American law (*i.e.*, American conflict-of-law rules require that the English order be honoured).

It is worth noting that even if the Convention did not require the child's return on these facts, the non-treaty law of many American states would recognise and enforce the subsequent English decree.[37] That is, the Hague Convention leaves in place other laws directing the return of children. In the United States, those laws are generally state enactments of the Uniform Child Custody Jurisdiction Act. In England, both the law as developed in guardianship and the European Convention supplement the Hague Convention.

---

35 *In Re J* establishes that, at least as to a non-marital child, the custodial parent who can remove a child without breaching anyone else's custody rights can thereby shift the child's habitual residence. To the extent that this analysis applies, subsequent litigation in the former state of residence occurs only after the child is no longer habitually resident there. If this is so, it is the law of the new habitual residence (England, in the case of a child lawfully brought here) that will test the wrongfulness of challenged acts (such as a retention in England) that occur after the child's habitual residence has shifted. See *supra* n.13; *infra* n.36.

36 These jurisdiction and recognition provisions are found in the Uniform Child Custody Jurisdiction Act. See Uniform Child Custody Jurisdiction Act ss 3, 7, 14 and Commissioners' Notes, 9 *Uniform Laws Ann.* 115 (West 1988). The expression "home state" is a term of art defined in the Act. *Ibid* s 2(5). For purposes of the example in the text, I have assumed that the child's home state was England at the time of its removal. Although the Act has been enacted by every American state legislature, not all states contain the provision extending these rules to the international sphere. See *Ibid* s 23. Because of the Act's influence, however, it is extremely likely that the same reasoning would be applied to determine the question of wrongful retention under the Hague Convention. That is, even a lawful taking could be transformed into a wrongful retention by a refusal to honour a subsequent custody order pronounced by the child's former residence that qualifies for recognition under the Act.

37 See *supra* n.36.

Exceptions and defences

Let me briefly identify the exceptions and defences that can alter the results I have just described.[38]

The first circumstance in which return will not be ordered is if the requesting party either had not actually been exercising custody rights[39] or had consented or acquiesced in the taking or retention.[40] There have been occasional cases in which acquiescence has been argued, but rarely has it been found. A decision to engage in negotiations rather than seek immediate judicial relief does not constitute acquiescence, nor does a person's apparent resignation to the situation while he or she is unaware of possible legal redress.

The more commonly litigated defences arise under Article 13(b) of the Convention, which permits a court to refuse the petition when there is a grave risk that the child's return will expose him or her to physical or psychological harm or otherwise place the child in an intolerable situation. The cases have made clear that not *any* danger will raise the defence, but only a grave risk of harm so serious as to create an intolerable situation for the child.[41] They have also made clear that a parent who has removed a young child, creating the difficulty now confronting the court, cannot successfully argue that the child would be endangered by an unaccompanied return to the other parent. Rather than permit the abductor to benefit by the position that he or she has created, the courts recognise that some harm is inevitable if a child has been abducted and must be returned. It is then the abductor's choice whether or not to return at the same time that the child does.

In this connection it is important to note that a child's ordered return is not necessarily to the other parent, but rather to the jurisdiction that will make the ultimate custody decision. In practice, courts often return young children in the care of primary caretakers who abducted them, sometimes with the financial assistance of the left-behind parent. This is particularly common where the abducting parent has alleged abuse or unusually difficult circumstances in the petitioning parent's home, and the petitioner offers undertakings to alleviate the court's concern instead of attempting to disprove the 13(b) allegations in that distant forum.[42]

Upon occasion, courts have also considered the defence under Article 13, paragraph 2, that a child who has obtained an age and degree of maturity that make it appropriate to take account of its views objects to its return. Rarely have these defences been permitted. Special circumstances, generally

---

38 They are discussed at greater length in my related publications. See Bruch, *International Child Abduction Cases, supra* n.5; Bruch, *In preparation, supra* n.5.

39 Art 13(a); see also Art 3(b).

40 Art 13(a).

41 See, *e.g., In re E (A minor) (Abduction)* [1989] 1 FLR 403.

42 English courts developed the practice of undertakings. For my analysis suggesting that this is a useful enhancement of the Convention in some cases, but contrary to the Convention's purposes in others, see Bruch, *International Child Abduction Cases, supra* n.5.

involving familial violence that was witnessed by teenagers and pre-teens, exist in the cases where children's objections to return have been honoured.[43]

Courts have been similarly reluctant to refuse returns on the Article 12 grounds that the return request was not commenced within a year of the child's removal and the child is settled in its new environment. These cases most typically involve children who were secreted, although sometimes the delayed request has been the product of incorrect legal advice when parents have been told they have no remedy, only to learn later of the Convention. As with the other defences, even if an asserted defence is established, it merely means that a court is *permitted* to refuse the return; it is not *required* to refuse it. Where the purposes of the Convention will be served by a return, courts show a reassuring willingness to enter an appropriate order.

Thus far, there has been virtually no use of the final defence to return – that it would be contrary to the fundamental principles of the requested state relating to the protection of human rights and fundamental freedoms.[44] This is probably thanks to the recent political changes in Eastern Europe. It may also be due to the fact that difficult cases have not yet arisen involving gender-based or religiously-based custody laws.

Conclusion

English courts have been thoughtful and prolific in interpreting the Hague Child Abduction Convention. Their opportunities to comment stem from this country's cost-free representation of foreign petitioners and the excellent co-ordinating work of its Central Authority, which is willing to take precedent-setting cases to the appellate level. On the whole, English opinions are sophisticated and appropriate.[45] As a result, England is making a marked difference in providing relief for children who have become caught in international family disputes.

Acknowledgements

The author expresses her appreciation to the Law Department, London School of Economics and Political Science and the Institut für Internationales Recht – Rechtsvergleichung, Ludwig-Maximilians-Universität, Munich, for their kind hospitality during the preparation of this work, to the United States Fulbright Commission and the Alexander von Humboldt Foundation (Germany) for their financial support, and to the many individuals who shared generously of their expertise, most particularly Gillian Noury and Diana Hulin.

---

43 The violence in these cases did not rise to the level that would have endangered the children, as required by Art 3(b), sometimes because it was visited upon the children's mother although witnessed by them.

44 Art 20.

45 Where they have missed the mark, for example, concerning certain aspects of the definition of habitual residence and some features of undertakings, things may yet get back on track as a result of their own continuing experience and the persuasive force of opinions from other countries.

Chapter 5

A Perspective on Surrogate Motherhood in Jewish and Israeli Law*

Pinhas Shifman
Jacob I Berman Professor of Family Law, The Hebrew University of Jerusalem

"Give me children or else I die... Behold, my maid
Bilhah, go in unto her; that she may bear upon my
knees, and I also may obtain children by her."
Genesis 30:1, 3.

Introduction

This article will address the attitude of Jewish and Israeli law with regard to
the legal and moral issues raised by the practice of surrogate motherhood.
At the outset, it should be emphasised that the term "surrogate mother" is
a misnomer. As employed in legal literature[1], a surrogate mother is a woman
who produces a child for a couple[2] by becoming artificially impregnated,
carrying the fetus to term, and surrendering all parental rights to the child
upon birth. However, since she is actually the biological mother of the
child, [3] a more precise label would be "surrogate wife", because she
performs the procreative function for the husband of the adoptive couple
in the place of his legal wife. The change in terminology is not mere
semantics, because it directs our attention to the fact that surrogate

---

* An earlier version of this paper appeared in the New York Law School Human Rights Annual, Volume IV (1987) at 555.

1 A great deal has been written on the legal issues raised by surrogate motherhood, even before the controversy over Baby M. See, *e.g.*, "Note, Contracts to Bear a Child" (1978) 65 *Calif. L. Rev.*, 611 [hereinafter "Note, Contracts to Bear a Child"]; Black, "Legal Problems of Surrogate Motherhood", (1981) 16 *New ENG. L.Rev.* 373; Wadlington, "Artificial Conception; The Challenge for Family Law, " (1983) 69 *VA.L.Rev.*465; Stumpf, "Redefining Mother: A Legal Matrix for New Reproductive Technologies", (1986) 96 Yale *L.J. 187* [hereinafter "Stumpf"].

2 This article will attempt to deal only with agreements between a married couple and a surrogate mother. This assumption, of course, does not preclude the possibility that such an agreement can be initiated by an individual, a homosexual couple, or an unmarried couple, and in dealing with existing cases these situations do arise. See *infra* n.40.

3 This study does not include the possibility of *in vitro* fertilization in which an egg is taken from the husband's wife, fertilised by the husband's semen, and implanted in the surrogate mother's womb. In this case, the surrogate mother is the gestational mother, but not the genetic mother. The matter is now regulated in Israel by Public Health Regulations (In Vitro Fertilization) 1989.

motherhood was not new to the 1980s, but instead existed as far back as biblical times. In that era, however, the surrogate mother was legally wed, prior to engaging in intimate relations, in addition to the sterile wife, unlike today's surrogate mothers whose contractual status is temporary, not sacred.

Following an examination of the religious duty of procreation, which might sanction the practice of surrogate motherhood, this study will focus upon the legal problems in Israeli law for determining the status of a child conceived through such methods. Israeli law, while built upon religious principles of marriage and divorce[4], does not necessarily follow religious law in issues of public policy.[5] Even if the practice of surrogate motherhood is not repugnant from a religious perspective, it must still be scrutinised from a secular point of view.

The religious duty to procreate: surrogate mother or surrogate wife?

Biblical law

Marriage in ancient Israel was polygamous. In addition, concubinage also existed. Accordingly, high birth rates were assured and marital sterility was not a problem.[6]

Sarah, Abraham's wife had borne him no children. She gave her maidservant, Hagar, to Abraham: "Behold now, God hath restrained me from bearing, go in, I pray thee, unto my handmaid it may be that I shall obtain children by her. And Abraham hearkened to the voice of Sarah. And Sarah, Abraham's wife took Hagar the Egyptian ... and gave her to Abraham her husband to be his wife."[7] This transaction culminated in the birth of Ishmael.

This same custom is reflected by Rachel, Jacob's wife. In grief for her barrenness, Rachel gave Bilhah, her maid, unto Jacob, saying: "Behold my maid, Bilhah, go in unto her, and that she may bear upon my knees, and I also may obtain children by her."[8]

One can infer that where a barren wife "gave" her maid to her husband for the purpose of bearing children it was the custom for such children to be adopted by the wife of their father, who thereby became their foster mother. The concubine thereupon relinquished all rights to the child, who became the legal child of the foster mother according to law. Hence, it was Rachel who gave the names Dan and Naphtali to the two sons born to Bilhah from Jacob.[9] "When Leah saw that she had left bearing, she took Zilpah, her maid, and gave her to Jacob to wife"[10] and Leah named the two sons borne by Zilpah.

---

4   Shifman, *Family Law in Israel* (Hebrew 1984).
5   Shifman, "Marriage and Cohabitation in Israel", (1981) 16 *Isr. L.Rev.* 439 (citing England, *Religious Law in the Israel Legal System* (1975) 168-77) .
6   Neufeld, *Ancient Hebrew Marriage Laws* (1944) 118-32.
7   Genesis 16:1-3.
8   Genesis 30:3-4.
9   Genesis 30:6-8
10 Genesis 30:9-13. The children were named Gad and Asher.

Adoption by the legal wife did not protect the child from abuse. After Hagar conceived, she became contemptuous of Sarah who, in turn, abused her. After Sarah had borne Isaac, she demanded the expulsion of Hagar and her son. Abraham reluctantly banished Hagar to the desert where she and Ishmael were saved from death by divine intervention.[11] Later, Abraham disinherited Ishmael; he gave his entire estate to Isaac while the sons of his concubines received only token gifts and were sent away.[12] In the case of Jacob, however, there was no discrimination between the children of his wives and those of his concubines; together, they were the progenitors of the twelve tribes of Israel.

The biblical tradition reflected in these legends illustrates a striking similarity to the general practice of other nations at that time. The Patriachs lived in the region of Harran, where the custom of concubinage was also practised, and whereby the wife, if childless, had to provide her husband with a handmaid in order to bear children. This custom provided that the master's wife would have authority over the child of the maidservant, in conformity with Abraham's practice regarding Hagar and Ishmael.[13] The practice followed that of other nations of the Near East.

Talmudic and post-Talmudic law

Talmudic law adduced the biblical precedent of Abraham. Sarah gave Hagar "to Abram her husband for a wife", in order that a child be born "after ten years."[14] Under the Talmud, if a man marries a woman who fails to give birth within ten years, he must take additional steps to fulfil his duty of procreation.[15] He is required either to divorce her or to take a second wife.[16] Polygamy, as well as divorcing one's wife against her will, was prohibited by the eleventh century ban of Rabbi Gershom.[17] Under appropriate circumstances, however, a man could obtain special dispensation permitting him to take a second wife.[18] Such a release would be justified where, due to his wife's sterility, the husband is prevented from fulfilling the commandment to "be fruitful and multiply."[19] In such a case, the husband, in theory, is not only permitted, but obligated, to take a second wife in order to fulfil this commandment.

---

11 Genesis 16:5-16. Genesis 21:9-19.
12 Genesis 25:54.
13 Neufeld, *supra* n.6, at 1 30-32; 12 *Encyclopedia Judaica* 1287-88.
14 Genesis 16:3.
15 Yevamot 64a.
16 *Ibid* Rashi. (R Solomon Yitzhaki, d 1105).
17 Feldman, *Birth Control in Jewish Law* (1968) 37-41 [hereinafter "D Feldman"] .
18 *Ibid* at 40-45.
19 According to Jewish Law, the commandment to procreate had been originally imposed upon men only. On the logic of this position, see D Feldman *supra* n.17, at 53-56. On the ramifications of this commandment in terms of the liberty of women to use contraceptives, see Biale, *Women and the Jewish Law* (1984) 198-218.

In practice, however, many scholars opposed the bigamous solution to the problem of childlessness, contending that the religious duty to procreate should yield to the need to maintain happiness and harmony in marital relations.[20] In one case, a man was advised to remain with his barren wife and compensate for not procreating by raising an orphan in his home.[21]

On one occasion, the concept of a surrogate wife was realised in a different way; it was suggested that the man temporarily divorce his wife and marry another woman conditionally for as long as was necessary to have children, then return to his first wife.[22] In practice, the idea that a childless marriage should be dissolved unconditionally had been limited to circumstances of marital rift. Conversely, the ideal of domestic peace and the undesirability of divorce justified the continuation of a marriage despite the presumed primacy of procreation as one of the objectives of marriage.

In the State of Israel, bigamy is prohibited by secular law.[23] Rabbinical authorities may, however, permit a person to take a second wife in exceptional circumstances. Upon the granting of such permission, the secular criminal penalties for bigamy no longer apply.[24] In one case, the Chief Rabbi refused a request made by a husband to allow him to marry a second wife in spite of the fact that the infertile first wife had consented to her husband's request. The High Court of Justice refused to interfere with the Chief Rabbi's interpretation of Jewish law which precluded bigamous marriage.[25] The biblical acceptance of a surrogate mother gave the woman the status of a surrogate wife; a status which is no longer available under modern laws prohibiting bigamy.

The use of extra-marital relations in order to fulfil one's religious duty to procreate is strictly forbidden by Jewish law. Would the result be different if the man had no sexual relationship with the mother who became impregnated by artificial insemination? In order to answer this question, one must first consider the general attitude of Jewish law toward artificial insemination.

Artificial insemination with the semen of a third party donor is considered by most rabbinic opinions to be both repugnant and contrary to Jewish ethics for a variety of reasons, particularly the possibility of incest and the difficulty in tracing the child's genealogy.[26] Where the risk of incest is minimal, some scholars approve of artificial insemination in order to

---

20 D Feldman, *supra* n. 17, at 45.

21 Responsa Big'dei Khuna (Fiorda 1807), Even Hatzer, No 1 cited in Pit'hey T'shuvah (Abraham Zvi Eisenstadt, d.1868), Commentary to the Shulkhan Arukh, Even Hatzer, No 154, sec (27); D. Feldman, *supra* n.17, at 45.

22 Responsa Me'il Tz'dakah, No 33, by R. Jonah Landsofer of Prague (d.1712); D Feldman, *supra* n. 1 7, at 42.

23 See Shifman, "The English Law of Bigamy in a Multi-Confessional Society:The Israeli Experience", (1977) 26 *Am J. Comp.* L. 79.

24 P. Shifman, *supra* n.4, at 178-80.

25 *Beeton* v *The Chief Rabbi*, 30(1) PD 309 (High Court 1975) .

26 See Shifman, "Paternity of Children Born of Artificial Insemination" (1981) 10 *Mishpatim* 63 (Hebrew); Rosner, *Modern Medicine and Jewish Law – Studies in Torah Judaism* (1972) 89-106; Drori, "Artificial Insemination: Is it Adultery?" in Rakover (ed), *Jewish Law and Current Legal Problems* (1984) 203.

preserve marital harmony and family integrity. If the surrogate mother is married, rabbinic opinion opposes the surrogacy arrangement on the ground that it could lead to incest and doubts as to the identity of the father who is presumed to be the woman's husband. Moreover, some scholars hold that the implantation of a married woman with semen from a man other than her husband is tantamount to adultery.[27]

Limitation of surrogate motherhood to unmarried women would minimise formal religious doubts as to the propriety of this practice. The identity of the father does not lie in doubt and an unmarried woman cannot be an adulteress. By artificial insemination of the surrogate mother, the man is fulfilling his duty to "be fruitful and multiply", without engaging in illicit relations. If this argument is correct, the procurement of a surrogate mother would be looked upon as a religious duty!

The difficulty lies, however, in the fact that the issue of the legitimacy of surrogate motherhood cannot be resolved on formal, technical grounds alone. Permitting such an arrangement creates a discrepancy between marriage and procreation which in the long run could lead to sexual permissiveness and disintegration of the family. Although rabbinic opinion has not yet addressed itself to the religious problems created by surrogate motherhood, several conclusions can be drawn from the parallel debate on test-tube babies. Rabbi Waldenberg believes this technique to be strictly forbidden because a man cannot fulfil his duty "to be fruitful and multiply" by any means other than sexual intercourse.[28] Rabbi Neventzal, who disagrees with this line of reasoning, expresses the view that the mere fact that a child had been conceived by artificial techniques does not lessen the value of a man fulfilling his duty of procreation. On the contrary, Rabbi Neventzal believes that the prohibition of test-tube conception techniques denies the husband the opportunity to fulfil his duty to procreate and might precipitate a serious challenge to marital harmony.[29]

Unfortunately, allowing a husband to fulfil his duty to procreate by the use of a surrogate wife does not resolve the fundamental question: Can the father deny the parental rights of the child's biological mother?

---

27 The commentators based themselves mainly upon the prohibition contained in the verse in Lev. 18:20: "And thou shalt not implant thy seed into thy neighbour's wife, to defile thyself with her." There are some who hold that adultery is prohibited because of the fear that the uncertainty surrounding the child of an adulterous union and the resultant confusion could lead to incest. Thus, in the above verse, they emphasise the words "and thou shalt not implant thy seed" and consider it to be adultery when a strange man implants his semen in a married woman, even though sexual intercourse has not taken place. Another approach stresses that the prohibition falls upon the desire to be implanted with strange semen, even without sexual intercourse, and as such, it is not sexual relations which are prohibited – as in the case of incest – but rather the implantation of seed.

An opposite approach regards sexual relations as being the basis for the prohibition of adultery, and therefore interprets the verse to contain a prohibition on "lying carnally". Drori, *supra* n.26, at 204-06 (footnotes omitted).

28 *Sefer Asia* 84-92 (Hebrew 1976). See also Steinberg MD (ed), Simons MD trans, *Jewish Medical Law* (1980) 106-10.

29 *Sefer Asia* at 92-93.

Parental rights of the parties under Israeli law

Biological parenthood and social parenthood

Who are the legal parents of the child? Fundamental concepts of Jewish and Israeli law which define legal parenthood conflict with modern legal theories which claim that the mentally conceiving parents have rights superior to all other parents.[30]

Traditional Jewish and Israeli law do not recognise the concept of an illegitimate child; children born in or out of wedlock are treated equally. Furthermore, unmarried parents are not, in principle, denied any rights toward their children. The factual, biological relationship is a sufficient basis for vesting parental rights, and the fact that the parent is unmarried does not by itself derogate his or her parental rights if he or she is willing to take responsibility for the child.[31] It seems that the encounter of the courts with artificial insemination and other new reproductive technologies necessitates a change in the traditional definition of parenthood from a purely biological definition to a socially oriented one.

Although many scholars of Jewish law are reluctant to recommend the use of new reproductive technologies, modern Israeli secular law has taken no stand as to their morality. The emerging viewpoint of Israeli law seems to be that upon the actual birth of a child to a surrogate mother, the best interests of the child must be the primary concern since the child bears no responsibility for the manner in which it was conceived. Furthermore, Israeli law will likely adopt the viewpoint that in a modern state, society should not be allowed to interfere in intimate matters of procreation by regulating reproductive technology. According to this view, the couple's decision is a personal one, based on their right to privacy, and must not be exposed to state interference. The first decision of the Israeli Supreme Court concerning artificial insemination by donor (AID) resulted in recognition of the legality of an agreement between spouses concerning the performance of artificial insemination.[32] By recognising the agreement and regarding it as imposing upon the husband a duty to support the child, the court has adopted by implication an approach which does not condemn, *a priori*, artificial insemination from a donor to a married woman whose husband gives his full consent to the act. This inference is important

---

30 See, *e.g.* Stumpf, *supra* n.1, at 207:
    Especially in situations where both the initiating parents and the surrogate mother want the child, case by case determinations of which set of parents might provide the best home environment would be unnecessarily intrusive and arbitrary. In surrogate parenting cases, the initiating parents should be the designated legal parents with sustained rights to the child. Indeed, in most cases of procreative collaboration, the parties will agree – and the legal presumptions proposed here reflect- that the initiating parents should raise the child as initially planned (footnotes omitted).
31 Shifman, "The Status of the Unmarried Parent in Israeli Law", (1977) 12 *Isr.L.Rev.* 194.
32 *Salma* v *Salma*, 34(2) P.D. 779 (Civ. App, 1980).

as a signal that the court ignored the attitude of most religious scholars to AID.[33]

The process which produced the present state of the law on AID in the United States may eventually emerge in Israel. In the United States the first step in the positive recognition of AID was taken on the basis of contract law.[34] Later, the idea was formulated and institutionalised in case law[35] and legislation[36] that a husband who consented to artificial insemination should bear the unequivocal status of father even without reliance on implied contract theory.[37] While the general legal doctrine behind this rule does not totally replace the idea of biological parenthood with consensual parenthood, the mere fact that the wife was fertilised through artificial insemination is not decisive. There is no dispute that where artificial insemination by husband (AIH) is performed the husband is the father of the child although the wife's pregnancy was the result of artificial insemination.[38] Conversely, the mere fact that a person gave his consent to take parental responsibility for a child does not grant him the status of parent to the child. If, for instance, a husband gave his consent to sexual relations between his wife and another man, he would not be considered, on the basis of his consent, to be the father of the child conceived in that situation.[39] Why, then, is a child conceived by AID deemed to be the child

---

33 Shifman, "First Encounter of Israeli Law with Artificial Insemination" (1981) 16 *Isr. L. Rev.* 250.

34 *Gursky* v *Gursky*, 39 Misc.2d 1083, 242 N.Y.S.2d 406 (Sup. Ct. Kings Co 1963). The court found that Mrs Gursky was induced by her husband's consent to be artificially inseminated and thus relied to her detriment upon her husband's wishes. The court chose to invoke the contract doctrine of equitable estoppel and found Mr Gursky primarily liable for support of the child. 39 Misc. 2d at 1088-89, 242 N.Y.S.2d at 412; *Cf In re Karin T* v *Michael T*, 127 Misc 2d 14, 484 N.Y.S. 2d 780 (Fam. Ct. 1985) (contract entered into by respondent - a woman attempted to change her feminine identity and live and act like a man and a father - with the mother and the doctor must inure to the benefit of the children); *RS* v *RS* 9 Kan. App 39, 670 P.2d 923 (Kan. Ct. App. 1983) (the court held that a husband who consents to his wife being artificially inseminated is estopped from denying that he is the father of the child and has thus, impliedly, agreed to support the child).

35 *People* v *Sorenson*, 68 Cal. 2d 280, 437 P.2d 495, 66 Cal. Rptr. 7 (1968); *In re Adoption of Anonymous*, 74 Misc 2d 99, 345 N.Y.S. 2d 430 (Sup. Ct. Kings Co. 1973) .

36 See *e.g.* N.Y. Dom. Rel. Law S73 (McKinney 1977); Cal. Civ. Code S 7005 (West Suppl 1980).

37 See *People* v *Sorenson*, 68 Cal. 2d 280, 437 P.2d 495, 498-99, 66 Cal. Rptr. 7, 10– 11 (1968) . This case involved statutory construction of s 270 of the California Penal Code Cal. Penal Code s 270 (West 1983). In controversy was the definition of the term "father". The court found the determinative factor was not limited to traditional concepts of a biological or natural father, but rather whether there exists the legal relationship of father and child. The court reasoned that it would be unfair to consider an anonymous donor of sperm as the "natural father", as he is "no more responsible for the use made of his sperm than is the donor of blood or a kidney." See also *In re Adoption of Anonymous*, 74 Misc. 2d 99, 105, 345 N.Y.S.2d 430, 43536 (Sup. Ct Kings Co. 1973) (The court held that a child born of consensual artificial insemination during a valid marriage is a legitimate child entitled to the same rights as a naturally conceived child).

38 The courts might, however, rule otherwise regarding AIH that took place after the death of the husband. If a wife was impregnated with semen deposited by her late husband in a sperm bank, it is submitted that the child could not legally be considered his son, since he did not take an active role in conception.

39 See *In Re Marriage* of LMS v SLS, 105 Wisc, 2d 118, 312 N.W. 2d 853 (1981) (a husband who consented to having his wife impregnated through sexual relations with a surrogate father, has the legal duties and responsibilities of fatherhood, including support); *In re Adoption of McFadyen* 108 Ill. App. 3d 329, 438 N.E. 2d 1362 (1982), cert. denied 460 U.S. 1015 (1983) (presumption of husband that he was the biological father of the child born to his wife was rebutted where the husband had a vasectomy and wife had relations with other men).

of the mother's husband, rather than the donor who supplied the semen for his conception? In the context of surrogate motherhood, the donor of the egg parallels the sperm donor in AID who consented in advance to relinquish all parental rights to the child.

To evaluate this problem, compare the case of a single woman using semen donated by a friend with the typical situation of a married couple employing AID. As to the former situation, a New Jersey court ruled that the friend who donates semen was the natural father of the child.[40] The court held that it is in the child's best interest to have two parents whenever possible and, therefore, no distinction should be made between natural and artificial conception.[41]

The result presumably would have been different if the semen came from an anonymous donor.[42] In the New Jersey case, the donor's active participation in the procedure leading to conception was cited as the basis of placing the responsibilities of fatherhood upon him.[43] An anonymous donor to a married couple, on the other hand, has no direct contact with the procedure or the mother. Although he is the biological father, he may not assert any rights with regard to a child born through the use of his semen because he did not consciously participate in the child's conception.[44] Although he supplied semen and placed it at the disposal of the doctor, the decision became the doctor's whether to use this semen, if at all, and if used, with which woman.[45] The wife's husband, who actively

---

40 *CM* v *CC* 152 N.J. Super. 160, 377A.2d 821 (Juv. & Dom. Rel Ct 1977). A donor of semen which was used by an unmarried woman artificially to inseminate herself, sued to obtain visitation rights to the child born as a direct result of the artificial insemination. The court found the anonymity of the sperm donor to be the dispositive factor. By donating his semen anonymously the donor impliedly gives it without taking on such responsibilities for its use. In such a situation, the person who consents to the use of the sperm, not his own, is responsible for fathering the child. For example, when a husband consents to his wife's artificial insemination from an anonymous donor, he takes upon himself the responsibilities of fatherhood. *Ibid* at 167, 377, A.2d at 824. But in this case, the donee received the semen from a friend, someone she knew and dated for two years. This friend intended to assume the responsibilities of parenthood when the child was conceived. Therefore, because of his consent and active participation in the procedure leading to conception, he will be treated as the natural father of the child and will be entitled to visitation rights. *Ibid* at 166-68, 377 A.2d at 824-25.

41 The court took no position as to the propriety of the artificial insemination between unmarried persons. It was concerned only with the best interests of the child in granting custody or visitation. For such consideration, the court will not make any distinction between a child conceived naturally or artificially. *Ibid* at 166-67, 377 A.2d at 824-25.

42 By donating his semen anonymously, the donor impliedly gives it without taking on such responsibilities for its use. *Ibid* at 167, 377, A.2d at 824.

43 "C.M.'s consent and active participation in the procedure leading to conception should place upon him the responsibilities of fatherhood." *Ibid* at 168, 377 A.2d at 825.

44 "[A] child conceived through heterologous artificial insemination does not have a "natural father", as the term is commonly used. The anonymous donor of the sperm cannot be considered the "natural father", as he is no more responsible for the use made of his sperm than is the donor of blood or a kidney ... With the use of the frozen semen, the donor may even be dead at the time the semen is used." *Ibid* at 164, 377 A.2d at 823, (quoting *People* v *Sorenson*, 68 Cal 2d 280, 66 Cal Rptr. 7, 10, 437 P.2d 495, 498 (1968).

45 By statute in California a "donor of semen provided to a licensed physician for use in artificial insemination of a woman other than the donor's wife is treated in law as if he were not the natural father of a child thereby conceived." CAL. Civ. Code S 7005, subd. (b) *In Jhordan C* v *Mary K* 224 Cal. Rptr. 530, 179 Cal App 3d 386 (1986) (because Mary did not obtain Jhordan's semen through a licensed physician and because the parties by all other conduct presented Jhordan's status as a member of the family, the court held Jhordan to be the baby's legal father).

participates in and consents to his wife's artificial insemination, will be treated as the child's legal father, instead of the donor who has relinquished control over the procreational use of his sperm. Surprisingly, some Jewish law scholars support this view.[46]

In brief, the general test under American law of the status of a parent is whether he actively participated in the child's conception, regardless of whether that conception took place artificially or naturally. When applying this test to a case involving surrogate motherhood, both genetic parents of the child, namely the husband and the surrogate mother, actively participated in the conception of the child: the husband by supplying his sperm, and the surrogate mother by supplying an egg, becoming impregnated, and carrying the foetus to term. While the husband's wife may assume a prominent role in the various stages leading to the birth of the child, and even take the initiative in seeking a surrogate mother, this does not automatically guarantee her status as the child's mother, since another woman, who is the biological mother, was so directly involved in the child's conception and birth. In other words, despite the tendency of courts and legislators to accommodate the needs of people trying to realise their right to parenthood through recent reproductive technologies, biological motherhood is still the starting point in the legal definition of parenthood.

All legislation on these matters must begin with a general theory of parenthood. Statutes have been enacted in many states in the United States in attempts to solve the legal problems of AID. Their scope, however, is generally limited to those situations where a married couple agrees to artificial insemination. By addressing one specific set of facts, these laws have not retained the flexibility required to address various situations. The provision that "the donor of semen provided ... for use in artificial insemination of a woman other than the donor's wife is treated in law as if he were not the natural father of a child thereby conceived"[47] was clearly aimed at absolving donors of legal responsibility for children born as a result of the use of their semen. Ironically, by applying this provision to the situation of surrogate motherhood, although the child is biologically the husband's, proof of paternity becomes virtually impossible.[48] The husband as well as the surrogate mother should be considered the child's parents inasmuch as both actively participate in the conception.

Waiver of parental rights by the surrogate mother

Assuming that, *ex definitio*, the surrogate mother is the legal mother of the child, what is the value of her waiver of parental rights and her advance consent to surrender the child for adoption by the husband's wife?

---

46 Rosner, *supra* n.26 at 98-99.
47 Cal. Civ. Code S 7005(b) (West 1983); see also 41 Unif. Parentage Act s 5(b) 9A U.L.A. 593 (1973).
48 "Note, Contracts to Bear a Child", *supra* n.1, at 614.

A distinction should be made between two different concepts in a surrogate motherhood contract: the agreement of the surrogate mother and the husband to produce a child; and the agreement of the surrogate mother to surrender the child and her parental rights to the child. The agreement of the surrogate mother and the husband to produce a child is not likely to be treated as repugnant to public policy in Israel where both the civil right to privacy and the religious duty to procreate coincide and the strong economic incentive of the surrogate mother to co-operate with the couple does not render the agreement immoral exploitation. On the other hand, payment given to the surrogate mother in exchange for releasing the child for adoption is likely to invoke the criminal law against the sale of babies. The Israeli Adoption of Children Law 1981, provides that "[a] person who otherwise than by permission of the court, offers or gives, or requests or accepts, any consideration in money or money's worth for an adoption ... is liable to imprisonment for three years."[49]

Nevertheless, surrogate motherhood is not necessarily prohibited by this provision inasmuch as it does not forbid payment for services rendered. The mother's consent to surrender the child for adoption may be invalidated, however, by a court on her application on the ground that it had been given before the birth of the child.[50] She would not be bound under Israeli law by her undertaking since, under the Supreme Court ruling, an agreement between parents that their child will not be recognised as the child of both parents has no validity.[51]

If the surrogate mother changes her mind and refuses to surrender the child, the court will be called upon to decide the custody dispute by determining the best interests of the child. Israeli law espouses the tender-years doctrine which gives the natural mother custodial preference concerning children up to six years of age unless there are special reasons to rule otherwise.[52] Grounds for paternal custody for a child under six years of age can be found if the father can raise the child in a two parent family.

In the absence of lengthy post-natal bonding between mother and child, the psychological attachments of the infant are far more difficult to determine, thus frustrating predictions of best interests.[53] In such a case, the court should do justice between the parties. Optimally, legal custody should be granted to the adoptive couple, because they have no other chance to realise their right to parenthood.[54] While the agreement is legally void if the natural mother refuses to surrender the child, it still retains

---

49 S 32, Penal Law 1977, s 364, prohibits relinquishing the custody of a minor for profit.
50 Adoption of Children Law, 1981, s 10.
51 *Merhav* v *Sharleen*, 26(1) P.D. 701, 704 (Civ. App. 1972).
52 Legal Capacity and Guardianship Law 1962, s 3.
53 "Note, Contracts to Bear a Child", supra n.1, at 621.
54 This consideration does not apply if the motivation for the surrogate motherhood agreement was not infertility of the husband's wife but rather her desire to avoid pregnancy as a matter of her own convenience. In such a case, it is submitted that no presumption of preference should be made in favour of the couple.

moral weight. The best interests of the child require that the court be guided by moral directives. The emotional trauma of a custody suit may cause more harm to the child than good from placement of the child with the more appropriate parent. The tender-years doctrine favouring the natural mother is a simple solution which disregards the fitness of any of the parties as parents. A presumption in favour of the adopting couple – the biological father and adopting mother – based on the surrogacy agreement, is also simplistic but ensures that the child will have a two-parent family. This final doctrine may be the only solution under Jewish and Israeli law where the two-parent family is the most favoured situation.

Chapter 6
Undoing What Comes Naturally – Regulating Medically Assisted Families

Derek Morgan
Senior Fellow in Health Care Law, Centre for Philosophy and Health Care,
University College, Swansea

"Children aren't happy with nothing to ignore
And that's what parents were created for"
Ogden Nash, Happy Days, (1933), The Parent.

"They fuck you up, your mum and dad.
They may not mean to, but they do.
They fill you with the faults they had.
And add some extra, just for you."
Philip Larkin, High Windows, (1974),
This Be the Verse.

In their complementary way, the introductory verses from Nash and Larkin raise questions about the relationship between parents and children. What either would have made of the technology of assisted conception we may only hazard. Genetic knowledge and reproductive medicine have developed in such a way since Watson and Crick's discovery of the structure of DNA, and particularly in the past two decades, that it is possible to envisage the development of new categories of birth, parenthood and family faster than vocabulary can be brought to the aid of understanding.[1] The discovery of the structure of DNA and the mapping of the human genome has given us a plot of human life. Aldous Huxley has even given us a title to the fabulous world which might be entered, and with which we can advertise the project. What we appear to know about the intimate structure and workings of gametes and embryos, foetuses and babies enables us to speak almost of a quantum theory of reproduction, to be set alongside a theory of general relativity – in which we factor the social, environmental, cultural, and emotional aspects of fertility, parenthood, individuation and society.

---

1   A recent contribution to this literature is Ruth Macklin, "Artificial Means of Reproduction and Our Understanding of the Family" (1991) 21 *Hastings Center Report* 5-11. Watson's provocative account of his work with Crick is detailed in his renowned volume *The Double Helix: A Personal Account of the Discovery of the Structure of DNA* (New York, Atheneum, 1968).

There are those who believe that work in present biotechnical research and associated infertility treatment services is like playing alchemy in the crucible of the genetic future. They suspect the danger that the atoms will enter new and unforeseeable trajectories and take on vectors and forces which cannot now be understood. In this vision, under the eye of the biotechnological clock we are moving towards some alchemical armageddon in which the horsemen of the apocalypse become the cavalry charge of the chromosomal chemists. For some, the sanctioning of research on human pre-embryos signals that the orders for that charge have already been given, and that the slippery slopes of disaster and destruction have already been tested and will exercise an inexorable gravitational pull.[2]

In parallel with this are doubts which have consistently been voiced about the wisdom of investing resources so heavily in the "reproduction revolution".[3] Against a background of serious, if contested, concern about the continuing rapid development and growth of population size in certain quarters of the globe and more explicit feminist arguments about technological fixes to the perceived problem of infertility and childlessness, there are fears that present imperatives address at several levels the wrong problem and certainly propose the wrong solutions.

The challenge is to obtain all the benefits and advantages of these developments in reproductive technology but to control these developments and guide them in the directions that we want. One of the major difficulties will be to identify the unwanted or unwarranted consequences, but a prior problem will be to agree upon which consequences are unwanted or unwarranted and how these are best to be avoided or minimised and what the opportunity costs are of having identified and chosen to regulate in one way rather than another. The types of control which could be envisaged include:

(i)   a private ordering approach, based upon individual control, responsibility and power;
(ii) professional self-regulation and control, through the medical profession, local research and institutional review committees, which has been a hallmark of medical regulation and supervision for many centuries;
(iii) community control, through national ethics committees and the courts;
(iv) legislative and regulatory control;
(v)   a combination or blending of one or more of these approaches.

Whichever is chosen will reflect the perceived judgment of the proper role

---

2   I do not deal in this essay with what Anthony Giddens has recently called "plastic sexuality" although this is an important analytical dimension in examining assisted conception. The links between the reproductive technologies and transformations affecting sexual relationships require a focus on "plastic sexuality" which is "decentered sexuality, freed from the needs of reproduction ... and from the rule of the phallus, from the overweening importance of male sexual experience". Giddens, *The Transformation of Intimacy* (Cambridge, Polity Press, 1992).
3   A term coined by Peter Singer and Deane Wells, *The Reproduction Revolution* (1984).

of the state in assisted conception. As McLean has suggested, "human reproduction is, in part regulated by law because it is seen as more than a merely private matter."[4] Most states have indeed eventually decided that some form of regulatory control through specially framed and implemented legislation is preferable, although the nature of that regulation and review differs markedly.

The existence of specialist clinics has revealed a global market for assisted conception.[5] At least in each "westernised" jurisdiction (and in many "developing" countries as well)[6] similar questions arise with respect to law, medicine and bioethics. But there are differences of a philosophical, economic, social, political and even geographical nature which are not easily (even if desirably) bridged. The use of contrasting responses to reproductive technologies helps illuminate different legislative and regulatory approaches which disclose some of the ambiguities of reproductive technology and the contrasting ways in which this might impinge upon or even compromise reproductive freedoms and also the plurality of moral responses.

Nonetheless, the need for such comparative reflection is underscored by the assessment of Jiri Haderka who has suggested that:

"It would be an illusion to think that further use of biomedical assistance to non-coital fertilisation can be stopped. Its application is so deeply rooted that it can be eradicated by no means in any of its forms, especially those connected with the use of donated gametes or embryos. No effect can be brought by outlawing some technology in one country or in a group of countries. Artificially induced births will continue to occur because pregnancy will be available in other countries which will permit them and the world becomes more and more interconnected and travels to this aim will be quite easy."[7]

---

4   Sheila McLean, "Reproductive Medicine" in Dyer (ed), *Doctors, Patients and the Law,* (Blackwell, 1992) pp89-105 at p89.

5   A singular but graphic example of what Bartha Knoppers and Sonia Le Bris have identified in "today's modern 'global village'... [which allows] citizens to practice 'procreative tourism' in order to exercise their personal reproductive choices in other less restrictive states." "Recent Advances in Medically Assisted Conception: Legal, Ethical and Social Issues" (1991) 17 *American J of Law & Medicine* 329-61 at 333, is provided by the report, carried in the Sunday Express on 5 July 1992 and rapidly disseminated elsewhere, of the policies of the Institute of Human Reproduction and Fertility in Rome, headed by Dr Serverino Antinoi. The report disclosed that he had provided infertility treatment to nearly thirty post-menopausal women over the age of 50, one of whom was now pregnant at the age of 60. In an associated "Heart of the Matter" television programme the woman disclosed that her reason for wanting to establish this late pregnancy was to succour for her otherwise uncontrollable grief at the loss of her son in a motor accident some months previously.

6   Pran Manga, "New Reproductive Technologies in the Third World: Heightened Human Rights and Ethical Controversies" paper delivered to the Third International Conference on Health Law and Ethics, Toronto, July 1992; suggests that "the largest product line" in new reproductive technologies is sex selection; estimates of the size of the market put this at $6 billion a year. And see Kussum Kumar, "Legal Implications of Medical Advancement" in Leelakrishan and Sadasivan Nair (eds), *New Horizons of Law* (Cochin, Cochin University of Science and Technology, 1987) pp199-212, esp at pp 199-204 and 210-12.

7   Jiri Haderka, "Medically Assisted Procreation and Legal Questions of Parenthood", paper presented at the VIIth World Conference of the International Society of Family Law, Opatija, June 1991, at p 19.

Even on the more sanguine assumptions of Bartha Knoppers and Sonia Le Bris the urgent need for comparative understanding is evident. They have identified a range of emergent assumptions about the necessary forms of limitation and prohibition of assisted conception, and a narrower area in which disagreement or national difference is more pronounced.[8] Thus they suggest that a general consensus exists in respect of access to assisted conception; that clinicians offering the service should be supervised or regulated (at least by medical colleagues); that legal considerations of paternity and maternity should be addressed; that confidential medical records should be established concerning donors and children; that embryonic life *in vitro* should be limited to 14 days; that time limits on storage be established; that posthumous implantation or insemination be prohibited; that commercial surrogacy agencies be prohibited; that participant consent be established and common conditions of donation be established; that reproductive technologies be free from commercialization; that sex selection of embryos for other than genetic disease be prohibited as well as forms of eugenic selection and that controls and prohibitions on extreme forms of genetic engineering, such as cloning, pathogenesis, inter-species fertilization and the creation of chimeras, be established. We can test these assessments against the jurisdictions studied, for although many common issues are addressed by these statutes or proposals, I have drawn from each different facets of the regulation of assisted conception in order to illustrate the argument.

On other areas there is, they argue, less or no agreement. For social, cultural, economic or religious reasons there is lack of unanimity on questions such as the remuneration of donors; access to information by children born following assisted conception; the maintenance of information registers; the donation, conservation and experimentation with human embryos; limitations on the number of children by donor and finally, on the genetic diagnosis of embryos. Of these differences, Knoppers and Le Bris comment:

> "... the possibility of a comprehensive policy, or of legislation encompassing all of these new technologies in each state, may never be forthcoming and may not even be desirable where it would run contrary to basic human rights and freedoms."[9]

This paper is what may be described as an introductory essay in the comparative anthropology of law. The two immediate purposes of this essay are first to explore the various ways in which different jurisdictions have responded to the regulatory challenge of assisted conception and associated research and secondly, to seek to make some observations on the ways in which laws, customs and values have been manipulated to produce pictures of the family and the way in which we want – literally and figuratively – to conceive of it in the twenty-first century. First I examine

---

8   *Supra* n.5 at pp 332-33.
9   *Ibid,* at p 333.

cursorily the United Kingdom's Human Fertilization and Embryology Act 1990, which exhibits what may be thought of as a "radical laissez-faire" approach; a system of regulated private ordering. The second review considers the Danish legislation of 1987 and 1992[10] which embodies a "cautious regulatory system". The third study is of the Austrian Act on Procreative Medicine[11] which came into force on 1 July 1992 and which exemplifies a "prohibitive licensing regime". Finally, I consider the proposals of the Law Reform Commission of Canada "Medically Assisted Procreation"[12] which may be characterised as a form of "liberal constitutional approach".

The United Kingdom Human Fertilization and Embryology Act 1990

This is a major and complex piece of legislation, seeking to tackle sensitive and difficult ethical, legal, personal and social problems which surround and attend infertility. Jonathan Montgomery has observed that it "provides the first attempt in English law to provide a comprehensive framework for making medical science democratically accountable."[13] The Act has four main purposes:

(i)   to regulate certain infertility treatments which involve keeping or using human gametes and to regulate the keeping of human embryos outside the human body;

(ii) to sanction and regulate embryo research, which is permitted until not later than the end of the period of 14 days beginning with the day when the gametes are "mixed", excluding any period of cryopreservation;

(iii) to prohibit the creation of hybrids using human gametes, the cloning of embryos by nucleus substitution to produce genetically identical individuals, and genetic engineering to change the structure of an embryo; and

(iv) to effect changes to the Abortion Act 1967.

---

10 Act No 503 of 24 June 1992, *Lov om et videnskabsetisk komitéststem og behandling af boimedicinske forskningsprojekter*, which came into force in October 1992.

11 The Austrian Act on Procreative Medicine (275 Bundesgesetz, mit dem Regelungen uber die medizinisch unterstutzte Fortpflanzang getroffen (*Fortpflanzungsmedizingestez - FMedG) sowie das allgemeinen burgerliche Gesetzbuch, das Ehegesetz und die Jurisdiktioinsnorm geandert werden, Bundesgesetzblatt fur die Republik Osterreich*) was enacted by the lower house of the federal Parliament (*Der Nationalrat*) on 14 May 1992.

12 Law Reform Commission of Canada, "Medically Assisted Procreation" Working Paper 65, Minister of Supply and Services, 1992.

13 Montgomery, "Rights, Restraints and Pragmatism: The Human Fertilisation & Embryology Act 1990" (1991) 54 MLR 524. Lord Mackay, the Lord Chancellor has said of the Act that: "It is an innovative and comprehensive piece of legislation which has brought hope and reassurance to many people", see House of Lords, Hansard, Vol 537, col 1366 (11 June 1992).

The Act establishes few fundamental prohibitions and otherwise exhibits what might be termed a radical *laissez-faire* approach; a system of regulated private ordering and professional supervision tempered with public scrutiny and input. The major vehicle to effect these directions is the Human Fertilization and Embryology Authority (HFEA), created under the Act and which came into being on 7 November 1990.[14] As a licensing body the Authority has power over public and private institutions to scrutinise and license, to approve, discipline and sanction the provision of assisted conception services and three main areas of activity; the storage of gametes and embryos, research on human embryos and any infertility treatment which involves the use of either donated gametes or embryos created outside the human body.

This licensing responsibility lies at the heart of the Authority's regulatory powers; "not only is it used to ensure that proper standards are maintained, but it also assists in informing the Authority about current and developing practice in the whole field of assisted conception."[15] Different parts of the Act apply to the collection, storage and usage of such gametes. Where a clinic performs AID using gametes from the couple alone, or where it undertakes a procedure such as GIFT – gamete intrafallopian transfer – using the couples own gametes, then the licensing conditions of the legislation do not apply. There are some provisions of the Act to be attended to, but controversially not the full blown licensing scheme.

In addition, HFEA is charged to:

- maintain a register of information concerning donors, treatment services and children born following licensed services;
- publicise services which centres and HFEA itself provides;
- produce advice and information to centres and publish a code of practice to which centres should adhere or aspire;
- provide information to donors, to potential patients and to children born following regulated services.

The Code of Practice which the Authority issued in July 1991 deals, *inter alia*, with the confidentiality of records kept in pursuance of the Act, arrangements necessary for securing compliance with the "consents" requirements of Schedule 3, screening procedures for donors of egg and sperm, guidance on the numbers of eggs or pre-embryos which should be transferred to the uterus, appropriate laboratory standards, qualifications and experience of employed staff at licensed centres, and the means of involvement of local ethics committees.

---

14 In what follows I have concentrated on only the outline of the 1990 statute and have taken the opportunity to make some observations upon the initial work of the HFEA. For a more comprehensive consideration of the legislation see Morgan and Lee, *Blackstone's Guide to the Human Fertilisation and Embryology Act 1990, Abortion and Embryo Research: the New law* (Blackstone, 1990). The introductory assessment of the work of the HFEA and the nature of the regulation undertaken by this Authority could in time be replicated for the other models here under consideration, but the United Kingdom is probably the most sophisticated system yet in operation and as such repays closest examination.

15 HFEA, First Annual Report (1992) para 12.2

Assessing the legislation, Montgomery observed that the forum within which the debates about infertility treatment and embryo research are to be carried out is structured by "a complex web of discretion, restraints, control and accountability." The HFEA will have considerable autonomy to develop its own standards of what is acceptable and good practice, and will not be limited to the framework established by Parliament.

> "Its interest therefore arises both from the solutions it adopts for particular issues and from the model of regulation on which it builds."[16]

In assessing the nature and thrust of the regulatory model, it is possible to draw on and read between the lines of the HFEA's first Annual Report. The Authority's glossy report encapsulates some of the fears to which the work of any regulatory body gives rise. Doubts will centre on whether some of the major issues with respect to assisted conception may be being glossed over and whether the focus of the Authority appears from the evidence of some of its early work to need radical readjustment.

There are a number of ways in which the HFEA was effectively snared by the interests of those whom it was set up to regulate even before the main body of the Authority's work had started. This is not, of course, to imply anything sinister or unexpected; one of the mainstream analyses of administrative, regulatory agencies focuses on the "capture" of the agency by the group, interest or industry which the agency was established to regulate.[17] Two examples will suffice. First, in paras 5.1 and 5.2 of the Annual Report the HFEA records claims that the confidentiality provisions contained in section 33 of the 1990 Act providing for restrictions on disclosure of information were "potentially dangerous" suggesting that centres were "not able to give information to others directly, even with the patient's consent." Three difficulties were suggested;

(i) that even in an emergency the licensed practitioner would be prevented from giving potentially vital information to the doctor handling the emergency;

(ii) that clinicians would be unable to communicate directly with a patient's

---

16 Montgomery, *op cit*, n.17, at p 526, p 524. I do not have the space here to rehearse the interesting constitutional position which HFEA and its predecessor the Interim Licensing Authority occupy; that forms a separate paper. There is, as yet, no accessible history of the ILA and its work, although one has been proposed by Jennifer Gunning and Veronica English, who each served as Secretary to the ILA. There are interesting parallels between the HFEA and the system of Boards which discharged administrative powers and responsibilities in the C19; for an introduction to the constitutional position of "Fringe Organisations" see Craig, *Administrative Law*, (Sweet & Maxwell) pp 107 *et seq*, and for an exposition of the importance in examining the link between legislative provisions and related concepts of public power requiring a distinct public law and suggesting one set of parameters for such a study see Prosser, *Nationalised Industries and Public Control* (Blackwell, 1986) pp 1-15.

17 For an introduction to this literature see, for example, Peltzman, "The Benefits and Costs of New Drug Regulation" in Landau (ed), *Regulating New Drugs* (1973), Bernstein, *Regulating Business by Independent Commission* (1955), pp 183–87. For an evaluation and critique of some of the standard "capture" theories see Guido Calabresi, *A Common law for the Age of Statutes* (Cambridge, Mass., Harvard University Press, 1982) esp at pp 46–51.

general practitioner or other hospital staff such as anaesthetists and theatre nurses; and

(iii) that a clinician might not be able to give proper instructions to a lawyer in the event of being sued by a patient because of the provisions relating to permitted disclosures of information.

These strictures arose from a reading of section 33(5) of the 1990 Act which was at best contentious, [18] and led directly to the passage of the Human Fertilization and Embryology (Disclosure of Information) Act 1992. This relaxed the restrictions on disclosure by adding further exceptions to those contained in section 33(6) of the principal Act.[19] The inspiration for the amendment came from the members of the medical profession whose clinical freedom had been abridged by the original section[20] and consultation on the proposed amendment was taken with the Royal College of Obstetricians and Gynaecologists, the General Medical Council and the British Medical Association.

The following paragraph of the Report deals with the fate of gametes and embryos stored before 1 August 1991.[21] In this, the medical profession was able to ensure an effective moratorium on the implementation of the Act. The ensnarement of the HFEA at this early stage by its supposed quarry, "professional people not much used to legislative control", [22] is a troubling reflection on the preparedness of the Authority to assume its regulatory functions and the confidence with which sceptical public opinion can be assured. We should recall that even the treatment licensing provisions of the legislation are controversial and that the infertility treatment services provision remains a contested area of medical practice and delivery.

The Report does disclose some interesting aspects of the Authority's relationship with the Treasury and other Departments of State. In this time of reproductive recession, when the profit margins of all private treatment including assisted conception are being squeezed, the reduction in the "tax

---

18 I have elsewhere attempted to outline an alternative reading which would have rendered amending legislation unnecessary; see Morgan and Lee, "Disclosure is Possible Under HFEA" (1992) 75 *Bulletin of Medical Ethics* 25-28 and the critical response from Leigh and Barker, "HFEA Confidentiality" (1992) 77 *Bulletin of Medical Ethics* 10-11. Of course, this interpretation of restrictions on disclosure of information in an "emergency" appears to proceed without acknowledgment of the effect on consent requirements of the House of Lords' decision in *Re F* [1990] 2 AC 1 in which Lord Bridge spoke of there being circumstances in which a doctor who failed to treat a patient being in need of treatment as in breach of a duty to treat. Lord Bridge said that it was "axiomatic" that "treatment which is necessary to preserve the life, health or well-being of the patient may lawfully be given without consent."

19 The Bill was given an informative Second Reading in the House of Lords on 11 June 1992, see Hansard, vol 537, cols 1366-1379, and also vol 538, col 551 and in the House of Commons vol 211, col 1153. Royal assent was indicated on 16 July 1992.

20 See "Correspondence" from, respectively, Brinsden and Craft, (1991) *British Medical Journal,* 3 August and 5 October.

21 For reports of the confusion see The *Independent* 24 July 1991 and 26 July 1991, and the HFEA's response in its *First Annual Report* (1992) para 5.2, p13. A similar problem has arisen following the enactment of legislation in Austria, see text.

22 Colin Campbell, Chairman of the Human Fertilisation and Embryology Authority, *First Annual Report* p2.

on the infertile" which the HFEA was able to negotiate with the Treasury will be pleasing to clinics, managers and, if passed on to them, patients. Originally, the government proposed that the HFEA should raise up to two-thirds of its operating costs from other than Treasury subsidy. Most of this would have come from the fees charged to clinics for licences, inspections and allied work undertaken by the Authority. In the course of its first year of operation, paragraph 6.2 of the Report discloses that the Treasury agreed to set the figure at 50%, and extrapolating from data in the report[23] the total operating costs of the HFEA for 1991-92 must be in the region of £1.2m.[24] The Authority acknowledges that it has no accurate estimate of the number of various *in vitro* fertilization and donor insemination treatment cycles being performed annually although it indicates that the future level of fees will in part depend upon this, as well as any requirements imposed by the Secretary of State and the Treasury and the costs of running the Authority (especially its licensing function) and its projected staffing costs.

This confession may be thought alarming and, while this position may be expected to improve in the course of the Authority's work, it reflects the general indiscipline to which self or voluntary regulation had been allowed to succumb by the medical profession.

The Danish legislation of 1987 and 1992

On 24 June 1992 the Danish Parliament passed Act no 503 dealing with Ethics Committees, the treatment of biomedical research projects and regulation of embryo research and donation and cryopreservation of human eggs and embryos.[25] This and associated legislation of 1987 embodies what may be called a "cautious regulatory approach"; although it is much less comprehensive in the coverage of assisted conception than any of the other initiatives surveyed here. In that sense, the caution expressed in terms of the regulatory model has to be set alongside the administration

---

23 It is surprising that this is not spelled out in the Annual Report either in s 9 (the organization and finance committee whose remit is identified as including "the preparation of the Authority's budget" p 25) or in s 11 (details of the authority's executive).

24 This is calculated on the basis of £28, 700 raised in initial treatment, storage and research licence application fees (see para 6.2); £360K raised from IVF centres based on the rate of £30.00 per IVF cycle and an estimate from the most recent ILA data of 12, 000 cycles p.a. and £210,000 raised from centres on the basis of £7.00 per DI cycle, estimated on a purely hypothetical figure of 30, 000 DI cycles p.a. The total here of £598K represents 50% of the HFFEA operating budget as now approved by the Treasury and the Secretary of State (it would be interesting to know what sort of horse trading had taken place between these two officers of state). The HFEA has (at September 1992) recently passed details of its budget to the Department of Health and the Secretary of State will in due course lay this before Parliament.

25 A commentary on the background to the Danish legislation may be found in Morgan and Nielsen "Dangerous Liaisons; Law, Technology, Reproduction and European Ethics" in McVeigh and Wheeler (eds), *Law, Health and Medical Regulation*, (Dartmouth, 1992). That paper was prepared as part of a project funded by a grant from the British Council, from which this paper has also benefited.

of the public hospital system in Denmark through which until very recently all health care, including assisted conception would have been provided.[26]

In April 1984 the Danish Minister of the Interior established a committee to investigate the ethical problems connected with genetic engineering, *in vitro* fertilization, artificial insemination and pre-natal diagnosis. The Committee's report, "The Price of Progress", was presented six months later. In it, the establishment of a central ethics council for the health system was recommended. Following the Danish Parliament's consideration of the report the Council of Ethics' work was initiated under the 1987 statute in January 1988. The legislation provided that a number of specific matters should be reviewed and that further legislative proposals should be laid before the Parliament in the session 1989-90 at the latest. The law of 1987 was enacted to provide what in effect amounted to a moratorium on embryo research and a restriction on the uses of assisted conception until the contemporaneously established Ethics Committee had had the opportunity to address the social, legal and ethical questions which it believed that these developments disclosed.

It is sufficient presently to observe that the "protection" given by the 1987 Act did not prevent a majority of the Ethics Council sanctioning very limited forms of experimentation – the proviso is that the object of the research, sanctioned by a regional as well as the central committee, must be the improvement of techniques of *in vitro* fertilization with a view to promoting pregnancy. Removing and fertilising eggs or embryos for any other purpose is however prohibited. The legal motives (explanatory Memorandum) appended to the Act make it clear that the main reason for accepting research but restricting it in this way is that *in vitro* fertilization is a recognised treatment and that research is accepted internationally as an integrated part of the development of treatment; prohibiting all research would mean consciously offering less optimal treatment than is possible.

Chapter 4 section 14 of the Act prohibits cloning, the production of individuals by fusion of genetically different embryos or parts of embryos prior to implantation (nucleus substitution) and experiments whose objective is to make possible the production of living human individuals which are hybrids with a genome containing constituent parts of other species (cross species fertilization). Chapter 2 section 5 of the legislation provides that any biomedical research project which includes research on living human individuals, human gametes which are intended for use in fertilization, fertilised human eggs and pre-embryos or embryos should be reported to regional ethical committees. There are presently seven such committees, established according to local government boundaries, and they comprise nine or eleven members, three of whom are nominated by the state authorised scientific committee, Den Centrale Videnskabsetiske Komite. The constitutional position of the Ethical Council is paralleled by

---

26 A similar assessment of the questions of access to treatment services and associated questions would be possible in reviewing the operation of the Danish public hospital system. A separate paper outlining the provision of assisted conception in Denmark is in preparation.

committees charged to oversee narcotics, alcohol, traffic safety, consumer questions, and the independent economic council, such that, unlike the HFEA, its establishment does not set the same precedent.

The central and regional committees are charged to oversee and where appropriate to approve research, although the Act does not contain a definition of that term. Section 9 provides that fertilised eggs may only be kept outside the woman's womb for 14 days from conception, excluding any period of cryopreservation. Fertilised human eggs which have been subjected to research must not be implanted into a woman's womb unless this can be done without risk of transmitting hereditary disease, defects, abnormalities or similar deformities. The donation of fertilised eggs is prohibited, although by virtue of section 13 (6) the Minister of Health may make further rules regarding cryopreservation and donation of human eggs, and further regulations securing donor anonymity. The legal motives specify that it is a pre-condition that the donation of unfertilised human eggs is only undertaken anonymously; while the legislation presupposes that it will only be permissible to cryopreserve eggs for a maximum of one year. The Act does not deal with sperm donation, although administrative provisions operated through the central Danish cryopreservation facility for sperm ensure that this will only be undertaken anonymously. There are, however, few regulations or prohibitions on the availability of sperm in Denmark, and it is possible to obtain and use fresh unscreened semen, either in the Rigshospitalet (University Hospital), Fertility Centre or on the "open market" of unregulated fertility specialists who operate in Copenhagen.

Civil law questions of family rights are not affected by this legislation because those questions are deemed to lie within the competence of the Ministry of Justice. Unlike the British legislation, the Danish Act does not aim to be as comprehensive or wide-ranging; and in neither case does the legislation present itself as a code covering all questions of assisted conception.

The Austrian Act on procreative medicine[27]

With the exception of Israel, Austria has more centres offering some form of assisted conception per head of population than any other country. There are 22 *in vitro* fertilization centres, with many more clinics (or "hospitals") offering various forms of artificial insemination. It is likely that the restrictive provisions of the 1992 Act – the main scheme of the Act is contained in the 25 sections of Artikel I – will ensure that this situation will dramatically change, at least in the short-term. The Act, which came into

---

27 This section draws on a longer analysis of the legislation in Morgan and Bernat, "The Reproductive Waltz" (1992) *J. of Social Welfare and Family Law* 420–26.

force on 1 July 1992[28], illustrates a "prohibitive licensing approach" to the regulation of assisted conception and has three main aims. First, it introduces a range of prohibitions in relation both to assisted conception treatment services and research. Secondly, it establishes a system of regulation of those limited treatment services which are to remain lawful after 1 July 1992, and introduces penalties for contravention of either the prohibited or regulated activities. Finally, the Act mirrors the United Kingdom's Human Fertilization and Embryology Act 1990 in dealing with what may be called the status and relationship considerations of assisted conception.

Prohibitions

A wide spectrum of prohibitions, backed with administrative penalty, discloses the essential antipathy with which assisted conception is held in Austria. All forms of assisted conception using donated gametes are prohibited with the exception of donor insemination *in vivo* – DI.[29] Thus, *in vitro* fertilization with donated semen or eggs is prohibited; gamete intrafallopian transfer (GIFT) with donated gametes is also prohibited. Heterologous embryo transfer where the embryo is not genetically related to the recipient woman is also prohibited, as is the mixture of semen from different donors.[30] Artikel I section 3(3) prohibits embryo transfer or embryo donation and provides that ova and embryos may only be used for women from whom they are genetically derived. This ensures that donated embryos or gametes may not be used to establish a surrogate pregnancy. Artificial donor insemination is even prohibited where the intending social father is fertile but carries an hereditary disease which is likely to be transmitted to any children.

Assisted conception is to be confined to married or stable heterosexual cohabitations; single women may not benefit from medically assisted conception. A woman who has been divorced or whose husband or partner has died while she has embryos frozen pending a further procedure is prohibited from making use of these stored embryos. In any event, such storage may not exceed one year, after which any stored embryo, or gametes, must be allowed to perish.[31]

In any IVF procedure which is permitted (essentially those using the couples' own gametes) Artikel I section 10 provides that a doctor may only cause as many eggs to be fertilised as are to be used in that treatment cycle. This is an important provision which abrogates the former freedom of Austrian IVF practitioners to fertilise an unlimited number of eggs or oocytes recovered from a woman's (possibly hyperstimulated) menstrual

---

28 The Austrian Act on Procreative Medicine (Act 275) Artikel V(1).
29 Artikel I s 3(2).
30 Artikel I s 9(3).
31 Artikel I s 17(1).

cycle and to store them for later use.[32] And while section 17 of the Act allows storage for up to one year, compliance with section 10 renders cryopreservation almost redundant. It will be rare now for "spare" embryos to be available for storage because it will not be possible to fertilise all recovered eggs intending to use only those with the "best" morphology for immediate use. The ability to cryopreserve gametes and embryos for up to one year appears effectively to cater only for the limited circumstances in which a woman becomes ill or unable to proceed with assisted conception treatment after fertilization but before the embryo transfer procedure.[33]

Destructive embryo research is forbidden under the terms of section 9(1) while section 9(2) prohibits any interference with the germ cell line. Section 9(1) provides that *in vitro* embryos may not be used for purposes other than medically assisted reproduction and, hence, may only be examined and treated as far as this is necessary in accordance with clinical practice. The same applies to ova and semen to be used in treatment services. A fine of up to 500K Austrian shillings (approximately £25K) may be imposed for violation of section 9 germ cell line or destructive embryo research. These absolute prohibitions stand in contrast with the requirements of section 17(1) that cryopreserved embryos which reach the end of the allotted storage period of one year must be allowed to perish.

Regulating reproduction

The main thrust of the regulatory provisions of Act 275 is that lawful assisted conception may be practised only by obstetricians and gynaecologists; previously no clinical or other restrictions existed. AIH may be administered in the private practices of such gynaecologists; all other assisted conception treatments (DI, IVF and GIFT using the couples' own gametes) must in accordance with the provisions of section 5 be conducted in specially licensed hospitals. Where DI is carried out other than in a specialised hospital licensed for that purpose a fine of up to 100K shillings may be levied.

Any practitioner who intends to offer assisted conception must apply for a licence from one of the nine provincial Governors' offices. The licence must be issued if the Office is satisfied of the personal and professional

---

32 Neither the Austrian legislation nor the UK Act goes as far as the German Embryonenschutzgesetz (ESchG- Embryo Protection Law) which prohibits the transfer of any more than three embryos in one cycle (see Bundesgesetzblatt: I, 2746; issued 13.12.90, in force from 1.1.1992). The UK's Human Fertilization & Embryology Authority's *First Annual Report* (1992) suggests that "The Authority believes that there is no longer any clinical justification for transferring more than three [embryos] in any circumstances. Indeed there are people who believe that the limit should be reduced to two." (para 7.4, p 21).

33 This is the rather cumbersome way in which the Austrian legislature has attempted to circumvent the legal problems which arose in the American case of *Davis* v *Davis* 15 Family Reporter 1551 (1989), on appeal to the Tennessee Court of Appeals (West Law 130807 (Tenn. App.) (1990)), discussed in Morgan and Lee, *op. cit.*, p 138. *Cf* the United Kingdom Act Sched 3 for a parallel attempt to pre-empt these circumstances. The Davis case is also analysed in Simon, "Honey, I froze the Kids: *Davis* v *Davis* and the Legal Status of Human Embryos" (1991) 23 (1) *Loyola University of Chicago Law J.* 131-54 and Robertson, "In the Beginning: the Legal Status of Early Embryos" (1990) 76 *Va. L. Rev* 437.

standards of the applicant. In assessing the latter, relevant personnel, procedures and equipment provision will be scrutinised. One ironic effect of this requirement is that the pioneer of Austrian IVF, Peter Kemeter, has been forced to suspend treatments as he has presently only a private practice. If he is to continue to offer the more medically advanced treatments he has to apply to be recognised as a specialised hospital, although the requirements are more of an administrative inconvenience than an effective screening procedure.

Section 17(2) of Artikel 1 restricts the ability of couples in an assisted conception treatment programme to direct what may be done with their gametes. While they may be stored in accordance with section 17(1), gametes and embryos may not be returned to their genitors nor to any other person other than for specified treatments. This section, inserted by the judiciary committee which examined the draft legislation, is intended to provide that genitors only have the right to retrieve their stored gametes and embryos for the purpose of using them in treatment with their own partner.

Before the sperm is used the donor and his semen must be examined (section 12). This must show that the donor is fertile and that the use of his gametes poses no health risks either to any woman undergoing treatment services or to any child which might be conceived as a result. Donor semen is thus always screened, but perhaps paradoxically the wife or partner of a fertile man who is the carrier of a genetic disease may not use DI. Their only chances of having a child is by adoption, adultery or abduction. Semen donors will not enjoy rights of anonymity.[34] Although this was earnestly discussed in the Judiciary Committee, where it was argued that the privacy interests of the donor should be balanced against those of the child, in the event, section 13(1) emerged as the compromise. On donation, the semen donor must record his consent that any child who may be born following the use of his sperm may, from the age of 14, request information of his identity. Clinics have a duty to keep records showing the names of donors, their birth date, birth place, nationality, residence and the names of the donors' parents.[35] The purpose of this last requirement is to ensure that where a doctor or clinic uses semen, there is no inadvertent insemination of a woman with semen donated by, for example, her brother.

In a more controversial regulatory gambit, Austrian legislators have provided that where an unmarried couple request treatment services they must first submit to an advisory procedure before a competent court or notary public. A doctor may not perform even medically indicated insemination using the couples' own gametes unless the legal consequences of the procedure have been explained to them by the court or notary.[36]

---

34 Artikel 1 s 20; for the UK position see the 1990 Act s 31 (4) and (5); the HFEA Code of Practice para 4(5) (e), subject to ss 34 and 35, and the Human Fertilization and Embryology (Disclosure of Information) Act 1992.

35 S15.

36 Artikel 1, Ss 7 and 8.

The most important is that the unmarried cohabitant has to acknowledge paternity of the child. The court or notary will issue the couple with a special licence which they must sign. Section 8(3) (iv) provides that this licence will specify the time within which the medically assisted reproduction may be performed, and that the licence may be issued either for one year or for the duration of the treatment until a pregnancy is established. This "reproductive regulation" is supplemented with a "tax on reproduction"; the couple must pay the court or notary charges of approximately 1000 Austrian shillings (approximately £50.00). This is one of the provisions of the legislation which may be challenged in the Austrian Constitutional Court, along with a second case in which a 45-year old woman who is incapable of producing ova is seeking to challenge the prohibition on egg donation. Her argument, based on Articles 8 and 12 of the European Convention on Human Rights (which is incorporated into Austrian law), is that the prohibition violates her privacy rights guaranteed under those provisions and her right to marry and found a family. While the scope of those articles is uncertain, and has been the subject of extensive commentary[37], the resolution of this case will be one of the first occasions in which a major European constitutional court has considered the ambit and application of the provisions in the case of assisted conception provision [38].

As with the UK Human Fertilization and Embryology Act, Act 275 contains no comprehensive transitional provisions. As happened in the United Kingdom in July and August 1991, there also is confusion about the legality of dealing with stored gametes obtained before the Act came into force on 1 July.[39] One particular case, which illustrates the problem, is of a doctor in Vienna who has frozen semen worth about £50, 000 at his clinic. The two different approaches are that semen or embryos obtained or created and stored before the commencement date are not covered by the Act, that they may be retained and used in treatment services and that the donors may remain anonymous. The alternative approach, which may be regarded as offending the constitutional provisions protecting propriety, is that the semen must be discarded thereby costing the doctor and his patients considerable expense.

The Law Reform Commission of Canada

In one of the final Working Papers published before its demise the Law

---

37 For example, in the voluminous United Kingdom literature reference might be made to Douglas, *Law, Fertility and Reproduction* (1992); and Douglas *et al*, "The Right to a Family" (1992) 142 *New Law* J. 488.

38 Article II of Act 275 is an addition to the 1811 Austrian General Civil Code (ABGB) which deals in part with filiation law and there are further technical amendments to the ABGB in Artikel III. These are more fully discussed in Morgan and Bernat, *supra*, n.27.

39 See, *supra*, at n.21.

Reform Commission of Canada (LRCC) published its review of, and recommendations on, Medically Assisted Procreation. This encapsulates what may be called a "liberal constitutional approach".[40] The recommendations of the LRCC have to be read in the light of their discussion of, and conclusion on, the effects of the Canadian Charter of Fundamental Rights and Freedoms[41], which establishes the constitutional background against which these proposals are made.[42] Thus, on the important question of access to assisted conception, the LRCC observes that it is imperative to respect the right to equality, and thus be limited only in terms of cost and scarcity of resources. Where limitation is necessary, selection should not be on the grounds rendered unlawful for discrimination purposes within the meaning of federal and provincial legislation.

Hence, discrimination should not be on the basis of family status, marital status, or sexual orientation.[43] Thus, the LRCC observes that the often-cited criterion of a stable heterosexual union[44] raises a number of questions of fairness; whether, for example, it is appropriate to apply this criterion to assisted conception when it is not applied to other forms of assistance to overcome infertility, such as hormone treatment or corrective surgery to overcome infertility. The objective of using the stability criterion – the welfare of the child – would, they suggest, "be more easily attained by ensuring proper support before, during and after the child is conceived."[45] Secondly, and perhaps more substantially, they argue that this type of criterion is "arbitrary and difficult to evaluate" and "involves the application of non-medical criteria by health professionals which creates or reinforces risks of discrimination."[46] The Commission concludes that "taking current social conditions into account" protection for the traditional family should not be incorporated in legislation at the expense of the right to equality under section 15 of the Canadian Charter of Rights and Freedoms.[47]

---

40 Law Reform Commission of Canada, Working Paper 65, *Medically Assisted Procreation* (1992). The Commission's work is separate from and independent of the Canadian Royal Commission on New Reproductive Technologies, chaired by Patricia Baird whose report is in the final drafting stages and is scheduled for publication early in 1993; see *Royal Commission Update*, August 1992.

41 Part I of the Constitution Act 1982, Sched B of the Canada Act 1972 (UK) 1972.

42 It is possible that the Royal Commission will come to alternative conclusions about either the scope or the effect of the Charter, and that its recommendations may be tailored in the light of that.

43 Recommendation 1, p 129, discussed at pp 124-29.

44 See Human Fertilization and Embryology Act 1990 s 13 (5), Austrian Act on Procreative Medicine, Act 275, Artikel l, s 3.

45 LRCC Report, at p 124.

46 *Ibid.* These are precisely the kind of judgments which clinicians are invited to make under the UK legislation. Researchers report a reluctance on behalf of clinics openly to discuss how in practice this sort of treatment criteria are being applied in the United Kingdom. The use in the United Kingdom of Ethics Committees to advise treatment-only clinics which are not licensed to carry out research (where the approval of an Ethics Committee must precede an application to HFEA for a research licence) has not been encouraged by the HFEA and at least one has in consequence discontinued its work. My own work with Linda Nielsen in Denmark has disclosed a much more open attitude and a willingness to discuss treatment criteria and other aspects of assisted conception.

47 *Ibid*, at p 127.

"Resolving the issue of access to medically assisted procreation technologies thus requires a thorough examination of the family unit at the dawn of the twenty first century. Are we prepared not only to accept single parent families and families with two homosexual parents, but also to place them on an equal footing, in terms of our social values, with families with two heterosexual parents? If so, should we not, in the interest of consistency, change our family laws to incorporate these new definitions? Or do we wish instead to make protection of the traditional family a public interest that would take precedence over the rights and freedoms guaranteed by the Charter and thus limit the right to procreate as we limit the right to marry in our society?"[48]

These questions are so much easier to state than they are to answer or resolve. The United Kingdom has gone as far as any other jurisdiction in allowing a *laissez-faire* attitude to access, with clinical discretion being permitted to act as a surrogate for state sanction and the medical profession confirmed as a form of legal order outside or alongside the state itself.

Apart from this, it is remarkable that many of the recommendations of the LRCC parallel the UK legislation of 1990 or the practices being established under the aegis of HFEA. Thus, the LRCC recommends that selection of gametes with specific qualities should be prohibited unless the object is to prevent the transmission of serious genetic disease and that the commercialization of donation of gametes and embryos should be prohibited and donors should receive only reasonable expenses. Gamete and embryo banks, which should be specially licensed, should be allowed to be reimbursed for reasonable associated costs. The twenty-two detailed recommendations may be grouped into three categories:

(i)   those concerning the conceiving of embryos and the donation of gametes:
(ii) those concerning status and parentage; and
(iii) those which set out the scheme of a regulatory system to oversee clinical and research work.

Conceiving embryos[49]

Before conceiving embryos for future personal use, the person or persons with control should stipulate in writing their intentions as to the fate of the embryo upon their death, abandonment of the parental project, expiry of the time limit on freezing, divorce or other dispute between the persons with control. Control over the embryos conceived using gametes from a couple should be exercised jointly by the partners; control over embryos conceived using gametes from only one of the partners and a donor should vest with the partner genetically linked to the embryos. The person with control over an embryo who donates it should before making the donation state in writing his or her consent to donation, and the conditions attached

---

48   *Ibid*, at p 126.
49   LRCC Report, at pp 139-46.

to it respecting its use. These conditions may be varied in writing at any time prior to the embryos' use; where control over the embryo is shared by two partners, both must agree to any change. Embryos conceived with donated gametes should vest in the bank or clinic which has the embryos in its possession and embryo use should be limited to implantation, experimentation, and destruction. Implantation should be prohibited beyond the time limit on freezing.

Parentage[50]

Provincial parentage laws should reflect intentions of couples using medically assisted procreation; actions to disavow paternity by a father who gave his consent or to challenge paternity by a third party following donation should not be allowed. It should not be possible to establish a bond of parentage between a donor and a child.

Children born as a result of assisted conception should be regarded as legitimate; children born as a result of post-mortem use of gametes or embryos should not be entitled to inherit unless there is specific reference to that effect in the will of the deceased producer.

Regulating reproduction[51]

A series of recommendations would establish a form of regulation which again is close to that undertaken by the HFEA. The LRCC would want to see federal and provincial co-operation to facilitate the establishment of a national body to establish a system of certification of clinics and banks and to oversee the work of licensed clinics. Clinics would be obliged to make returns to that body with a view to securing the safety of women in treatment programmes and the health of children who may be born through them. National standards should be established for screening donors and for the selection, screening and storage of gametes and embryos.

In an important recommendation, the LRCC suggests that efforts should be made to reduce the risk of multiple pregnancy and to promote the development of technologies that follow the normal cycle of ovulation; research with the objective of facilitating understanding of infertility and the reproductive processes should be encouraged.

Licensed clinics would be required to keep records on donors, recipients and any resulting children in order to allow physicians to link the donor to the recipient while protecting the anonymity of the parties. The legal parents of the child should be able to request disclosure of non-identifying information concerning donors, in particular social information such as ethnic origin, profession, education, religious affiliation and interests of the donor but identifying information should only be disclosed with the donor's consent.

---

50 *Ibid*, pp 146-48.
51 *Ibid*, pp 151-65.

The purposes for which the clinics might lawfully collect and store information would also be circumscribed. Data collection for the following objectives only should be permitted; to ensure access to medical and genetic information that may be needed to obtain optimum medical care; to meet the psychological needs of the child; to ensure that proper clinical reports are maintained; and finally to permit studies of the long-term effects of the various technologies used in assisted conception. Clinics offering treatment services should be required to provide counselling services before, during and after treatments in order that clients may obtain the information and assistance they might need concerning the specific problems involved.

Undoing what comes naturally?

In this essay I have tried to review some different approaches to the regulation of assisted conception in order to discover the pictures of family life which may be taken against the back drop of state interpretations put upon it. They are taken from broadly similar western societies and yet they disclose a rich variety of regulatory approaches, formal prohibitions and social aspirations. Each sets out to protect visions of individual and social life which are conceived as basic, fundamental or natural. Yet the paradox here is that, as Sheila McLean has observed:

> "... whatever one's views on investment in reproductive technologies, there seems to be wide agreement that increased efforts should be made to trace and prevent the causes of infertility ... What is interesting is that without the technologies themselves, it is unlikely that the causes of infertility would be so clearly known. In other words, the techniques which are designed to circumvent infertility may also point in no small measure towards information which in the future could render these services obsolete for a number of people."[52]

The Law Reform Commission of Canada proposes that any state or legislative intervention in medically assisted procreation should be aimed at promoting values that society holds as fundamental, such as the right to privacy and procreative autonomy, respect for the physical and mental integrity of patients, equality, the protection of life, special protection of children and those who are otherwise incapable of protecting themselves or vulnerable to harm or exploitation through incapacity.[53] Similarly, Knoppers and Le Bris suggest that five basic principles may be identified as needing to be to safeguarded; the respect for human dignity; the security of human genetic material; the quality of services; the inviolability of the human person and the inalienability of the human body.[54] Each or any of

---

52 McLean, "Reproductive Medicine" in Dyer (ed), *Doctors, Patients and the Law*, (Blackwell, 1992) pp 89-105 at p 90.
53 *Supra*, n.40, at pp 113-14.
54 *Supra*, n.5, at pp 333–34.

these offers a range of opportunities for state intervention or agnosticism. There are polar extremes, such as those shown by Austria and the United Kingdom, between which lies a spectrum of supportive roles which the state may assume in seeking to identify and secure those values which it feels to be challenged or placed at risk by assisted conception. A study of reproductive technologies is salutary not just in and of itself but also for the way in which it discloses snapshots from the family album; it throws into relief our understanding and appreciation of families and family life. The "reproduction revolution" has upset or dislocated what Stanley Fish has in another context called "the unreflective actions that follow from being embedded in a context of practice"; recombinant DNA research and reconstructed family life have transformed, literally and figuratively, doing what comes naturally.[55] The reproduction revolution has produced an "interpretive crisis"[56] which challenges us to re-examine and re-evaluate arguments and assumptions about "the family, " "relations, " and what is "natural". Christine Overall has recalled that to examine reproduction requires not just an understanding of nature, of what is biologically given:

> "it requires also an understanding of the social construction and organisation of sexual, procreative, and child care relationships. In fact, such an understanding calls into question the assumption that it is legitimate or even meaningful to speak of what is biologically given outside the context of the human interpretations put on it."[57]

Thus in any assessment it is imperative to recall that "Human beings are embodied beings" and an understanding of reproduction is essential to understanding human relationships and what it is to be human within the context of patriarchy.[58]

---

55 Fish, *Doing What Comes Naturally* (Clarendon Press, 1989), Preface p ix.
56 Fish, "Don't Know Much About the Middle Ages" in *Doing What Comes Naturally*, p 304, and see *ibid* at 358-59.
57 Overall, *Ethics and Human Reproduction; A Feminist Analysis* (Unwin Hyman, 1987) at p 5.
58 *Ibid* at p 5.

Chapter 7
Parenthood under Japanese Law

Norio Higuchi
Professor of Law, Tokyo University, Japan

Introduction

A parent-child relationship is one of the most basic and universal human relations. Significant differences exist, however, from country to country regarding regulation of this relationship. For instance, Soseki Natsume, one of the greatest novelists in modern Japan, had been adopted as a child and then after a few years returned to his original family, which experience continued to be a major theme for some of his later famous novels (Michikusa, Sorekara and others).[1] His adoption, and also his return, occurred long before 1926 when England first enacted its adoption law. Even after 1926, the English would no doubt have been perplexed or surprised to discover that the adopted child in Japan was "returned" to his biological family after a while without any interference by Japanese courts. The contrast between the two nations' customs and laws is striking.

We recognise two types of parent-child relations: biological and non-biological. The latter category, by definition, describes the situation in which an individual becomes a parent of a child with whom he has no blood tie rather than a child with whom he has a genetic relationship.

First, he or she may suffer from some medical problem which would make it impossible, or at least improbable, without medical assistance to have a baby. In Japan, for example, infertile couples are estimated to be 10-15% of all married couples, which means that about two million couples face difficulties even though they want to become parents.[2]

Some people, on the other hand, get pregnant so easily as to be totally unprepared to become parents. Some of them may resort to an abortion, a decision not to become a parent. According to the statistics by the Japanese Ministry of Health and Welfare, the number of abortions is gradually declining, while minors' abortions are increasing.[3] Others, who do not wish

---

1   Soseki Natsume (1867-1916) is one of the best known novelists in modern Japan. He stayed in England from 1900 to 1903, and he showed in his many writings keen insight into the inner conflicts of Japanese intellectuals towards the modernization.

2   See *e.g.*, Suzuki, *Taigai-Jusei* (*In-vitro* fertilization) 10 (1983).

3   Kohno, *Datai* (Abortion),135 *Hogaku Kyoshitsu* 56 (1991). According to this report, the total number of abortions was 486,146 in 1988 compared with 671,597 in 1975. As to abortions on minors, however, the number increased from 12,123 in 1975 to 28,596 in 1988. Yet, Kohno adds that minors' abortions are quite few in number, and that in Japan the largest age group receiving abortions is women in their 30s, not minors.

to resort to abortion, would give birth to a child and then free the child for adoption. Non-relative adoptions in Japan are, however, relatively few in number, about 3, 000 a year.[4]

In this paper, I do not intend to describe the current medical, social or psychological problems concerning parenthood in Japan. Rather, I shall apply a legal analysis to it in the context of Japanese law. It is one thing to say that any child has a pair of biological parents, and quite another to say that they are legally entitled to be the baby's parents. In most cases they are, but there are some exceptions in Japanese law as well as in other legal systems. Also with regard to the decision-making of childbirth, there may be some legal interventions upon an individual's decision whether to have a baby or not, especially in the case of assisted pregnancy.

In the second part of this paper I shall first outline the method of acquiring parenthood under the Japanese legal system. I shall make it clear that, although Japanese law is a code system, other legal norms, including case law and prevailing social norms have in fact played a more significant role in prescribing legal parenthood. In the final part, I shall turn to the current situation of biotechnological developments regarding infertility problems in Japan, and proceed to analyse legal responses to them. Here I shall refer to a recent survey on the Japanese public's attitude towards the new technological developments, from which I shall draw some predictions about Japanese legal responses in the near future.

Legal parenthood in Japan

Sources of Japanese law in general

To understand the laws of legal parenthood, we must first locate the principal sources of law under the Japanese legal system. This requires a brief look at the modern historical development of that legal system.[5]

A little more than a century ago, when Japan opened its gates to the outer world after 250 years of isolation policy, people felt a great fear that Japan might meet China's fate, that is, become colonised by western countries. To avoid this, they tried to modernise rapidly the whole country, including the legal system. They took as a model German and French systems where the word 'law' ordinarily means statutes. As a result, Japan adopted a code system, and the statutory law is paramount as the source of law, whereas court decisions are regarded as secondary. It follows that we should first look into statutory provisions to understand how to become a parent in legal terms under the Japanese legal system.

---

4   See generally, a report on the recent Family Court cases, (1992) 1 *Kasai-Geppo* 44-1.
5   The most basic English texts on Japanese law are Tanaka, *The Japanese Legal System* (Univ of Tokyo Press, 1976), and Noda, *Introduction to Japanese law* (Univ of Tokyo Press, 1976).

The Family Relations chapter of the Civil Code contains governing provisions.[6] Although this fourth chapter of the Civil Code was profoundly reformed after World War II, which reform was guided by the principle of democratization of the family, the paternity provisions and other provisions dealing with problems of legal parenthood were not subject to any great change in that reform. The relevant statutory scheme was established in 1898, a century ago, and there has been little, if any, change since then at least on the face of the statutory provisions.

To understand the statutory scheme for legal parenthood, one must keep in mind two types of classifications. First, the status of parenthood may depend upon whether the parents are married or not. Secondly, the process of establishing parenthood may differ by the gender of the parent. I shall first discuss the statutory provisions relating to paternity, and then those pertaining to maternity.

Paternity under statutory law

The Civil Code of Japan enumerates three ways for a father to obtain the legal status of parent.

(i)   If he is married and his spouse delivers a baby at least 200 days after marriage or within 300 days of the termination of marriage, he is then presumed to be a legal parent (s 772).[7] If he wishes to rebut this presumption, the husband, and only the husband, may bring a lawsuit for that purpose. However, there is a statute of limitation of one year which begins at his knowledge of the birth of the child.[8] Thus, if he is married and a baby is born, and if the husband does nothing for a year, he will be deemed a legal parent.

(ii)   If he is not married to a female who delivers a child, he may still make a voluntary acknowledgment to become a legal parent (s 779).[9] This

---

6   The Family Relations chapter covers sections 725-881 of the Civil Code. The Civil Code of Japan, originally enacted in 1896 and 1898, consists of five chapters: General Provisions, Property Rights, Contracts and Torts, Family Relations, and Succession.

7   S 772 Presumption of legitimacy.
     (1) A child conceived by a wife during marriage shall be presumed to be the child of the husband.
     (2) A child, born two hundred days or more after the day on which the marriage was formed or born within three hundred days from the day on which the marriage was dissolved or annulled, shall be presumed to have been conceived during marriage.
     (This English version was published by EHS, Inc. in 1975, and I use its translation in this essay.)

8   S 774 Denial of legitimacy. In any case mentioned in s 772, the husband may deny that the child is legitimate.
     S 775 Action of denial.
     The right of denial mentioned in the preceding section shall be exercised by an action against the child or the mother exercising parental power.
     S777 Statute of limitations
     An action of denial shall be brought within one year from the time when the husband became aware of the child's birth.

9   S 779 Acknowledgment.
     A child who is not legitimate may be acknowledged by its father or mother.

        acknowledgment is accomplished by his registration at the public office. Once he registers, he may not revoke his acknowledgement.

(iii) If he fails to acknowledge voluntarily his paternity the child, or a legal representative (typically the mother), may bring a paternity suit (s 787).[10] This the child may do at any time while his father is alive, and even after he died if it is within three years of his death.

Thus, under this statutory scheme, the marriage relationship, if it exists between parents, basically guarantees parenthood to the father and legitimacy to the child. On the other hand, when the child was born out of wedlock, either method of acknowledgment, through a father's voluntary registration or an involuntary imposition upon a father through a child's lawsuit, establishes the legal relationship of father and child.

At least three distinctive features are apparent in this rather simple legal scheme. First, legislators appear to be much more concerned with the marriage relationship of the parents than with the biological relation between the father and the child. Even if no real biological tie exists, a baby born to a married couple is strongly presumed to be their child. The husband is the only person who may legally challenge the presumption of legitimacy. Neither the child, the mother nor anyone else may challenge the husband's parentage.

Second, the Civil Code seems to emphasise the importance of legitimacy. The ways to obtain legitimacy are significantly limited to cases where a baby was born into a normal marriage relationship on the apparent assumption that the marriage relationship should coincide with sexual relations.

Third, and in contrast, lawmakers are quite generous in affording some legal status to the illegitimate child. A father, if he is the real father, may establish a legal relationship so easily through an *ex parte* registration of his acknowledgment that many foreigners may be surprised to learn that the father does not need the mother's consent before the registration. Also when the child wants his father's acknowledgment, the child may not be barred by any limitation of actions so long as the father is alive. And even after his death, the child may bring an action for paternity for three years.[11]

Also I should note here that Japanese law has been relatively generous to illegitimate children in their assertion of various rights. They have never been regarded as *filius nullius*, and have long had certain, though limited, rights against their parents. In legal terms, the illegitimate child has been a child of the birth mother, and has also been entitled to maintenance and even inheritance rights against the father. One must not forget that the illegitimate child has been a target of various forms of social discrimination, but as far as law is concerned, the illegitimate child has had a more

---

10 S 787 Action for acknowledgment.
     A child ... or the legal representative ... can bring an action for acknowledgement. However, this shall not apply after the lapse of three years from the time when the father or mother died.

11 It should be noted, however, that this was due to the 1940 statutory amendment, before which a child was barred from filing a complaint at the death of a father.

favourable status, at least in the past, under Japanese law in comparison with common law countries. We should, therefore, attach all the more significance to the fact that the child could obtain at least illegitimate status relatively easily.[12]

Paternity under case law

Neither Japanese judges nor most legal scholars, however, have been satisfied with this statutory scheme. During the last hundred years they have succeeded in reforming it in two ways.

First, case law widened the door to legitimacy. For instance, the statute does not recognise as legitimate a child who was born within 200 days of the parents' marriage. Of course the Civil Code does provide that if the parents make a voluntary acknowledgment, as they usually do, the child is legitimated from that time (s 789).[13] But what would be the status of a child, for example, whose father died 30 days after marriage but 30 days before the child's birth? Under the original act of 1898, which provided that a paternity suit might be brought only when the alleged father was still alive, there was no way for the child to establish a legal relationship with his father. And even after the statutory amendment in 1942, to the effect that the child had access to the courts for three years after his father's death, the child could have gained only the status of illegitimacy.

Case law developments relaxed the harshness of the Code. The Supreme Court, the highest court of Japan, as early as 1940 held that a child born within 200 days of marriage was legitimate, though the strong presumption of legitimacy under section 772 did not apply to this case.[14] As there was no presumption in this case, any person other than a husband could challenge the biological tie between the husband and the child, and the child might be required to establish a biological relation. But that would be easy for a real child.

The second judicial reform is much more important. It concerns the situation in which a child is strongly presumed to be the issue of a married couple but in fact is not. A 1969 Supreme Court case provides an illustration. A and B had been married for three years, and then they separated. After two and a half years separation, they formally divorced. But within 300 days of divorce, B had a baby. It was clear to all that the child was not the former husband's. But the statute says that there is a strong legal presumption that the child was born in wedlock, which is rebuttable only by the former husband's initiation of a lawsuit. The Supreme Court in

---

12 Now that common law countries have altered the unequal treatment of illegitimate children, at least some scholars bitterly criticise Japanese law for its surviving discrimination against the illegitimate. For instance, an illegitimate child is entitled to just half as much of inherited property as a legitimate child in the case of intestacy.

13 S 789 Status of legitimacy.
    (2) A child acknowledged by its father and mother during the subsistence of their marriage acquires the status of a legitimate child as from the time of such acknowledgment.

14 Supreme Court Judgment, 23 Jan 1940, 19 *Minshu* 54.

1969 held, that despite the statutory scheme, the child might bring a paternity suit against the real father.[15] Thereafter other courts naturally followed suit.

Thus the Japanese judiciary created an important exception to the original statutory law, which had attached more importance to family stability than to biological fact. Courts carved an exception for classes of children who would be prima facie legitimate, but were not covered by any statutory presumptions in section 772 in the following circumstances.[16]

First, when husband and wife had been long separated from each other and a baby was born, the strong presumption provision would not apply and, therefore, any interested party could bring a lawsuit to challenge the father-child relationship.

Second, the same could be true of cases where the husband was impotent. Moreover, this exception has now been further extended to cover any cases where scientific tests, such as blood testing and, possibly in the near future, DNA profiling can prove the non-existence of any biological tie.

These developments clearly show that Japanese courts have elevated the value of truth, in the sense of ascertainment of the real biological tie, above the value of a presumed family stability. The changes are so drastic in nature that we may conclude that the rule and the exception have been virtually reversed.

Maternal relationship under Japanese law

In determining the legal relationship between a mother and a child, again it is to the Civil Code that one must first look.

When a mother is married her child is strongly presumed to be born in wedlock, a legitimate child to the married couple. As for the unmarried mother, Japanese law provides that not only a father but also a mother may make a voluntary acknowledgment (s 779); and the provision regarding involuntary acknowledgment (s 787) makes no distinction whatever between a father and a mother.[17] It plainly prescribes that a child may bring an action for compulsory acknowledgment against "a parent" at any time the parent is alive. This suit would be barred only "after the lapse of three years from the time when the father or the mother died" (s 787).[18]

Thus we may easily conclude that Japanese law originally made no distinctions between a mother and a father with regard to the establishment of legal parenthood. Parenthood might be established, first, through the marital relationship, and secondly, in the absence of any marital relations, through voluntary acknowledgment by the parent or through a child's initiative by bringing a lawsuit.

15 Supreme Court Judgment, 29 May 1969, 23-6 *Minshu* 1064.
16 See, e.g. Yamahata, *Chakushutu Hinin to Oyako Kankei Husonzai Kakunin* (Rebuttal of Presumption of Paternity and Declaratory Suit for Non-existence of Paternity), (1991) 747 *Hanrei Times* 178-79.
17 See the cited sections of the Civil Code, *supra* n.9 and 10.
18 See s 787 in n.10 *supra*.

However, Japanese courts made another great change to this scheme. In 1962 the Supreme Court declared that there would be no requirement of acknowledgment to establish a legal mother-child relationship. It held that the fact of delivery was conclusive.[19]

This development also confirmed the clear trend mentioned above to narrow the gap between legal parenthood and biological truth. The result is that the blood tie, or natural biological truth, becomes predominant in the legal scheme.

Of course one can still imagine cases where legal parenthood does not coincide with the biological tie. For instance, suppose that a wife has a baby from her adulterous relationship, of which her husband is unaware, and one year has passed since the birth of the child. In such a case, it appears at first glance that there may be no legal way to deny the child his or her legal status of legitimacy. Even though the wife confesses the truth to her husband, and wants to raise the child with her lover as their child, it may appear that she has no legal means to do so if her husband does not bring a lawsuit to deny his paternity during the prescribed period of one year.

Surprisingly enough, however, even this is not true. Family Court Decree Act section 23 prescribes that any agreement between parties in conciliation proceedings before the family court may be made into a consent decree.[20] Thus even after the statutory one-year limitation of actions, the husband, wife and lover may reach an agreement that the child is that of the wife and lover, and then Japanese law will give the agreement formal recognition.

Japanese law of parenthood

To sum up so far, the original statutory scheme of Japanese law regarding the establishment of the parent-child relationship has been overturned almost completely. Courts and legal scholars in Japan have striven to make such a change for several decades. From these developments I shall draw a few conclusions about the nature of Japanese family law.

In the first place, contrary to the formal precept that the Japanese legal system is founded upon statutory law, that the statutes are paramount and cases merely secondary, in the family law area courts have boldly altered the literal meaning of legislation. The field of family law is by no means unique in this respect; courts have always played an important lawmaking role in Japan.

Secondly, one may wonder why this boldness has not been much criticised. How can the judiciary act contrary to express statutory provisions? I believe that the following are the really significant

---

19 Supreme Court Judgment, 27 April 1962, 16-17 *Minshu* 1247.
20 S 23 of the Family Court Decree Act reads, "When an agreement is reached among parties during the process of conciliation on the matters of parent-child relationship, marriage annulment, and divorce, the family court may make a consent decree in accordance with the agreement if it is found appropriate."

determinants of the parent-child relationship in Japan.

The first in order is agreement among the interested parties. If all the interested persons agree to a certain solution that is consistent with social mores, the law recognises it to be lawful without scrutinising in detail whether the solution coincides with biological truth. But if they do not reach agreement, then courts employ their own precedents to find a legal relationship as much in accordance with biological truth as possible. Where a resolution can be drawn from neither agreements nor precedents, then as a last resort the statutory solutions would apply.

In my opinion, the reason for this three-tier system is that courts respond with a certain sensitivity to the prevailing ideas or common sense of the Japanese people.[21] Courts have successfully changed the meaning of statutes, not because they have the formal power to do so, but because the direction they have taken has been correct from the popular point of view; their course has not been inconsistent with the prevailing ideas of the society.

The common sense among Japanese people is that a blood tie is very important. I asserted above that the paramount element in establishing parentage is agreement among the interested parties consistent with social mores. Suppose, for instance, that the husband, wife and lover agree that a child was born out of wedlock although in fact the husband is undeniably the real father. Japanese law could not make the agreement. Section 23 of the Family Court Decree Act, providing for enforcement of conciliation agreements, mentioned above, is never a trump to bring about false results. However, if the agreement reached coincides with the apparent truth concerning the blood relationship, then courts would not interfere with the agreement.

Artificially assisted conception in Japan

Development of birth technology in Japan

Let us consider how Japanese law is responding to the recent rapid development of biotechnology in the field of human birth. This response is related to the characteristics of Japanese legal development described above.

To begin with some basic statistics, Japan's population is about 120 million, and the number of infertile couples is estimated to be about two million, 10-15% of married couples. To those people the development of recent technology may make their dreams come true.

---

21 See, *e.g.* Hasebe, Ch 8 of his book, *Kenryoku e no Kaigi* (Questioning Constitution and Power) (1991). This chapter, original in Japanese, is titled, "Why Japanese people do not take rights seriously?" according to my translation into English. There Hasebe argues that Japanese courts have been reluctant to overturn or disturb the prevailing ideas of society even in the case of constitutional litigation where a fundamental individual right is involved.

So far, only two forms of artificially assisted conception are allowed in Japan.[22] One is artificial insemination, either by husband, which is called AIH, or by donor other than husband (AID). The other is *in vitro* fertilization. But this more recent invention is only used with married couples. Other artificial means, including surrogate motherhood, are totally prohibited. Interestingly enough, this prohibition is imposed not by law but by the internal ordinances of the Japan Association of Obstetricians.

There are no accurate statistics about these phenomena. It is believed that artificial insemination began to be used at Keio University medical centre in Tokyo some 40 years ago.[23] This medical centre has been renowned for its treatment of infertility problems. At least 10, 000 children have been born through this method at Keio medical hospital during the last 40 years, and one doctor has estimated that the current number is around 2, 000 per year.[24] The majority of these children were born through the AID procedure.

The first baby born by means of in vitro fertilization was born in 1983 in Japan, five years after the first success in England. A recent medical report stated that 387 children were born in 1989, and 496 women became pregnant through this method in the same year.[25]

Legal responses or no responses in Japan

Surprisingly, Japan has no court decisions regarding artificial insemination after 40 years of practice, and thousands of babies; nor have any laws governing the practice been enacted. Private agreements prevail.

At Keio University medical centre, where 70% of artificial insemination is of the AID type, this type of medical procedure is limited to married couples. The hospital always confirms that both spouses agree before initiating treatment. Donors of semen are recruited from among Keio university students. The institution keeps records about the donors, but not about which donor is the father of a particular child. The records are confidential and will not be disclosed. In fact, the medical centre has never received a request for disclosure.[26] Thus there is a complete system of agreements without any apparent disputes.

As for surrogacy, since all doctors are prohibited by their association from engaging in the practice, there is no surrogacy, no disputes, nor any laws at all.

---

22 See Ienaga, Japan (2) Artificial Insemination, in the Symposium "A Comparative Law Study of Artificial Human Reproduction", (1991) 53 *Comparative Law Journal* 75.

23 Professor Ienaga reports that the first AID female baby in Japan was born at Keio University medical centre in 1949 *Ibid*, at 75.

24 *Ibid*, at 77.

25 See Hattori, Japan (3) IVF & ET, in Symposium, *supra* n.22 at 53 *Comp. L.J. 84-85.*

26 Ienaga, *supra* n.22, at 77.

A survey

In November 1990 an interesting survey was conducted concerning Japanese attitudes toward artificially assisted pregnancy. The researchers made public at least part of the results at an academic society meeting in June 1991.[27]

The researchers randomly selected subjects from two groups[28]: the general public, and patients attending obstetricians for infertility problems. They asked each subject to fill out a questionnaire asking whether the subject approved of each of the following new technologies:

(i)   *in vitro* fertilization for a married couple;
(ii)   surrogate motherhood;
(iii) total surrogacy in which the surrogate mother has no biological link with the child; and
(iv)   AID.

Only (i) and (iv) are currently available in Japan. The number of subjects was relatively small (211 subjects from the general public and only 36 subjects from infertility patients), so one must be careful in interpreting the results, which were as follows[29]:

(i)   As to *in vitro* fertilization for a husband and wife, 56% of the general public approved, and only 17% disapproved. The opponents reasoned that the practice is unnatural. As for infertility patients, 75% approved, and only 2.7% disapproved as one would expect.

(ii)   The second question concerned a surrogate mother who contributes her own genetic material to the child she is to deliver for an infertile couple. 75% of the general public said no to this idea, and only 4.3% answered yes. Among infertility patients, however, only 47%

---

27 The reports and discussion are published in a 1991 issue of the *Comparative Law Journal*, *supra* n.22.
28 See Shirai, Japan (1) *Social Attitudes*, 53 *Comp. L.J.* at 61.
29 Survey on the attitudes toward new birth technologies (source: Shirai, *ibid* at 65-70).

| | General Public | | | Infertility Patients | | |
	For %	Against %	Don't know %	For %	Against %	Don't know %
(i) IVF for marital couples	56	17	27	75	2.7	22.3
(ii) surrogate mother	4.3	75	20.7	15	47	38
(iii) total surrogacy	14	59	27	25	30	45
(iv) AID	6.2	75	18.8	14	50	36

disapproved, and 15% approved. We could find at least a meaningful difference between the general public and infertility clients here.

(iii) As for total surrogacy where the surrogate has no biological link with the baby, 59% of the general public disapproved, while 14% approved. Among infertility patients, the respective figures were 25% and 30%. These results indicate that there existed somewhat less resistance among Japanese to the idea of the surrogate mother who acts only as a vessel for nurturing the foetus.

(iv) With regard to AID, 75% of the general pubic opposed the practice, and only 6.2% approved. Among infertility patients, those against outnumbered those in favour 50-14. These attitudes persist despite the fact that AID has been performed in Japan for more than 40 years.

I believe that we may infer from these results that Japanese attitudes are deeply influenced by the biological link. If new technology maintains the blood tie between a child and both parents, the public's hesitation to accept the technology will be considerably reduced.

Analysis of Japanese law regarding birth technologies

The absence of case law and statutes concerning AID demands an explanation. In my opinion, two prevailing social mores offer a key to this difficult question: the importance of the biological link, and the idea that married couples should have a child.

These two ideas may be inconsistent. As to AID, the biological link between parents and a child is incomplete, but it affords the couple an opportunity to have a child. In Japan, at least until today, these apparently inconsistent ideas have been harmonised in the following way. When a married couple has a baby through AID they have successfully satisfied the prevailing social mores that the husband and wife should have a baby, and also they have not expressly contravened the other prevailing idea that emphasises the importance of the blood tie, since they do not make public the lack of biological link between the father and the child. They register the birth as if both parents were the child's natural parents, and a public official accepts this fiction by taking no time to make scrutiny. If the agreement is not broken by any of the participants in this treatment scheme, no outsiders would suspect the non-existence of a blood relationship.

Suppose that the legislature tried to enact some statute concerning these issues. Whatever the statute's contents, it would destroy this delicate harmony. There would have to be a choice between the two prevailing ideas.

Needless to say, this harmonised system is not without de-merits. For instance, a child is denied any right to know the truth about the circumstances of birth. So long as the system does not plainly betray the truth, however, Japanese law pays great respect to the facts as they are officially stated.

The next problem is whether the Japanese will allow surrogate motherhood through the same process. This will be much more difficult, for, in the case of the surrogate mother, the difference between the rearing mother and the birth mother becomes inevitably apparent. Even if no disputes occur among the participants, it would be fatal to make public the inconsistency.

Finally, I should consider briefly total surrogacy. Here a complete blood tie exists between both parents and the child. The survey mentioned above showed that Japanese people are more tolerant of total surrogacy than of AID. Is it probable that total surrogacy will be legalised in Japan?

It seems to me that its probability of acceptance is higher than that of ordinary surrogate motherhood. Still, the probability is relatively low. The problem in this method is the difficulty of openly admitting that the birth parent and the rearing parent are not the same. Of course sometimes we have to accept this, as in adoption cases. But most Japanese have been quite reluctant to do so, and would not want to extend such situations too far.

Conclusion

I have outlined in this essay some characteristics of Japanese law with regard to legal parenthood. Its special features are its preference for the blood tie, its boldness in supporting legal change by case law in that direction (even to the point of contravening express statutory language), and its recognition of exceptions for agreement-oriented solutions, in at least a few cases, at the expense of biological truth. So far, the Japanese harmony-oriented scheme has been mostly successful, and courts have not been troubled by issues concerning AID children or surrogate mothers. Yet I expect that in the near future situations will occur where a choice has to be made plainly and openly between genetic truth and family stability. Only then will the true value of Japanese law be tested.

Acknowledgements

I would like to express my special thanks to Professor David Pearl and Dr Andrew Bainham for their kind invitation to The Centre for Family Law and Family Policy. I also thank Professor Robert Leflar of the University of Arkansas School of Law for his useful comments on an earlier draft.

Chapter 8

The Economic Consequences of Divorce in the United States

J Thomas Oldham

Professor of Law, University of Houston Law Center, USA,
Visiting Scholar, Wolfson College, Cambridge (1992)

Introduction

Many have questioned whether the United States remains the leader of the West in many spheres, but America clearly still unfortunately remains in the vanguard in terms of the propensity of its citizens to divorce.[1] Although America has had substantial experience with marriage dissolution during the past few decades, the private divorce law system is perceived by many as inadequate, and few public programmes have been created to deal with the refugees from failed marriages.

I will briefly outline in this paper the history of US divorce law, as well as the contemporary criticisms being levelled against current rules. Statistical evidence relating to a number of questions relevant to the economic consequences of divorce will be provided. I will then suggest certain ways in which the dialogue could be advanced regarding what would constitute "fair" rules for the economic consequences of divorce in America.

History of American private law rules regarding the economic consequences of divorce

Divorces are primarily regulated at the state level in America. Most states have permitted absolute divorce for quite some time.[2] In connection with a divorce, a spouse not at fault could receive alimony in most states, if the court determined that an award would be appropriate.[3] Rules

---

1 See Phillips, *Putting Asunder* (1990).
2 See Riley, *Divorce: An American Tradition* (1991).
   Of course, divorce historically could only be obtained if a fault ground could be established.
3 See Clark, *Law of Domestic Relations* 2nd ed (1987) [hereinafter "Clark, Second Edition"]; Vernier & Hurlbut, "The Historical Background of Alimony Law" (1939) 6 *Law & Contemp. Prob.* 197. Of course, not all innocent needy divorcing spouses received alimony. See Garrison, "Good Intentions Gone Awry: The Impact of New York's Equitable Distribution Law on Divorce Outcomes" (1991) 57 *Brooklyn L. Rev.* 621, 629 n.27 [hereinafter "Garrison, *Good Intentions*"].

regarding property division at divorce varied widely, however.

In community property states[4] a divorce court has always possessed the power to divide either spouse's accumulations during marriage, other than a gift or inheritance received by one spouse.[5] In some states, this community of acquests must be divided equally; in others, it can be divided equitably.[6] Post-divorce alimony could also be awarded in all states except Texas.[7]

States that adopted English rules regarding marital property are sometimes called "common law states". In many of these states, divorce courts did not originally have the authority to divide the accumulations of the parties at divorce.[8] (However, this statement should be tempered by noting that "lump-sum alimony" was available in many such states, and lump-sum alimony may have functioned in some instances as a property-division system.)[9] Post-divorce periodic alimony was possible in most cases,[10] if the recipient needed it and was not at fault.

The differences among the divorce law systems of the various states have narrowed during this century. Almost all common law states have now accepted some type of "equitable distribution" system where the divorce court has the authority to divide the accumulations of spouses during marriage.[11] Property division is now a common result of a divorce action; this remedy is distinct from the court's ability to award alimony (sometimes now called spousal support or maintenance).[12] Fault has become a much less important factor. All states except four permit unilateral no-fault divorce.[13] So, almost all states, regardless whether they are common law or community property states, now permit divorce courts to divide the accumulations of the parties during marriage and to award alimony. In all common law states and in most community property states, this property

---

4   The eight original community property states' rules are derived from Spanish and French principles regarding marital regimes. See DeFuniak and Vaughn, *Principles of Community Property* 2nd ed (1971); Reppy and Samuel, Community Property in the *United States* 3rd ed (1991). Wisconsin has recently adopted the Uniform Marital Property Act and has become the ninth community property state.

5   Washington courts may now divide all property owned by either spouse, regardless of when or how it was acquired. See Reppy and Samuel, n.4.

6   See W. Reppy and Samuel, *supra* n.4.

7   *Ibid.*

8   See Clark, 2nd ed; Kay, "Beyond No-fault: New Directions in Divorce Reform, " in Kay and Sugarman, *Divorce Reform at the Crossroads* (1990) at 6.

9   See Clark, *Law of Domestic Relations* (1968) at 447.

10 *Ibid.*

11 See Oldham, *Divorce, Separation and the Distribution of Property* (1992). The various states do not define the divisible estate identically; most, however, have adopted a system of community of acquests.

   In 1889, Kansas became the first common-law state to adopt something resembling an equitable distribution system. See Garrison, *Good Intentions*, at 627 in n.19. By 1939, about ten common-law states had adopted such a system. See Daggett, "Division of Property upon Dissolution of Marriage", (1939) 6 *Law & Contemp. Prob.* 225, 227. Mississippi is now the only state that has not yet clearly adopted some similar system.

12 See Oldham, *supra* n.11.

13 See Garrison, *Good Intentions*, at 637 n.61.

division does not have to be equal; the court is directed to divide the marital estate fairly.[14]

In addition to the power to award alimony and divide the marital estate, if there is a minor child of the marriage one parent may be ordered to provide post-divorce child support to the custodial parent. The presumptive child support award is calculated from guidelines according to one of a few types of systems that have been accepted by various states (income shares, percentage of income, etc).[15]

Fairness of the current system

Much has been written about the post-divorce economic suffering of a number of women under the American system.[16] This suffering has resulted from a number of factors, some easier to remedy than others. Although divorce courts have the power to divide the spouses' accumulations during marriage, in many instances this is not a particularly significant potential remedy. Most American couples who divorce are young people divorcing after a relatively short period of marriage.[17] It, therefore, may not be surprising that many couples do not have much property.[18] Property awards, therefore, frequently cannot significantly affect the post-divorce economic circumstances of the spouses.

Empirical studies have found that most divorcing spouses do not have much property.[19] This result obviously depends to some degree upon how one defines "property". In the past, divorce courts were reluctant to accept

---

14 There is some question whether common law states and community property states apply these standards in the same way. Although the statutory language governing property division in the various states is quite similar, it appears from anecdotal evidence that common law states have a greater tendency to emphasise financial contribution when the estate is being divided. In other words, anecdotal evidence (as well as some empirical evidence) suggests that housewives tend to receive less than half of the marital estate. See Weitzman, *The Divorce Revolution* (1985) at 108; Cohen and Hillman, *Analysis of Seventy Select Decisions after Trial under New York State's Equitable Distribution Law* (New York Women's Bar Association). Cf, Garrison, *Good Intentions* at 674. In contrast, again on the basis of anecdotal evidence, community property courts tend to grant more than half of the marital estate to a housewife. See *McNaby v McNaby*, 782 P2d 1291, 1296 (Nev.1989).

15 See Ellman, Kurtz and Bartlett, *Family Law*, (2nd ed 1991) at 355 *et seq*.

16 See Glendon, *Transformation of Family Law* (1989); Weitzman, *The Divorce* (1985). For a discussion of English couples, see *Revolution* and Maclean Eekelaar, *Maintenance after Divorce* (1986).

17 See notes 41-44 *infra* and accompanying text.

18 See Garrison, *Good Intentions* at 665.

19 See, *e.g.* Garrison, *Good Intentions* at 665; Weitzman, *op cit* n.14. I wonder whether this is changing somewhat, due to the increasing number of workers who are covered by private pension plans. For example, a recent study found that two-thirds of all American workers have pension rights (see Short and Nelson, US Dept of Commerce, *Pensions: Worker Coverage and Retirement Benefits: 1987*, at 1 (1991)). About 80% of full-time workers for medium or large firms have some types of pension coverage. See Bureau of Labor Statistics, US Dept of Labor, Bulletin No 2363, *Employee Benefits in Medium and Large Firms*, at 4, Table 1 (1990). Given the increase in the number of workers covered by pensions, this might increase the value of the divisible estate at divorce.

that any contingent right was property.[20] More recently, most courts agree that a contingent right can be divisible property.[21] So, courts have had little difficulty agreeing that contingent rights, such as an unvested pension right (that could be lost if the employee quits or is fired before the right "vests")[22], a right to receive a contingent legal fee after divorce in a case if the lawyer/spouse prevails[23], or an unliquidated cause of action[24], could be included in the marital estate, to the extent that the right was earned during marriage. Some critics of the American system argue that the current concept of divisible "property" needs to be enlarged.[25] These commentators argue that the most valuable "asset" acquired during marriage is a spouse's career. Under this theory, this "career asset" should be included in the marital estate. Its value should be the lifetime value of the spouse's increase in earning capacity that occurred during marriage. I have argued elsewhere that this is not a good idea.[26] In any event, most courts and legislatures have not accepted the argument.[27]

So, the private divorce law system must try to deal with a situation where the couple at divorce has few divisible[28] assets. What is a fair result? Based upon the model of a commercial partnership, one could argue that it would be appropriate to divide the pot of marital assets, award the custodial spouse "reasonable" child support[29], and the divorce court's job would be done. However, this attitude ignores a basic concern: spouses frequently leave a marriage with very different economic prospects. What is the appropriate response of private divorce law to this fact?

Many writers have documented the economic problems borne by divorcing women. When one looks at the picture painted by the data

---

20 See Weitzman, *The Marriage Contract* (1980).

21 See Oldham, *op cit* n.11.

22 See *Ibid.*

23 *Ibid.*

24 *Ibid.*

25 See Krauskopf, "Theories of Property Division/Spousal Support", (1989) 23 Fam. L. Q. 253. Blumberg, "Reworking the Past. Imagining the Future" (1991) 16 *Law & Soc. Inq.* 115.

26 See Oldham, *Book Review* (1992) 80 *Cal. L. Rev.* 1091. See also, Parkman, *The Recognition of Human Capital as Property in Divorce Settlements* 1987 40 *Ark. L. Rev.* 439: Kay, "Beyond No-Fault", in *Divorce Reform at the Crossroads* (1990) at 6.

27 See Oldham, *supra* n.11, Gregory, *The Law of Equitable Distribution* (1989). *Cf* O'Brien v O'Brien, 489 NE2d 712 (N.Y. 1985); *Elkus* v *Elkus*, 572 NYS2d 901 (App. Div.1991).

28 It is conceivable, but not likely, that a spouse could have valuable property that is not divisible under the community of acquests. See Garrison, *Good Intentions*, at 661 (finding that 37% of all divorcing spouses claimed such property; of the spouses who claimed such property, the average value of the property amounted to 26% of the total estate).

29 This method chosen to calculate this support obviously would be controversial. See Maclean & Eekelaar, "Child Support, Wife Support or Family Support?" in Maclean and Weitzman, *The Economic Consequences of Divorce* (1991) at 239. See also, Rhode & Minow, "Reforming the Questions, Questioning the Reforms, " in Kay and Sugarman, *Divorce Reform at the Crossroads* (1990) at 191; Garrison, *Good Intentions* at 737; Eekelaar and Maclean, *Maintenance after Divorce* (1986); Garfinkel, "Child-Support Trends in the United States, " in Weitzman and Maclean, *Economic Consequences of Divorce* (1991) at 205; Bruch, "Developing Standards for Child Support Payments", (1982) 16 *U. C. Davis L. Rev.* 49; Krause, "Reflections on Child Support" (1983) 17 *Fam. L.Q.* 109; Harrison, Macdonald, & Weston, "Payments of Child Maintenance in Australia" (1987) 1 *Int. J. Law & Fam.* 92.

regarding post-divorce outcomes for divorcing women, the image certainly bears more resemblance to the work of George Grosz than that of Claude Monet. Still, is this the fault of the private law divorce system? How should the fairness of the current system be evaluated?

Many more American married women work outside the home than ever before. For example, in 1957, 33% of married women worked.[30] By 1987, 68% of married women were in the work-force (see Table D).[31] Also, an increasing number of women are working year-round, full-time.[32] More women are graduating from university and professional school, and women are pursuing careers that have been traditionally male.[33] Of those women who have completed five or more years of college, 40% earn as much or more than their husbands.[34] Even after these advances, however, most women still earn substantially less than men. Although 18% of all wives earn more than their husbands, and another 8% earn about as much[35], the average wage of a female worker (who works fulltime, year-round) amounts to about 70% of a man's wage (see Table C).[36] Wives who worked year-round, full-time earned 57% of what husbands earned when they worked year-round, full-time.[37]

Some wives still do not work outside the home, of course.[38] Also, a number of wives work part-time or less than year-round.[39] The differences in post-divorce economic prospects between such wives and their husbands could be quite pronounced.

The information contained in the last two paragraphs suggests a question fundamental to any discussion of divorce reform: to what extent, if any, should the private law divorce system attempt to reduce differences in post-

---

30 See Shank, "Women and the Labour Market: The Link Grows Stronger", (1988) 111 *Labor Monthly Rev.* 3, 5.

31 *Ibid.*

32 See Goldin, *Understanding the Gender Gap* (1990).

33 Fifty percent of all college graduates in 1980 were female. See Goldin, *ibid* at 215. In 1985, women received 30% of all medical degrees, 21% of all dentistry degrees, and 38% of all law degrees. See O'Neil, "The Wage Gap Between Men and Women in the United States" (1991) 3 *Int. Rev. of Comp.Pub. Pol.* 351, 361, *Cf* King, "Occupational Segregation by Race and Sex, 1940-88" (1992) 115 *Monthly Lab. Rev.* 30.

34 See Glick, "Fifty Years of Family Demography: A Record of Social Change" (1988) 50 *J. Marr. & Fam.* 861, 865.

35 See *Earnings of Married-Couple Families.* 1987, Bureau of the Census, Current, Pop. Rep., Series P-60, No 165 (1989) at 6.

36 See Goldin, *op* cit n.32 at 61. The wage gap is below 70%, nearer 65%, if a mean is used rather than a median. See Table A.

37 See Earnings of Married Couple Families: *supra* n.35 at 2.

38 In 1988, 35% of all mothers with a child under 18 did not work. See *Handbook of Labor Statistics,* August 1989, Bulletin 2340, Table 57, at 242. This is "snapshot" information, and is in one sense misleading, because it shows only how many were not in the labor force at one moment in time. Of married women surveyed in 1989, 33% with children under 6 had not worked outside the home during the last year. Of those who did work, 36% did so part-time. Of married women whose youngest child was 6-17, 22% did not work at all during the past year, and 32% of those who worked did so on a part-time basis. Bureau of Labor Statistics, US Dept of Labor, Current Population Survey, March 1990 (unpublished data on file with the author).

39 Approximately 1/3 of all married mothers did not work full-time in 1988. See O'Neil, *The Wage Gap, supra* n.34. Only about one-half of all working wives work year-round, full-time. See Earnings of Married Couple Families; *supra* at 1.

divorce income? How one answers this question depends to a large degree upon how the marital commitment is perceived. If it is seen as a lifetime commitment largely unaffected by the decision to divorce, one might conclude that a divorcing party could owe the other, if financially dependent, substantial continuing post-divorce support, particularly if the dependent spouse did not want the divorce. In contrast, if marriage is viewed as a partnership dissoluble upon some minimal notice, a very different model results.

Although it might be useful for some aspirational purpose to perceive marriage as a lifetime commitment, the reality of contemporary American marriage seems quite different. One writer has estimated that two-thirds of all couples currently marrying will divorce.[40] Although the divorce rate has for the moment stabilised, during the past 30 years it has more than doubled.[41] The median duration of marriages that end in divorce, not counting the period of separation before divorce, is about five years.[42] About one-fifth divorce within three years of the wedding, counting the period of separation.[43] The median age of divorcing wives at the time of separation is younger than 30.[44] Most of these divorcing parties will remarry others, often quite quickly.[45] Most American couples, though certainly not all, are young people who have been married a relatively short time. Divorce rules must account for this serial marriage practised by most divorcing spouses. What model for post-divorce outcomes would best suit this scenario?

One model for post-divorce outcomes would be equality of result. However, it is difficult to justify this result for all marriages on a number of grounds. First, it seems to reflect a questionable assumption that marriage is a lifetime commitment, regardless if ended by divorce. Even if marriage is in some sense a lifetime commitment, shouldn't divorce have some effect upon the economic relations of the parties? Some continuing support obligation is inevitable in some circumstances, such as when the couple has a minor child, and in many cases when the couple divorces after a "childful" marriage of long duration, but it is not clear that the appropriate standard is equality of result. Although a detailed discussion of this question is beyond the scope of this discussion paper, I would suggest that a model of equality of result is not a useful one, particularly if it would be applied to all marriages. In America, the primary purpose of divorce precisely is to dissolve one family relationship and to form another.

Under a model of equality of result, one spouse is asked to compensate the other for the negative effects of all decisions made by the other spouse, including decisions made before the spouses met. It is not clear why one spouse should be responsible for all decisions made by the other.

---

40 See Martin & Bumpass, "Recent Trends in Marital Disruption" (1989) 26 *Demography* 37, 49.
41 See Glick & Lin, "Recent Changes in Divorce and Remarriage" (1986) 48 *J. Marr & Fam.* 737.
42 See Oldham, "Is the Concept of Marital Property Outdated?" (1984) 22 *J. Fam. L.* 263, 272.
43 *Ibid.* at 273.
44 *Ibid.*
45 See Goode, "World Changes in Divorce Patterns" in Weitzman and Maclean, *Economic Consequences of Divorce* (1991) at 11, 24.

Differences in earning capacity stem from many things, including decisions made before marriage and during marriage, as well as other matters, such as innate ability and career choice. It would be hard to justify asking a spouse to pay a portion of post-divorce earnings to the other spouse to remedy differences in earning capacity that stem from factors such as innate ability, career choice, or other decisions made before the parties met.[46]

Another model for post-divorce outcomes would focus upon career damage incurred due to family obligations.[47] The roles spouses assume during marriage obviously can affect earning capacity. If one spouse removes himself from the work-force for a significant period, this can have substantial career ramifications. For example, Professor Polachek has estimated that a person who stays out of the work-force incurs an annual loss of approximately 2% in seniority rights and pay raises, as well as .5% in human capital depreciation.[48] Many wives suffer this type of career damage during marriage. It, therefore, appears unlikely, particularly given the current policies of private employers and the US Government[49], that the difference in earnings between women and men will disappear soon.[50]

The "career damage" due to roles assumed during marriage can be substantial. One scholar has estimated that 40% of the "wage gap" between men and women is due to gender-based customs regarding roles assumed during marriage.[51] The wage gap cannot totally be explained by the different roles customarily assumed during marriage, however. For example, a Census Bureau study found that, when comparing the wages of men and women who worked year-round, full-time, the women's wages amounted to only 69% of the men's, even when only considering those women who had never experienced a work-force disruption (see Table G).[52]

---

46 Cf Blumberg, "Reworking the Past, Imagining the Future" (1991) 16 *Law & Soc. Inq.* 115.

47 See Funder, "Australia: a Proposal for Reform" in Weitzman and Maclean, *supra* at 143, 147; Eekelaar, *Regulating Divorce* (1991) at 83.

48 Conversation between the author and Professor Polachek, September 1991. The literature pertaining to human capital depreciation is quite large. See Mincer and Polachek, "Family investments in Human Capital: Earnings of Women" (1974) 82 J. *Po. Econ.* S76, S94-95; Mincer and Ofek, "Interrupted Work Careers: Depreciation and Restoration of Human Capital" (1982) 17 *J. Hum. Resources* 3, 4-5; Cox, "Panel Estimates of the Effects of Career Interruptions on the Earnings of Women" (1984) 22 *Econ. Inquiry* 386; Jacobsen and Levin, "The Effects of Intermittent Labor Force Attachment on Female Earnings", (paper presented at the American Economic Association Conference, Jan, 3-5, 1992, New Orleans, on file with the author).

49 See generally Kamerman and Kahn, *The Responsive Workplace* (1987).

50 See O'Neill, *Women and Wages, The American Enterprise,* Nov-Dec 1990 at 25, 33.

51 See Hoffman, "Divorce and Economic Well-being: The Effects on Men, Women and Children", Spring 1987 *Del. Law.* at 22.

52 See Bureau of the Census, Current Pop. Rep., Series P-70, No 10, Male-Female Differences in Work Experience, Occupation, and Earnings: 1984 at 2-3 (1987).
    Writers like Victor Fuchs would argue that this type of study underestimates career damage incurred by women. Dr Fuchs argues that women experience career damage not only due to actual workforce disruptions, but also due to other factors stemming from the assumption that a woman will have to spend a significant amount of her adult life caring for children. For example, a woman might choose a career, such as teaching, that would not be particularly lucrative but could be better combined with caring for a child. Such a career choice could affect earnings even before any career disruption. See generally Fuchs, *Women's Quest for Economic Equality* (1988); Fuchs, "Women's Quest for Economic Equality" (1989) 3 *J. Econ. Perspectives* 25.

I have stated above that I question whether the private law divorce system could or should always attempt to equalise the spouses' post-divorce economic circumstances, regardless of the cause of the disparity.[53] In my view, there is a much more compelling argument that a spouse should be compensated for career damage incurred due to a work-force disruption during marriage, particularly if the disruption was due to family responsibilities. In many instances the other spouse participated in this decision to leave the work-force, and in some sense enjoyed the benefits of it.

Other American writers have noted this "career damage" and have discussed how the private law divorce system might compensate for such damage.[54] Proponents of this new remedy are not in total agreement regarding the types of career damage that should be compensated. For example, Professor Ellman attempts to limit his awards to "financially rational" decisions to leave the workforce.[55] Professor Kay would not impose such a limit.[56]

While I believe there is merit in the arguments advanced by Ellman and Kay, I have serious reservations about the specifics of the policy advanced. First, under such a system a divorce court would always have to calculate the value of the career damage incurred by a spouse during marriage. This will be by no means a simple calculation. For example, imagine the "simplest" case: the spouse who had started a career before stopping work for a period. A number of assumptions will have to be made about the career path that would have resulted but for the career disruption. Most women who experience a career disruption are young, and the career path is not well established. For example, if a lawyer's initial job was working for a private firm, would she have stayed there and been promoted to partner?[57] Alternatively, would she have changed employers and eventually worked for a less lucrative employer, such as house counsel or the government? If a spouse did not begin a career before caring for children, the "career damage" calculation is even more confusing. In this instance, the spouse did not suffer career damage but merely deferred beginning her career. What compensation would be appropriate in this instance?

---

53 A few writers have endorsed this goal. See Rutherford, "Duty in Divorce: Shared Income As a Path to Equality" (1990) 58 *Fordham L. Rev.* 539.

54 See Ellman, "The Theory of Alimony" (1989) 77 *Cal. L. Rev.* 1; Kay, "Beyond No Fault: New Directions in Divorce Reform" in Kay and Sugarman, *op cit* n.8 at 6.

55 See Ellman, *supra* n.54 at 58. If a spouse left the work force to care for a child, this should be compensated even if not financially rational, according to Prof. Ellman. *Ibid* at 71. See also, Ellman, "Should the Theory of Alimony Include Nonfinancial Losses and Motivations?" (1991) *Brigham Young L. Rev* 257. *Cf* Carbone, "Economics, Feminism and the Reinvention of Alimony: A Reply to Ira Ellman" (1990) 43 *Vand. L. Rev.* 1463; Carbone & Brinig, "Rethinking Marriage: Feminist Ideology, Economic Change and Divorce Reform" (1991) 65 *Tul L. Rev.* 953.

56 See Kay, "Beyond No fault" in Kay and Sugarman, *op cit* n.8 at 6. Professor Kay believes that this award should no longer be provided at some point in the future when it is less difficult for women to work and raise children in the United States. See Kay, *Commentary* (1991) 57 *Brooklyn L. Rev.* 755, 764.

57 It is increasingly common in the United States for young lawyers to be asked to leave a firm after a few years of work. In the most competitive firms, fewer than 10% of lawyers who start working for the firm as a new lawyer remain and are invited to become partners.

So, the career damage remedy poses serious valuation problems. The calculation is very complicated and would be based upon very speculative assumptions. I fear that the remedy would lead to inconsistent results.[58] If such an unpredictable element would be added to the divorce bargaining process, this would discourage settlement and encourage litigation.[59] Also, substantial expert witness fees would be necessary to establish the case for career damage. If most spouses do not have much property to begin with, it hardly seems wise to add a new procedure that will further drain the estate. Finally, it is unclear what magnitude of award would result under such a system. A fundamental notion of the "no-fault" divorce system is that both spouses should be able to establish a better relationship with one another. If the career damage award would be so large that the obligor could not remarry, this would be inappropriate.[60] A related point would be when, if ever, under this system a spouse would be deemed unable to afford such an award.

Even if all husbands could afford to pay a career damage remedy, I question whether a career damage award would be fair in all cases. A basic argument in support of the career damage system is that the spouses mutually participated in the decision for the wife to leave the work-force. There is very little evidence to support this assumption. In fact, the only study I have seen regarding this issue suggests that the decision is unilateral in a surprising number of cases.[61] It, therefore, seems appropriate to limit such awards to situations where it is more likely that the decision was made jointly, or at least that both spouses more clearly "benefited" from the choice to leave the work-force. I, therefore, suggest limiting the divorce reform remedy focus to those spouses who raised a child together. In such a situation, both spouses benefit from one spouse staying at home and caring for the child. In other situations, a spouse probably leaves the work-force to avoid an unpleasant job or have more leisure time; the other spouse may in some sense benefit from the spouse being at home, but the spouse staying at home seems by far the principal beneficiary of the decision, and the equities favouring post-divorce compensation are less compelling.

---

58 For example, a minority of American courts have determined that a professional degree acquired during marriage is divisible property and the value is the increased earning capacity generated thereby. Courts have calculated very different values for similarly situated spouses. See Oldham, *Divorce, Separation and the Distribution of Property* (1992) at 9.02 [3].

59 See Glendon, "Fixed Rules and Discretion in Contemporary Family Law" (1986) 60 *Tul. L. Rev.* 1165.

60 One might argue that the current system leaves the wife destitute, so the career damage system would, at worst, only force men and women to switch places. Still, current American data suggest that, at least for women who divorce while younger than 30, it is very likely they will remarry. See Bumpass *et al*, "Changing Patterns of Remarriage" (1990) 52 *J. Marr & Fam.* 747; Cherlin, *Marriage, Divorce, Remarriage* (1981) 29. It is unclear that most men would be able to remarry under the career damage system.

61 See Brinkerhoff & Lupri, "Conjugal Power and Family Relationships: Some Theoretical and Methodological Issues" in Ishwaran (ed), *The Canadian Family* (1983) 202, 218.

A proposed system of post-divorce income sharing

American law traditionally has attempted to provide one set of rules for all divorces. Such a system inevitably has produced vague and sometimes even contradictory "factors" to be considered by divorce courts.[62] This system may serve the interests of some. For example, the interests of lawyers might be advanced because the vague rules leave substantial room for advocacy. Legislators are able to avoid making a clear decision regarding the controversial subject of the economic consequences of divorce. It is highly improbable that this system well serves the divorcing parties, however. A number of writers have commented that the current system yields arbitrary results, discourages settlement and increases the costs of divorce.[63] I believe most parties would prefer a system that yielded predictable, consistent results with low transaction costs.

There is a growing tendency among American commentators to want to restrain judicial discretion in divorce law matters.[64] I would be reluctant to remove all discretion from divorce judges regarding the economic consequences of divorce. There certainly are instances where a child or dependent spouse will have special needs that deserve consideration. Still, it would be useful to create presumptive results for divorcing couples. While the method chosen for the calculation of child support guidelines has been quite controversial, once the guidelines have been promulgated they have greatly helped parties (and lawyers) predict the result. Results are more consistent and settlement has been facilitated.[65]

The principal variable remaining under the American system is the award of alimony. Judges, lawyers and parties currently are given little statutory guidance regarding this factor of the divorce result.[66] Any attempt to promulgate a set of presumptive results for alimony awards will be at least as controversial as the process for the calculation of child support guidelines. However, it will be impossible to do this as long as there is a continuing effort to promulgate one standard for all divorces. I feel the dialogue regarding post-divorce economic consequences will only be advanced when it is acknowledged that different types of marriages present very different equities. The equities at divorce depend upon two basic factors: the duration of the marriage and whether the

---

62 See Oldham, *supra* n. 11.
63 See Glendon, *Abortion and Divorce in Western Law* (1987) at 96; Glendon, "Fixed Rules and Discretion in Contemporary Family Law and Succession Law" (1986) 60 *Tul. L. Rev.* 1165; Murphy, *infra* n.64.
64 See Murphy, "Eroding the Myth of Discretionary Justice in Family Law" (1991) 70 *N.C. L. Rev.* 209; Glendon, *supra* n. 63. *Cf* Schneider, "Discretion, Rules and Law: Child custody and the UMDA's Best-Interest Standard" (1991) 89 *Mich. L. Rev.* 2215.
65 See Murphy, *ibid* at 232-235.
66 For example, some researchers studying divorces in a county in Florida attempted to develop a "predictive model" for the award of alimony. The variations among judges were so large that no such model could be developed. See White and Stone, "A Study of Alimony and Child Support Rulings" (1976) 10 *Fam. L. Q.* 75, 80. Eekelaar has reported similar results in England. See Eekelaar, *Regulating Divorce* (1991) at 60.

parties had a child together.[67] It may be easier to arrive at some consensus about a "fair" post-divorce result if the presumptive result varies based upon whether the marriage was short or long, and whether the parties had a child.

Childless marriages present a relatively easy problem. I would bar alimony in all such marriages. Neither spouse normally would have suffered career damage due to childcare responsibilities.[68] Most such marriages either involve very short marriages, marriages of couples who both work year-round, full-time, or second marriages of people marrying late in life. The property division remedy should be adequate for such marriages.[69] There is no compelling argument in these circumstances for any continuing support responsibility after divorce. One might argue that a "long" childless marriage should impose some post-divorce support obligation. It would probably be fair in some instances, such as if one spouse was not working, to impose a short transitional support obligation while the divorce is being processed. Other than that, neither spouse should have a support claim.

If childless couples would not be granted alimony, this would affect a significant number of divorcing couples in America. A recent study found that 42% of divorcing couples had not had a child together.[70]

Reaching a consensus regarding "childful" marriages undoubtedly will be more difficult. I have suggested that the private law system should try in some way to compensate women for career damage incurred if they leave the work-force to care for children. An ideal proposal would compensate the mother, not increase the cost or hostility of the divorce process, and would not forever impede the husband's ability to remarry. There is substantial tension among these goals. I believe the best way to advance them is to adopt some form of income sharing after separation.[71]

Research suggests that the economic problems of young divorcing American women are transitional.[72] The greatest needs appear to be experienced shortly after divorce. If a system of short-term post-divorce income-sharing would be created, some of these needs could be satisfied. Also, if the sharing did not continue for too long a period, the husband would be free after a reasonable time to establish a new relationship.

---

67 Other writers have in the past emphasised the difference between childless marriages and "childful" marriages. See Eekelaar, *Family Law and Social Policy* 2nd ed (1984) at 86-87; Glendon, "Family Law Reform in the 1980s" (1984) 44 *La. L. Rev.* 1553, 1558.

68 This could occur if one spouse has primary custody of a child from a prior marriage and the other spouse assumes child care responsibility. This now rarely occurs in the United States.

69 I would include the remedies that have been developed by various states to reimburse a spouse who supported the other spouse during professional training. See Oldham, *supra* n.11.

70 Information provided to the author by the Natality, Marriage and Divorce Statistics Branch Division of Vital Statistics (National Center for Health Statistics, US Dept. of Health and Human Services).

71 A number of American writers have suggested various forms of this. See Singer, "Divorce Reform and Gender Justice" (1989) 67 *N.C.L. Rev.* 1103; Sugarman, "Dividing Financial Interests on Divorce" in Kay and Sugarman, *op cit* n.8 at 130.

72 See Hoffman & Duncan, "What Are the Economic Consequences of Divorce?" (1988) 25 *Demography* 641; Duncan & Hoffman, "Economic Consequences of Marital Instability, " in David and Smeeding, *Horizontal Equity, Uncertainty and Economic Well-being* (1985) 427, 437; Maclean, *Surviving Divorce* (1991).

I propose that the sharing period should begin at separation, and the duration should be the lesser of one-half the duration of the marriage (until separation) or three years.[73] This transitional award would in some ways resemble what is currently referred to as rehabilitative alimony. The transitional award proposed here would differ in some important respects, however. Rehabilitative alimony is now awarded only if the recipient desires training; this transitional award would not be conditioned upon a need for training. Also, rehabilitative support normally is now not awarded in a large amount; this transitional award contemplates equal income sharing during the period.[74]

This transitional model obviously would not work for all relationships. If the spouses have been married for a long period, the wife has been out of the work-force for some time, and it is unlikely the wife could establish a career, something more than a transitional award frequently will be necessary. But such a divorcing couple is certainly the exception in America today. Most divorcing couples are young and have not been married for a substantial period.

The income sharing model should be applied only to situations where career damage resulted due to the assumption of family responsibilities. I, therefore, would limit the income-sharing system to those marriages where a spouse experienced a substantial work-force disruption due to family responsibilities, and that spouse's earnings were significantly lower than the other spouse's at divorce. So, the system would not cover childless marriages or marriages where both spouses worked full-time throughout the marriage. Such situations would be governed only by child support rules and property division principles.

This transitional income-sharing model would not fully compensate many women for career damage incurred due to family responsibilities. However, it seems to be a workable compromise. Most studies suggest that divorced women have the most serious financial needs before they remarry.[75] A recent study of those women who divorced before age 30 and remarried found that the median number of years between divorce and remarriage was 2.8.[76] Another survey concluded that 89% of women who divorce under age 25 remarry, while 79% of those who divorce between age 25 and 29 remarry.[77] Fewer than two-thirds of those women divorcing in their thirties

---

73 This sharing would be in addition to child support and any property award.

74 If the couple has minor children, the question arises whether the sharing would be equal between households, or whether some notion of per capital equality should be achieved.

75 See Duncan & Hoffman, "A Reconsideration of the Economic Consequences of Marital Dissolution" (1985) 22 *Demography* 485; Hoffman & Duncan, "What are the Economic Consequences of Divorce?" (1988) 25 *Demography* 641.

76 See Glick & Lin, "Recent Changes in Divorce and Remarriage" (1986) 48 *J. Marr & Fam.* 737, 742.

77 See Bumpass *et al*, "Changing Patterns of Remarriage" (1990) 52 *J. Marr & Fam.* 747. This percentage may be misleadingly low in the sense that a number of divorced people cohabit instead of remarrying. See Smock, "Remarriage and Cohabitation Among Previously Married Women: Race Differentials and the Role of Educational Attainment" at 11 (National Survey of Families and Households Working Paper No 31, Center of Demography and Ecology, Univ. of Wisconsin-Madison).

remarried, and less than one third of those divorcing while over 40 remarried.[78] Many of these women, however, presumably would be women divorcing after a long childful marriage, and would not be governed by this transitional system. The transitional award suggested here would provide significant assistance for divorcing mothers when they most need it, without unduly impeding the ability of husbands to establish a new relationship.

I do not suggest that the transitional payment scheme will adequately resolve the current problems of divorced mothers. Increased government involvement in child support collection seems inevitable.[79] Also, more public resources will probably have to be allocated to the support of families with minor children.[80] Still, although the role the government chooses to play regarding divorced families certainly will be important, the goals of private divorce law also need to be clarified. I hope that the proposals set forth above advance the latter purpose, or at least will stimulate the debate about those goals.

---

78 *Ibid.*
79 See Kahn and Kamerman, *Income Transfers for Families with Children* (1983); Kahn and Kamerman, *Child Support: From Debt Collection to Social Policy* (1988).
80 See Krause, "Child Support Reassessed, " in Kay and Sugarman, *op cit* n.8. at 166.

Table A. Mean annual "earnings" for workers who work full-time*, year-round**

	Men	Women	Ratio of wages Women/Men %
1978	$17, 526	$9, 929	56.7
1988	$31, 093	$19, 854	63.9
† 1990	$34, 923	$22, 833	65.4

*   "Full-time" means 35 hours or more per week.
** "Year-round" means 50-52 weeks per year (counting paid vacations).
†   *Source:* Money Income of Households, Families, and Persons in the US: 1990, Current Pop. Reports, Consumer Income, Series p 60, no 174 (Bureau of Census, August 1991), at Table 29.

Source: Monthly Labor Review, Dec. 1990, at p 4.

Table B. Mean "income" for full-time, year-round workers

Age	Men	Women	Ration of income Women/Men %
15-24	16, 970	14, 848	87.4
25-34	27, 973	21, 526	76.9
35-44	38, 574	24, 421	63.3
45-54	42, 743	23, 931	55.9
55-64	42, 673	23, 088	54.1

Source: Bureau of Census, Series p-60, # 168, Money, Income and Poverty Status in the US: 1989 (at pp 49-50).

Table C. Mean earnings of married people, spouse present, who work year-round, full-time

Age	Husbands	Wives	Ration of earnings, Wives/Husbands %
15-24	17, 931	13, 529	75.4
25-34	27, 581	18, 366	66.5
35-44	35, 852	20, 379	56.8
45-54	37, 555	19, 481	51.8
55-64	33, 615	18, 714	55.6

Source: Bureau of Census, Series p-60, # 165, Earnings of Married-Couple Families: 1987 (at pp 17-19)

Table D. Labor force participation of married women, spouse present

Presence and age of Youngest child	Labor force participation rate%	% of employed women who work full time
None under 18	51.1	77.3
Under 18 (0-17)	66.3	69.8
Children 14-17	75.1	74.6
Children 6-17	73.6	71.7
Children 3-5	64.1	67.7
Children Under 3	55.5	67.2

Source: March 1990 Current Population Survey (unpublished data – Bureau of Labor Statistics – obtained by the author from John Stinson of BLS).

Table E. Labor force participation, divorced women

Presence and age of youngest child	Labor force participation rate%	% of employed women who work full time
No Children under 18	72.2	89.3
Children (0-17)	81.3	87.5
Children 14-17	87.2	92.4
Children 6-17	85.9	88.3
Children 3-5	78.4	85.4
Children under 3	57.6	83.3

Source: March 1990 Current Population Survey (unpublished data, Bureau of Labor Statistics, obtained by the author from John Stinson of BLS).

Table F. Labor force participation rates for women, 1988

Age	White	Black	Hispanic
20-24	74.9	63.2	62.3
25-34	73.0	73.7	60.9
35-44	74.9	78.1	62.1
45-54	69.2	68.3	57.9
55-64	43.6	43.4	41.6

Source: Handbook of Labor Statistics (August 1989) at Table 5, p 27.

Table G. Hourly wages, based on sex and work-force disruptions*

	No interruptions		
Age	Male	Female	Female/Male%
21-29	$7.98	$6.64	83.2
30-44	$11.60	$8.40	72.4
45-64	$12.60	$7.57	60.1
	One or more interruptions		
Age	Male	Female	Female/Male %
21-29	$6.77	$5.24	77
3044	$8.93	$6.85	77
45-64	$9.28	$6.98	75

* A "disruption" is defined as a break of service of at least six months.

Source: Current Pop. Reports, Household Economic Studies, Series p70, No 10, "Male-Female Differences in Work Experience, Occupation, and Earnings: 1984", US Dept of Commerce, Bureau of the Census (1987).

Chapter 9
A Poor and Lonely Old Age – Who Supports Ex-Wives in Retirement?

Judith Masson
Professor of Law, University of Warwick

Introduction

In the past poverty and loneliness in old age largely resulted from the death of one's spouse. The Social Security system recognised (and entrenched)[1] the wife's economic dependence on her husband but state widow's benefits were not designed to compensate fully for the loss of the husband's income.[2] Nowadays, fewer people are widowed during their spouse's working life but massive increases in divorce are producing continued growth in the proportion of the married who reach retirement alone.[3] Women whose working lives have been shaped by marriage and child care are likely to have pensions which are both inferior to their husbands' and inadequate for a comfortable retirement.[4] The way pensions are treated at divorce[5] and the limited rights ex-spouses have in their former partners' pensions[6] mean that despite adequate income before retirement many will have a poor and lonely old age.

Economic dependence of married women on their husbands which results from limitations on their ability to save for retirement is not a problem confined to the United Kingdom. Other jurisdictions have sought and found a variety of solutions, particularly the reallocation of pension

---

1 See Beveridge Report *Social Insurance* Cmd. 6404 (1942).
2 Abel Smith "Sex Equality and Social Security" in Lewis (ed) *Women's Welfare Women's Rights* (Croom Helm, 1983) p 89 ff.
3 Haskey, "Current prospects for the proportion of marriages ending in divorce" (1989) 55 *Population Trends* 34; Joshi and Davies *The Pension Consequences of Divorce* (EPR Discussion Paper No. 550 (1991)) 30.
4 Joshi and Davies *supra*, n.3, p.17; Davies and Ward, *Women and Personal Pensions* (EOC, HMSO, 1992) 9.2, 9.8.
5 Ellison, *Pensions and Divorce* (PMI, 1991) part II and see discussion *infra*.
6 Benefits may be paid from occupational pensions schemes to ex-spouses who are dependants of the scheme member, Inland Revenue IR 12 para 11.7. Less than 7% of men and less than 2% of women scheme members report that their former spouse retained benefits in their scheme, Gregory and Foster, *The Consequences of divorce: the report of the 1984 Consequences of Divorce Survey carried out on behalf of the Lord Chancellor's Department* (OPCS, HMSO, 1990).

rights between spouses at divorce or the redesign of benefit packages to fit with patterns of serial marriage.[7] Pensions remain the only substantial asset which cannot be effectively reallocated at divorce in England and Wales.[8] Failure to achieve change here is not due to inertia – both pensions and divorce law have been subject to continued review and reform in the past 25 years. Why then is it that reports and proposals have not lead to legislative reform?

This paper describes briefly the effect of divorce on women's pensions and the extent of the problem of post-retirement poverty which must be addressed. It examines the different approaches to and definitions of the problem of divorced women's pensions. It suggests that the failure of the government, the pensions industry, the Law Commission and family lawyers to agree about the nature of the problem and the need for (and likely source of) a solution to the problem have prevented sensible discussions. However, there are now some signs that a debate is beginning, but this will need to extend beyond private law approaches of dividing existing assets if it is to provide a solution. It is suggested that the pension system needs to be redesigned to take more account of the effects of caring responsibilities on employment and thus pensions. The final part of the paper looks at a possible comprehensive solution and considers whether there is likely to be sufficient will to pay for it.

The problem outlined

Most people who retire have a pension derived from a combination of state, employment and private sources. The state basic retirement pension is earned through contributions and credits over at least 9/10ths of the working life. Originally married women could choose whether they contributed or not; those who did not qualified for a reduced rate (Category 'B') pension through their husbands' contributions.[9] This option which currently affects 1.1 million women[10] is being phased out. These pension rights are protected[11] at divorce because the woman is permitted to use her husband's insurance record but she may receive a

---

7   See Ellison supra n.5 chap. 11 and von Maydell "Credit-Splitting (*Versorgingsansgleich*) at divorce" in Meulders-Klein and Eekelaar (eds), *Family, State and Individual Economic Security* (Kluwer, 1988) chap 42.

8   There is limited provision for Scotland in the Family Law (Scotland) Act 1985. This requires compensation for loss of pension but does not allow reallocation of pension assets because the restrictions in the Social Security Act 1975 apply throughout the United Kingdom.

9   Masson, "Women's Pensions" (1985) JSWL 319.

10 Department of Social Security, *Statistics* 1990 table H 104.

11 This was not always the case. Beveridge had suggested retraining grants for divorced women but these were not provided. The Morton Commission on Marriage and Divorce, Cmnd 7678, 1956 para 712-6 recommended permitting the use of the husband's insurance record and this was provided by the National Insurance (Married Women) Amendment Regulations 1957 (SI 1957 1322).

reduced pension if she fails to make full contributions after divorce.[12] Periods out of employment caring for children or elderly dependents are covered by "home responsibilities credits and thus do not reduce the amount of pension. The state basic pension protects women well from divorce and the effects of family responsibilities on their working lives but it provides only a low (and declining) standard of living. At £52.00 per week it represents approximately 25% of women's full-time average earnings.[13] Since 1980 the basic state pension has been uprated in line with prices not wages and this is predicted to lead to its decline to only 10% of average earnings by the year 2030.[14]

The low level of the state basic pension lead to provision for its supplementation by additional pensions through a system introduced by the Social Security (Pensions) Act 1975 and reformed by the Social Security Act 1985. Employees must now contribute to the State Earnings-Related Pension Scheme (SERPS), a contracted out occupational scheme or an appropriate private pension. In addition anyone may make further contributions, although tax advantages will only be available to those in employment and up to specified limits. All of these types of pension produce a retirement income which is related to either the contributions made or the final salary of the employee; in most cases both income and length of working life combine to determine the size of pension. The SERPS scheme provides limited protection for periods of home responsibilities but also produces pensions which are low[15] and currently only uprated in line with prices. Periods out of full-time employment have a double effect on pensions. They reduce the number of years during which contributions are made and, because they affect career progression, reduce the size of earnings.

Although SERPS takes some account of the former, neither it nor employers' schemes deal with the latter. In theory (but subject to Inland Revenue limits) an individual can opt out of their employer's scheme or SERPS in favour of a private pension but in practice this is unlikely to provide enhanced benefits because a substantial proportion of the value of an occupational pension is provided by the employer. (There are benefits of opting out of SERPS for part of the working life.[16]) Moreover, since those with low incomes can only afford to make low contributions to a private pension, a high proportion of their premiums will be absorbed by the administrative costs of the pension provided.[17]

---

12 27% of women but only 4% of men who have pensions on their own contributions receive a reduced pension.
13 Figures for 1991 calculated by Labour Research, see Davies and Ward, *supra* n.4 p 17.
14 *Ibid.*
15 The SERPS scheme will only reach maturity in 2018-19. The maximum pension will be 20/80ths of income between the National Insurance Lower and Upper Earnings Limits. This compares with occupational schemes which provide between 40/80ths and 40/60ths of final salary for someone who has worked for 40 years.
16 *Supra* n.4 p 55.
17 Davies and Ward *supra* n.4, chap 6.

Periods of dependency during marriage are reflected in lower income after retirement. Even where a woman has remained in employment her pension is likely to be lower than her husband's because workforce segregation has resulted in lower pay and fewer benefits (such as good occupational pension schemes) in jobs dominated by women.[18] On average, women's income in retirement is less than half that of men. Although there is little difference between the average incomes of single retired men and women this is not the case for married women whose average income is less than 30% of that for married men nor for divorced women whose average income is only 65% of that of divorced men.[19] Whilst the marriage remains intact the woman's retirement may be cushioned by her husband's income. However, if she divorces and does not remarry she is likely to fall into poverty, unless her working life has been relatively unaffected by marriage (putting her husband's career first, being a housewife) or domestic responsibilities (child care, care for elders).[20]

Women's dependency on their husbands' earnings or pension is recognised in the state, most employers' and some private pension schemes by the provision of a widow's pension related to the husband's earnings. Widower's pensions are also available but because of their more recent introduction, women's lower average earnings, and longer life expectancy, they are less valuable benefits. Many schemes also provide a discretionary lump sum payment on the death of a scheme member. Following divorce the ex-spouse no longer qualifies for a widow's or widower's pension although where maintenance is paid and the scheme member does not remarry an employer's scheme may provide a pension.[21] In addition, the former spouse loses the possibility of sharing directly the member's retirement benefits. In SERPS this amounts only to a fairly small supplement to their weekly income, but in employer's schemes there is usually a lump sum of up to four times final salary on top of a pension of between a half and two-thirds of final salary which may be inflation-proofed. Private pensions are used to purchase annuity contracts but some of the assets may be taken as a lump sum.

Current divorce law has only a limited effect on the pension consequences of divorce. Although the Matrimonial Causes Act 1973 s25(2) (h) requires the courts to have regard, *inter alia*, to "the value to each of the parties to the marriage of any benefit (for example a pension) which by reason of the dissolution ... that party will lose the chance of acquiring", there is no power to distribute assets from a pension fund. Payment of benefits other than on retirement or death would disqualify the pension funds from its valuable rights to special tax treatment.[22] Also pensions may be subject to a

---

18 60% of men but only 35% of women are members of occupational pension schemes. Government Actuary, *Occupational Schemes* 1987 (HMSO 1991).

19 Bone *et al, Retirement and retirement plans* (OPCS, HMSO 1992) tables 7.26 and 7.27.

20 Martin and Roberts, *Women and Employment on a lifetime perspective* (HMSO 1984).

21 *Supra*, n.6.

22 Inland Revenue IR 12 para. 7.20. The Social Security Act 1973, Sched 16, para 15 also precludes assignment of benefits.

"spendthrift" clause which prevents their being attached directly by a court to satisfy the member's obligations or debts.[23] It may be possible for a lump sum payable on retirement to be claimed but because only one application can be made following divorce for a lump sum this will require the court's permission to adjourn the application until retirement. This has only been allowed where the respondent is approaching retirement.[24] If there is no access to the pension fund the court can only attempt to evaluate the applicant's needs and legitimate expectations and attempt to satisfy these from the respondent's other resources. In most cases the present needs will more than absorb all the current assets but it may be possible to argue that the wife receives a greater share in the matrimonial home to compensate for her loss of pension.[25] Maintenance payments following the husband's retirement might seem the most obvious way to transfer part of his pension income to his ex-wife. However, this would only be possible if the ex-wife had not remarried and there was an existing order when the ex-husband retired. Such a scheme would not protect the ex-wife in the event of the husband's death prior to retirement. The policy of the "clean-break"[26] has largely removed this option in favour of making the parties independent of one another. Where dependency remains uncompensated the ex-wife's independence may be illusory and shift after her retirement from the husband to the state as she seeks Income Support.

Where loss of pension would cause "grave financial hardship" the court has the power to refuse a divorce but only where the petition is based on MCA 1973, s1(2) (e), five years' separation. In practice, very few decrees are sought on this ground and refusal is very rare. However, it may be useful in encouraging a scheme member to seek ways, for example the purchase of an annuity, to compensate his spouse for loss of pension rights.[27]

The failure of the pension system to cope with divorce and of divorce law to deal adequately with pensions have been apparent for some time[28], but only relatively recently have attempts been made to quantify the amounts of money and numbers of people concerned. Studies for the government by the EOC[29] and OPCS[30] are now providing clear and up-to-date information about the differences in men's and women's post-retirement income and explaining this in terms of their work histories and access to different types of pension provision. Despite increased employment

---

23 Ellison *supra* n.5. para 6.6.
24 *Morris* v *Morris* [1957] 7 yrs L.244 (gratuity payable with three years adjournment granted); *Roberts* v *Roberts* [1986] 1 WLR 437 (6 year waiting period, adjournment not granted). Even if the adjournment were granted the husband might avoid an order by taking a pension rather than a lump sum.
25 This is apparently the practice in Scotland where the Family Law (Scotland) Act 1985 requires fair sharing of pension assets but the same revenue and pension rules preclude access to pension funds.
26 MCA 1973, s 25A(2) (3) which require the court to consider time limited maintenance and to dismiss applications rather than make nominal orders.
27 *Julian* v *Julian* (1972) 116 SJ 763; *Parker* v *Parker* [1972] Fam.116.
28 See below for a detailed discussion of the responses to the problem.
29 *Supra*, n.4.
30 *Supra*, n.19.

opportunities and reductions in the periods spent out of employment whilst caring for children, women are still much less likely than men to be members of occupational pension schemes.[31] Most women will continue to have fragmented employment patterns and lower earnings which will continue to combine to provide them with poor pensions. The state basic pension is more important to women because it provides a higher proportion of their retirement income. If it continues to be uprated only in line with prices up to two-thirds of women (but less than one-third of men) will face poverty in retirement.[32]

The size of the elderly population is also increasing.[33] As divorce rates continue to rise[34] the proportion of this population who is divorced will also grow. It has been estimated that 13.5% of elderly women will be divorced by 2025.[35] As divorced elderly women have the lowest incomes amongst the retired[36], an increase suggests a further growth in the problem of poverty. However, in a comparatively affluent country such as the United Kingdom poverty reflects inadequate distribution of assets rather than an inability to provide. While consideration is being given to means of improving women's pensions and particularly the position of divorced women, research by Joshi and Davies[37] and by the EOC[38] suggests that neither changing divorce law nor focusing on occupational and private pensions will provide a solution. Both suggest that the answer lies in improving the basic state pension. If this is paid for by all tax payers it would also spread the costs of caring from carers, particularly those who get divorced, to the whole population.

Responses to the problem

Divorce law and the pensions system have both been the subject of major reforms twice in the last 25 years. These have not changed the nature of the problem of divorce and pensions although they have changed the way the problem is defined, and the numbers of people affected and amounts of money involved. Understanding of the problem has evolved so that it is increasingly accepted that it concerns the majority of divorcing women and relates to retirement benefits generally, not merely the loss of the potential widow's pension. However, two approaches have persisted – that there is no problem or that the problem is so complex that it is beyond any solution.

31 *Supra*, n.19 tables 6.2 and 6.4.
32 *Supra*, n.4. table 8.3.
33 Joshi and Davies *supra*, n.3. table 2.2.
34 Currently one marriage in three is expected to end in divorce with higher divorce rates for second and subsequent marriages, *Haskey, supra*, n.3.
35 *Supra*, n.33.
36 *Supra*, n.19 table 7.26. This presumes that married and cohabiting women have access to their partners' income.
37 *Supra*, n.3.
38 *Supra*, n.4.

Problem? What problem?

Despite long-standing inequality in employment opportunities, pay and pensions which reinforced women's economic dependency on their husbands, family law failed to recognise pension loss as a problem of divorce. This is in marked contrast to concerns about the wife's rights in the matrimonial home. Family law texts included at most the briefest mention of pensions.[39] Consequently solicitors were not alerted to or trained in this aspect of divorce settlement. Clients, except perhaps those close to retirement[40], probably did not raise questions of pensions at divorce; people, particularly younger adults, who form the majority of those who divorce, are often not well-informed about their pension rights and probably have even less knowledge of those of their partner. There is little evidence that the value of pensions has been taken into account in divorce settlements despite the provisions in the Matrimonial Causes Act 1973.[41]

The pensions industry has also largely been unconcerned with the problem. Pensions texts rarely refer to divorce[42], but this may reflect the fact that, because the courts have no power to touch the pension fund, divorce rarely impinges on the work of pensions administrators.[43]

The Law Commission first looked at divorce and pensions in 1967[44] when it canvassed views on a number of solutions: divorced wives' pensions (a proportionate share of the state and possibly an occupational widow's pension related to the length of the marriage); an allowance for loss of pension in the maintenance award; award of pension (an order which would require the pension fund to pay the wife a share of the husband's pension); award of a lump sum to compensate loss of pension expectancy; award of a deferred payment; a payment of premiums for a deferred annuity.[45] These were all rejected partly because none provided an acceptable and complete solution and partly because the Law Commission took the view that the problem would be "less serious and pressing" because of other reforms.[46] The rights to the matrimonial home conferred by the Matrimonial Homes Act 1967 and the availability of lump sum payments and property adjustments would enable women to be better compensated at divorce. Proposals for change to pensions were also thought likely to

---

39 See for example *Bromley's Family Law*, 4th ed (1971) 448. The 7th edition contains slightly more information but no main heading in the index. Similarly Passingham and Harmer, *Law & Practice in Matrimonial Causes*, 4th ed (1985) includes no reference.

40 There is some evidence that loss of pension rights leads to applications for judicial separation rather than divorce, Garlic "Judicial separation a research study" (1983) 46 MLR 719 at 721; Maidment, *Judicial Separation* (1982) p 52.

41 Eekelaar and Maclean, *Maintenance after divorce* (1986).

42 Joshi and Davies, "Pensions, divorce and wives' double burden" (1992) 6 *Int. J. Law and Fam.* 289, 298.

43 The recent concern in the industry seems to have arisen because the Scottish divorce provisions have led to requests from lawyers for valuations of pension rights.

44 LCWP No 9.

45 *Ibid* paras 190-207.

46 L.C. Report No 25 (1969 HC P448) para 112-114.

ameliorate the problem at least within the state scheme although these seem to have been misconstrued and were never implemented. The fact that a major asset, the pension, would remain untouchable was largely ignored.

At this point the Law Commission also noted that "innocent wives would be able to protect themselves by defending divorce petitions and remaining married, and seems to have been influenced by the fact that any loss would only be suffered by those who either wanted a divorce or were divorced because of their fault.[47] Considering that fault had previously determined whether a wife could claim any financial award on divorce, it is not surprising that loss of pension to such women was considered unimportant. But such responses reflect the view that pension benefits are discretionary payments to reward long service rather than entitlements which were being abandoned by the pensions industry.

The Law Commission considered pensions briefly again when they reviewed the financial consequences of divorce in the early 1980s. Despite recognising that the pension could be "an exceedingly valuable asset" they again minimised the problem, suggesting that the move to the clean-break would reduce the cases where preserving the contingent widow's rights might seem appropriate and that their proposals should not be delayed to enable pension problems to be solved.[48] A less sanguine view might have recognised that imposing a clean-break without access to this major asset would necessarily result in inadequate compensation for wives who would no longer be able to resurrect claims for maintenance. The Commission's most recent paper on matrimonial property makes no reference to pensions even though it recommends that property bought by one spouse during the marriage for the benefit of both – a definition which clearly fits a private pension with dependent's benefits – should be jointly owned.[49]

The government has been unwilling to recognise the existence of a problem for either divorce law or pensions. Although the Lord Chancellor's Department produced a consultative document in 1985[50] it has subsequently taken the view that there is no problem requiring legislation and the matter is one for pension schemes to manage by more generous rules for granting dependent's pensions.[51] This does not acknowledge any rights in the spouse's personal pension.

Awareness of the pension consequences of divorce increased during the 1980s and family lawyers started to seek ways of using the existing law to obtain compensation for their clients. However, the view is still expressed that pensions are only of concern to the relatively wealthy (where compensation is possible through use of other assets). There is also considerable complacency about the powers of the courts. Ellison in a book

---

47 *Ibid.*
48 L.C. No 112 (1981 HCP 68) para 33.
49 L.C. No 175 (1988 HCP 9) 19.
50 See *infra.*
51 See Hansard, Commons 16 June 1988 cols 375ff.

on pensions and divorce published by the Pensions Management Institute (PMI) concludes that "the position is broadly satisfactory ... the courts can and do take account of pensions rights in reallocating assets on divorce."[52] Such a view may well undermine the current reform proposals from a working party set up by the PMI.[53] Until the nature and extent of the problem is fully recognised by all concerned the prospects for reform are bleak.

Too difficult!

The complexity of pensions, particularly the split between the state and private sector and the diversity of private sector provision makes it extremely difficult to draft proposals which will make similar provision for those with similar needs while at the same time having comparable effects on individual scheme members and the schemes themselves. This difficulty increased after the Social Security Act 1986 extended the types of pension scheme which qualified to exempt a member from SERPS and allowed greater choice to those in employers' schemes. Solutions which seem simple for funded schemes where the pension must contain identifiable assets are not appropriate for pensions backed by insurance contracts particularly where surrender values are low. Similarly, methods of reallocating the member's pension are not necessarily appropriate for the widow's benefits.

It has also become clear that merely dividing existing pension assets will not compensate fully a wife whose working life has been interrupted by caring responsibilities.[54] The effect these have on her income persist after divorce and continue to affect her acquisition of pension rights. Compensation by way of a single payment at divorce could be adequate if resources were available but would not be based on an accurate assessment of her loss which cannot be calculated until the end of her working life. Similarly, the amount the husband can afford to pay from his pension savings is unclear because his future career and pension prospects cannot be known. Also any approach which is restricted to employers' or private schemes will exclude a substantial proportion of those who divorce.[55] These are likely to be those with the most limited assets.

A comprehensive system needs to include SERPS and thus the Guaranteed Minimum Pension (GMP) element in occupational schemes. If it allows access to the pension fund it breaches one of the requirements for approval by the Department of Social Security and the Inland Revenue. Reform thus involves issues of pensions policy and public expenditure.

---

52 *Supra*, n.5 para 15.2
53 PMI Consultative Document *Pensions and Divorce* May 1992 see also *Financial Times* 25 July 1992.
54 Joshi and Davies *supra* n.3, n.42.
55 *Supra*, n.19.

These functions make it impossible for either the Law Commission or the pensions industry to promote reforms, particularly in the face of a government view that legislation is not required.

The Law Commission concluded that a direct and complete solution to the problem of pensions and divorce could not be found in 1969.[56] Subsequently it has shied away from the issue, mentioning it only briefly when re-examining reallocation of property on divorce in 1980–81.[57] The Occupational Pensions Board (OPB) agreed that full compensation for loss of pension was impossible but did suggest both an increase in the court's powers on divorce and changes in scheme rules to allow survivors' benefits to be apportioned.[58] However, its suggestions were not taken up although they probably helped to shape the Lord Chancellor's Department's proposals. When these were rejected the government seems to have found further exploration too difficult and returned to ignoring the position.

A minimalist approach

A number of responses to the problem of divorce and pensions have focused exclusively on the loss of the contingent widow's pension. The OPB rejected the suggestion that the husband's personal pension[59] should be allocated to the wife because she "does not have any right to receive [it] during his lifetime." Instead she should claim maintenance which he could pay from his pension[60] – an option which was still available in 1976 although enforcement was often problematic. Both the OPB and the Law Commission supported allowing a divorced wife to claim part of the survivor's pension.[61] Such an award could protect a dependent ex-wife after her ex-husband's death but would not allow her to share the fruits of his employment during his lifetime. The Lord Chancellor's Department developed its proposals from these papers but took a very restrictive approach including only benefits above the GMP minimum and leaving the decision on quantum until after the husband's death.[62] These proposals were so limited that they would have had little effect on the problem and were rejected by both family lawyers and the pensions industry.

This method of compensating for lost pension does not fit well with the reforms to financial provision introduced by the Matrimonial and Family

---

56 *Supra*, n.46.
57 See *supra*, n.48 and accompanying text.
58 Occupational Pensions Board, *Equal Status for men and women in Occupational Pensions Schemes* Cmnd. 6599 (1976) para 13.41, 13.70.
59 The same argument would apply to any lump sum.
60 *Supra*, n.58 para 13.68.
61 OPB *supra*, n. 58 para 13.50; L.C. *supra*, n.45 para 197; n.48 para.33.
62 Lord Chancellor's Department, *Occupational Pension Rights on Divorce* (1985). Both limitations were directly contrary to recommendations of the OPB.Restriction to benefits above the GMP meant that no comparable changes were needed in state benefits.

Proceedings Act 1984. Provision of a widow's pension appears to encourage the ex-wife to remain dependent on the husband and prevents a clean-break. Either the ex-wife is vulnerable to her ex-husband's pension choices – for example moving to a private pension with no widow's benefits – or the ex-husband is restricted in the arrangements he can make. In any event she cannot make proper plans for her old age if she has to wait until her husband's death to know if she will receive an award.

Although reform based on the contingent widow's pension may be seen as limited, it has met with strong opposition from logically minded pension fund administrators who object that divorce ends marriage and thus widow's and widower's benefits should not be paid. This reflects a concern that a pension scheme might be made to provide a number of pensions in respect of any member which would be very costly and unfair to both other scheme members and employers who would inevitably have to pay higher contributions. Even if the member does not remarry, there is additional expenditure because schemes are funded on the basis that only some members will leave dependants. If the pension is shared between the ex-wife and widow there is little cost to the scheme[63] but the widow, who may have been as financially dependent as the ex-wife suffers.

Pension as capital

If the pension is viewed as a capital asset which may be invested to provide benefits it is more logical to focus on dividing the asset than any component parts. Where the scheme is not funded or is insured this approach may present problems, but these all turn on the valuation of the rights the scheme member has. A number of countries[64] have adopted this as a basis for dealing with pensions at divorce although none may have as complex a pension system as the United Kingdom. Also most operate some form of community of property regime; splitting the pensions savings made during marriage fits logically with the way other assets are treated although there may be restrictions so that pensions cannot be converted and spent before retirement. Such restrictions protect any state's investment in occupational pensions provided through tax advantages to pension schemes.

A number of proposals have been made for pension splitting in England and Wales although none has yet obtained official backing from the government, the Law Commission or the OPB.[65] Each would allow a wife to retain a preserved pension in her husband's scheme or transfer rights from

---

63 If the first wife dies before the widow and her share is not retransferred there is a saving.

64 Germany, Canada and various North American States. See Ellison *supra*, n.5. The Scottish system is also based on a concept of matrimonial property. Family Law (Scotland) Act 1985, s 10.

65 Institute of Fiscal Studies, Freedman *et al, Property and Marriage an integrated approach* (1988) and Labour Party (Meacher) *Pensions, Couples and Divorce* (1990); Law Society, *Maintenance of Capital Provision on Divorce* (1991); PMI *supra*, n 53.

it to a separate scheme. Splitting fits well with the current divorce law's notion of a clean-break but may not prevent poverty, particularly where the divorce occurs after a short marriage in which the wife has acquired long-term caring responsibilities. Equal division of the existing asset does not produce equal pensions because of the ex-wife's subsequent restricted employment and may not even ensure that her retirement income is adequate.[66]

Valuation and division remain major problems with pension splitting proposals for England and Wales. Under the Matrimonial Causes Act 1973 the court has wide discretion to redistribute assets so it would be logical if this applied to pensions as well. However, complete freedom over assets would allow the court or the parties to exchange the home for the pension and might leave the wife dependent on welfare benefits.

There are two alternative bases for valuing pensions in final salary schemes:

(i) "the cash equivalent" which is used to determine transfer values when an employee changes jobs; and

(ii) "the past service reserve" which is the amount the actuary calculates that the scheme should retain in order to cover the expected levels of benefit. Both are based on actuarial assessments and there is substantial room for differences of opinion, particularly in relation to "the past service reserve". The past service reserve may be as much as twice the cash equivalent.[67] Using this would, therefore, have a substantial effect on the outcome of splitting. Valuation of annuity contracts and other insured benefits is usually based on the surrender value of the policy which is typically very low. Competition between insurance companies for business from people who thought they might divorce might improve this.

It is also necessary to determine when the valuation should be made, at separation or divorce and exactly which benefits should be valued. In Scotland the legislation makes it clear that matrimonial property only includes that acquired during the marriage but the Matrimonial Causes Act 1973 applies no such restriction.[68] It would, therefore, be possible that on a second or subsequent divorce an English court would impose a split to remove pensions savings from the husband which had already been subject to a division.

The cost of producing individual valuations is potentially quite high although schemes must provide statements of cash equivalents each year to members who request them.[69] The greater the amount of discretion within the system the higher the costs of valuation will be. Settlements may also be more difficult to reach. Although discretion could allow the tailoring of the

---

66 *Supra*, n.3, n.42.

67 Scott "Pension rights on divorce" (1991) *J. Law Soc. of Scot.* 1, 3 (February).

68 If reform is introduced which allows the same degree of discretion in England and Wales as there is currently in relation to other property there will still be differences between the English and Scottish systems. These are unlikely to be welcomed by pensions schemes administrators who have members on each side of the border.

69 Occupational Pension Schemes (Disclosure of Information) Regulations 1986(S1 1986/1046).

solution to the individual's circumstances the future uncertainty and the limited impact of splitting may make a rule-based approach more advantageous to couples, if not to professional advisers. If pension splitting is to be introduced, a substantial amount of detailed work to produce regulations relating to different types of schemes and guidance for the courts will be essential. Proposals will need the full support of the government and the pensions industry. However, Joshi and Davies' work[70] indicates that it will not solve the problem of poverty among elderly divorced women. An understanding of the limitations of the system may encourage the search for further solutions but could lead to the abandonment of efforts to establish pension splitting.

Benefit design

The pensions industry likes to claim that it has responded to changes in society by developments in benefit design[71] although the most recent changes seem to have been provoked by EC Directives.[72] Many of the technical difficulties of pension splitting could be overcome by abolishing widows' and widowers' pensions and replacing them with a spousal benefit equal to that of the scheme member which would be preserved at divorce. Annuity contracts for married (or even unmarried) couples would also be in the form of two separate pensions. Although changes in benefit design are necessary to fit women's more fragmented working lives, this proposal fails to tackle the fundamental problem that an ex-wife is not able to earn equal pension after divorce. An adequate pension could be secured by the ex-husband making further contributions on her behalf, but this would offend against the clean-break.

A recent paper from the Equal Opportunities Commission recognises this. It shows that the introduction of private pensions has not improved the pensions position for most women because their incomes do not allow them to make sufficiently high contributions and concludes that the best and most straightforward way of reducing the risk of poverty is through significant increases in the level of the state basic pension.[73] The basic state pension is divorce-proofed and also protected against low income and caring responsibilities. If its level were increased it would protect against poverty but would still leave ex-wives at a disadvantage in comparison to their former husbands.

---

70 *Supra*, n.3.
71 PMI *supra*, n.53 para 15.
72 *e.g.* the inclusion of widowers' benefits and the equalization of pension ages.
73 *Supra*, n.4 para 9.9.

The price of pensions reform

While the existence of the problem is denied or ignored as too difficult, the cost is divided between the individual women and the state (all tax payers). Divorced women whose incomes take them above means tested benefit levels receive no compensation and others are supported to poverty level. In effect the state pays twice since it provides tax relief to pension funds in order to facilitate adequate pensions but is forced to pay again because the pension is not distributed. An increase in divorce may benefit those who bear the cost of occupational pension schemes (employers and members) if it means that fewer widow's pensions are paid, but lose if scheme members marry women who survive them for longer periods.

Pension splitting should redistribute pension savings and raise the income of divorced women bringing some above poverty level. However, such a system cannot be seen as purely redistributive without costs to the pensions industry or the state. Pensions managers are concerned about the cost of splitting, particularly the need to maintain more detailed records if valuation is based on the length of marriage, and of a large increase in the number of preserved pensions. In fact, pension splitting based on the cash equivalent can be seen to benefit schemes because they will have calculated the member's benefits on the basis of past-service reserve. Apart from administration the costs of splitting fall on the wife who receives benefits based only on a low valuation of rights existing at the time of divorce. If the amount of tax relief to pension schemes or individual pensioners increased, as it would if husbands could make good losses after splitting further costs are borne by all tax payers. Some of the burden would fall on people who have more limited pensions than the divorcing wives who benefit.

Recent changes in the design of state benefits have been introduced to cut the costs of provision, but it is clear that improvements in the basic state pension such as those proposed by the EOC and endorsed by Joshi and Davies would be very costly even though there would be some savings through reduction in claims for means tested benefits. The cost of improving the state pension falls disproportionately on lower income earners so long as contributions are not levied on earnings above the earnings limit. If improvements to the pension were achieved through increases in the contribution rate rather than changes in its structure or by taxation the burden would continue to fall on those with lower incomes.

The problems of divorce cannot be tackled by pension splitting nor by separation of pension benefits from the date of marriage because the dependency produced in marriage continues to affect pension rights long after divorce. The effect of that dependency on pensions can only be calculated when the wife retires, although it may be estimated earlier, but she needs to know what it is so that she can make the best provision for her old age. Although pension splitting at divorce does not provide a complete solution to the problem of pensions and divorce, it recognises that the wife has a legitimate claim to a share in all assets acquired through the husband's employment during the marriage.

Failure to make provision for dividing existing pension benefits reflects a view that some assets belong to the husband alone and should thus be protected at divorce. Alternatively that women who divorce prior to retirement disqualify themselves from a share in pension assets. Such views are out of keeping with the law on financial provision, even though English law as yet contains no definition of matrimonial property. A fairer distribution could be achieved if there were powers to require the husband to enhance the wife's pension rights after divorce. Such provision would recognise the long-term effects of marriage but conflict with the concept of the clean-break. However, that policy seems too firmly entrenched to be abandoned. Women with short marriages and fragmented working lives will, therefore, remain dependent on the state pension.

Improvements to the basic state pension are capable of benefitting more poor women than changes to pensions and divorce. However, the recent history of pension reform does not give any cause for hope that the necessary level of improvements will be made and sustained. Even if substantial improvements are made, they will not substitute for the benefits of sharing part of the occupational pension, particularly the receipt of a lump sum on retirement for women whose husbands have good occupational pensions and whose marriages last longer than average.

The most complete solution to the problem of pensions and divorce would be provided by increasing the basic pension and requiring splitting of all earnings related rights including the Guaranteed Minimum Pension. It would be fairer if the costs of improvement to the basic pension were met out of general taxation whilst those of pension splitting fell on the individuals concerned rather than the scheme or tax payers generally.

There is now sufficient information to demonstrate the nature and size of the problem and where the solution lies. It should now be impossible to suggest that there is no problem, that it is too difficult or that it should be solved by better legal advice or fairer pensions administration. Reform requires legislation to change both pensions and family law and public expenditure to improve the basic state pension.

Chapter 10

Reform of the Law of Intestate Succession

Gareth Miller
Professor of Law, University of East Anglia

Introduction

In December 1989 the Law Commission published their report on
Distribution on Intestacy.[1] They expressed the view that "a system which was
first devised in 1922 and has received only minor modifications since then
is quite inappropriate to modern social and economic conditions."[2] Few
would disagree that a general reappraisal of the rules of intestate succession
was opportune, and most of the recommendations in the report appear
acceptable and indeed desirable. However, the crucial and central
recommendation that a surviving spouse should in all cases receive the
whole of an intestate's estate was surprising and has proved controversial. It
is almost certainly the reason why no action has been taken to implement
the recommendations contained in the report. Such a rule would be clear
and simple and give rise to little or no disagreement in many, perhaps the
majority of cases. It would remove or reduce the difficulties encountered
by some surviving spouses under the present rules, but there would be
cases where such a rule would appear too simple and would frustrate what
are considered to be the legitimate expectations of other members of
an intestate's family in relation to what is seen as the property of that
family.

This paper will concentrate on the provision for a surviving spouse,
though this cannot be viewed in isolation from the claims of other members
of an intestate's family. However, it will first be appropriate to consider
briefly the task which a system of intestate succession is required to perform
and the size of that task.

---

1   L. C. No 187.
2   *Ibid* para 23.

The scope of intestate succession?

The rules of intestate succession are intended to provide for the disposition of the property of a person who has not left an effective will or not left a completely effective will. Accordingly they need to cover a number of situations. Thus the deceased may not have attempted to make a will at all. The deceased may have attempted to make a will but his attempt has failed completely because, (a) of defective execution, (b) it has been revoked unintentionally, *e.g.* by a subsequent marriage, (c) it has been rendered ineffective by subsequent events such as the death of beneficiaries or the sale of property specifically given, or (d) of invalid provisions. The deceased may have made a valid will but it is effective to dispose of only part of his property because, *e.g.* of defective drafting or subsequent events as mentioned above.

This variety of circumstances giving rise to an intestacy, complete or partial, should be borne in mind in considering the formulation of the actual rules of intestate succession. In particular while some may have chosen to die intestate – to adopt the statutory plan – or did not feel sufficiently strongly about the claims of particular beneficiaries to make a will providing for them, this is unlikely to be the case where the deceased left an ineffective will. There is no simple picture of a person who has died even wholly intestate. The existence of partial intestacy complicates the picture further.

The number of cases of total intestacy in which the rules must be applied is substantial as is apparent from the number of grants of Letters of Administration made each year as shown in the following table.[3] These account for about 25% of all the cases in which grants are necessary. Even where the deceased left a will so that a grant of Probate or Letters of Administration with the Will annexed is appropriate, the rules may have to be applied to cases of partial intestacy.

	1988	1989	1990	1991
Grants of Probate and Letters of Administration with the will annexed	172, 722	171, 964	182, 634	184, 291
Grants of Letters of Administration	61, 753	59, 919	60, 020	74, 071
Total number of Grants	234, 475	231, 883	242, 654	258, 362

The size of the task which the system is required to perform is an important factor in determining the form of the system.[4]

---

3   See the Civil Judicial Statistics.
4   See Plager, "The Spouse's Nonbarrable Share: A Solution in Search of a Problem" (1966) 33 *Univ. of Chicago* LR 681.

The formulation of the rules of intestate succession

The pre-1926 rules

Prior to 1926 the rules of intestate succession applicable to realty differed from those applicable to personalty. Under the rules of inheritance applicable to realty lineal descendants were entitled before ancestors, males were preferred to females of the same degree and among males of the same degree the eldest son was preferred. The rules applicable to personalty provided for a division between the children if there was no widow but if there was a widow she obtained one third and the children two thirds of the personalty. If there were no children the widow took one half with the other half passing to the father or mother of the intestate or in default to his brothers or sisters. On the death of a married woman, her husband took all her personal property if he survived her, to the exclusion of any children. If he did not survive, her personalty passed to the children. These two systems had evolved over a long period of time before being codified by Parliament.

Post-1925 rules

The Administration of Estates Act 1925 provided a new system of intestate succession applicable to both real and personal property.[5] The statutory system was based upon an examination of a large number of wills at the Probate Registry designed to ascertain the wishes of the majority of testators.[6] The same approach was taken by the Committee on Intestate Succession set up in 1950 which took into account statistics compiled at the Principal Probate Registry by taking a census of all wills proved over a certain period of time.[7] Amendments were made by the Intestates' Estates Act 1952 and the Family Provision Act 1966.[8]

The present system

The most striking feature of the system of intestate succession as it has developed since 1925 has been the extension of the rights of a surviving spouse at the expense of the children and other kin of an intestate. The rules were established in 1925 and developed in 1952 on the basis of provisions that testators then normally made in their wills. Accordingly this development must obviously reflect the wishes of those that made wills at

---

5   See Part IV.
6   See 2 Wolstenholme & Cherry's *Conveyancing Statutes* 1593.
7   Cm. 8310, para 18.
8   Some modification has however been made on policy grounds. See the Family Law Reform Act 1987 which changed the position in relation to illegitimate children.

least around 1925 and 1952.[9] However, the idea that the rules of intestate succession should reflect the wishes of the "average" or "typical" testator is probably no longer satisfactory, particularly in view of the more varied pattern of marriages.[10] Concern for the surviving spouse has also been an influence and this, together with the view that marriage should be regarded as a partnership of equals, have probably been more important considerations in the recent changes in the amount received by a surviving spouse and in efforts at reform.

The interest taken by the surviving spouse of an intestate after payment of funeral, testamentary and administration expenses, debts and other liabilities depends upon whether or not certain other relatives of the intestate also survive. If the intestate leaves no issue who attain an absolutely vested interest and no parent or brother or sister of the whole blood, then the residue is held in trust for the surviving spouse absolutely. If the intestate also leaves issue, then the surviving spouse takes the personal chattels absolutely and a fixed net sum (at present £75, 000) with interest to the date of payment, and subject thereto, the residue is held as to one-half upon trust for the surviving spouse during his or her life, and, subject to that life interest on the statutory trusts for the issue of the intestate. The other half of the residue is held on the statutory trusts for the issue immediately.

Finally, if the intestate leaves no issue, but is survived by one or more of one of the following, *i.e.* a parent, a brother or sister of the whole blood or issue thereof, then the surviving spouse takes the personal chattels absolutely and a fixed net sum (at present £125, 000) with interest to the date of payment. Subject thereto one half of the residue is held in trust for the surviving spouse absolutely and the other half is held in trust for the intestate's parents in equal shares or the survivor of them absolutely. If neither parent survives then that half is held in trust for the brothers and sisters of the whole blood of the intestate on the statutory trusts.[11]

If there is no surviving spouse then the residue is held on the statutory trusts for the issue. If there is no surviving spouse or issue then the residue is held in trust for the parents of the intestate in equal shares or the survivor of them. If the parents are dead then the residue will be held on the statutory trusts for the brothers and sister of the whole blood of the intestate, or if none for brothers and sisters of the half blood. In the absence of anyone so entitled the residue will pass to the grandparents of the intestate, and, if more than one, in equal shares. If they are all dead then the residue is held on the statutory trusts for the uncles and aunts of the whole blood of the intestate, or if none then for brothers or sisters of the half blood of the intestate. In default of anyone taking an absolute interest

---

9 See Glendon, *The New Family and the New Property* (1981) 21-22.
10 See L. C. Published Working Paper No.108, paras 4.2 – 4.3.
11 Administration of Estates Act 1925, s 46 as amended by the Intestates' Estates Act 1952 and the Family Provision Act 1966. S 1 of the 1966 Act empowers the Lord Chancellor, by order, to increase the amount of the statutory legacies. They were increased to their present figures by the Family Provision (Intestate Succession) Order 1987 (SI 1987/799).

under the foregoing provisions, then the residue passes to the Crown as *bona vacantia.*[12]

A surviving spouse has statutory rights to take a capital sum (calculated in accordance with the Act) instead of a life interest[13], and to require the residence in which he or she resided at the date of death and which forms part of the intestate's estate, to be appropriated in satisfaction of an absolute interest under the rules of intestate succession.[14] Where the statutory trusts apply then any member of the class must have been alive at the date of the intestate's death and must attain the age of 18 or marry under that age in order to obtain an absolute interest. Where a member of a class has predeceased the intestate issue of that person who are alive at the intestate's death and attain the age of 18 or marry under that age take through all degrees according to their stocks, in equal shares if more than one, the share which his or her parent would have taken if living at the death of the intestate.[15]

Defects of the present system

The position of the surviving spouse

The Law Commission found agreement that the principal defect of the present law is "the failure to ensure adequate provision for a surviving spouse."[16] This is because the statutory legacy is often insufficient to ensure that the surviving spouse is able to remain in the matrimonial home even though the estate is otherwise large enough to enable him or her to do so. Even if the legacy is sufficient to retain the home, it will often leave the survivor with very little on which to live or maintain the home.[17] The impact, however, varies. House values vary considerably from one part of the country to the other. The home may not have been wholly owned by the deceased spouse. If the spouses were entitled to the home as beneficial tenants in common then the deceased's interest in the home will form part of his or her estate and its value in relation to the amount of the statutory legacy remains important. If the spouses were entitled as beneficial joint tenants then the deceased's interest will automatically accrue to the survivor who will also be entitled to the full statutory legacy. While it is likely that most couples will have been advised that the automatic right of survivorship is one of the advantages of the joint tenancy the choice will not always have been a deliberate one especially in relation to other assets.[18]

---

12 *Ibid* s 46.
13 *Ibid* s 47A.
14 Intestates' Estates Act 1952, s 5.
15 Administration of Estates Act 1925, s 47.
16 L. C. No 187, para 17.
17 *Ibid* para. 18. In theory an application could be made under the Inheritance (Provision for Family and Dependants) Act 1975 but see *infra* (the text at n.22-23) for the relationship between appropriate provision under the intestacy rules and appropriate provision under the 1975 Act.
18 See L. C. PWP No 108, *Distribution on Intestacy* paras. 3.7-3.9 and L. C. No 187, paras 19 and 20.

The position of other members of the family

The Law Commission pointed out that under the present system the expectations of children will depend on the nature and tenure of their deceased parents' assets rather than upon the extent to which proper provision has been made for the surviving parent.[19] The hotchpot provisions applicable to children are complicated and have been much criticised.[20] In contrast there has been little demand for a change from *per stirpes* distribution to *per capita* distribution though this has caused much debate in the United States. The concept of "children of the family" has not been incorporated into the rules of intestate succession as it has into the family provision legislation. It would be difficult to incorporate such a concept with its in-built element of judgment into a system of fixed rights but the fact is that stepchildren are excluded from the rules of intestate succession. Their position is considered further in relation to family provision.

The rules also make no provision for cohabitants who must also look to the Inheritance (Provision for Family and Dependants) Act 1975 and claim as dependants.[21]

Reform

Fixed or discretionary system

Under the Inheritance (Provision for Family and Dependants) Act 1975 the court is given a discretionary power to order financial provision out of the deceased's estate for certain members of his or her family. This was preferred to a system of fixed rights of inheritance such as is common in the United States because it enables the court to fashion the solution appropriate to the circumstances of an individual case. The advantages and disadvantages of the two approaches are beyond the scope of this paper but it is clear that a discretionary system is feasible only where the potential number of cases is relatively small. Where a large number of cases arise every year a basic system of fixed rules is essential in the interests of certainty, ease of administration and expense. This is clearly the case with regard to intestate succession in contrast to the task faced by the system of family provision.[22]

However, while a basic system of fixed rules is essential, that system may provide for more than one situation. This occurs under the existing rules whereby the share of the surviving spouse depends upon what other relatives survive. This is carried further in the Uniform Probate Code under

---

19 L.C. No 187, para 21.
20 Administration of Estates Act 1925, s 49.
21 S1(1)(e).
22 See Plager, *loc cit* n.4

which the interest taken by the surviving spouse varies according to whether all the surviving issue are the issue of the surviving spouse as well as of the deceased.[23] Moreover, a system of fixed rules may be formulated in such a way as to enable a discretionary system to operate at the margins of the system of fixed rules.

Since the Intestates' Estates Act 1952 applications under the family provision legislation have been possible in the cases of intestacy.[24] There is only one reported case where a surviving spouse has applied for provision out of the estate of a person who died wholly intestate.[25] In many cases the surviving spouse will in practice inherit the whole estate, but even where this is not the case the standard of provision for a surviving spouse should on general principles be more generous than even the higher standard of provision for a surviving spouse under the 1975 Act. If the intestacy rules are intended to make the provision which a typical testator would have made one would expect this to be more generous than the minimum provision to which the survivor should be entitled under the 1975 Act for his or her maintenance and fair share in the family property.

Since the intestacy rules are based on a single model of a surviving spouse it is not surprising that the situations in which an application by a surviving spouse might be expected to succeed will be relatively few.[26] One situation where an application by a surviving spouse may be necessary is the where the deceased spouse has depleted his estate by *inter vivos* dispositions in favour of third parties so that there is only a small amount of property remaining on which the intestacy rules can bite. In such circumstances, the surviving spouse may need to make an application under the 1975 Act so as to take advantage of the anti-avoidance provisions of that Act and so increase the size of the net estate.[27] This was the case in *Jessop* v *Jessop*[28] where the Court of Appeal found it appropriate that the deceased intestate's severable share in a house vested in the names of himself and a cohabitant as joint tenants should be made available as part of the net estate to the extent necessary to provide a lump sum of £10, 000 for the applicant widow.

In the case of stepchildren and cohabitants, an application under the 1975 Act will be the only avenue open to them.[29] In neither case can the discretionary system be said to operate at the margins.

---

23 Ss2 – 102.
24 See now s 1 of the 1975 Act.
25 *Jessop* v *Jessop* [1992] 1 FLR 591.
26 The position would be different if the rules of intestate succession were to distinguish, *e.g.*, between spouses who had been the intestate's only spouse and spouses who had been the intestate's second spouse.
27 For the definition of "net estate" see s 25(1) and the avoidance provisions contained in ss 8-13.
28 [1992] 1 FLR 591.
29 A surviving cohabitant (or indeed a stepchild) may be able to establish a beneficial interest in property the title to which was vested in the deceased on the basis of a resulting or constructive trust or proprietary estoppel.

An application by a stepchild will be possible only if he or she has been treated as a child of the family in relation to a marriage of the deceased.[30] This may be the case even though the stepchild was an adult at the time of his or her parent's marriage to the intestate.[31] An application by a cohabitant will be possible only if he or she satisfies the conditions set out in paragraph (e) of s 1 (1) and s 1(3). In particular the court is required to balance the benefits received by the applicant from the deceased against the benefits conferred on the deceased by the applicant so as to show a degree of dependency on the deceased by the applicant. This has not been without its difficulties, but a more generous approach is now evident.[32] In the case of stepchildren and cohabitants provision is limited to maintenance in contrast to the more generous provision laid down for a surviving spouse. A broad view of maintenance has been taken in the case of applications by stepchildren in *Re Callaghan*[33] and *Re Leach*[34] where the property passed to brothers and sisters of the deceased under the intestacy rules. The Law Commission has recommended changes in the 1975 Act which would make it easier for cohabitants to establish a claim which would, however, still be based on maintenance.[35]

Arguments for giving the surviving spouse the entire estate

In a large number of cases the entire estate already passes to the surviving spouse because the value of the estate does not exceed the value of the statutory legacy. This is reinforced by the entitlement of the surviving spouse to the personal chattels and by the operation of the right of survivorship in relation to joint tenancies. The Law Commission pointed out that if the statutory legacy was raised to a level which is sufficient to ensure adequate provision for the surviving spouse, the practical result would be that this would cover the vast majority of cases.[36] There would remain a minority of cases where only a fraction of the estate was necessary to ensure adequate provision for the surviving spouse, but as the Law Commission says it would not be right for large estates to determine the rules for all intestacies and those with large estates are more likely to make wills. The problem of large estates where there may well be claims from a wider family group, could be dealt with to some extent without affecting the average estate by imposing a limit on the size of the estate which would pass to the surviving spouse. However, this is probably not the crucial issue in determining the basic system.

---

30 S 1 (1) (d) of the 1975 Act.
31 See *Re Callaghan* [1985] Fam.1 and *Re Leach* [1986] Ch 226.
32 See *e.g. Bishop* v *Plumley* [1991] 1 WLR 582.
33 [1985] *Fam* 1.
34 [1986] Ch 226.
35 L. C. No 187, para 59. They recommended a new category of applicant to cover those cohabitants who are already entitled to bring actions under the Fatal Accidents Act 1976, s 1 (3)(b).
36 L. C. No 187, para 30.

145

The crucial argument is that the solution proposed by the Law Commission would ensure support for the surviving spouse within the resources of the estate and would reflect the modern view of marriage as a partnership of equals. Moreover with increased life expectancy the need of surviving spouses for capital to provide for care is of growing importance and to be contrasted with the position of children who are likely to be middle-aged and well able to provide for themselves financially. If the children are minors or otherwise not yet self-supporting, then it is arguable that provision is better made for them through provision for the surviving spouse who can be relied upon to care for them at least where they are also the children of the surviving spouse. This view underlies the revised 1990 Uniform Probate Code which gives the entire estate to the surviving spouse where all of the decedent's surviving descendants are also the descendants of the surviving spouse and there is no other descendant of the surviving spouse who survives the decedent. It is said that "decedents do not perceive their own children as losing. Rather, they see the surviving spouses as occupying somewhat of a dual role, not only as their primary beneficiaries, but also as conduits through which to benefit their children."[37]

Arguments against

The rights of a surviving spouse depend entirely on status both at present and as envisaged by the Law Commission. Unless a marriage has been dissolved by a decree absolute of divorce or annulled by a decree of nullity in the case of a voidable marriage, the surviving spouse is and would be entitled in full despite the fact that the parties were separated unless a decree of judicial separation was in force.[38] The duration of the marriage is likewise irrelevant as is the fact that either or both parties had previously been parties to other marriages which is increasingly likely in view of the high incidence of divorce and remarriage. A system of fixed rules will inevitably produce some hard cases at the margins and it is difficult to see how such a system could in practical terms accommodate informal separation and unmeritorious behaviour on the part of the surviving spouse. It seems not unreasonable to leave such cases to be dealt with by appropriate wills.

The same view may be taken of the length of a marriage, but it is possible to formulate a more sophisticated rule whereby the whole estate will pass to the surviving spouse only if the marriage has lasted for a specified period. The elective share to which a surviving spouse is entitled under the revised Uniform Probate Code is calculated on an accrual basis ranging from 3% of the augmented estate where the marriage lasted between one and two years to 50% of the estate where the marriage has lasted 15 years or more, accruing first at 3% per year of the marriage, and, after 11 years at 4% per

---

37 Waggoner, "The Multiple-Marriage Society and Spousal Rights Under the Revised Uniform Probate Code" (1991) 76 *Iowa* LR 223 at 232.

38 See L. C. No 187, para 39.

year.[39] There is an element of artificiality, and perhaps arbitrariness, about such a system and it should be noted that this method is not applied by the Uniform Probate Code in the calculation of the intestate share of the surviving spouse, but to the elective share which is designed to perform the task performed by the Inheritance (Provision for Family and Dependants) Act 1975 in England and Wales and most common law jurisdictions.

In formulating a more sophisticated rule relating to the intestate share of a surviving spouse, the Uniform Probate Code has concentrated on the position where there are children who are not the children of both the intestate and the surviving spouse.[40] However, before considering the claims of children of previous marriages, it is important to consider the potential claims of children of the marriage in force at the date of death. The Law Commission's proposal ignores the interests of such children even if they are still minors. Nevertheless, there is much force in the view expressed by the Law Commission that the interests of such children are normally best served by their surviving parent being adequately provided for and restrictions on the use of property may inhibit the performance of this task.[41] If the surviving parent fails to care for the children satisfactorily then steps could be taken under the Children Act 1989.[42]

The greatest difficulty, however, arises in relation to surviving spouses of second or subsequent marriages where the intestate leaves issue of a former marriage. The Law Commission found that the majority of respondents in the public opinion survey took the view that such spouses should be treated differently.[43] Property which passes to the surviving spouse will certainly not pass to the children of the former marriage on the intestacy of the surviving spouse. Even if the surviving spouse makes a will, there may be a conflict between the claims of his or her own children and the claims of the deceased spouse's children by a previous marriage. Thus, even though a substantial part of the surviving spouse's estate may have been derived from the deceased spouse, it may pass to the surviving spouse's family rather than to the deceased spouse's family.

Nevertheless, the Law Commission concluded that the intestacy rules should not give issue of former marriages rights upon intestacy.[44] The first reason given is that this might mean that in some cases the surviving spouse would not receive adequate provision. This raises the question of what is adequate provision, or, indeed a fair share of the partnership property. Is the claim of a second or subsequent spouse who may have been married to

---

39 Ss 2 – 201. The "augmented estate" is defined in s 2 – 202 and includes not only property subject to certain *inter vivos* dispositions made by the intestate, but also property owned by the surviving spouse at the date of the intestate's death.

40 ss 2 – 102.

41 L. C. No 187, para 37.

42 S 15 and Sched 1. An application against the intestate's estate can of course be made by a child under the Inheritance (Provision for Family and Dependants) Act 1975, s 1 (1) (c) but an application can only be made with leave of the court after the expiration of six months from the grant of letters of administration to the intestate's estate.

43 L. C. No 187, para 41.

44 *Ibid* para 42.

the deceased for only a relatively short time for provision or a share in the intestate estate to be the same as a spouse who was married to the deceased for many years?

It is difficult to take into account the features of the marriage in formulating a fixed rule, but there is no reason why a fixed rule should not distinguish between cases where there are children by a previous marriage and those where there are not. This is done in the Uniform Probate Code which also distinguishes marriages where the surviving spouse has children who are not descended from the intestate. If that lower standard does not make adequate provision for the surviving spouse then an application under the Inheritance Act 1975 would be possible. While applications by the children of a former marriage are possible, they are limited in scope to maintenance. In this way the discretionary powers could become exercisable at the margins, whereas the formulation of the Law Commission allows little scope for the discretionary powers to refine the fixed system of rules.

Ways forward?

Identifying the problem

It now seems unlikely that the proposal of the Law Commission to give the entire estate to the surviving spouse in all circumstances will be implemented. The Lord Chancellor concluded that the views expressed recently in the House of Lords were "against legislating the Law Commission's scheme and in favour of a more elaborate proposal."[45] In considering what that more elaborate system might be, the first task is to identify the situation or situations in which the general rule proposed by the Law Commission is considered to be unsatisfactory. The main criticism seems to be concerned with the cases where the intestate left issue of a previous marriage.[46] However, it is not clear whether there is a widely held view that the length of the marriage to the surviving spouse is also a matter which ought to be taken into consideration. Where there are children of a previous marriage, the intestate's marriage to the surviving spouse may well have been entered into late in life and to have been of short duration, but this is not always the case. There is a very good chance that the previous marriage was determined by divorce and to have been of shorter duration than the subsequent marriage.

The crucial complaint of those who are unhappy with the whole estate passing to the surviving spouse seems to be the moral claim of the children of the previous marriage rather than a concern with the significance of the

---

45 Hansard HL Vol 538, col 177, June 16, 1992.
46 It may also be appropriate to consider the position where the surviving spouse has children by another marriage.

surviving spouse's contribution to the marriage. Nevertheless, a view must be taken as to whether the rules should attempt to take into account the contribution of the surviving spouse by having regard at least to the length of the marriage. The length of the marriage may also be thought to be an important factor in determining the level of support to which the surviving spouse is entitled.[47] However, while the surviving spouse's claim to support and to a fair share of the family assets on the basis of his or her contribution to the marriage partnership may be said to be the basis of provision for a surviving spouse under the family provision legislation, it is by no means clear that this is a sufficient formulation of the basis for a surviving spouse's claim on intestacy. The generally accepted objective in the latter case is a distribution which accords with provision made by a typical testator. In the absence of reliable evidence as to the provision made by testators for second or subsequent spouses, is it reasonable to expect the rules of intestate succession to do more than attempt to ensure provision for the needs and contribution of the survivor in a broad way leaving any deficiency to be made up under the 1975 Act?

The techniques

Having identified the problems, consideration can be given to the techniques to be utilised. There seem to be two basic techniques that might be employed either in the alternative or in combination, while special consideration may be appropriate with regard to the matrimonial home.

The first is to give the surviving spouse merely a life interest in the whole or part of the estate, at least above a certain figure either where there are children of the intestate or only where there are children of the intestate by a previous marriage. Apart from the disadvantage attaching to life interests, particularly where the capital is relatively small, this might not give the surviving spouse the capital needed for care in old age. Such a deficiency might be rectified where appropriate by an application under the family provision legislation where the court could take into account the appropriate level of support (and return for contributions to the marriage) according to the duration of the marriage and other factors.

The second approach is to give the surviving spouse a capital sum, which might be a specified sum or a fraction of the estate or a combination of the two. The capital sum could be fixed at a level which could depend on a number of factors. The existence of children of a previous marriage is a condition precedent to the application of this approach, but the amount might also take into account the existence of children of the survivor by some person other than the intestate. The length of the marriage could be taken into account, though this might be thought to introduce too much complication or if just one or two periods were selected, *e.g.* distinguishing between marriages which have lasted less than five years and those which

---

47 Should the surviving spouse's own property be taken into account?

have lasted more than five years, an element of arbitrariness. The result might be to leave the surviving spouse with inadequate provision to maintain herself. However, this depends entirely on what is regarded as appropriate.

Thus, where the intestate had married the surviving spouse say three years before his death when they were both aged over 60 and with children from previous marriages views will differ as to what the survivor should reasonably expect by way of provision from the estate. An application under the Inheritance Act 1975 would be open to the spouse who thought that the fixed provision inappropriate for his or her support and to give insufficient regard to his or her contribution to the marriage.

This leaves the question whether special provision needs to be made in relation to the matrimonial home. The first problem is to ensure that the surviving spouse can continue to live there for the rest of his or her life assuming this to be appropriate. A capital sum, which might be of modest size if the shortness of a marriage is taken into account or a fraction is utilised will not necessarily ensure this and a life interest has clear attractions in this respect. There will be cases where the only or principal asset available to provide a capital sum for the survivor will be the matrimonial home. Entitlement to a life interest will provide protection to the extent that the value of the house exceeds that capital sum. It would also produce fairness between the different forms of holding of the matrimonial home and between cases where the home forms a significant and perhaps major part of the intestate estate, and cases where it forms no part of the estate at all either because it is rented or because it is owned by the surviving spouse.

Conclusion

It seems clear that there is a substantial body of opinion that is unhappy with the surviving spouse receiving the whole of an intestate's estate in all circumstances. A more elaborate set of rules is necessary but the first requirement is to agree on the factors which will bring that more elaborate system into play. This brings into question the objectives of intestate succession and probably a reconsideration of the idea of a typical testator. Only then can a satisfactory attempt be made to deal with the problem. Moreover, any new system must be based on a clear idea of the relationship between the system of intestate succession and the system of family provision.

Part II
1995

Introduction

This collection of papers, like the first volume published in 1993, derives from an ongoing series of seminars organised by the Centre for Family Law and Family Policy at the University of East Anglia, Norwich, and led by academics both from the United Kingdom and abroad. The aim of the seminars is to analyse the law's response to the key policy issues affecting the family, and these essays illustrate the wide range of issues currently facing those who are working in this exciting and ever-changing field.

Although the topics under consideration are varied, they all seek to explore underlying themes critical to every aspect of family law. The fundamental question in this arena is the extent to which the law should prescribe within the unit we identify as the family. In a democratic and pluralistic society, what is appropriate in terms of intervention in families' conduct of their lives, is arguably the most difficult question that the law has to address anywhere. Central to this conundrum is the law's role in the protection of the most vulnerable members of the family against abuse or exploitation by those who are more powerful. Equally crucial though is the wider question of the function of the family unit within the fabric of society, and the use of the law as an instrument of social policy.

A significant recent development in family policy has been the emphasis on the notion of parental responsibility, evident in both the Children Act 1989 and the Child Support Act 1990. A prominent feature of this policy has been the promotion of the idea of the parental responsibility of genetic fathers for their children. In the first paper in this volume, Jane Fortin questions how important the blood-tie really is to parents and children, and suggests that the current debate as to whether there is a need for an automatic vesting of parental responsibility in a father for his non-marital child is misconceived. She contends, using the analogy of adoption law, that there is a clear case that social parentage should be privileged over biological parentage, and that, at present, legal policy and practice are confused and incoherent.

Frances Price discusses the rapidly evolving field of assisted procreation using gamete donation, where the lines between biological and social parentage have become well and truly blurred. In contrast to Jane Fortin, Price argues that the significance of genetic identity, whether to donors, recipients or the children produced as a result of donations, is not well understood. Since novel situations are arising all the time in reproductive medicine, and the law has already created inconsistencies, she suggests that there is an urgent need for research into the social processes involved in this highly controversial area of medical practice.

The paper by Sanford Katz addresses the question of decision-making in child custody cases in the United States. Although he focuses on the divorce process, much of what he says could be equally relevant to contests between biological and social parents. He highlights the changing fashions in custody dispositions over the years – the abandonment of the maternal preference rule, the emergence of joint and shared custody, and most recently the favouring of the primary caretaker – and he identifies the difficulties which the courts face in transcribing into practice the latest doctrinal shorthand.

The evolution of doctrine in cases involving children is the theme taken up by Mervyn Murch. He discusses the issues raised by the involvement of different professional groups in the system of legal adjudication of family matters. He examines how the clash of differing professional cultures can contribute to the often wholly unsatisfactory disposition of both public and private law cases. He looks at two connected issues in this regard: first, the organisational divisions in the system of family justice; second, the often competing professional values of different disciplines. In the course of his paper Murch evaluates the arguments put forward by those who believe that the autopoeitic nature of law inhibits co-operation with other professions. He argues forcefully against this view, and in favour of an inter-disciplinary approach. In particular, he advocates education and training as the answer, because, as he suggests, there is no alternative to achieving inter-disciplinary co-operation, however problematic.

One example of what can be seen as a failure to achieve an integrated inter-disciplinary approach, and the impact of this failure, is discussed by Gwyneth Boswell. She looks at what happens to children who commit very serious crimes such as murder, and their treatment within the criminal justice system. Her research shows that there is a disjuncture between two models of sentencing employed in respect of such young offenders, the treatment model and the punishment model. She discusses how many such young offenders will start their sentence at an institution oriented towards treatment, only to be moved to a punishment oriented institution when they are older. She argues that such a process almost invariably has an extremely negative outcome for the young people involved, and that there is an urgent need for a change towards a more coherent policy.

One of the most important shifts in policy relating to children brought about by the Children Act 1989, has resulted from the introduction of a threshold requirement to be satisfied before the majority of public support services may be made available to families. The test which must be met is that at least one child of a family seeking support from local authorities must be demonstrated to be "in need". In her paper, June Thoburn points out that this threshold not only conveys entitlement to be considered for provision by Social Services departments, but also bestows priority for education, health and housing services. Satisfying the statutory definition provides, in effect, a ticket to positive discrimination, and it is important, therefore, that the criteria should be clear and applied consistently. But she also asks whether parents feel diminished by having to prove to a social worker that their child is "in need", and identifies an urgent requirement for work to be done on the impact on parents' capabilities of being labelled by this terminology.

The next three papers in the volume are concerned with differing aspects of the state's obligations to protect human rights under international law. The papers examine not only the potential for conflict between state and individual, but also between notions of the rights of parents and those of children.

Carolyn Hamilton's paper looks at the nature of the parent's "right" to determine a child's religious education, and how this relates to the state's interest in controlling the content of the school curriculum. She assesses how the interests that particular communities have in preserving their religious and cultural identities in a pluralistic society, may come into conflict with the interests of the state in promoting cohesive social policies through the education system. She discusses the implications this has for what may be perceived as an individual child's best interests in relation to concepts of rights, for example, such as equality of opportunity, and discusses how, in the United Kingdom, parents who can afford to pay for private education can circumvent their dilemma.

Peter Newell, co-ordinator of the campaign to End Physical Punishment of Children continues this discussion in the context of corporal punishment of children. He argues that a child has a basic human right to personal physical integrity which should in no way be compromised for religious or cultural reasons. He discusses the inter-relationship between the tradition of physical punishment of children in the United Kingdom and child abuse, and his argument echoes that of Mervyn Murch when he calls for co-operation and a consensus against hitting children, amongst those involved professionally in child welfare and child law, in order to achieve a change in the culture.

Geraldine Van Bueren further explores the issue of the right of the child to physical integrity in her examination of the sexual abuse and exploitation of children. She too looks at the issue of cultural relativism and adopts a human rights perspective for her analysis, arguing this as the basis of a means of improving the protection of children. She argues that the conceptual framework of the debate needs to change before effective implementation of internationally agreed standards of child protection can be achieved.

The last two papers in this volume deal with the determination of the property rights of cohabitants. Together, these two papers represent a major contribution to the debate on the law relating to homesharers which is currently under consideration by the Law Commission.

Mika Oldham examines the inconsistency with which "homemaker services" are treated in English law, and the injustice of the way in which they are almost invariably undervalued. She argues for a proper recognition by society both of the worth of such contributions to the enterprise of family life, and of the problems posed for homemakers by their lack of financial security. In doing so she provides a comprehensive review of the different approaches which the law can offer to the solution of this problem.

Continuing the discussion, Patrick Parkinson addresses the question as to whether statutory reform can provide an answer. He looks in detail at legislative experience in Australia, and assesses this against the development of the caselaw in several common law jurisdictions. In this process he picks up and elaborates on some themes evident in the contribution by Thomas Oldham to the first volume in this series. Advocating a unified set of principles to encompass both married couples and cohabitees who satisfy certain criteria, Parkinson identifies parenthood as the key factor in distinguishing between different sorts of relationship, and different moral claims.

We believe that the contributions to this volume, as in the previous collection, provide academics, students and practitioners with an evaluation at the highest level of both theoretical issues and empirical evidence, and that these essays can justifiably claim to be at the "Frontiers of Family Law".

Contributors

GWYNETH BOSWELL is a Lecturer in Probation Studies in the School of Health and Social Work at the University of East Anglia, Norwich. She is chief author of *Contemporary Probation Practice* (1993) (with Martin Davies and Andrew Wright). Since 1991 she has made a particular study of young offenders who commit grave crimes, including the preparation of a report for the Prince's Trust, "Waiting for Change: An Exploration of the Experiences and Needs of Section 53 Offenders" upon part of which her chapter is based.

JANE FORTIN is a Solicitor and Senior Lecturer in Law at King's College, London. She has written widely on child law topics, and is co-editor (with Mary Hayes) of *Child and Family Law Quarterly* (formerly the *Journal of Child Law*). She runs a post-graduate course on child law and has developed a specialised diploma course for a wide range of professionals working in the child protection field. She is a council member of the children's charity, the Shaftesbury Homes and Arethusa, and is a part-time chair of the Child Support Appeal Tribunals.

CAROLYN HAMILTON is Senior Lecturer in Law at the University of Essex, where she is also Director of the Children's Centre, an inter-disciplinary centre for research into all aspects of children's lives. Recent publications include *Family, Law and Religion* (1995), and *European Family Laws* (1995) (edited with Kate Standley).

SANFORD N KATZ is Professor of Law at Boston College Law School, USA. He is the co-author of *Cases and Materials on Family Law: Legal Concepts and Changing Relationships* (1994) and he has written extensively in the field of family law over many years. He has been President of the International Society of Family Law and remains a member of its Executive Council.

MERVYN MURCH has been, since April 1993, Research Professor at the Cardiff Law School, University of Wales, where he specialises in the development of cross-disciplinary family justice studies. He previously taught law and applied social studies at the University of Bristol where he also founded and directed the Socio-Legal Centre for Family Studies. His published works include *Justice and Welfare in Divorce* (1980), *Marital Violence: the Community Response* (1993) (with Val Walker and Margaret Borkowski), *Grounds for Divorce* (1988) (with Gwynn Davis), *The Family Justice System*

157

(1992) (with Douglas Hooper) and *Pathways to Adoption* (1993) (with Nigel Lowe et al).

PETER NEWELL is co-ordinator of EPOCH, the campaign to end physical punishment of children, which was launched in 1988. He is also chair of the Council of the Children's Rights Development Unit. His publications include *Children are People Too: the Case Against Physical Punishment of Children* (1989) and *UN Convention on Children's Rights in the UK* (1991).

MIKA OLDHAM is a Fellow of Jesus College and a Lecturer in Law at the University of Cambridge where she teaches family and property law, and is Director of Studies for the LLM in family law. Her particular interests are in family property and comparative law.

PATRICK PARKINSON is an Associate Professor of Law at the University of Sydney, Australia. Originally from England, he studied law at Oxford and has an LLM from the University of Illinois. He taught at the University of Wales, Cardiff, before moving to Sydney. He has written extensively in the areas of family law, child protection, and the law on equity and trust, and is co-author (with S Parker and J Behrens) of *Australian Family Law in Context* (1994).

FRANCES PRICE is a Senior Research Associate at the Centre for Family Research at the University of Cambridge, having previously taught sociology at the University of Lancaster. She has conducted research and written widely on the social and ethical implications of the new reproductive technologies. Her recent publications include *Three, Four and More: a National Study of Triplets and Higher Order Births* (1990) (with B Botting and A Macfarlane) and *Technologies of Procreation: Kinship in the Age of Assisted Conception* (1993) (with J Edwards, S Franklin, E Hirsch and M Strathern).

JUNE THOBURN is Professor in Social Work at the University of East Anglia, Norwich. She has written widely on aspects of child and family law and social work practice, especially in the fields of adoption and child protection. Her book *Child Placement: Principles and Practice* (1994) (2nd ed) is widely used in the training of social workers.

GERALDINE VAN BUEREN is Senior Lecturer and Director of the Programme on International Rights of the Child at Queen Mary and Westfield College, London. She participated in the drafting of the Convention on the Rights of the Child at the United Nations. She has been a consultant to the Government of Uganda, the Commonwealth Secretariat and to Amnesty International on children's rights issues. She is co-editor in chief (with Michael Freeman) of *The International Journal of Children's Rights* and author of *The International Law on the Rights of the Child* (1994).

Chapter 11
Parenthood in Child Law – What is its Real Significance?

Jane Fortin
Senior Lecturer in Law, The Law School, King's College, London.

Introduction

Despite the growing tolerance of extended family networks created by increased unmarried birth and family breakdown, there remains considerable social uncertainty about the importance to be attached to the blood tie.

How important is the genetic link between parent and child and what legal recognition should be given to it? There appears to be very little clarity of thought or policy over this. On the one hand, there is legislation which treats the blood tie as having little legal significance. Thus section 27 of the Human Fertilisation and Embryology Act 1990 ignores the genetic link between the donor of an embryo and the embryo itself and states that the woman who carries the embryo to term is to be treated as the child's legal mother.[1] But another approach is to assume that the blood tie between parent and child carries an automatic significance which should be accompanied by legal responsibilities. Thus the Scottish Law Commission's 1992 Report on Family Law recommended:

> "In the absence of any court order regulating the position, both parents of the child should have parental responsibilities and rights, whether or not they are or have been married to each other."[2]

Further, at first sight, Lord Templeman's celebrated words in *Re KD* appear to inflate the importance of the bond between parent and child out of all proportion to its possible impact on the child itself. He stated in trenchant terms that:

> "The best person to bring up a child is the natural parent. It matters not whether the parent is wise or foolish, rich or poor, educated or illiterate, provided the child's moral and physical health are not endangered."[3]

---

1   Human Fertilisation and Embryology Act 1990 s 27(1). See also s 28(2) which treats the mother's husband as the legal father of a child conceived by sperm donation and not the donor.
2   Para 2.50 of The Scottish Law Commission's Report on Family Law (1992) Scot Law Com No 135.
3   [1988] AC 806 at 812.

In the course of considering this uncertainty, it is proposed first to discuss what appears to be confusion of thought underlying the proposals to reform the law relating to the status of unmarried fathers in this country. Next it is intended to consider the ambivalence apparent in the judicial treatment of contact disputes involving unmarried couples, and lastly the lack of coherence in the caselaw involving disputes between unmarried fathers and third parties over who is to bring the child up. In all three areas there appears to be considerable variation in perceptions over the weight to attach to the blood tie between the unmarried father and his child.

Law reform and the unmarried father

Ever since the English Law Commission's celebrated change of heart in 1982 over the legal status of the unmarried father[4], there has been increasing pressure to reform the law more radically, in order finally, to give him equality with the married father[5]. In particular, the fact that the unmarried father has to take some formal steps to obtain parental responsibility has been the subject of constant criticism. It was clear that the Scottish Law Commission's recommendation that all Scottish fathers should automatically acquire parental responsibilities in relation to their children, irrespective of their relationship with the mothers, would stimulate further calls for similar reforms in England and Wales[6]. But before advancing too far down this road, there should be some reflection on whether this reform would be of genuine benefit to those children who are born to mothers who have no good relationship with the fathers.

Dominated as it is by the welfare principle, few would deny that child law should reflect a good understanding of children's needs, and that this should underly the formulation of reforms relating to children and their relationships with their parents. Nevertheless, far from being justified by the child's own developmental needs, an approach to reform which attaches considerable significance to the blood tie between parent and child may actually harm the child. Child lawyers are not unfamiliar with the theories of child care experts such as Bowlby[7] and Rutter[8] who researched child attachment and its consequences. Bowlby's research indicated that during their early years, children who are deprived of a warm, intimate and

---

4   In the Law Commission's Working Paper No 74 on Illegitimacy (1979), the Law Commission had suggested that unmarried fathers should automatically acquire all parental rights and duties by virtue of their parenthood: para 3.16. The Law Commission resiled from that position in their subsequent report on Illegitimacy (Law Com No 118), see para 4.50, and recommended instead the present law, whereby the courts scrutinise the child's interests before permitting parental responsibilities to vest in the unmarried father.

5   e.g. Eekelaar, "Second Thoughts on Illegitimacy Reform" (1985) 15 *Fam Law* 261; Bainham, "When is a Parent not a Parent? Reflections on the Unmarried Father and his Child in English Law" (1989) 3 *IJLF* 208.

6   See Bainham, "Reforming Scottish Children Law – Sense from North of the Border" 1993) 5 *JCL* 3 at 7. In the event, this recommendation of the Scottish Law Commission did not find its way into the Children (Scotland) Bill published in 1995 and it seems unlikely that such a change will become part of Scottish law.

7   Bowlby, *Child Care and the Growth of Love* (Penguin, 1965).

8   Rutter, *Maternal Deprivation Reassessed* (Penguin, 1972).

continuous relationship with the mother, or a permanent mother substitute, run a grave risk of developing a range of disturbances in later life, including delinquency, affectionless psychopathy and difficulties in parenting their own offspring.[9] Goldstein, Freud and Solnit made child attachment theories accessible to lawyers by placing them in the context of legal disputes. It was they who instructed family lawyers so clearly that the child's psychological parent need have no blood tie with the child, explaining that:

> "Whether any adult becomes the psychological parent of a child is based thus on day-to-day interaction, companionship, and shared experiences. The role can be fulfilled either by a biological parent or by an adoptive parent or by any other caring adult – but never by an absent, inactive adult, whatever his biological or legal relationship to the child may be."[10]

It is difficult to understand how acceptance of the proposition that the most important person to a child is his psychological or social parent can be squared with the Scottish Law Commission's recommendation that a child's biological parents should have automatic legal responsibility for their child. Deech criticises what she calls "the unmarried fathers' rights movement" and points out that "to a child too young to understand the background to such a claim [the biological tie] it is meaningless unless accompanied by physical and social intimacy".[11] Since for at least some children born to unmarried parents the blood tie may carry little significance, there seems little justification for giving all unmarried fathers automatic equality with their married counterparts, when there is a risk that, in those cases where conflict exists between the parents, such a change will introduce additional stresses into the children's lives.

Such a reform is sometimes justified by the suggestion that the child is entitled to a legal relationship with his natural father, because this is part of the child's personal heritage, and to deny him this link is to deny him security of identity.[12] Such claims may be influenced by research findings focusing primarily on the child's developmental needs in the context of fostering and adoption, a rather different context to that of the parental custody disputes discussed by Solnit, Freud and Goldstein. As Thoburn has explained[13], in order to achieve self-esteem, children must have a sense not only of permanence, which is acquired through the love and care of their immediate family, but also a sense of identity, acquired through knowing about their birth families and past relationships. Recognition of this latter need has been a very potent force in producing changes in adoption law and practice. In particular, the Houghton Committee[14] were impressed by the research of Triseliotis[15] which drew attention to the shock felt by some

---

9   Bowlby, *op cit* n. 8 at 13-15.
10 Goldstein *et al*, *Beyond the Best Interests of the Child*, (Free Press, 1973) at 19.
11 Deech "The Unmarried Father and Human Rights" (1992) 4 *JCL* 3.
12 *e.g.* Bainham, *op cit* n. 6.
13 Thoburn, *Child Placement: Principles and Practice* (Wildwood, 1988) 31.
14 The Departmental Committee on the Adoption of Children (1972) Cm. 5107.
15 Triseliotis, *In Search of Origins* (Routledge & Kegan Paul, 1973).

adopted people when discovering by accident that they had been adopted, either from documents or letters or by chance remarks by people outside the family; and to the fact that many found it difficult to come to terms with a late disclosure of this information.[16] As a result of the Houghton Committee's call for greater openess in adoption[17], reforms were introduced allowing adopted people to discover the identity of their birth relatives.[18] Indeed it is now national policy for all adoption agencies to require from couples selected to become adoptive parents a commitment to tell their adoptees about the circumstances of their adoption. Thus it is no surprise that the Inter-Departmental Review of Adoption Law stated that: "It is now generally undisputed that many adopted people experience the need to know about their origins"[19] and stressed "It is essential that an adopted child of sufficient age and understanding is told that he or she is adopted and what this means". It also recommended that all agencies be obliged to advise adoptive parents that "it is fundamental to the welfare of the child that he or she is told (when of sufficient age and understanding) about his or her adoptive status."[20]

The information about a child's needs gained from adoption research and practice can usefully inform the discussion about how best to reform the law relating to the unmarried father. It indicates that all children have a need to know about their origins at as early an age as possible and that secrecy can be damaging and should be avoided at all costs. Interestingly though, the adopted children's need for information about their parentage is not necessarily also associated with an additional need to establish a relationship with their natural parents. This is borne out by the fact that many adopted children who obtain copies of their original birth certificates do not intend to seek out their natural parents.[21] This is easily explained by recalling the concept of the psychological parent. Thus whilst the adopted child may need to fill the gaps in his past by acquiring information about his birth parents, his need for love and affection is still fulfilled by his adoptive or psychological parents.

Thus by analogy, whilst all children born to all unmarried couples may require their need for a sense of identity to be promoted by a law entitling them to discover the identity of their birth father, there is no developmental need for that law to create a legal relationship between them and their fathers through the automatic vesting of parental responsibility. Indeed statistics show that many children born to unmarried couples may not need any change in the law, since the typical situation is one where the father is already living in a stable union with the mother – so the child's sense of identity and need for love is already well founded on a secure relationship

---

16 *Op cit* n. 15 at paras 300-301.
17 *Ibid* at paras 299-301.
18 See Adoption Act 1976 s 51 which enables adopted persons to obtain access to their birth records and s 51(A) which establishes an Adoption Contact Register. See also *Review of Adoption Law* Report to Ministers of an Inter-Departmental Working Group Consultation Paper (DoH, 1992) paras 4.1-4.10.
19 *Ibid* at para 31.3; see also 121 at para 15.
20 *Ibid* at para 27.4.
21 See (1983) *Adoption and Fostering* 7(2) 51.

with both parents.[22] In these cases, their successful cohabitation might certainly justify the father acquiring parental responsibility, as he may under the present law, but this would not necessarily promote the child's developmental needs.

In situations where the unmarried father has no existing relationship with the child, perhaps because his relationship with the mother was merely a casual and short-term liaison, the automatic acquisition by him of parental responsibility merely in order to give the child a sense of personal origins seems an over-drastic remedy which, rather than fulfilling the child's developmental needs, may instead cause damaging friction. Again, applying the analogies of adoption law, in such a situation, the child may indeed require his need for a sense of identity to be promoted by a law entitling him to discover the identity of his birth father, perhaps through the establishment of a paternity register. Indeed the Child Support Act 1991 makes the idea of a national paternity register very feasible. The Act's requirement that all mothers on income support identify the fathers of their children in order to facilitate the Child Support Agency's task of collecting maintenance from absent parents[23], means that this information will be recorded officially and could, like adoption records, be made available to persons authorised to see it.[23a] This innovation would not only address the child's need for a sense of identity with his past, but also give him what might be crucial information about his medical and genetic history. It was Katharine O'Donovan who in the course of criticising the continued secrecy surrounding artificial insemination by donor (AID) birth, pointed out that: "In its exclusive concentration on *psychological needs* the literature on the 'search for origins' overlooks the [more] practical reasons why their genetic parentage is of interest to children".[24] Nevertheless, experience gained from adoption practice suggests that the child has no developmental need for the blood tie to be invested with an additional legal relationship.

This approach is consistent with Eekelaar's views. He points out that English law has already developed a complex structure of parenthood which accommodates biological parenthood, legal parenthood and parental responsibility.[25] He criticises the assumption that biological parenthood and social parenthood should be linked, particularly when the Children Act 1989 allows parental responsibility to be detached from legal and biological parenthood and attached instead, through a residence order, to persons exercising social responsibility. He points out that the advances of medical science have achieved a situation whereby biological parenthood can now

22 By 1993, the rate of births outside marriage in the UK had reached over 30% ((1995) Social Trends Table 2.1). By 1988 around three quarters of these births were being jointly registered ((1995) Social Trends, 42).

23 Child Support Act 1991 s 6(9).

23a *In Re C* (1995) 1 FLR 201 Ewbank J held that the court had no power under s 50 Child Support Act 1991 to direct the Secretary of State to disclose information held by the Child Support Agency. The applicant was a boy of 17 who desired information about his father's whereabouts.

24 O'Donovan "What Shall we Tell the Children?" in Lee and Morgan (eds) *Birthrights* (Routledge, 1990) at 108. Emphasis added.

25 Eekelaar, "Parenthood, Social Engineering and Rights" in Morgan and Douglas (eds), *Constituting Families: A Study in Governance* (Steiner, 1994).

be established with near certainty. In the light of this and the growing tendency of people to take their genetic origins seriously, he suggests that biological parenthood should now be legally recognised in all cases but should carry no automatic responsibilities. He considers however, that parental responsibility should always be associated with the exercise of social parenthood and that it should be exercised automatically by married couples, but also acquired by longer-term cohabitees and step-parents.[26]

Eekelaar's suggested reforms would neatly solve the problem of how best to reform the law relating to the absent unmarried father. It would certainly deal more effectively with circumstances like those arising in *Re F*[27] than the outcome achieved in that case by the Court of Appeal. A baby girl, aged just over one, was being brought up by her mother in a stable family setting with her husband. The mother's transitory relationship with another man, B, had been terminated before the child was born. B, though he had never met the child, was convinced that he was her father. He applied for a parental responsibility order (PRO) and a contact order and sought DNA tests to establish his paternity. B's application was strongly opposed by the mother; she alleged that considerable disruption would be caused to the family unit if he was shown to be the child's father, because he would then apply for increasing contact with her.

The Court of Appeal approved of the refusal of Judge Callman, in the court below, to refuse the putative father's application for blood tests. Like Judge Callman, their Lordships were particularly influenced by the view that even if tests proved the applicant's paternity, any further application he brought for parental responsibility and contact would fail. In their view, since there was no realistic prospect of the applicant succeeding in obtaining either order, there was little point in exposing the child to the possible disadvantages of a blood test, with the accompanying disruption that the mother claimed would be inflicted on the household. It is a pity that the illogicality of Judge Callman's reasoning was accepted by the Court of Appeal. It would have been perfectly possible for the court to decide that although it might not necessarily benefit the child to meet her natural father, she should have the opportunity to discover the truth about her origins. Indeed, in the leading case of *S v McC; W v W*[28], decided twenty years earlier, both Lord Hodson and Lord Morris of Borth-y-Gest acknowledged this need in their judgments. Lord Hodson said:

> "it must surely be in the best interests of the child in most cases that paternity doubts should be resolved on the best evidence, and, as in adoption, the child should be told the truth as soon as possible."[29]

The Court of Appeal's decision in *Re F* had perfectly laudable objectives; it addressed the child's need for continued love and affection from those in her immediate family unit, undisturbed by the stress of interference from

---

26 Eekelaar, *ibid.*
27 (1993) 1 FLR 598. See a discussion by Fortin in "Re F: The Gooseberry Bush Approach" (1994) 57 *MLR* 296.
28 [1972] AC 24.
29 *Ibid* at 59.

outside.[30] But arguably the decision only addressed the child's short-term interests; the court placed considerable faith in the continuing success of the mother's current relationship and failed to give adequate weight to the child's need to discover the truth about her origins or genetic parentage. It is unlikely that in the event of the mother's marriage subsequently breaking up, the child, now older, would be grateful for the court's refusal to allow blood tests if she discovered the doubt surrounding her paternity. Eekelaar points out that the rationale for the Court of Appeal's decision in Re F[31], is that the child's biological parentage will not be accompanied by social parentage, and that its confirmation might disturb an existing parentage. If his own approach were followed, there would be no fear of directing blood tests on the application of a putative father like B, since there would be no expectation that their outcome would also be accompanied by the establishment of social parentage between him and the child. Legal parentage would carry no more than a biological identity.

It seems unlikely that those advocating legal reforms giving all unmarried fathers an automatic legal parental relationship with their children would be satisfied with the changes in the law suggested above, since these would only give the unmarried father the right to ensure that his child was given information about his identity and no more. Most critics of the existing law, including Eekelaar himself, have favoured the unmarried father being given complete equality with the married father.[32] But this change seems far more appropriate for the unmarried father who is living with the mother, and as discussed above[33], statistics show that these fathers are steadily increasing in number. It may make little sense to them to insist on taking active steps to gain a legal status relating to their children, particularly when the majority appear to be ignorant of the need to do so.[34] But if reforms were introduced to redress this situation, they should be seen clearly for what they were – reforms based on the needs of the unmarried father to be treated on an equal basis with the married father. They cannot be justified by theories about the child's developmental needs.

It should be noted that if English law were reformed so that all unmarried fathers acquired automatic parental responsibilities, it would then be difficult for the courts to resist applications for blood tests in cases like Re F. The putative father might then very reasonably claim that it would be against public policy to deny him the chance of proving the existence of an important legal status in relation to the child. If such a change were introduced, a putative father might have a better chance of success than

30 See also Re JS [1980] 1 All ER 1061, a case involving very similar facts to those in Re F, where the putative father's application for a determination of his paternity was treated with little sympathy by the Court of Appeal.

31 (1993) 1 FLR 598.

32 See Eekelaar (1985) 15 Fam Law 261; Bainham (1989) 3 IJLF 208.

33 See n. 22.

34 A recent report on the attitudes of cohabiting mothers to motherhood outside marriage, records that a substantial proportion of the mothers in the research cohort did not understand the legal position of their partner vis-a-vis their children and were mistaken about the legal implications of joint registration and remaining unmarried. S. McRae, Cohabiting Mothers: Changing Marriage and Motherhood? (Policy Studies Institute, 1993) at 71.

than B in *Re F* if he claimed the assistance of principles of international law. In *Re F*, B claimed a breach of Article 7 of the United Nations Convention on the Rights of the Child – which provides that a child shall have "as far as possible, the right to know and be cared for by his or her parents". It is unfortunate that Balcombe LJ failed to give adequate attention to this plea and in particular to the alleged breach of the first part of Article 7 – the child's right to know both parents. This he ignored entirely, focusing instead on the child's right to be cared for by both parents. In relation to this, he discounted B's claim by noting merely that joint care by B and Mrs F was acknowledged to be impossible.[35] There may also be scope for similar claims being brought under the European Convention of Human Rights. Article 6 guarantees everyone, in the determination of his civil rights and obligations, a fair and public hearing by an independent and impartial tribunal. Arguably, a decision to refuse an applicant a direction for blood tests constitutes a breach of this Article by effectively barring a claimant like B from obtaining a judicial hearing of his claim to paternity.[36]

Unmarried fathers and contact applications

Concern was expressed above over conferring on unmarried fathers automatic parental responsibilities; this was directed primarily at those situations where the fathers have not established any relationship at all with their children. By way of contrast, in cases where an unmarried father is applying for contact with his child, the child's own developmental needs may well justify the courts promoting a good relationship, if that relationship is one which has already been established between them. Even in those contact disputes where there has been no such ongoing relationship, the courts should be prepared to address the child's need for information about his father's identity and background.

Nevertheless, considerable confusion about the importance to be attached to the child's blood tie with his father appears to underly the judicial treatment of contact applications brought by unmarried fathers. In these cases, there appears to be considerable judicial ambivalence about the importance to the child of maintaining ties with his unmarried father in the face of opposition from his mother. Indeed, for some time emerging caselaw indicated a far greater likelihood of the courts viewing sympathetically a contact application brought by a married father, than such an application brought by an unmarried father. Interestingly, this difference in treatment was not apparent in the judicial approach to

---

35 *op cit*, n. 31 at 604.
36 See *K v United Kingdom* App No 11468/85 in which the applicant, an unmarried father, alleged, *inter alia*, breach of Art 6 arising from his inability to participate in care proceedings relating to his child. See discussed by Bainham, [1989] supra at 214. See also *K, Z and S v The Netherlands* App No 18535/91: The European Commission of Human Rights recently declared admissible an application brought by a Dutch couple claiming violation of Arts 8 and 14. They claimed that Dutch law prevented family law relations being established between the unmarried father and his child, because the mother was married to another man and the child was legally presumed to be that man's offspring.

parental disputes to decide which parent was to have day-to-day care of the child;[37] presumably because it was always abundantly clear in these disputes that the central issue to be assessed was the quality of the child's relationship with his prospective carer and not the father's status.

When it came to disputes over contact, as opposed to care, the courts' responses only seemed predictable when dealing with applications from married fathers. Thus the outcome of disputes between mothers and separated husbands over the extent to which the latter could retain contact with their children, on the whole reflected the assumption that if the husband had had a parental relationship with his child, its continuation would be beneficial to the child and should be promoted, even if there had been recent gaps in communication and even against the mother's strong opposition.

This judicial approach to contact applications by married fathers emerged relatively early. There was abundant caselaw, old and new, indicating that only the most exceptional circumstances would justify the court deciding that the married father should have no contact with his children.[38] Despite a new awareness of the need to consult the child, and the direction to that effect in the Children Act 1989[39], the courts might still order this contact to continue even against the clear wishes of reasonably mature children. Thus in *Re B*[40] Waite J, commented that the very limited contact he was ordering:

> "would on the one hand, prevent the father from becoming an unknown quantity in the children's minds, elevated, perhaps through absence, to a status inviting fear or fantasy in crucial teenage years. It would, on the other hand, avoid subjecting them during that crucial period to the distress involved in over-frequent contact with a figure who, perhaps through no fault of his, has become a source of distress or bewilderment to them and whom, in their present frame of mind, they would prefer not to see."[41]

These words made it clear that Waite J's approach was based, not on an automatic acceptance of the importance of the blood tie between parent and child, but on an acceptance that the child's developmental need for relationships with important people in his past life should be valued rather than being blocked off.

---

37   Butler-Sloss J in *Re O* (1992) 1 FLR 77 at 81 stated that she could "see no distinction in principle between a father who applies for the custody of his putative child and a father who applies for the custody of his child of the marriage."

38   *e.g. D v D* (1974) 4 Fam L 195: father released from prison having wounded his wife and murdered his brother-in-law given supervised access; *L v L* (1989) 2 FLR 16 father who had sexually abused his 5-year old daughter given supervised access. See also *H v H* (1989) 1 FLR 212: father who had sexually abused his 11-year old daughter given supervised access. See more recently *Re F* (1993) 2 FLR 830 where the Court of Appeal disapproved of the court below dismissing the father's application for contact, despite the evidence of his dishonesty, violence and involvement with drugs and glue sniffing.

39   Children Act 1989(3)(a).

40   (1992) 1 FLR 140: despite their father's bizarre and embarrassing behaviour, and despite the opposition of the two children of the marriage, aged 11 and 12, their father was awarded quarterly supervised contact. Per Waite J [CA] it was quite clear from the evidence that if the court had allowed the contact visits to terminate, as the children and their mother wanted, the children would lose all touch with their father.

41   *Ibid* at 146.

For a significant time the higher courts often appeared far less sympathetic to claims for contact brought by unmarried fathers. In cases where the mother opposed the unmarried father's claim for contact, the courts showed little of Lord Templeman's veneration for the blood tie between the father and his child.[42] Indeed the higher courts signalled disapproval of the lower courts justifying such contact by placing "a disproportionate weight"[43] on the blood tie between the father and his child. They seemed particularly concerned to avoid the natural father disrupting any new family unit the mother might have established and appeared to accept with little reservation the mother's claims that her new partner has replaced the natural father in the child's affections. Indeed in some cases, like Re W[44], the courts appeared to adopt a faintly moralistic approach to the mother who had married a man, not the child's father, and was now bringing the child up in a newly formed marital unit. Thus in that case, Heilbron J considered that:

> "The magistrates did not take into account that this mother had been fortunate enough to find and fall in love with a man against whom not a word of criticism had been made, who had offered marriage and who accepted with love and kindness her child by another man... For a mother in these circumstances to seek to make a fresh start in marriage, with the blessing of her own family and that of her fiance's, must be, one would have thought, not only very desirable for her, but very much in P [the child's] interests."[45]

These words implicitly suggested that since this unmarried mother's new partner had, through marriage, conferred respectability on her and her child, the child's father should not be allowed to disrupt things for the new marital unit. Nevertheless, in fairness to Heilbron J, apart from the first eight weeks of the child's life, the father had never had any contact with his son, and by the time of the contact application, the boy was already 2-years old. So there was little question of nurturing a relationship with an adult already important to the child. But the decision of no contact did nothing to promote the child's sense of identity with his past, and although Heilbron J did envisage his being told the truth about his paternity at some time in the future[46], there was obviously a danger that this might never happen. It is in circumstances like this that the establishment of a paternity register might be very appropriate.

The decision in Re W, where there had been no real relationship between the child and his father was less worrying than two other cases, Re C[47] and Re SM.[48] The facts of the two cases were not dissimilar to each other. In Re C, although the parents had not cohabited, the father had had very frequent contact with his daughter until she was 18-months old, when the mother

---

42 In Re KD [1988] AC 806 at 812.
43 See Heilbron J in Re W (1989) 1 FLR 163 at 172. See also Sir Stephen Brown P in Re SM (1991) 2 FLR 333 at 339.
44 Re W op cit n. 43.
45 Ibid at 168.
46 Ibid at 173.
47 (1991) 21 Fam L 417.
48 (1991) 2 FLR 333.

reduced it. On the father's application, the magistrates had granted him an order for generous contact – twice a week, including staying contact overnight. On appeal, Ewbank J reduced the amount of staying access, commenting that the magistrates' view that it was in the child's best interests to get to know the non-custodial parent and spend time with him, was a particularly unusual approach in relation to illegitimate children. This approach was worrying, since it implied an assumption that the developmental needs of a non-marital child were significantly different from those of the child of a marital union.

Fortunately, Ewbank J's attitude to non-marital children did not lead him to terminate contact altogether; this was the outcome in *Re SM*. There the father had visited his daughter once a month, until she was just under 2-years old, when the mother re-married her ex-husband and refused further contact. The magistrates listed their reasons for ordering contact to continue, and showed a sensitive appreciation of its value to the child and the fact that continued contact could be made to work successfully "by reason of the maturity of all the parties and the affection to the child expressed by all parties".[49] Sir Stephen Brown P allowed the mother's appeal against the order and criticised the court welfare officer for referring to the theoretical general principle in favour of access between a child and his natural parent, without indicating in what way *this* child would gain any positive benefit from continued contact with her father. But arguably this criticism was unjust. In the first place, it is always difficult to see how predictions about the strength of a future relationship can be anything but theoretical. Moreover, such a requirement implicitly created a rebuttable presumption that contact would not be beneficial, which the father had somehow to rebut. It was entirely unclear how the father could establish with any certainty what positive advantages would spring from it. It was encouraging to note that Hollis J in the later case of *Re H*[50] specifically disagreed with the need to establish some positive advantage for the child in the access taking place.[51] Sir Stephen Brown P may also have underestimated the wisdom of the welfare officer's assertion that:

> "L [the child] could only benefit from contact with her father and his parents. Experience shows that if access is established while the child is still young, it can become an accepted and pleasurable part of life and a good relationship formed with the absent parent. Disruption is more likely to occur if the child learns the truth at a later date".[52]

Both Sir Stephen Brown in *Re SM* and and Heilbron J in *Re W*, were influenced by the information that the child thought of the mother's new partner as his or her real father, and referred to him as "Daddy". In such circumstances, both judges considered that it would be confusing to introduce a new father into the picture. This approach was unsatisfactory for two reasons: first, it underestimated a child's ability to "have multiple

---

49 *Ibid* at 335.
50 (1993) 1 FLR 484.
51 *Ibid* at 487.
52 (1991) 2 FLR 333 at 338.

attachments" in his life – a child is perfectly capable of relating well to a number of people[53] and will work out for himself the feelings he attaches to them – by contrast the names he attaches to them are learnt from adults. Second, and of greater importance, is that it gave the mother a most effective and relatively easy method of blocking the unmarried father's claim for contact. Parents can manipulate their children and it is a simple step for a mother to teach her child to call her new partner "Daddy" and to treat him as a father.

In many of these cases, a mothers' implacable hostility to an unmarried father's contact claim appeared to reinforce the court's reluctance to equate his position with that of his unmarried counterpart.[54] Many decisions indicated that the courts were unclear in their own minds over what importance to attach to the unmarried father who wanted contact against the wishes of the mother. Certainly there was an absence of the certainty displayed when dealing with contact applications brought by married fathers, or any acceptance that contact is intrinsically beneficial. Indeed, as the discussion above indicates, the reverse presumption often seemed to apply. Thus in these disputes, far from inflating the importance of the blood tie, the courts seemed tempted to ignore its existence altogether.

More recently, however, the judiciary has been at pains to emphasise the potential benefit to a child of retaining contact with both natural parents. Thus Wall J has indicated that the present law on contact could be summarised by three propositions: that wherever possible the child should get to know his estranged parent and cogent reasons should be given for denying contact; that no court should deprive a child of contact to a natural parent unless wholly satisfied that it should cease and it should be extremely slow to reach this conclusion; and lastly that it is the normal assumption that a child would benefit from continued contact with a natural parent.[55] It is notable that Wall J did not qualify the wording of any of these three propositions for application to unmarried as opposed to married parents. This modern approach has also been linked with a new preparedness to "get tough" with mothers displaying an implacable hostility to the father's desire for contact[56], even in cases where the couple had never married. Thus Booth J in Re P[57] was content with the magistrates' conclusion that despite his

---

53 Schaffer, *Mothering: The Developing Child*, (Fontana, 1977) 108. See also Butler Sloss LJ in *Re H* (1994) 2 FLR 776, who stressed the need to recognise the importance of some people in a child's life with no biological relationship to him, at 783.

54 *e.g.* in *Re D* (1993) 2 FLR 1, the Court of Appeal agreed with the court below that the mother's implacable hostility towards the unmarried father was a factor justifying the departure from the "general principle that a child should grow up in the knowledge of both his parents", see per Waite LJ at 7. The mother and her parents had alleged that the father had treated her with violence, drank to excess and dabbled in drugs; they did not trust his promises of being a changed man; contact application dismissed.

55 Wall J set out these propositions in *Re M* (1994) 1 FLR 272 at 279 and in *Re D* (1995) 1 FLR 495 at 504.

56 "... judges should be very reluctant to allow the implacable hostility of one parent (usually the parent who has a residence order in his or her favour), to deter them from making a contact order where they believe the child's welfare requires it" per Balcombe LJ in *Re J* (1994) 1 FLR 729 at 736.

57 (1994) 2 FLR 374.

mother's extreme anxieties[58], the child would benefit from knowing his unmarried father as he grew up. It is too early to predict whether this caselaw heralds a fairer "deal" for unmarried fathers bringing opposed applications.

In many contact disputes between unmarried parents, there is not only the risk of the child losing touch with his father, but also of the child being kept in ignorance of the truth of his paternity. Recent caselaw however, indicates that some courts, if reluctant to allow contact between the unmarried father and child when opposed by the mother, are even more reluctant to allow the unmarried father to be sent away empty handed. Instead he may be provided with a compromise – being granted a PRO instead of a contact order. As *D v Hereford and Worcester CC*[59] and *Re H*[60] established, the inability of the father to enforce the parental responsibility order in such a way as to promote an active relationship between him and the child[61], does not justify refusing to grant him the order entirely. The rationale for such this approach is that a parental responsibility order, far from being entirely nugatory, will give the father other more long-term benefits, such as the right to veto the child's adoption. It was adopted by the Court of Appeal in *Re C and another.*[62] Although the court felt unable to allow the unmarried father contact with his two young children because of their mother's implacable opposition, it nevertheless granted him a parental responsibility order. Mustill LJ said:

> "Whichever way the future goes, it seems to us that the link which the father established with the boys in their earliest months is worth maintaining, for his sake as well as for theirs, and would justify the making of a PRO at this stage."[63]

This approach may be acceptable in those cases where there is genuinely no reasonable hope of establishing a good ongoing relationship between the child and the father. It is however, hardly fair to the father who already has a good relationship with his child, since although it avoids dispatching him from the child's life entirely, it also prevents him having any clear psychological role in relation to the child. There is also a risk that in cases where the mother is opposed to continued contact, despite the father's excellent relationship with his child, the courts will be tempted to grant the father a PRO as a easier alternative to imposing a contact order on a reluctant mother. Thus in *Re H* the father appealed from the refusal of the court below to give him either a contact order or a PRO, despite the fact that he already had a genuine and loving relationship with his son, now aged two. On appeal the Court of Appeal confirmed that the stability of the child's home could not be undermined by giving him contact, in the face of the attitude of the boy's step-father, a most unstable character, who threatened

---

58 Though the magistrates considered that the father had behaved in a highly irresponsible way towards mother and son, treating her with unjustifiable unkindness and violence, and despite the evidence of the mother's doctor that renewed contact would significantly risk the mother's mental health, they considered that she was capable of putting the child's needs before her own and coming to terms with this.

59 (1991) 1 FLR 205.

60 (1991) 1 FLR 214.

61 For example by opposing the Local Authority in their plans for the child whilst in Local Authority care.

62 [1992] 2 All ER 86.

63 *Ibid* at 93.

to leave the mother if contact was ordered. Although the courts at both levels agreed that in normal circumstances the child would have the right to grow up knowing his real father and building a relationship with him, they felt that this was impossible in view of the acrimony existing between the three adults. In the circumstances, the Court of Appeal thought the father was entirely qualified to be granted a PRO straight away to enable him to oppose any adoption application the step-father might mount. It is doubtful whether this outcome was in the child's long-term best interests. The step-father effectively bullied his wife and the court into allowing him to get his own way; more might have been achieved for the welfare of the mother and child by calling his bluff and ordering contact, albeit against his wishes.

Despite the obvious risks of utilising the PRO as a means of avoiding difficult decisions over contact, its use does, at the very least, promote the child's sense of identity, insofar as the mother is unlikely to omit telling the child of the father's existence. Moreover it ensures that the natural father retains not only the right to veto the child's adoption, but also the right to supplant any testamentary guardian, on the mother's death.

Disputes between the unmarried father and third parties

As discussed above, in the past the courts often treated the unmarried father's application for contact, if opposed by the mother, as being presumptively disruptive. By contrast, in those cases where he is seeking care opposed by a third person, he has always been treated far more favourably, solely by reason of his blood tie with the child. But here the courts exhibit considerable confusion over what factors they should attempt to assess when faced with this type of dispute. As illustrated by the decision in *Re K*[64], the outcome of such disputes appears to be influenced more by the identity of the disputants than by an assessment of the quality of their relationship with the child.

In *Re K*, the child's parents had formerly cohabited but the mother had suffered from continuous psychological problems and finally took her own life. Their child was thereafter brought up very happily for the next year by the mother's step sister and husband. The father successfully appealed to the Court of Appeal against the refusal of the court below to have the child returned to him. Both Fox LJ and Waite J criticised the judge below for not applying *Re KD*[65] to justify what they saw as a rebuttable presumption that there was a "right of every child, as part of its general welfare, to have the ties of nature maintained wherever possible with the parents who gave it life".[66] Waite J went further and criticised the judge below, for carefully assessing the households of the competing claimants, in order to decide in which the child would achieve a greater sense of security and stability. Instead, he should have been asking whether "there are any compelling factors which required him to override the *prima facie* right of this child to an upbringing by its surviving natural parent".[67] Similarly, Fox LJ could see no ground for ordering:

---

64 [1990] 3 All ER 795.
65 [1988] AC 806 at 812.
66 [1990] 3 All ER 795, per Waite J at 800.
67 *Ibid* at 800.

"that the father should be displaced from his normal role in the care and upbringing of his child... no circumstances had been demonstrated which made it necessary that, in the interests of the welfare of the child, the father's 'right' to bring him up should be displaced."[68]

It is remarkable that in this context, the Court of Appeal found it appropriate to use the language of "rights" when dealing with the relationship between the unmarried father and his child – in stark contrast to the appellate court's earlier rather grudging approach to opposed contact applications.

It is submitted that the decision in *Re K* is unsound for a number of reasons. First, the Court of Appeal applied *Re KD*, which involved an entirely different issue to that being dealt with in *Re K*. In the former case, the mother was not seeking to take over the child's care; the dispute was between her and the local authority caring for her child, now a ward of court, about her continued access to the child. Thus unlike *Re K*, it had nothing to do with disputes between private individuals about the future care of a child. Nor did *Re KD* establish any presumption that a child should be cared for by his parent as against a third party. Indeed the so-called "presumption" referred to by Fox LJ and Waite J in favour of the claims of the natural parent is entirely contrary to the House of Lords decision in *J* v *C* in 1969.[69] Further, even if *Re KD* did establish such a presumption, the court could only decide whether it was rebutted by considering all the evidence relating to the merits of both households; an impossible exercise without a careful and detailed assessment.

Finally, neither Fox LJ nor Waite J in *Re K* made any real attempt to evaluate the *quality* of the father's relationship with his son, as opposed to applauding him for his good qualities as an adult. Indeed the welfare officer had not even seen the child with his father. Waite J pointed to:

"the father's qualities of steadfastness and concern, as well as the father's record as a man who had made considerable efforts to match loyalty with realism throughout the ups and downs of a family relationship marred by the tragic impact of mental illness, [which] made this a case in which a risk of physical or emotional damage to the child of a very high order would have been necessary to dislodge the primary claim on R's welfare of an upbringing by his father."[70]

Thus in this case, in stark contrast to contested contact disputes, the court appears to have assumed that a good relationship existed or would exist between the child and his father, simply because of the existence of the blood tie between them. Arguably, this approach is just as dangerous to the child's welfare as the assumption that the natural father's claim for contact is detrimental to the child unless he can satisfy the court that this is not the case.

It was correctly predicted that the approach taken in *Re K* would be adopted in subsequent cases.[71] In the Court of Appeal's decision in *Re H*[72] Lord Donaldson MR warned against this happening, and admitted that he was:

---

68 *Ibid* at 799.
69 [1969] 1 All ER 788. See per Lord Macdermott who specifically stated that there was no presumption of law respecting parental rights, at 823. See also Eekelaar's comment on *Re KD* in "Access Rights and Children's Welfare" (1988) 51 *MLR* 629.
70 [1990] 3 All ER 79 at 800.
71 See Walsh, "Contradictory Trends in the Application of the Paramountcy Principle" (1992) 4 *JCL* 63.
72 (1991) 2 FLR 109.

"slightly apprehensive that *Re K* may be misconstrued... it is not a case of parental right opposed to the interests of the child, with an assumption that parental right prevails unless there are strong reasons in terms of the interests of the child... all that *Re K* is saying, as I understand it, is that of course there is a strong supposition that, other things being equal, it is in the interests of the child that it shall remain with its natural parents. But that has to give way to particular needs in particular situations."[73]

Unfortunately *Re H* was only an interim decision and Lord Donaldson's cautionary words were not mentioned by the Court of Appeal in the more recent case of *Re O*[74]. There the mother had placed her baby for adoption and subsequently implacably opposed the natural father's application to look after the child himself. Again the words of Lord Templeman in *Re KD* were quoted by Butler Sloss LJ:

"The best person to bring up a child is the natural parent. It matters not whether the parent is wise or foolish, rich or poor, educated or illiterate, provided the child's moral and physical health are not in danger."[75]

These words were particularly apt in *Re O*, since the father's character was far from perfect. Not only had the judge below described him as a liar, but it appeared that he was unable to form lasting relationships with women and two of the women he had had relationships with in the past retained unhappy recollections of these. Moreover, Butler Sloss LJ described the evidence surrounding the child's birth as indicating a great deal of selfishness and unkindness on the part of the father towards the mother.[76] Nevertheless, neither the trial judge nor the Court of Appeal considered that these defects were of sufficient importance to displace the parental "right" of the child to be cared for by his father as opposed to a stranger.[77] Indeed, Butler Sloss LJ emphasised that it would be "social engineering" to suggest that the father's known defects should be balanced against some idealised adoptive parents who might be discovered by the adoption society.[78]

In practical terms, the decision in *Re O* was inevitable. The weakness of the mother's opposition to the father's care of the child, was that by the time the case came before the Court of Appeal, he had been caring for the child for three months and had demonstrated practical parenting skills. The social worker who visited him four times, had formed the view that he had established a very good relationship with the child. By contrast, the mother did not wish to care for the child herself, and no prospective adopters had yet been found. Despite these circumstances, as Walsh points out[79], there is the obvious danger that by investing the parental blood tie with presumptive importance, the interests of natural parents will be given greater weight than those of the child. Further, *Re O* may signal a slippery slope in terms of acceptable standards of parental character. The fact that the Court of Appeal has allowed a father with considerable defects of character to retain care of his child, may strengthen the claims of other fathers with even worse defects to reclaim their children presently being cared for capably and happily by third parties.

---

73 *Ibid* at 113.
74 (1992) 1 FLR 77.
75 [1988] AC 806 at 812.
76 (1992) 1 FLR 77 at 80.
77 *Ibid* at 80.
78 *Ibid* at 79.
79 (1992) 4 *JCL* 63 at 66.

Conclusion

It is apparent that lawyers, academics and practitioners alike, show considerable uncertainty over what significance to attach to the blood tie between the child and the unmarried father. When considered in the context of the child's developmental needs, this blood tie may have little immediate significance for the child, particularly in circumstances where he has formed good attachments with permanent carers who are not linked to him by blood. Nevertheless, the child also has a psychological need both to know about his natural parents and to have appropriate contact with people who were important to him in his past. Placed in a legal context, these factors indicate that reforming the law by vesting parental responsibility in all unmarried fathers cannot be justified by the children's developmental needs, although there may be other good reasons for such a change. Moreover, children of unmarried parents, just like other children, need to know about their past and the identity of their fathers.

The two areas of caselaw considered above indicate judicial uncertainty over the position of the unmarried father. Although there can be no binding precedents in cases to do with children[80], considerable notice is taken of decisions of the Court of Appeal and in both these areas of caselaw, the Court of Appeal's record of inconsistency is unsatisfactory. The caselaw on disputes involving unmarried fathers is ambivalent to the point of hypocrisy. It cannot be satisfactory that in those disputes involving third parties wishing to bring up a child, opposed by the natural father, the Court of Appeal takes the view that it matters not whether he is wise or foolish, rich or poor; as the father, he is presumptively the best person to bring up his child. But if the natural father simply wants contact, opposed by the mother, the outcome may be quite different. And as illustrated by *Re F*[81] he may not even be allowed the means of proving his paternity through blood tests.

This discussion shows that lawyers may misuse theories about children's developmental needs to invest ideas for reform and judicial decision-making with a spurious value. More clarity would be achieved by adopting Eekelaar's suggested approach[82], which is to detach biological parentage from social parentage. Recognition of the former would not therefore carry more than recognition of identity. Social parentage would be exercised automatically by married couples but would have to be acquired by other people, such as long-term cohabitees and step-parents. This separation would allow the courts to determine the outcome of disputes over social parentage by assessing only what is most important to the child – the quality of his relationship with each of the disputing adults, free of the distracting influence of the blood tie factor. Until it is accepted by the courts and reformers alike, that there is no need to link biological parentage with social parentage, confusion and incoherence will inevitably continue.

---

80 See per Stamp LJ in *Re K* [1977] 1 All ER 647 at 649.
81 (1993) 1 FLR 598.
82 Eekelaar, "Parenthood, Social Engineering and Rights", *op cit.* at n. 25.

Chapter 12

Conceiving Relations: Egg and Sperm Donation in Assisted Procreation

Frances Price, *Centre for Family Research*
Faculty of Social and Political Sciences, University of Cambridge

Introduction

Human reproduction is more than simply a "family" affair. Lawyers know all too well that the relations between persons in the business of reproducing can be both novel and unanticipated. Nowhere is this so much in evidence than in contemporary reproductive medicine, the only branch of British medicine to become the subject of recent statute law: the Human Fertilisation and Embryology Act 1990. Certain scientific and clinical procedures involving human gametes and embryos came under review and license by a statutory body, the Human Fertilisation and Embryology Authority (HFEA) which was established in 1991.[1] At the last count, there were 101 licensed centres, largely in the private sector of medicine, offering what the Act refers to as "treatment services".

Clinics offering assisted conception hold out the prospect of a solution to problems for which people are willing to pay considerable sums of money. Further, over the past decade, access to procedures developed in conjunction with the management of infertility have been extended to fertile people. In vitro fertilisation (IVF) is no longer only a means of by-passing infertility in women with blocked fallopian tubes.

However, to date, few lawyers have confronted the social and legal relations which may be forged between those persons who, with medical assistance, engage in procreative projects. In this context, the contemporary use of donated human eggs and sperm to facilitate pregnancy has brought about a change in what is regarded as possible. This is a particular form of facilitation which has opened up many novel issues concerning the communication of risk information to donors and recipients.[2] These issues are likely to become more pressing as the genetic

---

1   Morgan and Lee *Blackstone's Guide to Human Fertilisation and Embryology Act 1990.* (Blackstone, 1991).

2   Royal Society *Risk: analysis, perception and management* Report of a Royal Society Study Group (1992).

basis of many disorders becomes known, and as genetic technologies are introduced into donor screening. The pressure on the British Government to regulate work with embryos was exacerbated by the complexities introduced by the use of donated gametes. New dimensions of risk and uncertainty arise and there are likely to be new allocations of responsibility for the consequences of the donation.[3]

In the licensed centres in the United Kingdom there is now a substantial gamete donation programme, as clinical indications for the use of donated gametes have been extended to include failed IVF and post-menopausal status. The third Annual Report of the HFEA records that more than 1500 sperm donors and 1000 egg donors have been registered with the HFEA since August 1991, when the Authority became established.[4] There is, however, a marked shortage of donated gametes, which has led to more extensive recruitment "campaigns" for donors, and renewed concern about what information to gather and what to share with parties to the donation or with any child born of the donation. The entire programme is underwritten by a number of taken-for-granted assumptions and practices involving the donor, which centre on ideas about parenthood and kinship and the relationship between the donor, the recipient and her partner. It is these assumptions and practices that fuelled the recent furore over the use of foetal eggs to establish pregnancies.[5]

Background to gamete donation in the United Kingdom

The pressure on the British Government to regulate scientific and clinical work with embryos, which led to the Human Fertilisation and Embryology Act 1990, arose not least because of the complexities of using donated eggs and sperm. Egg donation became possible only with the techniques that were developed as part of IVF, and the first reports of pregnancies following the transfer of donated eggs did not appear until the early 1980s.[6] But many centres rapidly adopted the practice, and donor egg programmes are now established worldwide.[7]

Egg donation is the only method by which women with primary or acquired ovarian failure can achieve a pregnancy. However, women with functional ovaries may also enter an egg-donation programme if they do not respond to ovulation stimulation, or following repeated failure of IVF, or if they are carriers of severe genetic diseases. Yet current methods of obtaining eggs from adult women are not without risk, and eggs have always

3   Jalbert *et al* "Genetic Aspects of Artificial Insemination with Donor Semen: The French CECOS Federation Guidelines", (1989) *Am J Med Gen* 269-275.
4   HFEA 3rd Annual Report (1994).
5   *e.g.* Dillner "Use of Fetal Eggs for Infertility Treatment is Banned" (1994) *BMJ* 309, 289-290.
6   Trounson *et al* "Pregnancy Established in an Infertile Patient after Transfer of a Donated Embryo Fertilised In Vitro" (1983) *BMJ* 286, 835-838. Lutjen *et al* "The Establishment and Maintenance of Pregnancy using In Vitro Fertilisation and Embryo Donation in a Patient with Primary Ovarian Failure" (1984) *Nature* 307, 174-175.
7   Cameron *et al* "Oocyte Donation: A Review" (1989) *Brit Jo Obst Gyn*, 893-899.

been in short supply. "Spare" eggs from women undergoing IVF or gamete intra fallopian transfer (GIFT) were the original source for donor programmes. But as it became possible to cryopreserve embryos, women and men claimed this opportunity to freeze their embryos for their own use at a later time.

By comparison, the use of donor sperm has a long history predating IVF, and following the Peel Report of 1973, donor insemination has been made available within the National Health Service. As medical interest in, and public awareness of, male infertility has increased, the practice of using donated sperm in assisted conception techniques has also grown. Sperm dysfunction remains one of the main and most elusive problems of contemporary infertility practice, and demand for donor insemination has been bolstered by the relative absence of effective treatments for male infertility, although this may change in the wake of new techniques involving the microinjection of a single sperm into an egg, to circumvent infertility among men who produce few or immotile sperm.[8]

The supply of egg and sperm donors

Both the recruitment and screening of donors is managed by centres licensed by the statutory authority, the HFEA. Donor insemination and the transfer of embryos created from donated eggs can be performed only in these centres, and all donors must be placed on a central register.

The contemporary demand is for donors who are healthy, free from transmittable genetic disorders and sexually transmitted diseases, and who have gametes with high fertilising potential. On these grounds, many prospective sperm donors are rejected.[9] The recruitment of sperm donors presents acute problems, many of which were highlighted in a recent survey of the licensed centres offering treatment using donor sperm, conducted by Dr Rachel Cook and Professor Susan Golombok on behalf of the HFEA.[10]

This survey found that following an intensification of recruitment effort between 1989 and 1992, more men offered themselves as sperm donors. Yet the supply of donors has remained steady, because more of these potential donors are being rejected. The overall situation may have worsened, however, as a result of an increase in demand. In the year following the implementation of the 1990 Act (1992), there was an increase of almost 30% in the number of patients treated by donor insemination.

Moreover, a large majority of prospective egg donors withdraw from donation programmes at an early stage – as a recent study at the regional IVF unit at St Mary's Hospital in Manchester noted.[11] In addition,

---

8   van Steirteghem *et al* "Intracytoplasmic Sperm Injection", in *Balliere's Clinical Obstetrics and Gynaecology* 8(1), 85-93.

9   Golombok and Cook "A Survey of Semen Donation: Phase I – the View of the Centres". (Report to the HFEA, 1993).

10 *Ibid.*

11 Horne *et al* "The Recruitment of Oocyte Donors". (1993) *Brit Jo Obs and Gyn* 100, 877-878.

many men and women of certain ethnic groups appear reluctant to donate.

Recruiting sperm and egg donors

The Chairman of the British Andrology Society, Dr Chris Barratt, has called for a "constant campaign", "vigorously maintained", to recruit sperm donors.[12] Similarly, in a recent issue of the *British Journal of Obstetrics and Gynaecology*, the team from the regional IVF unit at Manchester wrote of the need for greater "publicity" in the media, as well as active recruitment by GPs, directed to "groups of women who are likely to consider egg donation".[13] There is considerable disagreement among clinicians, however, about how best to target suitable donors. For instance, suggestions that women students and men attending antenatal clinics or undergoing vasectomy should be approached, have met with resistance.

Among clinicians, opinion is also divided about the practice of seeking egg donations from women undergoing sterilisation, or from the friends or relations of women who seek donated eggs, or from women who are undergoing infertility treatment.

Little is known about why individuals do, or do not, choose to become donors. Previous research on gamete donation has focused primarily on attitudes of donors and recipients of donation, on the issue of anonymity and on the consequences of secrecy.[14] Recruiting campaigns are likely to continue to prove ineffective and perhaps even counter-productive, in the absence of knowledge of the expectations of would-be donors, and the sources of reluctance of many suitable volunteer donors.

Screening sperm and egg donors

Assisted reproduction with donated gametes usually implies screening the donor for certain transmittable infectious diseases such as HIV and hepatitis B, as well as diseases thought to have a large genetic component, such as asthma and diabetes. Some genetic selection is generally accepted as being necessary, but this is typically based on assumptions about genetic make-up, based on information provided by prospective donors about their family history, rather than on direct genetic tests. Only some clinics test donors for cystic fibrosis carrier status, for instance. There is also considerable variation in practice in the United Kingdom and throughout the world concerning which infectious agents are tested for, whether donors are rescreened (and how frequently), and the procedures used to elicit a full

---

12 Barratt "Donor Recruitment Selection and Screening", in Barratt and Cooke (eds) *Donor Insemination*, (Cambridge University Press, 1993).

13 *Op cit*, n.11.

14 Daniels and Taylor "Secrecy and Openness in Donor Insemination" (1993) *Politics and the Life Sciences* 12, 155-170. Robinson *et al* "Anonymity of Gamete Donors: A Survey of Attitudes" (1990) *Jo Reproduction and Fertility* abstr ser 5, 67.

sexual history.[15] There is also uncertainty as to the best way to select sperm of high fertilising potential, since the standard variables of number, motility and morphology of sperm are generally insufficient to diagnose infertility reliably.[16] Opinions differ as to whether screening should be extended to the recipient – to allow "matching" of donor and recipient, in an attempt to avoid the accumulation of "risk factors" for either genetic-based or acquired diseases in a child born of the donation.[17] For instance, some clinics match sperm donors positive for cytomegalovirus to recipients who also test positive for the virus.[18]

The British Andrology Society (BAS) has produced guidelines for the screening of sperm donors, which is:

> "limited specifically to the protection of the offspring of donor insemination treatment from heritable genetic disorders and the offspring and recipient women from infection"[19]

These guidelines are to be reviewed in November 1994. The Code of Practice of the HFEA, revised in 1993, requires that centres "should as a minimum" follow these guidelines. It also states that "centres should adopt whatever is current best practice in the scientific testing of semen samples and of donors of gametes".

In Britain at the moment, genetic risks are generally assessed by taking a detailed family history. Cytogenetic tests to detect chromosomal abnormalities may sometimes be carried out. The BAS guidelines currently state that karyotyping of donors "would appear advisable", but this is "not considered mandatory". The BAS advises: "Whether or not to karyotype a donor depends on one's judgement of how small a risk one can afford to ignore."

The prospect, and public anticipation, of genetic screening using DNA tests raises further questions concerning which genetic diseases should be screened for, and by what means.[20] Should the donor be informed of the results? Should prospective recipients also be screened, so that risk factors can be assessed? Several leading clinicians in the field have expressed different views and practices concerning these matters.

---

15 Barratt and Cooke "Risks of Donor Insemination: A Review" (1990) *Int Jo Risk and Safety Medicine* 1, 113-115. American Fertility Society (1993) *Guidelines for Gamete Donation, Fertility and Sterility* 59, suppl 1. Novaes *Les Passeurs de Gametes* (Presses Universitaire de Nancy, 1993).
16 Jeyendran and Zaneveld "Controversies in the Development and Validation of New Sperm Assays" (1993) *Fertility and Sterility* 59, 726-728.
17 Selva *et al* "Genetic Screening for Artificial Insemination by Donor (AID): Results of a Study on 676 Semen Donors (1986). *Clinical Genetics* 29, 389-396.
18 *Op cit*, n.12.
19 British Andrology Society, "British Andrology Society Guidelines for the Screening of Semen Donors for Donor Insemination" (1993) *Human Reproduction* 8, 1521-1523.
20 ten Kate *et al* "Effectiveness of Prevention of Cystic Fibrosis by Artificial Insemination by Donor can be Markedly Improved by DNA-analysis of Sperm Donors, (letter) (1989) *American Jo Med Gen* 32, 148-149.

The rationale for anonymity

Anonymity and secrecy surround the recourse to donor gametes in reproductive medicine in the United Kingdom and many other countries in Europe, and became institutionalised in the context of sperm donation. Anonymity with "matching" was brought into the practice of sperm donation explicitly to conceal assistance. Perceiving male infertility to be particularly stigmatised, medical bodies such as the Royal College of Obstetricans and Gynaecologists (RGOC) advised that neither donor nor the recipient couple should know the other's identity.[21] Anonymity would further prevent the intrusion of a "third party" into the couple's sphere and support the stability of the "family". Anonymity, along with secrecy that entails "not telling" the child, disguises the "anomalous" nature of the child's conception.[22] There is currently a heated controversy in the United Kingdom over "telling" the child, and speculations about the consequences of disclosure or secrecy.[23]

As donor insemination became widely available as a service in reproductive medicine, the practice of matching donor to recipient came to form a crucial part of the culture of concealment. To help disguise the substitution, the RCOG recommended that "donors should have the same physical characteristics as the husband".[24] Today, clinics typically attempt to match the donor with the recipient's partner on a few explicit criteria: eye colour, hair colour and blood type. Height and body build are also likely to be taken into account. Egg donors and recipients may both be asked to complete forms about their physical characteristics to facilitate "matching".

The prevailing approach to the recruitment of sperm donors bolsters anonymity and secrecy. The practice of offering male students small financial inducements in exchange for their sperm encourages male donors to trivialise the process of donation. The assumption is that donors attribute little significance to the process. For instance, Golombok and Cook's survey (1993), enabled Susan Golombok to conclude that the typical sperm donor was "a student donating for beer money"[25] The sperm itself then appears to become a resource on par with other donated material such as blood.

---

21 RCOG *Report of the Royal College of Obstetricians and Gynaecologists Ethics Committee on In Vitro Fertilisation and Embryo Replacement or Transfer* (Royal College of Obstetricians and Gynaecologists, 1983).

22 Haimes, "Recreating the family? Policy considerations relating to the new reproductive technologies" in McNeil, Varcoe and Yearley (eds), *The New Reproductive Technologies* (Macmillan, 1990).

23 Glover, *Fertility and the Family: Report on the Reproductive Technologies to the European Commission (The Glover Report)* (The Fourth Estate, 1989). Bolton *et al*, "A Comparative Study of Attitudes Towards Donor Insemination and Egg Donation in Recipients, Potential Donors and the Public" (1991), *Jo Psychosomatic Obstetrics and Gynaecology* 12, 217-228.

24 *Op cit*, n.21.

25 Vines, "Double standards for egg and sperm donors" *New Scientist* 3 September 1994, 8.

Egg donation

The practice of using donated eggs, however, differs from sperm donation in several ways – not least that egg retrieval is physically invasive, with attendent medical risks.[26] Further, egg donors in Britain are not paid, and are said to be altruistic, motivated by the desire to help another woman to have a child.[27] Moreover, contemporary egg donation may be conducted between known parties – usually sisters but sometimes other relatives or friends. It has been anticipated that such requests will increase.[28]

Complex relationships between donor, recipient and their partners arise as a result of both anonymous and known donations. For example, a study by Roberta Lessor, of egg donation between sisters in a large university IVF centre in the United States, has documented the unprecedented difficulties that arise. For instance, the sister donor does the "work" of a patient, despite not being perceived as one. One donor sister said:

> "It's like being a hero. You go out on the field and do something, and everybody says, of course, that's what you're supposed to do, that's the honourable thing to do. But somebody from time to time has to ask how you're feeling."[29]

Little is known about what people think it appropriate to disclose about the process of donation. But there is now considerable evidence from British licensed centres to suggest that women donors and recipients alike often do tell others of their experience, even if the donation has been conducted anonymously. At one centre, 80% of egg donors told friends, relatives or doctors[30], and many clinics now encourage donors and recipients to seek publicity in the media.

Issues around disclosure were also a major theme in Lessor's study. She reported that recipients are more guarded than are their donor sisters in disclosing egg donation to other family members, friends and colleagues. Some recipients told her of their distress when their husbands or donor sisters revealed information about the donation prematurely or inappropriately. For example, most of Lessor's recipient sisters approved disclosing to their mothers, but several had reservations about their sister donor telling their boyfriends. Boyfriends, when told, sometimes disapproved, and were concerned about limitations on their sexual access to the donor and the effect on the donor's future fertility. Lessor also points to the difficulties that the sister's husband may experience, for instance, in knowing how to behave towards one's "sister-in-law, the egg donor".

---

26 Smith and Cooke "Ovarian Hyperstimulation: Actual and Theoretical Risks (1991) *BMJ* 302, 127-128.

27 Price "Assisting Fertilisation: Clinical Practices and Public Concerns", in Chard and Richards (eds) *Obstetrics in the 1990s: Current Controversies* (MacKeith Press 1992).

28 Lessor "All in the Family: Social Processes in Ovarian Egg Donation Between Sisters" (1993) *Sociology of Health and Illness* 15, 393-413.

29 *Ibid.*

30 Power *et al* "A Comparison of the Attitudes of Volunteer Donors and Infertile Patient Donors on an Ovum Donation Programme" (1990) *Human Rep* 5, 352-355.

If you assist conception, you assist relationships – as studies of the social processes in egg donation serve to underline. One of the major findings of a recent project funded by the Economic and Social Research Council, directed by Professor Marilyn Strathern, was that people who had no particular interest in, or personal experience of, assisted conception made sense of developments in the field of reproductive medicine through their existing knowledge of kinship, and what they already know about how to sustain social relationships in an appropriate manner.[31]

Fetal eggs

The recent debates about the possibility of using fetal ovarian tissue as a source of donor eggs brings to the surface fundamental assumptions about kinship and social relationships. The idea of using fetal eggs gained currency by analogy with donor insemination, where medical mediation maintains a separation of donor and recipient. The principle of anonymity is intended to eliminate the possibility of a relationship with the donor; and anonymity combined with matching is intended to conceal medical assistance. A fetus that has no name and can make no claim may seem the ideal candidate, the perfect source of eggs in a climate of opinion which favours separation, secrecy and anonymity. The eggs would seem to come with "no strings attached".

Yet contemporary research suggests that the donor and recipient relate to one another in important ways. Even in anonymous donation the donor is envisaged as an adult who has, through human agency, voluntarily donated. The contemporary donor is envisaged as a person who comes forward and is appraised for infectious and genetic disease and subsequently accepted as a substitute. The donor is theoretically traceable if something goes wrong, and can be held legally liable if he or she has failed to disclose medical or family history. The fetus, by contrast, is not imaginable as a substitute for the woman recipient. Moreover, the fetus cannot *act* as a donor, nor have personal characteristics that could form the basis of a "match". Further, to talk of a parent, even of a genetic parent, always invokes the idea of potential social relations.[32]

The prospect of using fetal eggs to produce a child – of "skipping a generation" – upsets our everyday thinking about kinship.[33] Insofar as fears are expressed, they reflect the profound discomfort produced by considering the relational consequences of disturbing categories already in place. The evident scale of this discomfort is also strong evidence for cultural constraints on who the donor should be.

---

31 Edwards *et al, Technologies of Procreation: Kinship and the New Technologies* (Manchester University Press, 1993).
32 Strathern, *Reproducing the Future,* (Manchester University Press, 1992).
33 Hall "Fears of Skipped Generation Raised by Use of Tissue" (1994) *The Independent,* 26 July 1994.

"Ethnic" issues

The donor effectively vanishes from view when a "good enough" match is secured. However, if the "difference" between donor and the recipient couple is perceived as marked, controversy may ensue. Politically salient notions of "difference" may come to the fore, particularly when donation appears to violate "racial" boundaries.

Simone Novaes has described two contentious cases which were reviewed by the centrally-organized French sperm bank, Centre d'Etudes et de Conservation de Sperme (CECOS).[34] In one case, the bank was unable to provide sperm that satisfied the CECOS criteria for matching blood type, and in the other, skin colour. In each case, the couple had requested that CECOS disregard the "mismatch" and allow the woman concerned to undergo donor insemination.

The first couple were allowed treatment on the grounds that the blood type mismatch was not visible – "not immediately apparent". Moreover, the couple concerned had already told the sperm bank of their intention to tell others that they had sought donor insemination. The second couple, faced with a prospect of no CECOS donors of "appropriate" ethnicity, had requested insemination with "European" sperm, and had accepted the prospect of a child with features different from their own. Novaes reports that only after a "lively discussion" was the couple accepted, and then only on a technicality – on the grounds that the CECOS bank could not observe its own "matching" rules because it did not have sperm from donors from a wide range of ethnic groups. But the bank ruled that its decision in this case should not create a precedent.

British newspapers recently heralded the claim that a "British black woman" – identified in one paper as "Afro-Caribbean" – was about to be given "a white woman's egg".[35] This procedure was justified by clinicians on the grounds that the recipient's partner was said to be of "mixed race", and thus any child born of his sperm would also be of mixed race whether a "black" or "white" egg was used.[36] Just over a week later, the *Guardian* reported that a National Health Service fertility clinic in Nottingham "has turned down an Indian couple's request for the wife to be implanted with a white woman's eggs. No Indian eggs were available."[37]

In clinical practice, the perceived need to "match" donor and recipient creates special difficulties. For "administrative" purposes, medical practitioners may be concerned to classify their patients into apparent "racial" or ethnic groups.[38] Yet such classifications are not only theoretically contentious, but socially problematic in their reinforcement of the

---

34 Novaes, *op cit* n.15.
35 Donegan " 'Designer' Baby Sparks Race Choice Row", *The Guardian*, 31 December 1993.
36 Timmins "Couples Barred from Choosing Race of Babies", *The Independent*, 1 January 1994.
37 Anonymous article in the *Guardian*, "Egg Request Refused", 12 January 1994.
38 Sharma, "What is an Ethnic Group?" in Clarke and Parsons (eds), *Culture, Kinship and Genes* (Macmillan, 1995).

outmoded discourse of race.[39] In this way, the language of justification and legitimation employed by clinicians who seek to facilitate pregnancy through the use of donated gametes may come to reflect popular notions of "race", and reaffirm them by vesting them with the mantle of medical authority.

Conclusion

What is going on here? Why is secrecy and anonymity apparently of paramount importance in sperm donation but not consistently in egg donation? Why is there a shortage of donors, and why, in particular, are many men and women of certain ethnic minority groups especially reluctant to donate?

Gamete donation remains one of the most controversial areas of medically assisted procreation, and may become more so as genetic technologies are introduced into the selection and "matching" of donors and recipients. Who will make the decisions about selection, and on what basis, and who will bear the responsibility for the consequences?

The meaning of "donation" in the context of human reproduction – as eggs or sperm are in transition between persons – also needs further exploration. We need to know more about the expectations of the donor and the recipient couple to know how to "recruit", and whether and how to attempt to "match" donor and recipient. Advances in human genetics have contributed to our increasing preoccupation with notions of genetic identity and genetic "health" – a cultural undercurrent that is at odds with the culture of concealment shrouding gamete donation. The current mixture of known and anonymous donations can only exacerbate tensions between secrecy and "telling", and between what is possible to sustain and what is felt desirable to sustain. What significance do donors and recipients place on notions of genetic identity and genetic health? What are they told, and what do they want to know about the nature of screening tests and their outcome?

Further research is needed to explore the novel social and legal situations created by gamete donation. *In vitro* fertilisation using the couple's own gametes is very different. Because the couple have been helped to conceive a child that they might have had without medical intervention, the treatment has no special implications for relationships within the family, nor does it raise substantive issues of information that are of consequence to the child. But when reproductive services rely on gamete donors, the intervention has implications for the child – giving it at least one anonymous "genetic" parent – and involving health care professionals in

---

39 Frankenberg *White Women, Race Matters: the Social Construction of Whiteness*, (Routledge, 1993); Harding (ed) *The 'Racial' Economy of Science* (Indiana University Press, 1993); Macbeth, "Ethnicity and Human Biology" in Chapman (ed), *Social and Biological Aspects of Ethnicity* (Oxford University Press, 1993); Tizzard and Phoenix, *Black, White or Mixed Race?* (Routledge, 1993).

decision-making about the identity of the donor that has fundamental consequences for the child.

There is an urgent need for a deeper understanding of the social processes at work in gamete donation, as issues of responsibility and risk in this area go largely unexamined. Our ideas about gamete donation are intimately related to wider cultural understandings of the way relationships are appropriately created and sustained. As gamete donation programmes continue to expand world-wide, we need to ask, how do people think about these new relationships in human reproduction, and in what circumstances will they support them?

Chapter 13

The Judge and Child Custody Decision-making in the United States

Sanford N Katz

Professor of Law, Boston College Law School, Newton, Massachusetts, USA

According to the latest statistics, more than a million children each year have experienced a family divorce in the past twenty years.[1] At the present time, about 26% of all children under the age of 18 live with a divorced or separated parent, or a step-parent. In 1990, six million – or 9.5% – of all children in the United States were living with a divorced single parent. One projection is that nearly half of all the children born in 1994 will spend some time in a one-parent family because of either single parenthood or divorce.

These statistics are startling when one considers that a major focus in the United States by politicians has been on "family values". The conventional description of "family" is of a male and female, mother and father, and a child established by biology or adoption. This description is outdated given the current statistics and social trends. Today, the single-parent family – usually a mother and her child or children – is the fastest growing family in the United States. Children living apart from their families in foster care number about 442,000, and the number of children living outside of their home other than in foster care in 1988 (the latest date) is about 760,00.[2] There is no reason to think that either figure will decline very significantly in the next decade.[3]

Divorce has been a part of American life since colonial times.[4] Art, literature, film and the popular media have all contributed to the development of a myth about the enduring stability of marriage and the family in the United States. It is only now, in the closing years of the

---

1   For a full discussion of the statistics quoted in this article, see Shiono and Quinn, "Epidemiology of Divorce" (1994) 4 *The Future of Children* 15.

2   See Behrman and Quinn, "Children and Divorce: Overview and Analysis" (1994) 4 *The Future of Children* 4.

3   *op cit* n.2 at 14.

4   For a historical perspective on American divorce from colonial times to the present, see Riley, *Divorce: An American Tradition* (Oxford University Press, New York, 1991). Riley writes at 5: "Although the divorce rate had been rising since the mid-1600s, it reached an unexpected high during the 1880s: one out of fourteen to sixteen marriages ended in divorce.

  One hundred years later, the divorce rate had climbed to a new zenith: during the 1980s approximately one of two marriages ended in divorce. Americans, a people who love weddings, romance, and living happily ever after, had generated the highest divorce rate in the world."

twentieth century, that a realistic picture is emerging of the variety of types of families and family-like arrangements that exist in the United States.

Divorce laws and procedures have changed radically in the past 30 years.[5] Grounds for divorce have been construed liberally, no-fault divorce has been added to all jurisdictions in the United States and divorce procedures have been simplified considerably.

Today the most common way of securing a divorce is through a no-fault system whereby the parties seek to dissolve their marriage by stating that their marriage has either "irretrievably broken down" or that the couple are "incompatible."[6] It is rare that divorce cases are litigated on the basis of proving a fault ground such as cruelty, desertion or adultery. The major focus of matrimonial litigation is on how marital property is to be is distributed and who should be assigned the custody of children.

Deciding which parent should be assigned custody of children has always been the most troubling part of divorce. Child development experts suggest that in an ideal world children should be raised by their birth parents – for psychological, sociological and economic reasons.[7] But, of course, that is not always possible. Death or divorce of parents, war and its dislocation of families, and for a variety of reasons prevent the ideal from happening. Thus the role of a judge in a child custody dispute in which there are competing claims, is to assess the strengths and weaknesses of the claimants, keeping in mind the specific needs of the child.

But it must be remembered that the vast majority of divorce disputes are negotiated and settled privately in lawyers' offices.[8] And, unless there are some obvious inequities or an agreement that is clearly detrimental to a child's welfare, judges usually approve the privately negotiated agreement.[9] It is when no agreement has been reached and a case is tried before a judge that a judge makes his or her own decision.[10]

---

5   See Katz, "Historical Perspective and Current Trends in the Legal Process of Divorce" (1994) 4 *The Future of Children* 44.

6   For a discussion of fault and no-fault divorce and the consequences of each system, see Katz (above) n. 5) at 46-50.

7   The statement of the ideal of being raised by one's biological parents comes from the author's discussions with Anna Freud.

8   Mnookin *et al* "Private Ordering Revisited: What Custodial Arrangements Are Parents Negotiating?" in Sugarman and Kay, *Divorce Reform at the Crossroads* (Yale University Press, 1990) at 60-67.

9   See, *e.g.* Massachusetts General Laws, CH. 208 31 (1994): "Where the parents have reached an agreement providing for the custody of the children, the court may enter an order in accordance with such agreement, unless specific findings are made by the justice indicating that such an order would not be in the best interests of the children."

10 Weyrauch, Olsen and the author have written: "Trial judges like to point out that since they are the ultimate decision makers, with the responsibility of looking out for a child's welfare, they are not bound by private agreements. They also reason that since a child is not a chattel, it cannot be bargained away for consideration. Yet these invocations are mostly ritualistic; the judge in fact incorporates the private agreement in his decree. The implication, at least outwardly, is that the parents' agreement coincides with the best interests of the child. Incorporation also establishes the power of the judge to modify the agreement later and to hold a custodian in contempt if the custodian violates a provision of the agreement, now a court order." Weyrauch *et al, Cases and Materials on Family Law Legal Concepts and Changing Human Relationships* (West Publishing Company, 1994) at 838-839.

The conventional standard judges use to decide custody is "the best interests of the child." Judges have defined the standard in a number of ways, generally with the principle goal of promoting a child's physical and emotional well-being. For a long period of time – as with the assignment of marital property – there were no statutory factors which a judge had to follow when deciding a custody case. A judge used his or her own discretion. And, a litigant's remedy for an adverse decision was to appeal it to a higher court on the basis of the judge's abuse of his or her discretion. This is changing; not that judges no longer have discretion, but that most state statutes now incorporate some definition of "the best interests of the child"[11] or in certain kinds of dispositions, like "shared custody," require that litigants present guidelines for parenting to the trial judge for his or her review.[12]

It is extremely difficult to engage in legal research on a national scale in the United States concerning child custody matters in the trial courts because of the large number of courts and the even larger number of cases that are heard – and the fact that trial court decisions are rarely published so as to be readily available for research purposes. Observational and anecdotal research are usually the basis for statements about how judges decide custody cases. Research can be done on statutory trends and appellate cases because state statutes and appellate cases are reported and available in libraries and computer programs. Yet it should be understood that fewer than 1% of all child custody cases in divorce are appealed. Thus, researching child custody cases heard in appeals courts does not give a total picture of the law of child custody in the United States.

Why a judge decides a case in a particular way and what evidence is particularly persuasive is difficult to determine. Lawyers spend hours preparing cases, utilising mental health experts, especially psychologists and psychiatrists, in order to convince a judge that the parent the lawyer represents will be the better custodian. Lawyers are critical players in the courtroom drama in that they present the story of the marriage as a narrator would do. In addition, and in a certain sense, they act as directors of plays sketched by clients. Lawyers flesh out the story, shape the characters, suggest the right affect, and decide what the climax will be and when it will occur. As in any other litigation, the performance of a lawyer in court may be the most critical factor in determining the outcome of a case rather than the facts or the law.

---

11 One model used by many states in drafting child custody statutes is the Uniform Marriage and Divorce Act s 402 [Best Interest of Child]: "The court shall determine custody in accordance with the best interest of the child. The court shall consider all relevant factors including: (1) the wishes of the child's parents or parents as to his custody; (2) the wishes of the child as to his custodian; (3) the interaction and interrelationship of the child with his parent or parents, his siblings, and any other person who may significantly affect the child's best interest"; (4) the child's adjustment to his home, school, and community; and (5) the mental and physical health of all individuals involved. The court shall not consider conduct of a proposed custodian that does not affect his relationship to the child." The full Act is reproduced in Weyrauch, *op cit*, n. 10 at 1105.

12 *e.g.*, Massachusetts General Laws, MGI Ch 208 s 31.

How do lawyers approach custody cases? Lawyers try to involve the judge in the case by appealing to both the judge's intellect and emotions. Lawyers know that a judge must decide the case on the basis of "the law" which means that the judge must be able legally to justify his or her decision (no matter how reached) and protect it from being attacked on appeal.

From reading child custody statutes and appellate custody cases, it is apparent that changes have occurred and are occurring both in legislatures and in courts. The maternal preference rule – often referred to as the tender years presumption (upon divorce, assuming a mother has nurtured the child and is fit, infants should be assigned to her rather than to the father) – is no longer stated as the reason for a decision, although an outcome of a case may indeed reflect a judge's preference for a mother over a father. Men have opposed the maternal preference doctrine because of the unfair advantage it gives mothers. In order to be assigned custody in a divorce case where the maternal preference was operable, a father had the heavy burden of proving a mother unfit, perhaps even neglectful. One scholar has suggested that the maternal preference rule which is generally thought of as favoring women because of their child-rearing capabilities, was rather a manifestation of a policy of keeping women in the home caring for children rather than out in the workforce competing with men.[13]

Morality and life style of the custodian are still relevant in child custody decisions and alternative life styles may be tolerated or not, depending on the specific facts of the case (*i.e.*, sex of the child and the sex of the custodian to whom the child is assigned) and the particular judge and jurisdiction.[14] Overall, it appears that continuity of care or the *status quo* (assuming the adult custodian is fit) is usually preferred over all other considerations.

Child custody statutes are subject to change depending on the vogue or fad of the moment and the political climate. For a long time it was customary to award a child to one parent (called the custodian) with visitation by the other (labelled "non-custodial parent"). In the United States, this usually meant that the mother was the custodian and the father was the non-custodial parent. Lawyers generally tried to dissuade their male clients from pursuing custody for two reasons: it was probably a

---

13 See Olsen, "The Politics of Family Law" (1984) 2 *Law & Ineq Jo* 1, 15.

14 In *Jarrett* v *Jarrett*, 78 Ill.2d 337, 400 N.E.2d 421 (1979), the Supreme Court of Illinois held that a mother who cohabited with a man to whom she was not married was morally unfit to continue to have custody of her three children (ages 7, 10, and 12) and modified a custody order depriving her of custody and assigning the children to their father. The US Supreme Court denied a writ of certiorari with Brennan J and Marshall J dissenting in an opinion which argued that Mrs Jarrett's living with a man and having sexual relations with him should not result in a conclusive presumption that Mrs Jarrett was morally unfit to be a custodian of her children (See *Jarrett* v *Jarrett*, (1980) 449 US 927).

In *Roe* v *Roe*, 228 Va. 722, 324 S.E.2d 691 (1985), the Supreme Court of Virginia held that a father who lived with another man with whom he had a homosexual relationship was not fit to continue to have custody of his 10-year old daughter. The court stated: "The father's continuous exposure of the child to his immoral and illicit relationship renders him an unfit and improper custodian as a matter of law."

fruitless endeavor and also, bringing such an action might damage the reputation of the mother. For a long period of time it was generally understood that if a mother was not assigned custody of her child, she was probably unfit. A non-custodial mother was stigmatised by her status. But during the 1960s and 1970s social mores changed. Women pursued their own careers independent of motherhood and a generation of fathers who manifested a serious interest in caring for their children on a day-to-day basis, sought custody. Fathers found, however, that they had difficulty in convincing a judge that times had changed and that they too could raise their children and be good parents.[15] When men were denied custody, often because they were unrealistic about their ability to undertake the responsibilities of parenthood (not having performed certain fundamental tasks of parenthood during marriage) and their unavailability for child care, they discovered that as non-custodial parents they had more obligations than rights. Fathers complained that as a non-custodial parent they were being left out of the day-to-day activities of their children. To mention just one, school authorities would not release school information to non-custodial parents nor would teachers ordinarily notify non-custodial parents about a school conference concerning their children. Of course, one method of remedying such a state of affairs would be to include notification in the divorce and custody decree. But unforeseen problems created further difficulties and left the non-custodial, who might be seriously interested in all aspects of his child's upbringing, out of plans for the child.

Joint custody (or as some jurisdictions label it "shared custody") became an alternative disposition to custody to one parent and visitation to another and was advanced in part in the late 1970s by fathers who thought that they had been abandoned in child custody cases.[16] Today joint custody generally means that both mother and father are jointly responsible for making decisions about their child. In a certain sense, a joint custody disposition is an attempt to recreate the intact family. It is obvious that joint custody requires unusually co-operative and financially sound parents to make it succeed. Various kinds of joint custodial arrangements have developed; for example, children living with one parent but visiting the other on certain days of the week. This arrangement might have been identical to the old method of custody to one parent and visitation to the other, except that in a joint custody arrangement both parents are legally responsible for making decisions about their child's life. Another arrangement is for the child to live with each parent for certain segments of time. This physical arrangement would require, of course, double homes.

As already stated, successful joint custody requires co-operative parents

---

15 For a discussion of the role of the father in custody matters, see Thompson, "The Role of the Father After Divorce" (1994) 4 *The Future of Children* 210.

16 For a discussion of joint custody, see Katz, "Joint Custody" (1985) 2 *Comp Law* (Nihon University) 29. Also see Kelly, "The Determination of Child Custody" (1994) 4 *The Future of Children* 121.

and those who have made a relatively healthy post-divorce adjustment. Obviously, warring and bitterly hostile parents would find it difficult, if not impossible, to communicate with each other and reach mutual decisions about their children on a rational basis. Further, it is said that joint custody should be a disposition suggested by the parents themselves, not thrust upon them by a judge who cannot make up his or her own mind. But a parent's motivation for seeking joint custody should be explored. Do parents have an unrealistic view of post-divorce life, especially the economic aspects? Does a father, for example, think that by becoming a joint custodian his child support obligation will be reduced? That is, does a father believe that in order to reduce his support payments he ought to seek custody, although his employment really will not allow for the day-to-day responsibilities of joint parenthood?

The findings of empirical research on joint custody have resulted in a new look at the disposition, especially as to whether in fact joint custody is truly joint and whether it lessens conflict.[17] Some feminist writers have felt that an award of joint custody may reflect a minimisation of the role a mother has played in rearing her children and they have called for major changes, some recommending the revival of the maternal preference rule and others for statutory enactment of the primary caretaker standard.[18] Joint custody has probably not fulfilled the strong expectations that it was desired to meet – including equal child-rearing responsibilities. Good intentions by lawyers, judges and litigants are not enough for a disposition to succeed. The realities of everyday living can prove to be extremely difficult in a divorced family where each of a child's activities may need joint parental approval, whereas in an intact family one parent can and ordinarily does act on behalf of both parents. In addition, any number of unforeseen factors and events can enter into the equation for success. Perhaps one of the most important unforeseen facts is that human relations are not frozen. Time and events prompt change. Spouses remarry, children mature, resulting in children having different needs and a different relationship with adults.

The child custody disposition that has caught the interest of academics, feminists, judges and law reformers in the past decade is the primary caretaker preference.[19] The primary caretaker is the adult who has cared for the child on a day-to-day basis and who wants to and plans to continue in that role after divorce. Supporters of the disposition see it as psychologically sound in that it legally sanctions a fundamental precept in child psychology and child development – that of continuity of care by an

---

17 See Mnookin *et al* "Private Order Revisited – What Custodial Arrangements are Parents Negotiating?" in Sugarman and Kay *op cit* n. 8 at 37-74.

18 See Carbone "A Feminist Perspective on Divorce" (1994) 4 *The Future of Children* 183.

19 For a discussion of the historical roots of the tender years presumption and the arguments for and against the primary caretaker presumption see Katz, " 'That They May Thrive' Goal of Child Custody: Reflections on the Apparent Erosion of the Tender Years Presumption and the Emergence of the Primary Caretaker Presumption" (1992) 8 *Jo of Contemp Health Law and Policy* 123.

affectionate and nurturing parent who wants to continue in that role trumps all other considerations.

At first blush, the primary caretaker preference seems to be reasonable. It is a neutral standard that does not speak in terms of mother or father. Either can be a primary caretaker.[20] Yet certain fundamental questions must be asked. The first concerns any preference in child custody. As already mentioned, the maternal preference rule has been abolished as being unfair because it required the father to prove that the mother was unfit, not that he was fit. Fathers viewed the preference as giving the mother a procedural advantage in a child custody case. Further, it turned the divorce case into a kind of child protection case. In other words, for a father to gain custody of his child he had to prove that his wife and the mother of his child was neglectful or had abandoned her child.

A major criticism of the primary caretaker preference is that it looks backward, not forward. It makes the assumption that the person who has had the primary responsibility for raising a child will continue in that role after divorce. This may or may not be the case. At the present time with so many parents both working outside of the home, neither is likely to be available on a continuous basis during the day. Rather, workers in day care centres and baby-sitters will perform the parenting function on an hour-by-hour basis, with parents continuing that function after they arrive home from work. Thus it is not unusual for judges to review parenting plans and determine, as between two fit parents, who has the better plan. Where both parents are fit and intend to use the same child care provider, the judge is faced with an incredible problem. Would the flip of a coin be an appropriate method to resolve the custody dispute?[21]

In discussing legal reforms concerning custody, sight is often lost of the child – who should be the major focus. In other words, child custody should be a child-focused inquiry in which the decision-maker asks the question: who among the adult claimants will provide the child with a safe environment and the appropriate affection, nurturing, and stimulation on a continuous basis, taking into account the child's age, physical and emotional development, attachments, special relationships and needs. Each one of these factors is important and the priority that must be given to each depends on the individual case. More often than not, the adult who can fulfill the child's needs post-divorce is the person who provided for the child pre-divorce: the primary caretaker. This does not necessarily mean that there should be a statutory preference for the primary caretaker if

---

20 In *Pikula v Pikula*, 374 N.W.2d 705, 712 n. 2 (Minn. 1985), Wahl J wrote: "The primary parent preference, while in accord with the tender years doctrine insofar as the two rules recognize the importance of the bond formed between a primary parent and a child, differs from the tender years doctrine in significant respects. Most importantly, the primary parent rule is gender neutral. Either parent may be the primary parent; the rule does not incorporate notions of biological gender determinism or sex stereotyping."

21 In *Beyond the Best Interests of the Child* (The Free Press, 1973), Goldstein *et al* write at 153: "A judicially supervised drawing of lots between two equally acceptable psychological parents might be the most rational and least offensive process for resolving the hard choice."

such a preference were to mean that a judge could not inquire into the quality and quantity of care the primary caretaker gave and will continue to give (with financial support from the non-custodial parent if necessary) to her or his child.

There are no magical solutions in child custody contests. No amount of statutory factors and parenting plans can nullify the judge's experience and intuition. Experienced judges who have listened to custodial contests for years develop their own sense of what is workable in a given case. There is no way to study such a phenomenon or to review it, but it is as much a part of child custody law as any statutory factor. In contested child custody cases the judge is endowed with enormous powers even when statutory factors must be followed and findings of fact must be issued. Ultimately it is the judge who profoundly affects the child's interest.

Chapter 14

The Cross-disciplinary Approach to Family Law – Trying to Mix Oil with Water?

Mervyn Murch
Professor, Cardiff Law School

Introduction

This paper focuses on aspects of inter-professional collaboration (and competition) in the emerging family justice system of England and Wales. It is thus concerned with the inter-disciplinary mix of law, welfare and child health which infuses the practice and structure of a distinctly hybridised system of jurisprudence. In this context I touch on the proposition advanced by Michael King and Christine Piper (1990)[1] that the autopoietic nature of law makes it particularly difficult for lawyers to collaborate effectively with the health and welfare professions providing services for children and families.

Inter-disciplinary relationships within the family justice system

First a brief reminder of some of the contexts in which a degree of inter-professional collaboration is now built into the family justice system. Most obviously there is the partnership between guardians *ad litem* and solicitors from the Law Society's Child Care panels which provide for separate representation of children in public law child protection proceedings.[2] There is also the important liaison role which guardians *ad litem* now play in arranging expert medical evidence and advising justices' clerks about time-tabling in order to avoid unnecessary delay. A central thrust of the Children Act 1989 and its approach to child protection is the improvement of inter-agency co-operation.[3] The grim catalogue of child abuse inquiries which proceeded the Act, and sadly many subsequent tragedies, highlight failures of inter-agency collaboration.[4] This includes not only the front-line

---

1   King and Piper *How the Law Thinks about Children* (Gower, 1990).
2   Hunt and Murch *Speaking Out for Children* (The Children's Society, 1990) 54.
3   DoH "Child Abuse: A Study of Inquiry Reports" (HMSO, 1991).
4   *Ibid.*

child protection agencies but also the important relationship between the courts and the local authorities.[5] Thus the administrative mechanisms of the family court service and business committees set up under the Act aim to provide local fora in which a multi-professional approach to improved co-ordination and collaboration can take place.

In so-called "private" matrimonial child related proceedings, court welfare officers have to work with court officials and solicitors. Likewise, in the growing domain of alternative dispute resolution we find that comprehensive mediation increasingly involves lawyers and social workers working together as "co-mediators"; a practice which could develop substantially if proposals in the Lord Chancellor's recent white paper find their way into legislation in the next year or so.[6]

The medical and legal professions have traditionally had an uneasy relationship because in some respects they have very different professional values. Even so medical practitioners of various kinds (especially child psychiatrists and paediatricians) frequently have to give evidence in child related cases: some get to know the legal ropes and cope well with the court experience, sometimes getting so absorbed into the court culture as to be almost regarded as part of it. By contrast others hate the court domain and find themselves at odds with the whole legal paraphernalia and its approach to children and their family problems.[7]

The case for a cross-disciplinary approach to family justice studies

As these inter-professional relationships have developed in and around the family justice system it is not surprising to find that increasing recognition has been given to their educational implications. For example Waterhouse J writing of the judicial approach to child abuse in 1989 remarked:

> "We hope that with experience we are better equipped to exercise our wide discretion more correctly in the best interest of the children with whom we have to deal, but we are not professional doctors, psychologists or social workers ... Our duty (as judges) is to evaluate the evidence before us and the greater the exchange of views between those involved in child care the greater is the hope that the correct or at least the best solution will be found."[8]

Later when the Children Act 1989 was being implemented the Lord Chancellor, Lord Mackay of Clashfern observed[9] that family law

> "is not an area where a knowledge of the black letters of the law takes one very far ... In my view we must exert ourselves to ensure that the studies of judges

---

5 DoH "Working Together under the children Act 1989 – a Guide to Arrangements for Inter-agency Co-operation for the Protection of Children from Abuse" (HMSO, 1991).

6 Ld Ch Dep "Looking to the Future: Mediation and the Ground for Divorce – the Government's Proposals" (HMSO, 1995).

7 King and Trowell *Childrens' Welfare and the Law: The Limits of Legal Intervention* (Sage, 1992).

8 Waterhouse J "Allegations of Child Abuse: The Courts' Approach" in Levy (ed) *Focus on Child Abuse – Legal, Medical and Social Work Perspectives,* (Hawksmere, 1989).

9 Ld Mackay of Clashfern, Ld Ch *The UpJohn Lecture* (1991).

and magistrates, or social workers and other professionals, and not least the lawyers are informed by each others disciplines and views and that the study itself is based on a common core and common perspectives".

Such a view underscored the flurry of inter-disciplinary training events that accompanied the introduction of the Children Act 1989, not least the series of seminars organised by the Judicial Studies Board. Even so in some respects, as I hope to show, such views and activities fail to acknowledge the complexities of the inter-disciplinary approach.

Rhetoric is not enough

We have to get beneath the rhetoric of inter-professional collaboration, which so often is all that appears in official publications, in order to examine why it can be so difficult to put it into practice. My current Nuffield-sponsored educational project "The Development of Family Justice Studies"[10] starts from the proposition that because the work of the family justice system is inter-disciplinary in character, the training of those who work within it needs to be organized on a cross-disciplinary basis, at least at the post-professional level. Those working in the family justice system not only need to understand each other's roles and appreciate what they have in common, they also need to know where their professional knowledge and values differ and where this can lead them into disagreements. These professional differences of opinion and perceptions often confuse clients and at worst invite manipulation and the playing off of one agency against another. At present – insofar as there is any serious post-professional study for those working in the family justice system – such thorny issues are often avoided and there is very little shared learning. Why is this?

In part it may be because most professional and post-professional education is organized in single disciplinary "ghettos". One can understand the reasons for this. It assists socialisation to the particular constituent professions – solicitors, barristers, justices' clerks, guardians *ad litem*, court welfare officers, Local Authority social workers, psychiatrists, paediatricians etc. Also it is probably easier to organize training this way and there is always a momentum against change. Nevertheless this traditional form of professional education can too easily allow unhelpful stereotypes of other occupations to develop and go unchallenged. Douglas Hooper and I have elaborated this point elsewhere.[11]

Another reason may be that much emphasis is placed in training, especially for lawyers, on the imparting of knowledge rather than on the development of collaborative skills. This may be because most of us assume that we already know how to collaborate – that it is something we acquire in the early days of our socialisation and education. At a certain surface level this may be true. We are constantly employing to varying degrees our

---

10 The Development of Family Justice Studies Project (April 1993 – March 1996), Cardiff Law School.

11 Murch and Hooper "*The Family Justice System*" (Family Law, 1992).

normal relationship skills to manage the selection/rejection tasks of everyday life; for example deciding who to work with, when and how closely, and who to avoid if we possibly can! But how much of this is task related? Certainly it will not do when it comes to working professionally with emotionally charged child welfare and family issues which can provoke acute anxiety, where the dangers of projective identification can be intense and where often no one practitioner or service can provide all that is required. When faced with this sort of work we need to take a more considered, disciplined approach to collaborative practice.

The educational task

In our professional education of lawyers, medical practitioners and social workers, I suggest we need to address the subject from a number of perspectives. This will involve some understanding of the sociology of organizations, the cultures that develop within them, and how certain occupations acquire status and power sometimes at the expense of others. It will also involve paying attention to the psychology of small group behaviour; for example understanding how groups draw boundaries, reward group loyalty, protect group privacy and develop other institutional defence mechanisms – all social forces which can impede collaboration. We also need to acquaint ourselves with insights from individual psychology in order to better understand and ascertain why some people are good collaborators and others not, and similarly why some are more competitive than others. This involves understanding how professionals learn to understand, trust and respect each others' competencies. In other words, we need to know about our own and other people's valencies in these respects – valencies which can be either reinforced or challenged by group processes in the work setting. Allied to all this is a need to improve our understanding of the ways in which clients can manoeuvre us and exploit these valencies.[12]

A challenge to reflective practitioners

Theoretical understanding of such matters has to be translated and applied to the practitioners' subjective professional life if it is to assist practice. For this reason I pose the following questions:

– Could you consider for a moment some recent work which involved you in dealings with someone with a different professional background from your own?
– How well were you in tune with their professional caste of mind?
– Did you feel you shared the same professional values?
– How well did you understand the intellectual frameworks and knowledge base which they used?

---

12 Woodhouse and Pengelly *Anxiety and the Dynamics of Collaboration* (Aberdeen University Press, 1991).

Next ask yourself whether you find it easier to work with people educated professionally in your own discipline – law, social work or whatever it may be? If you do, what exactly accounts for this? Is it simply because you feel you have more in common, that you speak the same professional language and hold the same values? Alternatively you might feel something of an outsider in your own profession and disagree strongly with some of your colleagues over the approach they adopt; in which case you might care to reflect why that is? Is it something about you or something about them? A difference perhaps between being something of a conservative or a radical within your own professional circle? Do you view people from other occupations with a certain uncertainty, mistrust or even distain? Do they represent something a bit foreign to you? Do you ever find yourself thinking about people from other occupations in stereotypical terms? How do these stereotypes match the realities and how do they influence your dealings with other professional groups? How easy do you find it to see and relate to the person behind the professional persona?

Reflecting on these sorts of questions and testing their realities can sometimes help us to overcome what might be recurrent obstacles to successful inter-professional collaboration. Professional supervision, or client-centred case consultation[13], are other methods of professional support which can address such problems at an individual level when they persist. In this paper I am more concerned to consider some of the structural forces which institutionalise professional rivalry and competition within the boundaries of the family justice system, and which make the tasks of collaboration more difficult. Before I do so I first need to remind you of some of the distinguishing features of this particular branch of civil jurisprudence.

Some distinguishing features of the system

In broad terms one could say that the primary task of the family justice system is to administer the civil law as it affects intimate family relations. Thus the first point to note is that it is a system with an essential unity of purpose. This itself gives a certain unifying authority to the jurisdiction's work. This involves a protective function for vulnerable family members who may be oppressed, neglected or injured within the privacy of the home – particularly children, women and the elderly. It also involves regulating certain legal changes of status such as adoption and divorce. It provides a framework for the resolution of dispute mostly between family members (private law), but also where families come into conflict with the welfare and educational authorities of the state over the upbringing of children (public law). The nature of dispute resolution ranges from encouraging settlement by negotiation and mediation, to more traditional court-based adjudication, which following the Children Act 1989 now operates through

---

13 Caplan *The Theory and Practice of Mental Health Consultation* (Tavistock, 1970).

a three tiered system of courts of first instance (Magistrates Family Proceedings Courts, Care Courts and Family Hearing Centres based on the County Court administration, and the Family Division of the High Court). As far as the court system is concerned, the intention is that family proceedings should be free of the stigma of criminality.

The Law Commission[14] has highlighted some other significant features. First, that most important decisions involve not merely the findings of relevant facts but also the exercise of wide discretion which is often more akin to the management of the family's future than to more traditional adjudication upon their past. Second, that many issues involve the future of children for whom delay in completing proceedings may be highly detrimental. Third, unlike other legal actions, a large part of the court's work with families consists of approving decisions already agreed between the parties, where the need for adjudication is minimal. Fourth, in contested cases the promotion of desirable settlement is increasingly seen as a task for the court. Fifth, in disputes about family matters the emotions of everyone in the court (including the tribunal) are often likely to more deeply engaged than in most other forms of litigation. In addition one might add that most family proceedings are protected by a degree of privacy, a value which can constrain the sharing of information between professional services within the system.

Structural and administrative fragmentation exacerbates professional rivalry

Despite the unity of purpose and these underlying distinctive values, the system remains structurally fragmented in a number of respects. I argue that these exacerbate the dangers of professional "tribalism" and promote inter-professional rivalry and competition rather than collaboration; the more so whenever there is either no superordinate co-ordinating authority or if it is too weak. True, the Children Act 1989 was accompanied by a number of administrative measures (court business and court service committees) designed to minimise these problems, but these have still to prove their practical value, and are certainly not yet strong enough to erode the legacy of traditional rivalries which still imbue the organizational culture of the system's constituent elements. Also we should not forget that increasingly for a number of years the traditional dominance of professional lawyers has been challenged by social workers of various kinds working within and across the boundaries of the system. Thus there are undercurrents of professional rivalry which tend to work against the overt collaborative task promoted by these new measures.

Boundaries between organizations have to be successfully crossed in any collaborative endeavour. Consider for a moment some of the more obvious boundaries running across and through the family justice system. At a national policy level there are three ministries involved. The Lord

---

14 Law Commission 172 (HMSO, 1988) "Review of Child Law: Guardianship and Custody".

Chancellor's Department, responsible for the courts, private family law, legal aid, and the work of the official solicitor; the Department of Health which is the lead ministry where public law child protection is concerned and which is responsible for the development of panels of guardians *ad litem* and reporting officers (GALRO).[15] The Home Office retains a continuing interest in the civil family court welfare work of the probation service.

Next consider the court structure. Although in recent years this has come under a unified administration under the authority of the Lord Chancellor, ancillary court welfare services continue to be divided between three services each accountable to a different ministry, even though many of their functions overlap and the work essentially requires a common professional knowledge and skill base, *i.e.*: the divorce court welfare service, GALRO panels, and the child-related work of the Official Solicitor. The future of mediation services (variously provided by the voluntary sector and the probation service) currently appears to await the outcome of proposals for divorce law reform.

In addition to these organizational splits, which are largely historically determined and which have a dynamic which will be resistant to reorganization, the system as a whole holds a number of competing social values in suspension – for example, considerations of justice and welfare, each of which can excite heated debate concerning the interpretation and application of law and legal process in particular circumstances. Here again individual valencies come into the picture. Some legal practitioners are more adversarial in their approach while others are more conciliatory. Court welfare officers and guardians *ad litem* can likewise differ in their particular philosophical beliefs; partly because they have a different professional heritage, (the probation service for one, local authority social work for the other), and partly because some are more inclined to rehabilitate families' while others are more concerned to save the child regardless of family attachments and loyalties. Medical practitioner's who come to court as expert witnesses, being more conditioned to a therapeutic approach to family conflict than lawyers, may hold quite different conceptions of what amounts to relevant evidence. One could cite many other examples of differences in professional value which orientate the professional's approach.

The autopoietic nature of law: how serious an obstacle to collaboration is it?

In addition to all these structural and attitudinal splits with which the family justice system is riven, there are those who argue that there is something about the lawyers' world view and approach to child and family welfare issues which is fundamentally at odds with those of other occupational

---

15 These are considered officers of the court even though administered by Local Authorities while supposedly independent of them.

groups, particularly those educated in what is sometimes rather loosely described as child welfare science. Thus Michael King and Christine Piper in their challenging book *How the Law Thinks about Children*[16], argue that a multi-disciplinary approach to family justice is not really possible. Using propositions developed by the German legal sociologist Gunther Teubner[17], that law is essentially a powerful, closed, self-referring and self-sustaining (autopoietic) system of thought, they suggest that legal process will inevitably "enslave" all other disciplines which come within its portals and distort other views to fit its own particular intellectual discourse. This leads King and Piper to the view that the legal approach to child welfare matters is bound to suffer from the following basic shortcomings.

First, it oversimplifies the child's social world, excluding from consideration, for example, environmental factors such as poverty, bad housing, social security provision and taxation – matters which the judicial process generally cannot address in any meaningful way. Thus they assert :

> "Those who are critical of the problem-solving capacities of law in children's cases will not improve matters by trying to change its reductionist tendencies by bringing about reforms to make law more responsive and more sensitive to the particular demands of these issues. The autopoietic nature of law precludes any fundamental changes both in the procedures for reality construction and in the epistemic framework within which law's semantic artifacts are produced and reproduced. All that changes are the accounts of people and relationships within law's social world constructions. These new accounts are constructed in ways that enable them to fit easily into the pre-existing categories and classifications that law provides·"[18]

Of course one could respond that much the same thing applies to other intellectual discourses; that, for example, behaviourist or psycho-dynamic theories have their own autopoietic character which tends to alter accounts of people and their relationships in order to accord to the basic tenets of the discourse.

Second, King and Piper argue that the legal approach traditionally individualises parent/child relationships and tends to "root them" in notions of individual morality and responsibility. Thus a functional systemic view of family interaction upon which various models of family therapy and mediation have been developed cannot be properly encompassed by the legal process. They write:

> "There have been, and no doubt there will continue to be, more attempts to substitute for this mediatory role a scientific enquiry into a child's welfare. These attempts cannot fully succeed as long as the law continues to "think" about children's issues in terms of individualised relationships between children and parents and our analysis suggests at least within western contemporary society, the law cannot think about children in any other way. Whatever changes are made to the criteria from state interventions, to the

16 King and Piper *op cit*, n. 2.
17 Teubner n. 2 *Law as an Autopoietic System* (Blackwell, 1993).
18 *op cit*, n. 2 at 123.

rules of evidence and procedure and to the definitions of the legal relationships between parents and children, the legal discourse and the semantic artifacts it produces seem always to be rooted in notions of individual morality and responsibility. In disputes between parents therefore the law 'thinks' about children's needs in relation only to the normative acceptability of the competing alternative solutions offered by each parent."[19]

While as a generalisation this view may have a certain validity, particularly as it applied to court practice before the Children Act 1989, I think King and Piper have failed to appreciate where it now clearly has to be modified. Take for example those instances when courts refer cases to child welfare experts for assessment and then simply accept the experts recommendation – quite often now making "no order" in accordance with the principle of section 1(5) of the Act. Similarly where mediation is arranged though the agency of the court it generally accepts the resulting settlements, sometimes as a basis for a subsequent order if that is what the parties and the children wish. Moreover it seems to me that in pursuing this argument, King and Piper fail to acknowledge how very often notions of individual morality and responsibility lurk behind the semantic artifacts of the child welfare scientists, notwithstanding that those "experts" may accept notions of the unconscious as determining certain behaviours which by definition is beyond the control of the individual. I would suggest that child psychiatry and child welfare services may be no more immune in this respect than legal practices.

Third, King and Piper suggest that the legal approach concentrates decision-making on dyadic relationships – child/mother, mother/father etc. – and thus excludes factors seen as irrelevant to these relationships, ruling out other versions of reality which it is unable or unwilling to handle. Again it seems to me that law is not alone in this tendency. In the child welfare field, different schools of thought will tend to shape and focus practitioners' thoughts in ways which include favoured or familiar perceptions while excluding others. For example those using family systems theory will focus on the interactions of the whole family, whereas those adopting a child development perspective may view the child's early attachments as the crucial factor.

Fourth, King and Piper argue that the very nature of the litigation process, particularly if based on the adversarial model of justice, encourages distortion and exaggeration. Parties are obliged to defend their corner and press their case to the limit, notwithstanding that children's proceedings under the Children's Act 1989 are "officially deemed to be an enquiry into the future welfare of the child". Again, one readily sees a certain validity in this observation, yet on reflection one might argue that any form of dispute or interpersonal conflict tends to generate a defensive dynamic which encourages exaggeration and polarisation. The legal process merely reflects this in its procedures. But one can equally argue that the judicial

---

19   *Ibid* at 123-4.

process overall structures the arguments, tends to contain and limit their excess, and in civil law weighs the balance of probabilities as far as the *evidence* is concerned – all processes which tend to correct exaggeration. Further, what King and Piper refer to as "distortion" could as easily be simply described as selectivity; a feature which inevitably occurs when human beings are obliged to choose between the relevant and the irrelevant. Such choices and decisions are made by therapists, social workers and mediators every bit as much as lawyers, according to the values of their particular discourses. These too will be reflected in the "rules" of their particular processes although this may not be so explicitly stated or readily accessible to the client/patient family or child. Here traditional legal principle of "open justice" may have some advantage.

Fifth, King and Piper argue that law is reductionist in its approach to child welfare matters – reducing the findings of child welfare science to simple rules of thumb, such as "continuing contact between child and non-custodial parent is a good thing". Even here one could argue that law is not alone in this tendency. Indeed there is much evidence to suggest that social work is recently being strongly developed and managed along similar lines. Thus we find a developing corpus of professional guidelines and rules of "best practice" limiting the individual social worker's professional discretion. Likewise in medicine, protocols associated with medical audit may share similar functions, setting standards of "best practice" which in time may well come to be regarded as "rules".

All this means that while not totally dismissing the validity of the so-called autopoeitic nature of law and the problems it may pose for collaborative work between the disciplines, I find King and Pipers' arguments somewhat overstated. I realise at this point I may be obliged to explain my own favoured theoretical approach to the problems of collaboration in the family justice system.

Institutional defences against anxiety

Perhaps because following my legal education I was professionally trained as a social worker at a time when psychodynamic theories were in vogue, I find the writing of Isabell Manzies Lyth[20] and Woodhouse and Pengelly especially helpful in attempting to understand the institutional barriers (and the barriers in the mind) to collaboration between services in the family justice system. The nub of this approach is that:

> "major impediments to inter-professional collaboration originate in the unconscious needs of practitioners to use the structures of their agencies and professional groups to manage task related anxiety."[21]

---

20 Menzies Lyth "The Functioning of Social Systems as a Defence Against Anxiety" in *Containing Anxiety in Institutions: Selected Essays Vol 1* (Free Association Books, 1985); A Psychoanalytic Perspective on Social Institutions" in *The Dynamics of the Social: Selected Essays* Vol 1 (Free Association Books, 1989).
21 Woodhouse and Pengelly *op cit* n. 12 at 228.

Almost all family proceedings have a potential to provoke acute anxiety, touching raw nerves in practitioners called upon to deal with them; child neglect, family violence, the breaking and remaking of family relationships, separation and loss and much more. Menzies' seminal work concerning the management of nursing services in hospital,[22] showed how rigid institutional procedures developed as an unconscious means of protecting nurses from the anxieties provoked by dealing with seriously ill and dying patients. This was evidenced by the nurses' compulsive adherence to administrative and technical procedures which distanced them from personal involvement with patients. We can see similar processes at work in family law work. For example I suggest that often in many family courts one can observe depersonalised isolation of litigant parents and children in the courtroom while the professionals act out their respective roles in the litigation drama, using a "clubby" professional language which can be quite baffling and alienating to the family.

Important to this way of thinking in our consideration of collaboration is the notion of the agency or work group as a defence which protects the practitioner's professional identity and status and which sustains professional self esteem when competence is challenged both by the client/family's situation and/or by practitioners in other settings with different professional perspectives. Woodhouse and Pengelly's study suggests that at the institutional level there are various aspects to this; for example because of differential agency function, different aspects of a client/family's problematic behaviour which provoke anxiety may be "channelled" and attributed to particular professionals (the lawyers, the court welfare officers etc.) working within the network of services dealing with the particular family. Thus they suggest that disturbed and disturbing behaviour within a family can manifest a variety of individual and collective defences of projection and "splitting" which tend to get "mirrored" in divisions between practitioners working with particular members of the family:

> "This incessant projective redistribution of unmanageable anxiety between agencies can only serve to rigidify the structures and practices through which (agency) members attempt to ward it off. In the relevant service network constellated by a given case, the practitioners involved may be impelled to use institutional defences (such as fight and flight) not only internally against their own, but externally against each other to the detriment of collaboration".[23]

Sometimes, as in the child sexual abuse crisis in Cleveland in 1987, this gives rise to inter-agency behaviour in which groups of practitioners from different agencies form defensive coalitions against those from another which appear to adopt an opposing view. Dynamics of this sort may also explain some of those situations when for example, in child proceedings, a

---

22 *op cit*, N. 14.
23 Woodhouse and Pengelly *op cit* n. 12.

guardian *ad litem* operating in partnership with a children's solicitor appears almost routinely to criticise the work of the local authority social services department.

Conclusion

To return now to the question posed in the title; are we in effect trying to mix oil with water in our attempts to develop a cross-disciplinary approach to family law? I appreciate that in drawing attention to some of the problems and complexities, particularly as they apply to collaborative practice between the relevant professions, I may appear to have been suggesting that the game is not worth the candle; that it might be better, as King and Piper suggest, to develop policies and practices which wherever possible avoid bringing children and their families into contact with the judicial process and subjecting them to the lawyers' caste of mind. Few would disagree with that. Litigation should always be a last resort – if only because of the problems of delay and expense. In child protection for example there may well be a case for a more restrictive use of courts, particularly in marginal cases where Local Authorities appear to differ widely over whether to institute court proceedings (a matter which is currently being researched by Hunt and Macloed in Bristol for the Department of Health[24]) Also, there may well be areas – such as uncontested adoption and undefended divorce – where judicial process is now little more than a symbolic ritual. But it is utopian to believe that the judicial process in family matters can be entirely replaced by therapeutic methods based on child welfare science. The behavioural and social sciences are not exact, and in any event contain schools of thought which themselves often take on an autopoetic quality. As others have observed, theories which are developed in a given field will reflect that particular culture and the systems of thought prevailing in it. Moreover civil liberty considerations associated with the state's extensive powers to intervene and regulate family life, particularly where there are allegations of child neglect and abuse, makes it inconceivable that judicial process can be dispensed with. Also the children's rights movement seems likely to increase rather than diminish the range of proceedings in which children can be separately represented by lawyers in partnership with guardians *ad litem*. So child related litigation is firmly with us. This means we have no alternative but to oil the wheels of collaboration by better understanding of the related processes.

At the end of the day, the case for adopting a cross-disciplinary approach to family justice studies rests on two main arguments. The first is the need to improve inter-professional collaboration in the service of children and their families in order to avoid the risks of harm which can otherwise result,

---

24 "Statutory Intervention in Childcare Proceedings Research Project" (Socio-Legal Centre for Family Studies, University of Bristol).

as the Maria Colwell case[25] demonstrated. But the educational effort to bring about improved practices of this sort will need to be substantial and sustained, and even then will often be hard to quantify and may be difficult to justify in strict cost benefit terms.

The second argument which I favour is more general, namely that broadly-based professional education is more likely to produce intellectual honesty, well balanced minds and sound judgement than narrow specialisation. A practitioner with a reflective self-critical approach to learning is a safer proposition when wielding power over other people's lives, than one who is fixated by a single set of ideas and intoxicated by dogma however fashionable. I suggest that most practitioners, given the chance at an appropriate stage in their professional development, have the intellectual capability to understand, integrate and even apply a range of discourses and theoretical frameworks. But this will not happen if their teachers are too specialised and are themselves not given to broad-ranging reflective thought. This is why I believe we have to urgently review and reorganize our current educational practices and structures which in my opinion fail to prepare practitioners sufficiently for work in the family justice system. We need a more concentrated, integrated and co-ordinated approach particularly at the post-professional level. We need to strike a better balance between a common core of knowledge and specialist thinking. Overall, the aim should be to produce practitioners with an expanding understanding of children and their families and of other practitioners' roles and expertise; practitioners with the will and opportunity to regularly update their professional education. We will also need to concentrate more on skill development and disciplined thought rather than on the mere acquisition of knowledge (which knowledge will in any event be increasingly contained in readily accessible computerised data-bases, which are bound to become more open to the "customers" of our services as well). At the very least a cross-disciplinary approach to learning should make us more aware of our professional limitations, and of the skills and insights that others have to offer in the pursuit of justice and welfare for the child and the family.

---

25 Report of the Committee of Enquiry into the care and supervision provided in relation to Maria Colwell (1974) (The Field Fisher Report).

Chapter 15

Section 53 Offenders – Waiting for Change

Gwyneth Boswell

Lecturer in Probation Studies, University of East Anglia, Norwich

Introduction

This paper provides a brief résumé of research conducted by the author for The Prince's Trust Young Offender Group during 1991, and then – drawing on its title "Waiting for change"[1] – uses the findings to try and illustrate the meaning of that phrase for young offenders sentenced under section 53 of the 1933 Children and Young Persons Act for serious offences, and to criminal justice professionals who work with them. The ensuing discussion will address the need for change in the sentencing process, in the young offenders themselves, in the nature of their custodial careers and in emphasis – from cure to prevention.

Waiting for change

The legal framework

Young offenders, who have committed serious offences, and whom the court deems cannot be dealt with in any other way are sentenced under the Children and Young Persons Act 1933, section 53 of which makes special provision for juveniles convicted on indictment by the Crown Court of murder or other serious offences. Section 53(1) provides that a person under the age of 18, convicted of murder, be detained during Her Majesty's pleasure in such place and under such conditions as the Secretary of State (the Home Secretary) may direct. Section 53(2) (amended by the 1961 and 1991 Criminal Justice Acts and the Criminal Justice and Public Order Bill 1994) provides that a person between the ages of 10 and 17, convicted of an offence for which an adult may be sentenced to 14 years' imprisonment or more, or for indecent assault on a woman, and for whom

---

1 Boswell, *Waiting for Change: An Exploration of the Experiences and Needs of Section 53 Offenders* (The Prince's Trust, 1991).

no other disposal is considered suitable by the court, be detained in such place and under such conditions as the Home Secretary may direct. The period of detention must be specified in the sentence, and must not exceed the maximum period of imprisonment with which the offence would be punishable in the case of an adult.

The section 53 population

On 1 February 1991, there was a total of 615 section 53 offenders spread across the child care and prison systems, whose ages ranged from 12 to 47 years. Of these, 135 were held in the child care system (a range of Community Homes, Secure Units and Youth Treatment Centres (YTCs)) and 480 in the prison system (267 in Young Offender Institutions (YOI) and 195 in adult prisons). About one third (212) were serving a section 53(1) sentence; 370 a section 53(2) determinate sentence; 26 a section 53(2) life sentence; and 7 a section 53 recall from licence. Ninety of these offenders were over the age of 25 and serving indeterminate sentences. They had all served at least 8 years, and most of them considerably more. Only 31 of the entire population were female. Twenty-two per cent of the 15 to 20 year age group were black.

Basis of the research

Evidence was collated from the foregoing statistical information, relevant literature, discussions with institutional staff, and interviews with a representative group of 25 section 53 offenders held in a variety of institutions. The interview schedules covered five key subject areas which had been identified through exploratory work with other groups of section 53 offenders and staff and with an ex-section 53 offender who had been all the way through the child care and prison systems and out on licence to the probation service for four years. These subject areas were offending behaviour; the psychological effects of a section 53 sentence; opportunities for education, training or employment; social skills learning, and the rehabilitation process. The respondents were asked two questions under each of these headings relating to their own experiences (see Appendix). Staff were asked the same set of questions relating to their role in helping the respondents in these five areas. Before discussing the results of this survey, let us consider the sentencing process which sets in motion the custodial careers of these young offenders.

Waiting for change in the sentencing process

The use of section 53(2) determinate sentences rose quite steeply during the 1980s, almost trebling over the decade. As a NACRO study showed[2] the widening of the net in respect of offences of robbery and burglary (though the latter was later removed by the 1991 Criminal Justice Act) and of children jointly charged on an indictable offence with an adult, made a significant contribution to this increase. The question that this sentencing increase raises is whether section 53(2) is being used by sentencers as a means of circumventing the 12-month maximum YOI sentence; and if it is, what implications this has for the 17-year olds who now fall into the category of "young persons" for the purposes of the new youth courts and for young people convicted of indecent assault under the 1991 Criminal Justice Act. Early indications are that section 53(2) sentences were beginning to rise steeply during the second quarter of 1993. The 1994 Criminal Justice and Public Order Act's inclusion of all 10-13 year olds under the potential umbrella of section 53(2) also has considerable implications for the continuation of that rising trend. Alongside that issue rests a serious concern relating to the report's findings of gross over-representation of young black people, especially in the 15 to 20 year age group, where they comprise 22% of the prison population. Why that situation obtains is something that policy-makers and practitioners clearly need to address.

In contrast to the increase in determinate sentences however, was the finding of less than 30 section 53(2) lifers in the system during 1991 – which suggesting that sentencers in recent times have been inclined to use this disposal only with extreme caution. An example of this trend was the sentencing in 1992 of a 12-year old girl in Newcastle for the manslaughter of an 18-month old child. She was given a section 53(2) determinate sentence of five years, which again follows the pattern of greater leniency towards the offence of manslaughter than hitherto. One of the most famous uses of section 53(2) life was in respect of Mary Bell, convicted of manslaughter in 1968 at the age of 11, and who then served about 12 years of a life sentence – first in a Local Authority secure unit and then in closed and open prisons. In fact, as Sereny[3] noted, the judge had wished to make a hospital order under the Mental Health Act 1983, but no suitable hospital could be found, and thus Mary ended up as a section 53(2) lifer. A particularly interesting aspect of her case was that it was seen as so exceptional at the time that it was instrumental in reversing the 1969 Children and Young Persons Act provisions to abolish custody for children under 17. Given the recent publicity in relation to the 11-year old boys convicted of the murder of James Bulger, this is a salient piece of history for lawyers and policy-makers to study. In addition, whilst there is no legal alternative to a section 53(1) sentence for the crime of murder, there is at least partial evidence from the Dartington Social Research Unit[4] to suggest that many of those who commit homicidal offences are first offenders who

---

2   NACRO Working Group, *Grave Crimes ... Grave Doubts, Report on Sentences made under Section 53 of the 1933 Children and Young Persons Act* (NACRO, 1988).

3   Sereny, *The Case of Mary Bell* (Arrow Books, 1972)

4   Bullock *et al*, "Secure Accommodation for Very Difficult Adolescents: some Recent Research Findings", (1990) 13 *Jo Adolescence* 205-16.

in fact do not reoffend. This would suggest that perhaps there are more appropriate and cost-effective ways of dealing with these young people than locking them up for indefinite numbers of years which indeed, as the survey showed, can cause them to become thoroughly institutionalised and literally lost in the prison system for 20 or more years.

To illustrate this "lost in custody" syndrome, I should like to recount the story of Thomas, aged 40. Thomas has now served 24 years of a section 53(1) sentence for the murder and sexual assault of an 8-year old girl. The long list of prison establishments where he has been held suggests that there are very few prisons in the country he has not sampled during his sentence. He has no tariff date given by the judge, because they did not exist when he was sentenced. He has had one day out in 24 years, when he was taken for a day in the countryside, and he treasures the memory of this greatly. More recently he has been tested in open conditions, but has by now become so institutionalised that he could not cope with the individual responsibility and decision-making. He is thus now back in a category B prison, in a vulnerable prisoners' unit and being greatly helped, he says, by seeing a student probation officer on a regular basis. Though staff are trying to encourage him to go on normal location to aid his release prospects, he fears doing so because of attacks by other prisoners when he has done it previously. This man appears indefinitely trapped in the prison system because of the nature of his offence and the institutionalisation which is a by-product of his sentence. As highlighted earlier, there are 90 people over the age of 25 in the prison system, who are either Thomases or potential Thomases and on the whole they are not recognised as section 53 offenders, but simply treated like all other adult long-termers. It is crucial for anyone working with someone like this to recognise that the adult is not the same person as the adolescent who committed the offence, and indeed has gone through one of the most important of life's developmental phases in completely unnatural surroundings. It seems doubtful that this is in keeping with the intention of the 1933 Act (a rehabilitative and individualised measure, stating that every court should have regard to the welfare of the child or young person). Is there, then, a different and more effective way of sentencing young persons who commit these grave crimes which ensures appropriate protection for the community without counter-productive institutionalisation and a consequent long-term drain on prison service resources, not to mention the increasing risk of suicide in custody?

Waiting for change in the young offenders

Section 53(2) determinate sentence offenders *are* given a date for release, and following the 1991 Criminal Justice Act are now eligible for remission, to apply for parole, and to have custodial remand time taken off their sentence. Hitherto the lack of these facilities has produced for these young people a double dose of custody which their adult counterparts did not receive. But those sentenced to life and Her Majesty's Pleasure, do not have any dates for release (other than a "tariff date" which is the earliest point at which they become eligible for release – subject to Parole Board and Secretary of State's recommendation). What, in effect, they have to demonstrate in order to have a chance of release, is that they have changed sufficiently not to constitute a risk to the community. What this means is that justice and welfare issues become blurred and young people can be detained beyond the period when they would be eligible for parole, perhaps because they are insufficiently informed about the nature of a section 53 sentence, or they don't know how to present their case, or because staff themselves are unfamiliar with the intricacies of Section 53, and do not give them the right advice. What follows is a description of some of the experiences of young offenders and staff in respect of the difficult task of demonstrating change in the individual offender.

> *Chris*, a section 53(2) lifer, who is 20 and black, was brought up in Africa, moving to England at the age of 13, a traumatic and confusing event for him. He still finds the language difficult and does not think any allowance has been made for his lack of understanding. It is difficult enough, he says, even for people whose native language it is, to express themselves articulately at case reviews and on parole applications. No one has really explained to him what section 53 means, and he would have liked someone to help him make sense of his offence, so he can feel sure he will not do it again. He periodically gets very depressed both about his custodial experiences and about not knowing the date of his release after 5 years inside. He feels in need of access to information, counselling, and attention to the special needs of being a black offender serving an indeterminate sentence.

> *Eric* is 26, and black. He has served 11 years of a section 53(2) life sentence for rape. Eric's tariff date of 10 years is now past, and he will not have another parole hearing for 18 months. He is intelligent and articulate, reads *The Guardian* and listens to BBC World Service. He talks reflectively and remorsefully about his crime, and feels he is now a very different person from that 15-year old. He considers that he has been stereotyped because of his colour and bearing and because he will not conform to the low status ascribed him. He thinks the language and decision-making around his case has been racist. He does not know what he has to do to get out. He definitely feels he has missed out the stage of normal youthful development and worries about how this will affect him on release. The worst thing though, he says, is "the way people look at you, believe you're still an animal, won't let you forget, won't let you move on."

Clearly there are implications in both these cases for the kind of contact criminal justice professionals have with indeterminate section 53s, their awareness of surrounding racial and cultural issues, and the need to supply them with information and guidance about their position.

A psychologist in the child care system, when asked about the psychological effects of being a section 53 offender serving an indeterminate sentence, described the attendant difficulties of individual change in this way:

"There is a lack of attention to [staff] explaining the implications of an indeterminate sentence and so they get more depressed than is necessary. They go through peaks and troughs, decide to co-operate for a while, then ask themselves what the point is. Many young adolescents are egocentric, and this situation just makes them feel more sorry for themselves which makes treatment more difficult. It is hard for staff to know how to treat kids who are going to go on to the prison system. Should you equip them for prison, or equip them for rehabilitation? They're a lurking presence because they are there indefinitely – and because of it, they can often be neglected."

Another psychologist referred to the "downgrading" of activity that occurs when young people are transferred to the prison system. Sex offenders who may have had sympathetic and structured treatment at a YTC, for example, become very vulnerable in the Prison system, and may have to go on to Rule 43 (*i.e.* be segregated) for their own protection. Staff at adult prisons sometimes advise transferred new prisoners not to reveal the true nature of their "grave" crime to their companions for fear of reprisal. This re-engages them in the very process of denial which they and their previous set of staff have been working so hard to eradicate. Generally, young offenders find that the message they had received about the importance of treatment and working to understand what caused their offending is replaced by another message – that they are there to serve the punishment element of their offence, and should simply get on with it as best they can.

These accounts of those serving indeterminate sentences, then, seek to illustrate the need for the following changes:

- the need for ongoing help in trying to understand and change their behaviour;
- the need for information both to themselves and staff about the nature of a Section 53 indeterminate sentence;
- the need for help to articulate their case both verbally and on paper;
- an adherence to the institution's race relations policy and those of outside organizations such as the probation service;
- clarity about whether to equip offenders for prison or for rehabilitation;
- a continuity of expectation from child care to prison system.

All of these points serve to emphasise the need for various information and consultant facilities, which, in fact, form part of the report's recommendations.

Waiting for change in an offender's institutional career

Some of the discussion in the last section has begun to give an indication of what the psychologist referred to as the "downgrading" process, as young offenders move through long-term sentences and from the child care system, to the YOI system and then to the adult prison system. The report has endeavoured to highlight the ways in which this happens by pointing to five key problem areas referred to earlier: working with offending behaviour; psychological effects; education, training and employment; social skills learning; and rehabilitation. It proved useful to locate this section 53 career along a continuum which has treatment at one end and punishment at the other, based on the so-called welfare and justice models of sentencing developed by juvenile justice experts such as Rutherford.[5] This issue is complex, but for the purposes of the present discussion can be simplified by explaining that the welfare or treatment model concentrates on the offender and dealing with underlying individual problems, whilst the justice or punishment model concentrates on the offence and just deserts – the infliction of an ill suffered for an ill done – which should apply to all offenders equally. The latter is a model with which those called upon to implement the 1991 Criminal Justice Act are by now becoming familiar.

What is fascinating about section 53 offenders is the way that many will begin their sentences under some form of treatment model (and indeed some will end their sentences in that setting), but others, especially the long-termers, will transfer at 18, 19 or 20 years to YOIs and then to the prison system – which may be open but is often closed because of the nature of the offence and a perceived risk to society – and where both offenders and staff will say they are going to serve the "punishment" element of their sentence. Simultaneously, as they move along this continuum, there is a general decrease of opportunity in the five key areas, though there are, of course, exceptions to this, and there are differential entry and exit points on the continuum. So here you have this odd notion of someone receiving intense therapy, counselling, family work, education, occupational and social skills for a period, say three years, much of which is then likely to evaporate rather than be seized and built upon towards a point of rehabilitation. At the same time the transition from childhood to adulthood is taking place in quite unnatural circumstances – the "lost youth" syndrome. Again, as a psychologist commented:

> "The time warp in an artificial environment is a problem, because there is no encouragement to grow up. What gave you 'street cred' at 15, won't at 22 or 23 because your friends will have moved on from that years ago."

Many of the young offenders seen by the author echoed their concern about that situation. In addition, as they move along this continuum, these young people experience a life in waiting – waiting for mobility, waiting for a tariff date, waiting for a parole date – and all the intermediate stages of waiting that are entailed in the bureaucratic process. All in all, the road from treatment to punishment, from indeterminacy to determinacy, is a hard and unmotivating one for young offenders to travel. Availability of

5   Rutherford, *Growing out of Crime* (Penguin, 1986).

social skills opportunities and volunteers from the home area, as the report suggested, could help fill an important gap here, and consistency from social workers and probation officers seems crucial.

A change in emphasis from cure to prevention

Clearly diversion from section 53 at the court stage is one major preventive remedy which solicitors, barristers, probation officers and social workers need to think about in relation to their pre-sentence work with these offenders. In particular, they should avoid giving sentencers the impression that a section 53 sentence is a measure which will afford offenders the "treatment" or "therapy" they need. In reality this is a very "hit and miss" affair. In addition to this point, however, it should be noted that evidence from staff and offenders alike suggests that anything between 50 and 90% of these section 53 offenders, most of whom are male, have been abused in one way or another as children, and in some cases are re-enacting with their own victims the acts which have been perpetrated upon them. This again is partial evidence which comes from case records, staff, and the young offenders themselves (and is currently being more thoroughly researched by the author) as shown in the following three profiles in the report – but as a phenomenon it pops up again and again:

> *Jerome's* father died when he was five. His stepfather physically and sexually abused him. Jerome became involved with an evangelical movement, and subsequently became friendly with one of its female members, developing inappropriate fantasies about the relationship. Realising his feelings were not reciprocated, he physically and sexually assaulted her, causing serious and lasting injury. He had no previous convictions. The original charge was attempted murder, but this was reduced, and he was, unusually, told that he should serve a minimum of 3 years. He had served two years seven months and a first parole review was due in three months.
>
> He had weekly counselling sessions which, together with some of the group encounter sessions, had helped enormously. From being arrogant, Jerome could now be more honest with himself and others. If he felt something, he worked out what it was, and tried to act on it appropriately. He felt very aware of the pain he had caused, and for that reason did not believe he could do it again. The message had reached him that his victim had forgiven him.
>
> He had obtained several AEB exams and a GCSE. Encouraged by the YTC to maintain family contact, he wrote to and telephoned his family regularly. His mother and sister visited every three weeks. A probation officer visited him and his family regularly. He had just been granted escorted "mobility" for a day trip to a place of his choice.
>
> Jerome had been confused and "numbed" for a year after his sentence. What keeps him going now is his belief that he should pay for what he has done, and learn to understand his crime, how the childhood abuse contributed to it, and how to avoid offending in future. "But it's a hard thing to live with."

At the age of 15, *Oliver* argued with a friend in the road over an old difference of opinion. He lost his temper, hit his friend over the head with a brick, then stabbed him. The friend subsequently recovered. Oliver was sentenced to two and a half years under section 53(2) for assault occasioning actual bodily harm. Although he had not been conscious of it at the time, Oliver had perpetrated this attack at the same spot as his father (now serving a long prison sentence) raped a 10-year old girl. It later emerged that his father had also sexually abused Oliver and his two sisters.

Oliver had 6 AEB exams, but didn't want education in prison: "I'm no good at anything except Art." People had helped him see that he needed to understand and control his anger. He was currently being assessed for allocation to a YTC (and has subsequently been transferred to one). In the meantime he was finding YOI life very difficult. He was undersized, and was being bullied there. He had regular contact with his mother and probation officer. He found it very depressing, knowing he might have to serve the whole sentence with no earlier release on parole. (This was prior to the 1991 Criminal Justice Act amendments). It seemed a matter of chance as to whether the therapy he needed to make the links between his father's and his own behaviour would be available to him during this period.

Eleanor was brought up in children's homes, with a history of emotional problems, self-mutilation and eating difficulties. She had five previous convictions, two for soliciting, two for assault, and one for criminal damage. Her current conviction was for murder of her boyfriend when she was aged 17, following his consistent sexual and physical abuse of her. She pleaded not guilty, was found guilty, but came to believe she was legally ill-advised.

She was studying basic English and maths, health and fitness and art, and was trying to get a Child Care Certificate. Although the Home Office had agreed to her going out of the prison to conduct a child study in pursuit of this, the prison was very sensitive about public reaction should the media get hold of the information. They were looking at ways round the problem, but it was felt that she might have to forego taking the qualification.

Social skills training had not been offered in this prison, but she hoped it would be available when she was transferred to an open prison. This had to happen before she could be released, and might be decided by the Local Review Committee which was due to meet later this year, two years prior to her "tariff" date. (Since this interview took place and one year after the expiry of this date, Eleanor has still not been released). In the meantime she had been allowed out of the Prison three times, for shopping, and to visit her family. She had also been out to an art lecture in the city, and felt the prison staff were very pro-active about arranging such opportunities.

She had close contact with her family, though some of them lived abroad. She had a series of probation officers, most of whom were supportive and visited regularly, and had found the contact of a prison-based student probation officer very helpful. She planned to live with a friend in another part of the country on release.

Having complained about sexual harassment from workmen at her last prison, she had been moved here so that the complaint could be investigated. This had unsettled her, as had a Local Review Committee "knockback" last year, for which she had not been given any reason. She would have found counselling and guidance about this, her experience of abuse, and the other "uncertain" aspects of a section 53 sentence, extremely valuable.

If the prevalence of high levels of physical and sexual abuse which appear above should become validated, it would highlight a very serious situation indeed, which requires further in-depth research over a long-term period, so that earlier means of prevention might be found. This would, for example, encompass educational policies (such as "parenting" classes), improved identification of families at risk, the greater facilitation for children reporting incidents of abuse and so on. It would also have important implications for the kinds of questions which lawyers, psychologists, psychiatrists, social workers and probation officers ask of young people who have committed grave crimes at the pre-trial stage when explanations and defences are being drawn up.

Conclusion

In conclusion, this paper has endeavoured to provide a flavour of what the expression "waiting for change" means to section 53 offenders. Its contents have been very much based around death and damage, ignorance and confusion, and another kind of waiting, which is waiting to live again. Being a Boswell, I sometimes find it appropriate to quote my namesake's account of the *Life of Johnson*.[6] Johnson once wrote to his patron Lord Chesterfield – as a section 53 offender like Thomas might write to one of us as a criminal justice professional about the experience of institutionalisation.

> "Are you not one who looks with unconcern on a man struggling for life in the water, and, when he has reached ground, encumbers him with help? The notice which you have been pleased to take of my labours, had it been early, had been kind; but it has been delayed till I am indifferent and cannot enjoy it; till I am solitary, and cannot impart it; till I am known, and do not want it."

There is, I think, a huge message there for criminal justice professionals about the need for legal knowledge, critical understanding and timely intervention in the lives of this small but singular group of offenders, who in all senses of the phrase are "waiting for change".

---

6   Boswell, *Life of Johnson (GB Hill, 1769)*.

Appendix

The interview schedule

1. *Offending behaviour:*
   What means are employed to help you understand why you offended? Do you consider that this process will assist in stopping you re-offending in the future?

2. *The psychological effects of a section 53 sentence:*
   Do section 53 offenders need extra help to understand the nature of their sentence? If so, should this come from an independent source, or from someone who has experienced it firsthand?

3. *Education/training/employment:*
   What provision is currently made in your institution for education, training, and employment? Do you expect this provision to continue at the next institution to which you are likely to be transferred? (If applicable).

4. *Social skills learning:*
   Are you given any help in the area of social skills learning? (If necessary, examples were given). If so, what is the nature of this help?

5. *The rehabilitation process:*
   Are you encouraged to maintain regular contact with your family? How does your social worker/probation officer help you to maintain links with your home area?

Chapter 16

The Children Act 1989 and Children "In Need"

June Thoburn
Professor in Social Work, University of East Anglia

Introduction

The subject of this paper is Part III of the Children Act 1989 and its impact on children "in need". "In need" is specifically defined in the Act as the threshold for the provision of support services to children and their families.[1] Before the 1989 Act there was no clear boundary between those families who could or should be offered services by Social Services departments, and those who should not. Social workers made more or less arbitrary decisions in each case as to whether children and their families appeared to need their services. After the implementation of the Act if the child is not "in need", a social worker would be acting *ultra vires* if she or he spent any more time with them than was necessary to reach a conclusion that the child did not cross the "in need" threshold, except when services are provided which the Act stipulates may be provided for children who are not "in need".[2] This "need" trigger is therefore an extremely important one. If, for example, a 15-year old is assessed as crossing the "in need" threshold, she or he can be provided with accommodation by the Local Authority, and if the Authority provides accommodation it is required to maintain the young person or supplement other sources of income if this is necessary to meet identified need until the age of 18, and to provide a range of support services, including in some cases cash help and maintenance payments, until the age of 21. By passing through this assessment gateway the young person will become potentially eligible for a range of services worth a considerable sum of money which will otherwise be denied.

It is for this reason that I consider that Part III of the Act is by far the most important, in that it will have a major impact on the lives of many more children and young people than will be affected by those parts of the legislation which require the involvement of the courts. It is interesting to ask, therefore, why it has received so little attention in training courses and debates in the literature, which have tended to concentrate on measures of

---

1   Children Act 1989, s 17(10).
2   *Ibid*, s 18(2).

compulsion, such the Child Assessment Order, which will be used very rarely.

The legislators intended that there *should* be a fundamental shift from working with family members through the exercise of compulsion, to working in partnership with parents, children, and relatives, or at least towards using negotiation skills if it was not possible to work in partnership. Section 17 (1) of the Act states:

> "It shall be the general duty of every Local Authority to safeguard and promote the welfare of children within their area who are in need, and so far as is consistent with that duty, to promote the upbringing of such children by their families."

The emphasis is on helping children and promoting their welfare *within their own families*, and it is made clear that:

> "any service provided for a particular child "in need" may be provided to family members of that child if it is provided with a view to safeguarding that child's welfare" [3]

So not only does section 17 provide a gateway to services for the *child*, but also to members of the family. Prior to the Act's implementation there had been a lengthy period when the "paramountcy principle" was interpreted as meaning that it was unnecessary to work with parents, especially if the child was away from home. Under the Children Act, provided that it will help the child who is "in need", the worker may offer services to the other members of the family.

The following example indicates how important this is. If a child has a severe disability a parent will often spend a great deal of time with the child who has the disability. In such circumstances it would be appropriate to offer services such as holidays to the other children in the family who don't have disabilities even though they may not themselves be "in need", because it would help the household to run more smoothly by taking some pressure off the parents, and thus help them to meet the needs of the child with the disability. Another example is that of a child who is missing a lot of school because the mother is depressed. It might make more sense, although the child might be considered to be neglected and therefore "in need", or even "in need of protection", to pay for the *mother* to have a holiday if that will help to prevent a more serious mental illness from developing.

The threshold to services for children "in need"

The threshold to services as defined by section 17 is therefore of considerable importance to both parents and children. Section 17 (10) lists three groups of children. A child is in need if:

---

3   *Ibid*, s 17(3).

"(a) He or she is unlikely to achieve or maintain or have the opportunity of achieving or maintaining a reasonable standard of health or development without the provision of a service."

The definition will, of course, depend on an interpretation of a "reasonable standard of health and development" and whether or not this particular child will fall below it now or in the future if a service is not provided. The Act goes on to say that mental, emotional and physical health are to be considered, and that development means emotional, physical and educational development.

Let us for example take a child living in homeless families' accommodation. I would find it very hard to see how a young child living with parent(s) in bed and breakfast accommodation was having the opportunity to achieve a reasonable standard of health and development. Such children tend to have to change schools frequently so their educational development is at risk, and may be exposed to physical and sexual abuse because of the other people living in the accommodation, especially homeless single men, possibly including men with criminal records for offences against children. Another example is that of a young person of 16 who is sleeping rough. It would be hard to put up a case that that young person's health and development is *not* being impaired, and that she or he *does* have the opportunity to achieve a reasonable standard of health or development without the provision of accommodation, income and a range of other services. I certainly would not make a professional assessment that either of these two are not "in need" unless they are extraordinarily resilient or, in the first case, have exceptionally caring and competent parents.

Section 17(10)(b) involves a threshold which in many ways resembles the threshold for care or supervision orders. The child is judged to be "in need" under this sub-section if his or her health or development:

"is likely to be significantly impaired or further impaired without the provision of services".

This definition is quite close to the definitions of significant harm or likely significant harm in sections 31 and 47 which are required to be evidenced in order for a care order to be granted. The difference is that under section 17 the significant impairment does not need to result from an action or inaction on the part of someone with parental responsibility, or from the child being beyond control as it does with a care order.

The third group of children "in need" are those with a clearly defined disability. Some children with serious health problems or handicapping conditions may not come under this particularly tight definition, but may nevertheless qualify for a service under sub-sections (a) or (b).

In talking about children who are homeless or living with their parents in homeless families accommodation I have noted the possibility of whole groups being defined "in need" and thus qualifying for priority services under the Act without the indignity of a separate assessment. A group of mothers in Sheffield are claiming that young children in high-rise flats are children "in need" because of the limited play space and the dangers associated with playing unsupervised in the play area at the bottom of the block. They want a grant to help them provide supervised play facilities. Some authorities around the country are identifying certain areas and providing a range of services such as local play schemes, credit unions, and food co-ops. An interim report of research by Aldgate, McBeath and Tunstill, included in the Second Annual Review of the Children Act[4], lists the priority groups identified in this way by different Local Authorities.

The wording of Part III is supplemented by three Department of Health documents which clarify its intentions.[5] These documents may be used as a manual of what is generally accepted by professional social workers as good child and family social work practice. The Guidance is clearly written and all child care solicitors and social workers should have their own copies. The Guidance on Family Support explains that the legislators *did* intend that there would be a shift of emphasis and priorities towards family support and away from compulsion.

> "Local Authorities will need to review all their existing child care policies, their priorities will need to be re-examined."

> "The Act's emphasis on family support and partnership with parents requires Local Authorities to adopt a new approach to child care services."[6]

Services to be provided for children in need and their families

Schedule 2 to the Act suggests the following services might be helpful to parents and to children "in need", but the guidance also encourages flexibility in deciding about how to meet individual needs:

- advice, guidance and counselling;
- home help (including laundry services);
- occupational, social, cultural and recreational activities;
- assistance with travel to make use of these facilities;
- assistance with holidays for the child and family;
- family centres;
- day care for the under fives and out of school and holiday care for those who are under eight;

---

4   DoH, "Report of the Secretary of State on the First Year of the Children Act 1989" (HMSO, 1993).

5   *i.e.* "Principles and Practice in Regulations and Guidance" (HMSO, 1989); "Introduction to the Children Act" (HMSO, 1989); and "Regulations and Guidance" vol 2 ("Family Support") and vol 3 ("Family Placements") (HMSO, 1991).

6   DoH, "The Children Act 1989. Regulations and Guidance" *op cit* n. 5 above.

– accommodation for those whose parents are unable to care for them, and respite care for children whose families are under stress.

Local Authorities are required to take reasonable steps to tell people that the services are available and who might be eligible for them. The Government itself took a very positive step by producing and distributing attractive and readable leaflets for parents and children.[7] These were meant to be available in libraries, health clinics, as well as Social Services offices. I make a point of giving copies to social work students going on placement and strongly advise them to give them to parents and older children on their caseloads. I regret to say that it does not appear to be common practice for social workers to do so.

As well as taking steps to ensure that children who might be in need and their families receive information, Local Authorities have to maintain a register of disabled children in their area, and they have to assess the needs of the child who may be "in need" at the same time as assessments required by other legislation such as the 1981 Education Act.[8] In providing these services authorities are required to pay attention to the racial, cultural and religious needs of any minority groups who are resident within the area, and they may, in exceptional circumstances, give cash.

A most important change to note is that the provision of accommodation is one of the family support services. For those who are familiar with the previous legislation, this view of accommodation as a service is very different from the notion of "voluntary care" which was something which social workers were required to prevent from happening.[9] The Act recognises that most parents can benefit from a short break from their children and that families under stress, whether because of environmental pressures or personal problems or problems to do with the children, may be especially helped by periods of respite care for the children.[10] Following the Act, accommodation of a child is a *service* to be provided as appropriate alongside day care and the other support services.

The process of meeting need

Given the value of services to families under stress, it is important that families should know to what extent they can exercise their right to claim them. In other words families need to be given a clear statement of whether the child meets the threshold requirements for the provision of services.

7   DoH, "The Children Act and Local Authorities – A Guide for Parents" and "The Children Act and You – A Guide for Young People" (HMSO, 1991).
8   The Children Act 1989, Sch 2, para 3.
9   Child Care Act 1980, s 1. For an account of the development of the concept of "prevention", see Thoburn, "The Role of the Local Authority" in Triseliotis and Marsh (eds) *Prevention and Reunification in Child Care* (Batsford, 1993).
10   Aldgate, "Respite Care" in Triseliotis and Marsh *op cit*, n. 9 above.

Once a child and family have crossed the threshold and have been given this information, discussions can begin about the services likely to be helpful, and, as the Guidance makes clear, it is at this stage that the Local Authority must decide about priorities. It is also important to note that there is a corporate responsibility:

> "Where it appears to a Local Authority that any authority could, by taking specified action, help them in their functions under Part III, the Social Services Department can request the help from the authority for the person and the authority shall comply with that request unless it is against their statutory duties."[11]

Crossing the section 17 "in need" threshold thus not only conveys entitlement to be considered for the provision of *social work* and other Social Services Department provisions, but also should bestow some priority for education, health and housing services. I stress housing because it is a scarce commodity, particularly for poor families with young children and for those young people who can no longer live in the family home.

Many Social Services Departments do not seem to have grasped this point. Because of the pressure on resources made worse by council tax capping and the need to make sure that their scarce resources are only used by those in greatest need, they often employ gate-keeping strategies when parents or young people request assistance. Prior to the Act this was an understandable reaction to the fear of being swamped – as social workers were the gatekeepers for their own time and their own services. After the implementation of the 1989 Act, that sort of attitude is particularly worrying because they are not only gatekeepers for their own services, but also gatekeepers to priority consideration for services from housing, education and health. It might be inappropriate for *social work* services to be offered in response to the need which has been assessed, but by giving the family the information that the "in need" threshold has been crossed, social workers enable family members to be referred for priority assistance by one of the other services.

My emphasis on the support provisions of the Act, and indeed the inclusive nature of the wording of section 17, may come as some surprise to those who are familiar with the workings of Social Service Departments and may recognise two statements which are very frequently made. One is, "we only work with statutory cases" and the other one is, "we only do child protection work, and don't do preventive work". I consider that both of these show a basic misunderstanding of the legislation. First of all section 17 *is* statute. The Act says that Local Authorities *must* provide services for children "in need". It does not say they *may* do so, although it does not go on to say which specific services must be provided to meet any specific need.

As well as being contrary to the spirit and indeed the letter of the Act, such statements are factually incorrect. Research studies of past and present

---

11 Children Act 1989, s 27.

practice show that social workers spend most of their time on family support work. This is because a child who may be in need of protection is almost always a child "in need" under the section 17 definition. So in many cases there is a choice for social workers: to offer their services under the compulsory routes by using the courts, or under the voluntary route of using Part III of the Act. Research indicates that most services for children who may be in need of protection are provided under Part III. Schedule 2 of the Act makes it clear that this is what was intended:

> "The Local Authority shall take reasonable steps by the provision of services under Part III of this Act to prevent children in their area suffering abuse or neglect."

It does *not* say "shall prevent children suffering abuse or neglect by using the courts", it says by "using Part III".

Children who may be in need of protection, including those who are the subjects of section 47 investigations, should wherever possible be offered services as children "in need" on a voluntary basis. Only when it is not possible to negotiate ways of protecting a child with those who have parental responsibility is it appropriate to institute court proceedings. So what social workers may mean when they say "we don't do preventive work" or "we only do child protection work" is that they are concentrating their resources and efforts on those who cross the section 17(10)(b) threshold, that is, on cases where there is a likelihood of significant impairment of health or development without the provision of Part III services.

Unfortunately the end result is that for a number of cases where children are in high need under the terms of section 17, their cases are unnecessarily turned into section 47 (child protection) investigations. A mother suffering from depression may tell the health visitor that she is "at the end of her tether" and the health visitor makes a request to the Social Services Department for a day care placement. On receiving the response that day care places are reserved for children who are in need of protection, the family or the health visitor can be pushed into saying that there are times when the child might be vulnerable to abuse as a result of stress in the family. The response then is that a day care placement may or may not be provided but the family carries the unnecessary additional burden of having the child registered as a child "in need of protection". This is why child protection statistics across the country are so varied in that some agencies run their "in need" services under the "in need of protection" administrative provisions of Area Child Protection Committees.[12] It is possible to find that of two adjacent teams – with similar problems within their communities – one will have very few children on its child protection register, and having investigated an allegation under Section 47, will provide the necessary services under Part III of the Act without considering it necessary to register except in very serious cases, whilst the register in the

---

12 DoH, "Working Together under the Children Act 1989: a Guide to Arrangements for Inter-Agency Cooperation for the Protection of Children From Abuse" (HMSO, 1991).

adjacent area is swollen by cases which could more appropriately be assisted through section 17 provisions. The latest child protection register figures demonstrate that the proportion of children on registers varies between Authorities – for example from 6.9 per thousand children under 18 in Nottinghamshire to 3.1 per thousand in Hackney. One can certainly not account for the difference between these two Authorities by the explanation that Hackney families have fewer problems than those who live in Nottinghamshire.[13]

The problems resulting from running child care services through child protection procedures are threefold. First, it is contrary to the Children Act philosophy of working in partnership and enhancing parental responsibility wherever possible; second, it is a dis-welfare to the family and the child to be unnecessarily labelled as an abused child/abusing family. Finally, it is a much more costly way of giving a service, because not surprisingly, families object to being unnecessarily labelled as abusers – so social workers have to spend a great deal of their time calming people down and attempting to explain that being on the child protection register is essentially benign and is a price worth paying to receive the needed services.

Conclusion: advocacy for children in need

To conclude, I argue that the "in need" threshold provides a label for positive discrimination for the provision of a wide range of services. Once over that threshold – once there is a recorded status that a child is "in need" – support services can be marshalled from the voluntary and statutory agencies.

It is, of course, not quite as easy as it seems. First, resources may be so inadequate that it may seem pointless to family members and their advocates to go through the process if the one service they need – say a day nursery place – is not available because it is already filled by children deemed to be "in need of protection". The response I would make to those who take this line is based on a "rights" perspective. Unless the parent or young person is told whether or not they have crossed the threshold, they are denied the possibility of making representation against the decision, either that the child is not "in need", or that they are not a sufficiently high priority to receive the requested service. If a Local Authority fetters the discretion of professional workers by re-defining "in need", so that whole groups – most likely those who come under section 17(10)(a) are left outside the threshold, there is certainly an argument to be made that an application for Judicial Review may be appropriate.

---

13 DoH, "Children and Young People on Child Protection Registers Year Ending 31 March 1992: England" (HMSO, 1993).

Second, there may be a negative impact for many parents of having to provide evidence to show that their child is "in need". It may feel to them that they are somehow at fault or diminished as parents. It is important that research is undertaken to attempt to identify the impact on parents of this terminology and to consider whether they *do* appear to be diminished in their parenting capacities and self-esteem by having to prove to a social worker that their child is in need. Some of my colleagues who are researching the implementation of the Children Act – most notably Aldgate, Tunstill and McBeath whose research is included in the report to parliament on the first year of the Act[14] – believe that it is a stigmatising term, especially if it is linked with Social Services Departments which are associated in the minds of many with parental failure and thus stigma. We do not yet know how willing families will be to approach the Social Services Department and demonstrate that their child is "in need" in order to receive services which may be essential to the achievement of a reasonable standard of health or development.

It is important to know if there *is* a deterrent element in the definition or the way it is incorporated into practice in view of the potential value of the services which might be made available. The assessment has to be based on a professional interpretation as to whether this particular child in this set of circumstances meets one of the section 17 criteria. There cannot be agency-imposed limitations on this professional assessment. When plans were being made to implement the Act, some Local Authorities prepared guidelines which would have meant that only children in need of protection were allowed across the Section 17 threshold. The Department of Health sent a "Dear Director" letter saying that this re-definition of the Act was not permissible and this advice was written into the Guidance:

> "The definition of "need" in the Act is deliberately wide to reinforce the emphasis on preventive support and services to families. It has three categories; a reasonable standard of health or development; significant impairment of health or development; and disablement. It would not be acceptable for an authority to exclude any of these three – for example, by confining services to children at risk of significant harm which attracts the duty to investigate under section 47. ... This guidance does not lay down firm criteria or set general priorities because the Act requires each authority to decide their own level and scale of services appropriate to the children "in need" in their area. However, because the definition is in the Act, a local authority cannot lawfully substitute any other definition for the purposes of Part III."[15]

I conclude by returning to the point I started with. Part III of the Children Act has the power to make a profound impact on the life chances of children and young people, but only if they and their parents are aware of their rights under this Part of the Act. I hope that law centres, advice workers and solicitors will be proactive in helping parents, and young people, to put forward the best case possible to claim these rights.

---

14 *Op cit*, n. 4 above.
15 DoH, "The Children Act 1989. Regulations and Guidance", vol 2, 5-6.

Chapter 17

The Right to a Religious Education

Carolyn Hamilton
Senior Lecturer in Law, University of Essex

The extent to which parents should be able to determine the education of their children according to their religious beliefs and convictions, and the extent to which the state should be able to control the nature and form of a child's education, are recurring issues. The twentieth century has seen increasing control by the British Government of both the content and extent of the school curriculum, as well as the establishment of minimum educational standards. At the same time, English society has become more pluralistic, with growing numbers of persons whose cultural and religious views are not those of the majority.

The aim of this paper is to seek to determine what a democratic society owes to a child in terms of education; in particular, what weight the legislature and the courts ought to give to the concepts of equality of opportunity and pluralism, and how community religious concerns can be balanced with an individual child's best interests. In attempting to determine whether England has achieved the right balance, this paper will examine the requirements of international treaties and declarations, and the extent to which the current English position meets the standards contained in these instruments. The paper seeks to examine the freedom of religious bodies to set up their own schools in England, and the powers of the state to regulate such schools, bearing in mind international obligations.

The right to education

Education is no longer simply a matter of individual concern, or state concern. It is now recognised as a fundamental right, and as such should be available to everyone. Article 26 of the Universal Declaration of Human Rights[1] provides that every person has a basic right to education. This right is repeated in other international instruments, such as the United Nations

---

1   Adopted and proclaimed by General Assembly Res 217A (III), 10 Dec 1948.

Convention on the Rights of the Child[2], the International Covenant on Economic, Social and Cultural Rights[3], the European Convention on Human Rights[4], and the Declaration on the Elimination of All Forms of Intolerance and of Discrimination based on Religion or Belief.[5]

These instruments also describe in general terms the appropriate form of education to be provided by a state. The Universal Declaration of Human Rights states that education shall be directed to the full development of the human personality and to the strengthening of respect for human rights and fundamental freedoms, and shall promote understanding, tolerance and friendship among nations, racial and religious groups, and further the activities of the United Nations for the maintenance of peace.[6] The International Covenant on Economic, Social and Cultural Rights follows the aims of the Universal Declaration but, in addition, requires that education shall enable all persons to participate effectively in a free society.[7] The United Nations Convention on the Rights of the Child is rather more specific. It provides that the education of a child shall be directed to the development of the child's personality, talents and mental and physical abilities to their fullest potential, and towards the development of respect for the child's parents, his or her own cultural identity, language and values, for the national values of the country in which the child is living, the country from which he or she may originate, and for civilizations different from his or her own.[8]

While a state is generally free to set up its own system of education, there is a qualification to this freedom for a state which is a party to one of these international instruments. Article 2 of Protocol 1 of the European Convention on Human Rights states that in the exercise of any functions which it (the state) assumes in relation to education and to teaching, the state shall respect the right of parents to ensure such education and teaching in conformity with their own religious and philosophical convictions.[9] This right of the parents is echoed in the International Covenant on Economic, Social and Cultural Rights and the Convention Against Discrimination in Education[10] and in the International Covenant on Civil and Political Rights.[11]

---

2   Art 28: "States Parties recognise the right of the child to education". This Convention was ratified by the UK in 1991.
3   Art 13: "The States Parties to the present Covenant recognise the right of everyone to education." This Covenant was ratified by the UK on 20 May 1976, T.S.6 (1977) (Cmnd 6702).
4   Art 2 of Protocol 1: "No-one shall be denied the right to education." The UK ratified the Convention in February 1951, but the Convention has not been given statutory form.
5   As a Declaration of the UN, this instrument does not need ratification by individual states, but acts as a benchmark or standard setter, that all member states should seek to aspire to.
6   Art 26(2). Repeated in Art 5(a) of the Convention against Discrimination in Education. Adopted on 14 Dec 1960 by the General Conference of UNESCO. The UK ratified the Convention on 14 March 1962, T.S.44 (1962) (Cmnd 1760).
7   Art 13(1).
8   Art 29 UN Convention on the Rights of the Child.
9   Although the UK has ratified the European Convention on Human Rights, it has entered a reservation in relation to Art 2 of Protocol 1.
10 See Art 5(b).
11 Art 18(4).

Following from this right of the parents, the relevant Conventions and Declarations recognise the right of individuals or bodies to establish and direct their own educational institutions, provided that the education in such establishments conforms to minimum standards laid down by the state.[12]

The Status of International Instruments

Although the United Kingdom has ratified the Conventions, Covenants and Protocols[13] mentioned above, it is not legally bound to uphold the provisions contained in them. England is a "dualist" legal system and thus, before courts can enforce the provisions of treaties – as these instruments are collectively known, the provisions must be transformed into domestic legislation through the passing of a statute by parliament.[14] While parliament should seek not to enact legislation contrary to its international obligations, and while the English courts will, where possible, construe a statute so as to give effect to the United Kingdom's treaty obligations, the provisions of a treaty will give way where parliament's intent is clearly expressed and to the contrary.[15] Thus in *R* v *Chief Immigration Officer Heathrow Airport ex parte Salaman Bibi*[16] the court refused to allow the provisions of the European Convention on Human Rights to take precedence over domestic legislation, even though the domestic legislation was clearly contrary to the provisions laid down in the Convention.[17] However, the courts have taken the provisions of the European Convention "into account as guidelines to statutory interpretation or even to fill in gaps in the common law".[18]

---

12 Art 29(2) United Nations Convention on the Rights of the Child; Art 13(3), (4) International Covenant on Economic, Social and Cultural Rights; Art 5(b) Convention Against Discrimination in Education. The Commission has held, in Appl 10233/83, *Family H* v *UK* [1984] D & R Vol 37, 105-118 that Art 2 of Protocol 1 "implies the right for the state to establish compulsory schooling, be it in state schools or private tuition of a satisfactory standard, and that the verification and enforcement of educational standards is an integral part of that right".

13 Conventions, Covenants and Protocols are regarded as treaties, according to the definition section in Art 2(1)(a) of the Vienna Convention on the Law of Treaties.

14 In the absence of such transformation, the rules contained in these international treaties have no legal force. See *Maclaine Watson* v *DTI* [1989] 3 All ER 523 per L Oliver at 544-5 and L Templeman at 526. For an example of parliament directly incorporating a treaty, see the Child Abduction and Custody Act 1985 which directly incorporates the Hague Convention on Civil Aspects of International Child Abduction, thus giving the Convention the force of law.

15 See Davidson, *Human Rights* (Open University Press, 1993) ch 3 for a clear discussion of the status of treaty obligations.

16 [1976] 1 WLR 979.

17 For a further discussion on this issue see *Brind and Others* v *Secretary of State for the Home Department* [1991] 1 All ER 720, where the Hse of Lds held that the UK's courts would seek to interpret domestic legislation in accordance with the Convention where this was possible, but there was no corresponding presumption that the courts would review the exercise of administrative discretion on the basis that the discretion has to be exercised in conformity with the Convention. Lord Ackner, reinforcing the view that Conventions only have legal force if contained in a statute passed by parliament, commented that to do otherwise would incorporate the Convention into English law by the back door.

18 See Fawcett, *The Application of the European Convention on Human Rights*, (Clarendon Press, 1987) and *Waddington* v *Miah* [1974] 1 WLR 683.

The Universal Declaration of Human Rights, passed by the General Assembly of the United Nations is also regarded as a treaty. Its status in English law is unclear. Although not technically legally binding, the general view is that either the Declaration is an authoritative interpretation of the Charter declared by one of its organs – in this case the General Assembly – or that the Declaration is a part of customary international law. Customary international law is deemed to be part of English law and statutes are to be interpreted so as not to conflict with customary law. Again, however, if a treaty is in direct conflict with an English statute, the statute will take precedence.[19]

The international instruments relevant to education have not been expressly incorporated into English law, although parts of some instruments are reflected in English legislation. The rights provided for in the instruments are thus unenforceable in a court of law, with the exception of the provisions of the European Convention of Human Rights. An individual may make an application to the European Commission on Human Rights in Strasbourg, claiming that one or more rights contained in the European Convention on Human Rights has been violated, provided that domestic remedies have already been exhausted.[20] However, even if legally unenforceable, these international instruments provide a very useful and important standard by which English policy and legislation in the field of education can be measured.

Equal Opportunity and Pluralism

One starts with the assumption that a democratic society must offer its children equality of opportunity – a right to receive an education of equal quality to that received by the majority, while at the same time recognising the need to protect pluralism. Pluralism requires that the state respect the religious wishes of all groups, whether that of the majority or the minority.[21]

For certain religious groups, secular education, as represented by the National Curriculum taught in state schools, constitutes a threat to its religious beliefs. For others, it is only certain elements of the secular curriculum that are offensive. If the state allows a religious community total freedom over the education of its children, the child's equality of opportunity may be threatened. However, if the state restricts the freedom of a religious community to educate their children too greatly – to ensure equality of opportunity – it runs the risk of being regarded as intolerant,

---

19 For a further, and much more detailed, discussion of the role of customary law, see Starke, *Introduction to International Law*, 11th ed (Butterworths, 1994).

20 See Arts 25 and 26. On 14 January 1986 the UK made a declaration under Art 25 recognising the right of individual petition under the Convention in respect of events occurring after that time. The declaration was originally made for five years but has been constantly renewed. There are occasional calls in Parliament to reconsider automatic renewal.

21 See Art 2 of Protocol 1 European Convention of Human Rights and Art 29 United Nations Convention on the Rights of the Child as examples of international instruments protecting pluralism.

insufficiently pluralistic and possibly in breach of the provisions of Article 2 of Protocol 1. The tension between these two principles, that of equality of opportunity and pluralism, becomes most acute in relation to orthodox religious groups of virtually any denomination. The role of the courts and legislature in England, when faced with a conflict between these two principles, has been to try and maintain a balance between the needs of children within their society to receive an adequate education, while at the same time respecting the parents' religious conviction. The balance has, on occasions been a precarious one, sometimes tilting towards the state and sometimes the parents. Rather troublingly, the state does not have any established criteria for balancing these two principles and, indeed, applies different balances according to whether the child is privately or publicly educated.

While international instruments provide that states must respect minority rights and the parents' religious beliefs, it is fair to ask whether parents should have any right to control their child's education where this conflicts with the child's right of equality of opportunity. It has been held by the European Commission in *H* v *United Kingdom*[22] that the state has a right to establish compulsory schooling. Thus it is acceptable for the state to exercise a right of control over the child, by insisting that the child shall receive education for a certain number of years, and of a basic minimum form, even in the face of religious and philosophical objection from the parents. Should the right of the state to insist that the child shall receive education extend to ensure equality of opportunity? If the parents have no right of control over their child's education, and each child within the country received the same education, one could argue that the child was at least being provided with equality of educational opportunity, allowing each child to be in a position to fulfil his or her potential as far as this was possible within the system offered. It may well be that the child would choose never to fulfil this potential, but at least the choice would exist.

However, such a view, while perhaps reasonable within a homogeneous society, becomes less acceptable in a society which is racially and religiously mixed, with cultural differences which parents wish to preserve in their children. International instruments recognise the rights of minority cultures to preserve their religious and cultural identities, and accept the concept of pluralism. Once it is recognised – as it has been in the United Kingdom – that parents should be able to send children to private religious schools, a balance between these two conflicting principles must be reached by the state.

At the other end of the spectrum is the view that the state should not intervene at all, and should give parents complete freedom over the extent and content of their child's education. This is not a view that has been taken seriously in the United Kingdom.[23] The compromise that appears to

---

22 Appl No 10233/83. 6 Dec 31984 D & R Vol 37 105.

23 See the Education Act 1944 which insists on minimum standards and a certain level of curriculum. Neither is it the intention of the Government in relation to new religious schools, which, if funded under the Education Act 1993, will have to adhere to the National Curriculum.

have been reached is to permit those parents who object to the "secular" education offered by state schools to take their children out of the state system of education, into a lightly controlled private sector school system that caters for their particular religious belief.

Such a compromise raises the question, however, of why, if the state is willing to allow children to be educated according to the parents' religious values in private school, can not the same opportunity be offered to children in a state school? Is it, after all, fair that only those who can afford it should be allowed to maintain their cultural and religious identity in the way they choose, while those who are poor must take what the state offers. The United Kingdom has recognised the validity of such a claim in relation to certain religious groups and has provided for the possibility of state funding for schools run by certain religious denominations.[24] This is a trend likely to increase under sections 49[25] and 96 of the Education Act 1993, which allows a body of persons to establish a grant-maintained school, or change the character of an existing grant-maintained school with the approval of the Secretary of State for Education. Once approval is granted, the state will fund 85% of the capital costs of a school and the running costs[26], but the school, as a maintained school, would be required to follow the National Curriculum. Such schools, while allowing parents to choose a "religious education" for their children, would still incorporate the secular education of the state system. Such a requirement would not satisfy many orthodox groups of different religions who object to the secular curriculum *per se*, or certain aspects of it. Private schools are not, of course, obliged to follow the National Curriculum, and thus some religious groups have argued that neither should religious schools which receive state funding.

Two questions are raised by this argument. First, is the state obliged under Article 2 of Protocol 1 of the European Convention on Human Rights, to offer state-funded education in line with parents' religious and philosophical convictions; second, is an insistence that state-funded religious schools follow the National Curriculum a breach of Article 2? It can be argued that such attention to religious and philosophical convictions is unnecessary where a school is religiously neutral, that all state-funded schools should be strictly non-denominational, and that religious identity should be preserved by education outside school hours. This was an approach favoured by the non-conformists in earlier debates on religious

---

24 There are 4,903 voluntary Church of England schools, 2,200 Roman Catholic schools, 22 Jewish schools and 31 Methodist schools. Out of a total school population of 6,768,081, 1,618,950 pupils are educated in Church schools: *The Independent* 6 August 1992. There are no state-aided Muslim, Hindu or Sikh schools, although this is likely to be remedied speedily by the Education Act 1993.

25 This covers proposals by promoters to set up new grant-aided schools. S 48 allows the funding authority to establish a new grant-maintained school, while s 96 allows for applications to be made to the Secretary of State to make a significant change to the character of a school. Thus a school with a predominantly Muslim population could seek permission to change the school's character and make the school a Muslim grant-aided school.

26 Loans will be available from the Funding Agency for Schools to enable groups to raise the 15% necessary. In April 1994, 20 groups had already expressed interest in obtaining such a loan.

education, and is the approach of the American public school system. However, many religious groups would also find this approach unacceptable, as the need to preserve their religious identity depends upon children not being exposed to a Western, liberal education and its attendant ideology, which conflicts with their principles. Many groups feel that substantive instruction cannot be separated from religious ideas. Thus, in the teaching of English, they would assert that no books should be read that conflict with a child's particular religious beliefs. Likewise, for those groups that take creationism rather than evolution as their creed, the teaching of evolutionary principles in science lessons would be unacceptable.

To what extent should the state recognise these parental concerns and by doing so suborn the child's needs for equality of opportunity in the modern state? If too much control is given to the state there is always the fear that this will lead to cultural oppression of a minority. It is the history of such oppression that led to the international instruments preserving the rights of cultural minorities, many of whom had been subjected to genocide or cultural suppression during World War II and after. However, in a Western, technological, liberal society, the question posed is rather different. It is one of the degree of recognition to be given to religious groups which do not fit into the ethos of the Western, liberal state, and which are seen by the majority to disadvantage their children educationally as a result of their religious beliefs.

In England, the issue has not been ruled upon by the court in relation to state-funded schools, but it has been the object of discussion within Parliament and the Department for Education. The Department and Local Education Authorities have issued circulars to try to accommodate a limited number of religious objections, such as those relating to "immodest" school uniform or mixed physical education lessons. There has also been a willingness to accommodate religious objections where the matters objected to are peripheral to the requirements of the National Curriculum, but not where the teaching objected to is central to the National Curriculum.

Certain fundamentalist Protestant groups, particularly the Plymouth Brethren, object to the use of audio-visual aids in schools. Such aids are commonly used at elementary level to teach a wide range of subjects. The Minister of State for Education has expressed his willingness for children to be excused from viewing television programmes where these are used as a teaching aid:

> "the use of television and radio programmes and videos as a medium for teaching is not a requirement of the National Curriculum ... DES Circular 3/90, which was issued on 6th March with the National Curriculum Order for technology made clear our hope that schools would have regard to parents' views in their choice of media for teaching purposes."[27]

---

27 Stated in a letter dated 19 Aug 1992: see *Hansard* 20 Dec 1990, 589.

Where such groups have also sought to exempt their children from certain secular courses which offend their religious beliefs, however – such as information technology (IT) which involves the use of computers, classified as audio-visual aids – the Government has been unwilling to accommodate their religious objections. In 1989, in reply to a Parliamentary Question on the right of withdrawal under Article 2 of Protocol 1 of the European Convention on Human Rights, the Minister of State for Education stated that Article 2 did not give parents a general right to withdraw children from secular courses, and that, as a matter of policy, the Government would not allow parents to withdraw children from the secular curriculum in maintained schools on the grounds of religion or conscience, but that those parents remained free to make alternative arrangements.[28] In other words, while the Government was not prepared to allow children to be educated in accordance with their parents' religious convictions in state-funded schools, the opportunity remained for parents to put the child into a private school where their religious objections to portions of the secular curriculum could be catered for.

The same issue was raised again in 1990 during a parliamentary debate, and more extensive reasons as to why the Government would not allow parents a right of withdrawal where a course was religiously offensive were given. The Secretary of State relied on three factors. The first of these was the need for plurality: all children should receive a broad and balanced education. The second was the need to provide children with equality of opportunity: all children should be fully prepared for the opportunities, responsibilities and experiences of adult life and not be disadvantaged by receiving anything less than a full and broad curriculum.[29] The third reason was the administrative inconvenience of such a request. If the Plymouth Brethren were allowed to withdraw their children from IT, then other parents might well expect to be allowed to make similar claims on grounds of religious objections to other parts of the curriculum. The end result, according to the Secretary of State, would be an undermining of the basic idea of a National Curriculum.

But what of the right contained in Article 2 of Protocol 1 requiring that the state shall respect the right of the parents to ensure teaching is in conformity with their religious convictions?

> The Government's view is that the Article [2 of Protocol 1 of the European Convention on Human Rights] does not require a state to provide education in accordance with the particular religious or philosophical convictions of parents. Nor does it prevent the state from including in the school curriculum matters that do not accord with some parents' convictions, provided – this is

---

28 See *Hansard* 23 Oct 1989, 321.
29 The Secretary of State found it essential that children should be prepared for the world in which they live. This is not a view that the Government hold in relation to private schools, which are allowed to offer a very much narrower curriculum, and not one that necessarily prepares them for the modern world. See below, *R* v *Secretary of State for Education ex p Talmud Torah Machzikei Hadass School*, the *Times* 12 April 1985.

a big proviso – that the material is presented in an objective, critical and pluralistic manner. We believe that the requirements of the National Curriculum are compatible with Article 2."[30]

Interestingly, the Government does not apply the same rigorous attitude to the need for a full and broad curriculum, and equality of opportunity, to those children whose parents choose to place them in private schools.

Private education and compulsory schooling

The freedom of any individual or body to set up their own educational institution, and for a parent to send a child to such a school is provided for in the United Nations Convention on the Rights of the Child, the International Covenant on Economic, Social and Cultural Rights and the Convention Against Discrimination in Education. This right is echoed in section 76 of the Education 1944. However, there is no inherent right to make the state pay for the establishment or running of such schools. Indeed, the United Kingdom has entered a Reservation to Article 2 of Protocol 1 of the European Convention on Human Rights, to ensure that the state is not under an obligation to provide such schools itself.[31]

The freedom to run private schools is, however, circumscribed both by international and national requirements. International instruments require that an institution shall conform to certain minimum standards set down by the state, while English legislation requires that the education offered should be efficient and suitable, and that all independent schools must be registered. A further limitation is laid down by Article 5(c)(1) of the Convention Against Discrimination in Education which, while recognising the rights of members of national minorities to carry on their own education activities, provides that the right must not be exercised in such a manner as to prevent the members of these minorities from understanding the culture and language of the community as a whole, and from participating in its activities, or in a manner which prejudices national sovereignty.

All private schools in England and Wales are subject to supervision by the Secretary of State. Section 70 of the Education Act requires that all schools

---

30 *Hansard* 20 Dec 1990, 54. Timothy Eggar, Minister of State for Education. It is difficult to know exactly what is meant by 'pluralistic' in this context, but it is most likely to mean "broad and balanced" or not representative of any one particular viewpoint. In some cases this is exactly what the parents object to.

31 The Reservation stated that in view of certain provisions of the Education Acts in the UK, the principle affirmed by the second sentence of Art 2 is accepted by the UK only so far as it is compatible with the provision of efficient instruction and training, and the avoidance of unreasonable expenditure. Further, in *Belgian Linguistics*, ECHR Ser B, Vol 1, 279), the European Commission held that Art 2 of Protocol 1 does not put a positive obligation on the state to provide a specific type of education, it merely imposes a negative obligation – not to take any action which might prevent those under their jurisdiction from setting up their own schools and providing their own education.

must be registered.[32] In starting a school, a proprietor must initially register the school, but this registration is regarded as provisional until there has been an inspection of the school, and notice has been given to the proprietor that the registration is final.[33] If the inspectors are not satisfied with the school, under Part IV of the Act the Secretary of State may serve on the school a notice, known as a Complaint.[34] The Complaint sets out those matters to which objection is taken, the measures necessary, in the opinion of the Secretary of State, to remedy those matters, and the time to be allowed for making the necessary changes (not less than six months) – unless the Secretary of State finds them unredeemable. The Secretary of State may also object to registration on a number of grounds, including the unsuitability of the premises or accommodation, or the nature of the instruction offered to pupils, which is required to be "efficient and suitable", having regard to the sexes and ages of the pupils.[35]

Where a complaint is served, there is a right to appeal[36] by "referring the Complaint" to an Independent Schools Tribunal. The Tribunal has wide powers, including the power to order that the school be struck off the register unless the requirements are, subject to modifications made by the Tribunal, complied with to the satisfaction of the Secretary of State. Non-compliance with the requirements of a Complaint can also result in the school being struck off, and may ultimately result in criminal sanctions.

There has been little in the way of caselaw on these sections. For the religious schools the all-important question is whether the education they offer, while in accordance with their religious beliefs and values, will be regarded by the state as "efficient and suitable" instruction for the pupils attending the school. This issue was addressed in the case of *R v Secretary of State for Education and Science ex parte Talmud Torah Machzikei Hadass School.*[37] The school provided the traditional form of education as required by the Belz section of the orthodox Hasidic Jewish community. After an inspection, authorised by the Education Act 1944, a Complaint was served. In particular, it was alleged that the instruction at the school was not efficient and suitable having regard to the ages and sexes of the pupils. The school was given six months in which to remedy the deficiency or close down. Although there was a right of appeal on receipt of a Complaint to an Independent Schools Tribunal, the school in this case decided to seek judicial review in addition, as a more appropriate procedure, to have the

---

32 It is an offence to conduct an independent school which is not registered or is only provisionally registered under s 70(3) or s 70(3)(A) unless an application has been made within one month from the time the school was first set up. The Education (Particulars of Independent Schools) Regulations 1982 specify the details of the school to be given to the Registrar.

33 An independent school will not be registered if the proprietor or the premises are disqualified.

34 Under s 71 of the Act.

35 Other grounds are that the proprietor or a teacher are not fit persons to act in those roles or that there has been a failure, in relation to a child provided with accommodation by the school, to comply with the duty imposed by s 87, Children Act 1989.

36 Under s 72, Education Act 1944.

37 *The Times* 12 April 1985.

Complaint notice quashed.[38] It was contended by the school, that if they were required to comply with the part of the Complaint relating to "efficient and suitable" instruction, it would be quite impossible for the children at the school to be educated in accordance with the traditions of the community to which they belonged and in accordance with the requirements of their religion. If the Complaint were upheld, it would mean that children belonging to the Hasidic community in England would not be able to receive the same traditional education as the Hasidic communities of America and Western or Eastern Europe.

The High Court had first to decide the extent of the power of the Secretary of State to interfere with the education of children in accordance with the traditions of a religious sect and the wishes of their parents who are members of that sect.

Woolf J in giving his judgment circumvented the issue. He held that the Secretary of State in applying section 71 and in deciding whether or not efficient and suitable instruction was being provided had to take into account the wishes of the parents. This is underlined by Article 2 of Protocol 1. When dealing with a school to which members of a minority sect are sent by their parents, the Secretary of State should bear in mind that the education being provided is the education which the parents want the children to have. This is particularly so where the parents regard it as a religious requirement that their children be educated in this particular manner. However, though the wishes of the parents are an important consideration, they are not the sole consideration, and the Secretary of State is permitted to have a policy setting down minimum requirements to be applied to all schools irrespective of the background of the children sent to that school and the wishes of their parents.

Counsel for the Secretary of State conceded that the education proposed by a religious school would still be suitable if it primarily equipped a child for life within the community of which he or she is a member, rather than the way of life in the country as a whole, so long as it does not foreclose the child's options in later years to adopt some other form of life if the child wishes to do so. What amounts to a "foreclosing of options" was not discussed and no guidelines were provided. The judge agreed with counsel for the school that the Secretary of State is not entitled to require the school to become a mini-state school[39], but the Secretary is entitled to regard a particular form of education as being too narrow. What minimum standards may the Secretary lay down for a religious school? The answer of

---

38 A Complaint was also served in relation to the premises, which the school did not dispute and which they had taken steps to remedy. The school sought to have Part C of the Complaint relating to instruction quashed by means of judicial review rather than appealing to the Tribunal under s 72, Education Act 1944.

39 This is an interesting statement in view of the fact that England's state schools must teach to a National Curriculum. One might assume that if Parliament had passed legislation that all children should be taught to the National Curriculum, including those taught in private schools, this would be a breach of Art 2 of Protocol 1, as suggested by L Woolf's statement – or would the National Curriculum be regarded as only a "minimum standard" of education?

the Court is not particularly illuminating: only those standards necessary in the Secretary of State's opinion to make the education "suitable". Nonetheless, it is now clear that the Secretary of State should be sensitive to the traditions of minority sects and only interfere with them so far as this is necessary to make the school "suitable".

Little more guidance on "suitability" is given. The court heard that most of the teaching in the school was conducted in Yiddish, although the children also learned Aramaic and Hebrew, but secular subjects were taught in English for between $1-1\frac{1}{2}$ hours in the afternoon – an amount of time considered insufficient by the Inspectors. But how much time should be given? The judge held that it would be difficult to find justification for a requirement that specific subjects, such as drama and music, that were not acceptable to the community should be taught. The judge also expressed doubt as to whether the Secretary of State was justified in requiring a specific number of hours to be allotted to secular subjects. However, excessive requirements by the Secretary of State did not justify granting relief by way of judicial review, as this would involve quashing the whole Complaint. The Complaint would have to be taken before the Independent School Tribunal which could, if it wished to, amend the Complaint.

While the view of the Secretary of State that an education would be suitable if it primarily equips a child for life within the community of which he or she is a member, rather than the way of life in the country as a whole, provided that it does not foreclose options in later life is laudable, it may be that the two views are irreconcilable, or indeed contradictory. The school was very clear on the academic instruction that needed to be offered, and as such it would not enable a child who chose to leave the community easily to fit in to British society. In some cases a child might not even be able to speak fluent English.

The tension in the Secretary of State's position was further exposed by the judge's doubts as to whether the Secretary of State was justified in requiring a specific number of hours to be devoted to secular subjects. Without such a requirement how could a child ever hope to have any form of equality of opportunity to an English child – limited as he or she would be by language and a complete lack of any modern technological or scientific education, and isolated from the larger, outside world. How could such a child, who chose to leave such a group, participate effectively in the economic, and perhaps more importantly, the democratic process? It is arguable that a child who received such an education could always seek employment as an unskilled worker, but it is difficult to defend the level of education in question as providing equality of opportunity. Allowing a child to be educated within such an ideological, social and educational enclosure undoubtedly upholds the principle of pluralism, and defends the right of the community to continue and perpetuate its way of life, but it does not provide equality of opportunity.

Some would argue that a child at such a school is receiving a stimulating, intellectually challenging education, and that this should be the only concern of the state. It is clear, however, that intellectual challenge does not, of itself, make an education "suitable", if it does not equip those children to compete on equal terms with their peer group in the wider world.

A further argument, often advanced by orthodox religious groups[40], is that such groups are economically self-sufficient. Thus, as orthodox Jews are not often recipients of welfare benefits and are supported by members of their own community, the state should not have a right to intervene. This is at best a limited argument, and at worst an irrelevant one. Any child who decides to exercise his or her options and leave the enclosed community will lose the support of that community; such support is dependant on the child fulfilling his or her role within the religious community. If a child is to retain any choice, and if the state is to ensure that the child's option are not foreclosed in later life, an education providing equality of opportunity is a minimum requirement.

The High Court in *Talmud Torah*, while giving consideration to the provisions of Article 2 of Protocol 1, did not refer to the wider range of international instruments which the United Kingdom has ratified, or which act as standard setters, and thus did not address the issue of whether English law is in line with the provisions contained in international instruments. Had there been such a consideration, the court may well have reached the decision that its own concessions towards pluralism and the upholding of parental values, had gone too far. Article 5 of the Convention Against Discrimination in Education limits the rights of parents insofar as education received should not be exercised in such a manner as to prevent the child from understanding the culture and language of the community as a whole. It is not at all clear that the education provided to the children in the *Talmud Torah* school met this requirement. Further, the Declaration on the Elimination of all Forms of Intolerance and of Discrimination based on Religion or Belief, while providing that the child has the right to religious education in accordance with the wishes of the parents, states that the best interests of the child shall be the guiding principle. There appears to be no discussion in the *Talmud Torah* case of what constitutes the best interests of the child, or indeed any discussion of a child's right to education and equality of opportunity. Such a decision also sits uneasily with the guiding principle of the Children Act 1989, which makes the child's welfare a paramount consideration in any question relating to the child's upbringing.

The Convention on the Rights of the Child requires that the education of a child be directed to the development of the child's personality, talents and mental and physical abilities to their fullest potential, and towards the development of respect for his or her own cultural identity. It may well be that not only are these aims unrealistic and idealistic rather than practical, but that they also set up an irreconcilable tension where the element of

---

40 See *Wisconsin* v *Yoder* 406 US 205, 32 L Ed 2d 15, 92 S Ct 1526 (1972) where the same argument was advanced in relation to the Amish community.

respect for the parent's religious beliefs requires that the child not reach his potential within the modern state where he or she now lives.

The *Talmud Torah* case illustrates very clearly the difficulty that occurs when rights are in conflict. The state in this case was asserting a right on behalf of the child to an effective education, while the school was asserting the right of parents to educate their children in conformity with their religious wishes. The High Court, while not resolving the issue of the validity of the Complaint, may have tilted too far towards the rights of parents. One wonders whether the decision that the education would be suitable if it primarily equipped the child for life within his or her community would stand if parents wished their daughters to receive an even more restricted education, different to the education given to their sons. In many orthodox forms of religion[41], a girl's role is defined as one of wife and mother, within the confines of the home, with education directed towards enabling them to fulfil this role. Following parental wishes in this instance may very well lead to girls receiving an inferior education both to that received by boys within their religious community and to girls generally. The Convention on the Elimination of all Forms of Discrimination against Women specifically forbids this.[42]

Conclusion

How should a state resolve the conflict between respect for a parent's religious convictions and the need to provide a child with equality of opportunity? The best interests of the child is the guiding principle in both domestic legislation and international instruments. However, little consideration has been given as to what form of education is in the best interests of the individual child. A child's best interests must require that he or she receives at least equality of opportunity from the education system, whether in a state school or a private school. It is difficult to argue that it is in a child's best interests to receive only a restricted education and inequality of opportunity, although it might be in the best interests of the religious community. While every effort should be made to ensure that children are educated in accordance with their parent's religious beliefs and convictions, that right of the parents must be subsidiary to the right of the child to equality of opportunity in education. On examination, standard-setting international instruments may not provide adequate direction to enable a state to achieve an equitable balance between equality

---

41 For instance in Hasidic Jewish communities, orthodox Muslim communities and fundamentalist Christian groups.

42 Art 10: States Parties shall take all appropriate measures to eliminate discrimination against women in order to ensure them equal rights with men in the field of education and in particular to ensure, on a basis of equality of men and women ... (b) access to the same curricula, the same examinations, ... (c) the elimination of any stereotyped concept of the roles of men and women at all levels and in all forms of education ...

of opportunity and pluralism – having given too little consideration to resolving conflicts between a child's rights, and best interests, a parent's rights, and the needs of the child's religious community.

The Education Act 1993 is to be welcomed as a step towards a possible resolution of the clash of interests. The new provisions allowing for the establishment of new grant-maintained schools, and applications to change the character of existing schools, will, undoubtedly result in a greater number of religious schools, particularly amongst those religious communities such as the Sikhs, Hindus and Muslims who have not previously received state funding for their religious schools. While on the one hand promoting the rights of parents to have their children educated according to their religious convictions and beliefs, the Act also promotes equality of opportunity by requiring that such schools teach to the National Curriculum. This will provide children with the same range of education as they would receive in a non-denominational school, whilst also allowing for extra religious teaching if a school so chooses. It is unlikely that many religious minorities, who have had great difficulty in adequately financing their own religious schools, will be able to resist the lure of state aid. Those private religious minority schools which do exist suffer, on the whole, from a lack of finance, resulting in poor premises, poor facilities and a limited teaching staff, all of which have been the subject of complaint by school inspectors. State funding will allow for the provision of acceptable facilities and a full teaching staff, and will make minority religious schools very much more attractive to the parents of that community. Provided that the Government stands firm, and does not accede to requests from minority religious bodies that the National Curriculum should not apply to religious schools, equality of opportunity may be achieved. The last remaining act for the Government is to safeguard those children who will continue to be educated in private schools, and extend the application of the National Curriculum to cover them as well.

Chapter 18
Why We Must Stop Hitting Children

Peter Newell

Co-ordinator of "EPOCH – End Physical Punishment of Children"

On a Kilroy-type programme on Tyne Tees television early in 1993, soon after the tragic murder of James Bulger, there was a debate on whether smacking should be made illegal. A mother intervened early in the programme to say that she had started slapping her baby when he was eight months old, to teach him the difference between right and wrong. The interviewer winced when she demonstrated on his arm that she was not talking about "little taps". Her mother sitting next to her nodded vigorously, and about a third of the audience of 50 or so warmly applauded.

A journalist on a well-known English women's magazine left a message on my answer-phone recently in the EPOCH office in London: "I'm preparing an article on the pros and cons of smacking children ..." she began.

It was just one of thousands of examples which EPOCH has collected of the strange public attitudes we still have to violence and children. Would any journalist pose the same question about women – "the pros and cons of slapping your wife", or about pets – "the advantages and disadvantages of hitting your cat"? No – our society – most societies, condemn every form of inter-personal violence, except physical punishment of children.

In 1991 the only other legalised form of inter-personal violence – marital rape – was declared illegal. But when it comes to children, the law draws a protective circle not around the child, but around the punishing parent or other carer. It is just over a century since we first legislated in the United Kingdom against cruelty to children (70 years after the first legal protection for animals). And when that legislation was debated, the primary concern of MPs and peers was to ensure that in seeking to limit cruelty, they did not interfere in any way with parents', teachers' and others' rights to hit – to physically chastise children. So that first Act – the Prevention of Cruelty to and Protection of Children Act 1889 – included statutory confirmation of these rights.[1] This defence has been re-enacted without change or even debate in succeeding laws on cruelty, including the still current Children and Young Persons Act 1933. The statute reflects the traditional common law defence of "reasonable chastisement". The still-quoted leading

---

1   Parliamentary Debates, 3rd ser (1889), vol 337, cols 1379-86; vol 338, col 956.

judgment is that of Chief Justice Cockburn, in the case of *R* v *Hopley* in 1860:

> "By the law of England, a parent ... may for the purpose of correcting what is evil in the child, inflict moderate and reasonable corporal punishment, always, however, with this condition, that it is moderate and reasonable".[2]

That is where our law still rests on violence to children.

Courts' interpretation of what amounts to "reasonable" chastisement has changed, but not consistently, and in recent months we have seen the confusion that judges' discretion to decide what is "reasonable" causes. There has been a little rash of cases involving parents using belts on their children. In March 1993 a father who belted his 5- and 8-year old sons was acquitted of assault in a Bristol Magistrates Court. In the same month at Bristol Crown Court another father who belted his 8-year old son was given a suspended prison sentence. Still in the same month, in Worcester a man who belted his 6-year old son was convicted of assault and given a two-year suspended sentence, but it was lifted on appeal. He had admitted using the belt on all his children – and his wife. Then in April in Southampton a judge quashed on appeal a mother's conviction for assault – she had caused heavy bruising with a slipper, noticed by her nine-year old daughter's teacher. The judge commented: "In the words of one of my colleagues, the world is going potty if a parent can't slipper a child".[3] I highlight these cases simply to show the extent of judicial approval for heavy forms of violence to children, not, I can assure you, to engender a Tory-Party-Conference-style enthusiasm for utterly irrelevant retribution and imprisonment.

We need to be clear from the beginning that hitting children is very common in the United Kingdom. John and Elizabeth Newson in 1985 found two thirds of a large sample of mothers admitting that they were already smacking their baby before the age of one; earlier, they had found that 22% of 7-year olds had already been hit with an implement, and another 53% of 7-year olds had been threatened with an implement.[4] Following the tragic murder of 2-year old Jamie Bulger in Liverpool, and the continuing ill-informed debate on youth crime and parenting, we have seen children scapegoated. It is easy to see why: they are smaller, less articulate, have no vote and no voice in national debates. But the scapegoating, the calls for more and "stronger" discipline are all part of the problem of violence in society, not part of the solution.

Child abuse – defined as extreme forms of violence against children – has become an acknowledged problem, although really only in the last 30 years, with public discussion and to some extent public concern escalating over the last few years. I find the idea that Henry Kempe "discovered" child battering in the 1960s, which appears in most child abuse textbooks, rather

---

2   *R* v *Hopley* (1860) F & F 202.
3   *Daily Express*, 20 Apr 1993.
4   *The Extent of Parental Physical Punishment in the UK*, Newson and Newson, (APPROACH, 1990).

insulting to the generations of children who had been experiencing it for centuries. The concept of child abuse is one designed by adults, not children, which may perhaps explain its incompleteness. From the beginning, the concept has had built into it an assumption that reasonable chastisement, punishment that involves deliberately hurting and humiliating children, is acceptable. The definition of child abuse, in both common and professional usage, has condoned an arbitrary, and quite high, level of physical and mental violence to children: hence those court decisions. The campaigns which ended the social and even legal acceptance of violence against women did not promote any parallel concept; they did not define "acceptable" levels of violence to wives or partners. That was probably because in those campaigns, adults were advocating on behalf of adults. The current concept and definition of child abuse does a disservice to children as long as it goes on tolerating some level of violence to them.

If children are to have the status they deserve, as individual people, it is their right to physical and personal integrity – to protection from all forms of inter-personal violence – which must be upheld. This is not demanding extra protection, or special laws – merely the protection that the rest of us take for granted. But of course, if anything, as children are smaller and more vulnerable, one would expect more not less legal protection of children's physical integrity. The task of child protection in relation to physical and sexual child abuse should be to uphold the child's right to physical integrity. In relation to sexual abuse, we at least accept the child's right to say no. But when it comes to physical punishment, which even in its minor forms is an invasion of the child's physical integrity, there is no right to say no.

In proposing that the definition of child abuse should be based on the child's right to physical and personal integrity, rather than some arbitrary level of "significant harm", I am not implying that there should be more intervention in families, or more prosecutions, because that would be most unlikely to be in children's interests. It is surely clear enough that many existing interventions add a level of abuse by involving professional input. The purpose of re-definition is to put child protection on a logical basis, with its roots in children's rights.

The UN Convention on the Rights of the Child

Since 1989, we have had new international authority for upholding children's right to physical integrity. In November of that year the United Nations General Assembly adopted the Convention on the Rights of the Child. That Convention had by July 1994 been ratified by 161 countries around the world. The United Kingdom ratified a little late in December 1991. The Convention was ten years in the drafting and provides the first set of internationally validated detailed minimum standards for treatment of the world's children. It represents a huge opportunity for raising the status of children throughout the world, moving them up the political agenda everywhere, and thus more urgently co-operating to solve the major ills facing them.

The Convention in its preamble emphasises the "equal and inalienable rights of all members of the human family", and also children's rights to "special care and assistance". Article 2 insists that all the rights within the Convention must be available to all children without discrimination of any kind. Article 19 asserts children's right to physical integrity:

> "States Parties must take all appropriate legislative, administrative, social, and educational measures to protect the child from all forms of physical or mental violence, injury or abuse, neglect or negligent treatment, maltreatment or exploitation including sexual abuse, while in the care of parent(s), legal guardian(s) or any other person who has the care of the child".

Thus the Convention makes it clear – reading Article 19 with Article 2 – that the right to physical integrity is an absolute right, one which neither culture nor religion, tradition nor material circumstances should limit. In considering physical punishment and humiliation of children, it is important to emphasise this. No longer can religious fundamentalists use selective quotations from Proverbs to justify using "the rod of correction"; nor can others suggest that the issue is simply about differing cultural practices of child-rearing.

Religious justifications for using physical punishment are particularly rife at the moment. Religious fundamentalism, with roots in America, is catching on here, and there are now about 45 schools in the United Kingdom connected with an organization called Christian Education, where corporal punishment, or correction as they term it, is administered with a wooden paddle. These schools are registered as independent schools; they are operating legally and using biblical quotations (selective quotations) to justify beating children. Recently the new edition of James Dobson's *Dare to Discipline* was published here, aimed at Christian parents, and advocating corporal punishment with implements.[5] This issue is not about promoting one way of child-rearing over another: it is about extending a fundamental human right – taken for granted by adults in most societies – to children. We must not allow religion, culture, or tradition to intimidate us from upholding children's right to physical integrity.

The United Kingdom Government, by ratifying the Convention is now committed to implementing it for all children. But how are we going to move forward from where we are now in terms of social attitudes and the law, towards really respecting children as people with the same right to physical integrity as the rest of us? The major problem is that this is a highly personal issue. Whether or not we experienced physical punishment or abuse as children (and most of us did), whether or not we have hit our own

---

5   Dobson, *Dare to Discipline*, (Kingsway Publications, 1993).

growing children, we have all been conditioned by living in a society which accepts deliberately hurting and humiliating children as a legitimate way of punishing or treating them. Our experiences as children and as parents get in the way of logical and "professional" consideration of the arguments and the evidence. We do not want to think badly of our parents, or of ourselves. As Alice Miller has written, if this was simply an intellectual matter, we would have stopped hurting and humiliating children decades ago.[6] Our use of language reflects the culture and gives away our attitudes to hurting children: "a good hiding", "six of the best", "a healthy smack" etc. The use of special words like "smacking" to describe violence when it is directed at children makes us more comfortable with the action.

Newspapers, or at least the tabloids, reflect these attitudes, while at the same time adopting a salacious, shock, horror approach to child abuse – an entirely different thing. A particularly graphic example: in 1989 5-year old Sukina Hammond died, according to her paediatrician, from pain, shock and exhaustion following a beating by her father because she would not spell her name. When he was convicted the *Daily Star* went to town, calling for the death penalty and even "praying" that Hammond's fellow prisoners would "make him suffer some of the pain he inflicted on tragic Sukina". Just a month earlier, EPOCH had published a report by John and Elizabeth Newson covering their research on prevalence of physical punishment, and its links with later delinquency. The *Daily Star*'s response was a little leading article which read: "Children who have been smacked by their parents are more likely to end up as criminals says a report. Not smacked hard enough perhaps".[7]

I have dwelt on the fundamental human rights argument against physical punishment and humiliation of children because it is the most important one, and should be sufficient. Of course there are many supporting arguments. There are mountains of research papers on the potential and actual ill-effects of physical punishment and deliberate humiliation in childhood, the dangers of "accidental" injury, the link with the development of violent attitudes and actions in childhood and later life, the escalation to more serious abuse etc.[8] There are no papers detailing positive effects of hitting children, because it teaches children absolutely nothing positive. It is a potent lesson in bad behaviour.

Turning to the research on links between physical punishment and child abuse, the extraordinary thing – only explicable in terms of the very personal nature of the issue – is how anyone could seriously suggest that the two can usefully be considered separately. There are a lot of published research findings from various countries on the origins of serious physical abuse, showing that many perpetrators of physical abuse explained (and in some cases justified the abuse) as legitimate chastisement, which maybe

---

6   Miller, *For Your Own Good: The Roots of Violence in Child-rearing,* (Virago, 1987).

7   "Clouts that make louts", *Daily Star* 3 Oct 1989; *Daily Star* "A life for a life", 25 Nov 1989.

8   A referenced review of research findings on "What's Wrong with Hitting Children" appears in Newell, *Children are People too – the Case Against Physical Punishment,* (APPROACH, 1989).

went a bit too far (the concept of over-chastisement). Some studies suggest this was so in 40% of cases, others suggest 80 or 90%. The handbook *Understanding Child Abuse,* by David Jones and others, states that it is "very noticeable that parents who injure their children, at whatever age and however seriously, more often than not relate the event to a concept of punishment, even when they accept that they went 'too far'".[9]

Many child protection co-ordinators, many paediatricians, many professionals and many parents prefer to keep physical punishment and child abuse in two separate boxes, whatever the evidence that daily confronts them.

How could anyone who has overcome their personal conditioning, seriously doubt that physical child abuse is punishment? Of course there are factors that make it more or less likely to happen, and more or less likely to be serious. To challenge physical punishment, we have to challenge the culture, see beyond the conditioning to respect children as individual people with rights.

I meet a very wide range of adult excuses for not consistently upholding children's right to physical integrity. Some sound at first more respectable than others perhaps. For example ...

> "Many families are suffering increased levels of poverty, homelessness, overcrowding and stress. We should give priority to these structural issues before we try to change these commonly accepted forms of discipline".

There is much wrong with that argument. First, it presents a stereotype that "poor" parents are particularly prone to hit and humiliate their children, which is not particularly borne out by research. Second, it implies that discouraging physical punishment and humiliation may increase, rather than reduce stress. But most important, it ignores the children's rights imperative for acting now. Why should children wait while we try to create a social utopia that looks further off than ever? Can you imagine anyone raising a similar excuse for avoiding challenging domestic violence against women; let's wait for full employment for men ... . This issue is not in competition with challenging poverty, inequalities, homelessness etc.

Another excuse:

> "By focusing too narrowly on physical punishment, there is a danger of encouraging other more damaging ways of abusing children – emotional abuse and so on"

EPOCH has been careful to include deliberate humiliation alongside physical punishment as harmful and counter-productive, and to have a wide definition of physical punishment which includes dangerous restriction of liberty of children – when time out leads to locking children in rooms or cupboards. In some countries where there is an explicit ban on physical punishment, the legislation bars humiliation too. Of course the focus of the campaign is on positive discipline, above all on ways of

---

9   Jones *et al, Understanding Child Abuse,* 2nd edn (Macmillan Education, 1987).

encouraging acceptable behaviour which also encourage the development of self-discipline.[10] But as I have indicated, there is a particular injustice in the current legality of physical punishment, in contrast to all other inter-personal violence.

These may be important arguments to go through, but all too often they do seem like diversionary tactics, arising from individuals' unwillingness to challenge their conditioning.

Failure to challenge violence

Our global failure to reduce inter-personal violence of every kind, including child abuse, owes so much to the hypocrisy of our attitudes to violence towards children, our failure to challenge logically and consistently the violence meted out daily to children by their parents and other adults: the hypocrisy epitomised by the mother in the supermarket: – "You – must – not – hit – your – little – sister": interposing the words with blows, or the schoolteacher beating the boy for bullying. We tell children they must not hit each other – that's bullying; they most certainly must not hit or humiliate an adult. So it is nothing less than gross hypocrisy to go on defending our right to hit and humiliate them.

The evidence of the links between physical punishment and all kinds of violence has recently been sifted by a number of major commissions around the world. Set up because of concerns at the levels of all kinds of inter-personal violence in society, and seeking strategies for prevention, they have come to the conclusion that ending physical punishment of children through legal reform and education is a vital first step, removing the potent modelling of violence as a useful way of sorting out conflicts which is passed on by the punishing parent to the child. In Australia, the National Committee on Violence concluded in 1989:

> "The greatest chance we have to prevent violence in society is to raise children who reject violence as a method of problem-solving, who believe in the right of the individual to grow in a safe environment". [11]

A two-year study by a governmental Commission in West Germany reported in 1990 and proposed as its first recommendation that Germany should follow other European countries in banning physical punishment:

> "The parental right to chastise, which makes violence a legitimate means of child-rearing, implies the risk of abuse. The borderline between permitted correction and forbidden abuse is neither fixed nor defined clearly".[12]

---

10 EPOCH distributes a wide range of leaflets and booklets for parents and other carers on positive discipline. For details, send SAE to 77 Holloway Road, London N7 8JZ.

11 National Committee on Violence, *Violence – Directions for Australia* (Australian Institute of Criminology, 1990).

12 Prevention and Control of Violence, Governmental Commission, West Germany, 1990.

In 1985, the Committee of Ministers of the Council of Europe had come to a similar conclusion in drafting a recommendation on reducing family violence:

> "It is the very assumption that corporal punishment of children is legitimate that opens the way to all kinds of excesses and makes the traces or symptoms of such punishment acceptable to third parties".[13]

Worldwide progress to end physical punishment

Finally, I will describe, more positively, the progress towards ending physical punishment of children worldwide. First, in the United Kingdom, there has been substantial progress towards prohibiting it outside the home: in state-supported education abolition came into force in 1987. Independent schools are the only institutions in the United Kingdom where adults can still beat children with impunity. But they have to choose pupils whose parents are paying the fees. Those supported by the state are covered by abolition. The Government's view, expressed in a recent letter from the Minister to EPOCH, is that "if parents wish to express their choice by sending their children to schools which still practise corporal punishment, they should be allowed to do so". You must have the choice to pay to have your children beaten. There is a complete refusal to recognise that the issue is about children's rights – not parents'. Last May (1993) in the House of Lords, an attempt to end this anomaly and extend abolition to all pupils was defeated by 128 votes to 121. As you can imagine, the phrase "It never did me any harm" echoed around the chamber.[14] Another Article in the UN Convention covers school discipline, which "must be administered in a manner consistent with the child's human dignity and in conformity with the Convention" (Art 28(2)) – *i.e.* in conformity with Article 19, without any form of physical or mental violence.

Under the Children Act for England and Wales, regulations and guidance have ended physical punishment in all children's homes, in private and local authority foster-care, and in all group day care including child-minding (the day care reform applies in Scotland too). But in 1993 magistrates in the London Borough of Sutton challenged the clear guidance which suggested that childminders should not smack minded children, by upholding an appeal from a minder, Anne Davis, against Sutton Council's refusal to register her. She had declined to give a no smacking undertaking. The decision was appealed by the Authority, but in March 1994 the High Court dismissed the appeal.[15] The judgment was not about the rights and wrongs of smacking, but illustrated that the guidance under

---

13 Council of Europe Committee of Ministers, Rec R85/4, Explanatory Memorandum (1985).
14 *House of Lords Hansard*, 10 May 1993 cols 971-991.
15 *London Borough of Sutton* v *Davis* (1994) 1 FLR 797.

the Children Act was not sufficient to implement the Government's clearly expressed policy that there is no place for physical punishment outside the family home. The Government could have saved a lot of taxpayer's money by issuing regulations under the Children Act – or more explicit guidance. Many organizations, led by the National Childminding Association, are urging it do so. The childminder involved was heralded by large sections of the media as a martyr for the cause of parent's rights: the real martyr was the 4-year old minded child. Anne Davis has since launched an organization, named Families for Discipline. Only in England, surely, could the 1990s see a new organization dedicated to preserving the right to hit children. But apart from the offensive anomaly of fee-paying pupils in private schools and the hiccup in Sutton, the end of physical punishment has reached the door of the family home.

In other countries there are now clear models for legal reform and education campaigns to show how to finish the job. It appears that only six countries have so far banned all physical punishment of children. Sweden was the first, in 1979, when its family law was amended to read:

> "Children are entitled to care, security and a good upbringing. Children are to be treated with respect for their person and individuality and may not be subjected to corporal punishment or any other humiliating treatment".

Finland followed: its 1983 Child Custody and Rights of Access Act stated:

> "A child shall be brought up in a spirit of understanding, security and love. He shall not be subdued, corporally punished or otherwise humiliated".

During the 1980s, four more European countries banned all physical punishment: Denmark, Norway, in 1989 Austria and in 1994 Cyprus.[16]

The commonest argument the campaign against physical punishment of children meets is that this is a matter of parents' rights – the law should not invade the family. Of course the law does already invade the family in many ways, including invasions to protect all adult family members against inter-personal violence. When Sweden's prohibition came into effect in 1979, a group of Swedish parents belonging to a particular religious group made an application to the European Commission of Human Rights in Strasbourg, alleging that the new law breached their rights, guaranteed under the European Human Rights Convention, to respect for family life and privacy. The Commission dismissed the application, saying:

> "The actual effects of the law are to encourage a positive review of the punishment of children by their parents, to discourage abuse and prevent excesses which could properly be described as violence against children."

It also stated:

> "The existence of legislation prohibiting all corporal punishment of children, but which does not provide for any sanction in this respect, cannot be considered as an interference in the exercise of the parents' right to respect

---

16 For a detailed account of the legal reforms in Scandinavian countries see Newell *op cit*, n 8.

for family life. Neither does the fact that corporal punishment of a child by his parents may expose the latter to criminal prosecution for assault, by the same standards as assault of a person outside the family, constitute an interference with the exercise of this right".[17]

What the Swedish law does is to place in civil law a clear statement that no physical punishment or other humiliating treatment of children is permitted – which has removed any lingering doubt that the criminal law on assault applies equally to physical punishment of children by their parents or anyone else. In Sweden, in 14 years since this law was implemented, there has only been one single prosecution of a parent for "ordinary" physical punishment. A detailed assessment of the effects of the Swedish law and the accompanying education campaign has shown its entirely positive effects.[18]

It is interesting to note that wherever the need to represent children's interests formally at government level has been recognised by the appointment of a children's ombudsman or children's commissioner, this issue of challenging physical punishment has been adopted as the first, or an early priority. Thus in Sweden it was the government-appointed Children's Rights Committee which proposed the 1979 law. In Norway it was the world's first children's ombudsman who was most influential in achieving legal reform. In Germany, the KinderKommission has recommended similar legal reform. And in 1993 the New Zealand Commissioner for Children proposed legal reform and launched an extensive education campaign.

There will soon be more progress in Europe: in 1992 the German Minister of Justice committed herself to introduce similar legislation within two years. In Switzerland, a governmental working group on child abuse has proposed constitutional change to give children an equal right to physical integrity, and in Poland a similar proposal has been made by a commission considering constitutional change and children. Outside Europe, in Canada the Federal Ministry of Justice recently announced that it would review the equivalent of the defence of "reasonable chastisement", and at the same time launch a public information campaign on positive discipline. In September 1993 at the Second African Conference on Child Abuse in Cape Town over 600 representatives from 15 African countries unanimously adopted a resolution supporting moves to eliminate all physical punishment by legal reform and education. Namibia recently declared school corporal punishment unconstitutional, and launched a vigorous education campaign directed at parents and communities as well as schools.

In the United Kingdom the governmental Scottish Law Commission in its Report on Family Law, published in May 1992, proposed strict limits on parents' rights to use physical punishment, proposing that any use of implements, and any striking of a child which causes or could cause injury,

17 European Commission on Human Rights, decision on admissibility of Application 8811/79: *Seven Individuals* v *Sweden*, 13 May 1982.
18 See Newell *op cit*, n 8.

or pain or discomfort lasting more than a very short time should become a criminal offence. An opinion poll found more than 90% of the representative sample of Scots believed that it should be illegal to hit children with implements. But the Commission failed to uphold children's right to physical integrity, leaving what it termed "the safe disciplinary smack" alone.[19] Its proposal is currently under consideration by Scottish ministers.

The campaign "EPOCH – End Physical Punishment of Children" was launched in 1989. It has made physical punishment a much more public issue in Britain. It has made available material on positive discipline, distributed over a million copies of leaflets and booklets, both to individual parents direct, and in bulk through local authorities and health authorities. EPOCH also held two very well-publicised National No Smacking Weeks, one launched by Esther Rantzen, and the second by Claire Rayner.

EPOCH has lobbied the Government, and met ministers. In a postscript to a 1992 letter to EPOCH, which confirmed the Government view that the concept of reasonable chastisement and current law protect children sufficiently, the Health Minister Virginia Bottomley wrote that she was "sympathetic to the case for doing more to change the culture".

Most important, we have converted a powerful coalition of over 50 professional and child welfare organizations to support legal reform. These now include the NSPCC, the Health Visitors Association, the British Association for Community Child Health, the National Children's Bureau, Save the Children etc. There are still a number of eminent medical and other bodies missing from the list, although of course no organization publicly supports physical punishment. Some local authorities, health authorities and trusts have agreed to formally support EPOCH's campaign. EPOCH gets increasingly impatient with organizations who dither and sit on the fence and thus effectively support deliberately hurting and humiliating children. In the current context of increased pressure on parents to take more responsibility for their children, to use "more" discipline, the unspoken implication is that this means hitting children harder, humiliating them more. It is as yet unspoken – no Government minister has actually advocated corporal punishment, but the vacuum, the lack of positive advice, given the cultural conditioning, is dangerous.

The culture is certainly resilient. We need a professional consensus against hitting and humiliating children. With such a consensus there is some hope that the culture could change quite quickly. Those involved in child welfare, children's law and child protection have a particular responsibility to make sure that definitions of child abuse, and a pre-occupation with extreme forms of physical, psychological and sexual violence to children, do not obscure the child's right to physical integrity. That right must be unequivocally acknowledged in our laws, in public attitudes, and in our individual behaviour towards children we live or work with.

---

19 Report on Family Law, Scottish Law Commission, HMSO, Edinburgh 1992.

We do not need more evidence, or more research. What we need is an end to individual and collective hypocrisy in our attitudes to violence and children, a recognition of the conditioning that has allowed us for so long to justify hurting and humiliating them. And we need action – individual and collective – to create a climate in which legal reform to give children the same protection that the rest of us take for granted, becomes a non-controversial imperative.

Further details about the campaign EPOCH – End Physical Punishment of Children may be obtained from EPOCH, 77 Holloway Road, London N7 8JZ, tel: 0171 700 0627.

Chapter 19

Combatting Child Sexual Abuse and Exploitation – Further Considerations on Human Rights Approaches

Geraldine Van Bueren

Senior Lecturer in Law, Director, Programme on International Rights of the Child,
Queen Mary and Westfield College, London

Introduction

The sexual abuse and exploitation of children, albeit in different guises, is universal. In part this is due to the subordinate status of children and to the cloak of invisibility which has clung to them through the ages. Sexual abuse within the family has not traditionally been regarded as a human rights issue, and even where protection against sexual exploitation is conceptualised as an aspect of human rights, it is classified as a health or economic issue requiring only progressive – in contrast to immediate – implementation. Hence it is assumed that a petitioning system would have no relevance for children in this area and further, that the Convention on the Rights of the Child, which was established to work on a co-operative basis, would not operate as effectively if it were to incorporate a child petitioning system. In an attempt to increase the protection of children at their most vulnerable, this paper argues that the prevention of child sexual abuse and protection of children from exploitation ought to be conceptualised within the general framework of international human rights law.

Child sexual abuse

Sexual abuse and exploitation of children violates the inherent dignity and worth of the child and usually involves cumulative breaches of several rights – the most common being unlawful interference with family life, breaches of privacy rights, health and leisure[1] – all of which are equally essential for

---

1   Arts 16, 24 and 31.

the healthy development and survival of the child. The two concepts of child sexual abuse and exploitation are expressly set out side by side in the Convention on the Rights of the Child.[2] Yet no clear distinction was made during the drafting of the treaty, probably because both are broad and overlapping concepts which risk being limited if defined. Nevertheless, a distinction ought to be made as the causation may sometimes be different, and states need to adopt different strategies both to prevent and to reintegrate child victims.

Child sexual abuse has been defined as:

> "involvement of dependant, developmentally immature children and adolescents in sexual activities they do not fully comprehend, to which they are unable to give informed consent, or that violates the social taboos of family roles."[3]

The definition includes paedophilia, incest and any intra-familial relationships of a sexual nature which risk damaging the healthy sexual development of a child. In contrast with the sexual exploitation of children, child sexual abuse may raise more fundamental issues of culture and indigenous tradition.

The Convention on the Rights of the Child does not limit the responsibility of the state only in regard to parents but also obliges the state to take measures to prevent sexual abuse by any person responsible for the care of the child.[4]

In contrast to the sexual exploitation of children, child sexual abuse was not expressly prohibited by international law until the adoption of the Convention on the Rights of the Child, partly because the sexual abuse of children, particularly within the family, raises the dichotomy of public and private law. It is the public sphere which traditionally has been regarded as the province of international law. Yet the creation of new rights for children has raised issues as to the limits of state responsibility. State responsibility defines the limits of government accountability in international human rights law which arises only when acts by an individual can be attributed to the state.[5] Hence acts of private individuals lie beyond the traditional nexus. Such a blinkered perspective of the potency of international law is not inherent to it, as the potential of comparatively recent jurisprudence of Inter-American and European regional human rights fora illustrate. Where the state does not commit the principal abuse however, it may still be held responsible if it fails to prosecute or detect the abuse carried out by those acting in their private capacities.[6]

There is sometimes resistance to using international human rights law

---

2   Art 34.
3   See Kempe, "Incest and Other Forms of Sexual Abuse" in Kempe and Helfer, *The Battered Child* (1980) at 198. For the history of child sexual abuse see Moll, *Sexual Life of the Child* (1913).
4   Art 19(1).
5   Brownlie, *Principles of Public International Law* (Oxford University Press, 1990) at 435.
6   See Shelton, "Private Violence and Public Wrongs and the Responsibilities of States" (1990) 13 *Fordham Int LJ* 1.

because it is perceived to be confrontational, pitting the child against the state. Yet in specific cases there is simply no alternative. Unless child sexual abuse is regarded as a human rights issue the child would be without a remedy. *X and Y* v *Netherlands*[7] arose because a father was unable to prosecute an institution for the mentally disabled in which he alleged his daughter had been sexually assaulted. His proposed action failed because under Dutch law at the time, only his daughter had the *locus standi* to bring the action. The European Court of Human Rights having previously established that Article 8 of the European Convention on Human Rights imposed positive obligations on a state[8], held that a sexual assault "involved fundamental values and essential aspects of private life" and that effective measures were therefore essential. Hence Article 8 of the European Convention may place a state under a duty to adopt measures aimed at securing respect for private life even between individuals. This, however, does not mean that the state will always be held responsible under international law for the violent acts of all private individuals, but in the sphere of child sexual abuse the European Court has established the necessary link. In *X and Y* v *Netherlands*, the European Commission of Human Rights specifically commented upon the mental suffering of children as a result of sexual abuse, concluding that "mental suffering leading to acute psychiatric disturbances falls into the category of treatment prohibited under Article 3" which prohibits torture, inhuman and degrading treatment.[9]

In *Velasquez-Rodriguez* v *Honduras*,[10] state accountability was also held to extend to responsibility for acts committed by private individuals amounting to torture, and the disappearance of individuals where the pattern of abuses pointed to state complicity. Treaty law may be applied where the state refuses to take responsibility for a consistent pattern of institutional child sexual abuse. Importantly, the court determined that an illegal act which breaches human rights law and which, because it is an act of a private person, is not directly imputable to the state, can lead to international responsibility of the state – not because of the act itself but because of the failure "to prevent the violation or to respond to it as required by the Convention."[11] The court also concluded that where human rights violations by private parties are not seriously investigated the parties are in a sense aided by the government making the state responsible on the international plane.

It is also submitted that a similar action would lie under the International

---

7   (Ser A No 91), Judgment of the European Court of Human Rights 26 Mar 1985.
8   *Marckx* v *Belgium* (Ser A No 31) Judgment of the European Court of Human Rights 1979. See generally Connelly, "Problems of Interpretation of Article 8 of the European Convention on Human Rights" 35 *Intl and Comp Law* 567.
9   *op cit*, n. 7.
10   Inter-American Court of Human Rights (Ser C No 4 1988). State responsibility was engaged because there was a consistent pattern of abuse linking the para-military group's action to the state.
11   *Ibid*, Para 172.

Covenant on Civil and Political Rights, as according to the Human Rights Committee, the right to be protected against arbitrary or unlawful interferences with privacy "is required to be guaranteed against all such interferences and attacks whether they emanate from State authorities or from natural or legal persons."[12] Such an approach has implications for institutional and intra-familial abuse generally, but the potential of such an action is severely limited by the fact that the Convention on the Rights of the Child lacks an individual petitioning mechanism.[13] Children are not able to bring a petition to the Committee on the Rights of the Child alleging sexual abuse within a particular state. However, the basic principle still holds and the Committee on the Rights of the Child will be entitled to question a state in public on its report if the state lacks the necessary measures to prevent and, where appropriate, prosecute child sexual abuse.

One question which will undoubtedly arise for consideration by human rights fora is whether child sexual abuse is a universal concept or a culturally relative one. Cultural relativism implies a recognition that the viewpoint of those within communities are as valid as those outside. It is applicable to concepts of child abuse generally.[14] Familial corporal punishment, for example, is an issue where cultural norms are diverse even within one continent.[15] However, to take a stance of extreme cultural relativism in each and every action concerning children would not only be irresponsible, but would also undermine the fundamental notion of minimum standards of treatment to which children are entitled as human beings. It would mean suspending judgement of the treatment of children in many areas.[16] An extreme stance of cultural relativity – as opposed to cultural sensitivity or cultural pluralism – would provide states with a gaping loophole equivalent to pleading act of state in justification of human rights violations.

One of the principal areas where opinions are sharply divided is whether female circumcision ought to be regarded as a specific form of torture; as cruel, inhuman and degrading treatment; or as sexual abuse, or whether it should continue to be regarded as a traditional practice prejudicial to health. Within the framework of the UN Convention on the Rights of the Child the prohibition of female circumcision comes within the abolition of the traditional practices prejudicial to the health, and is a specific facet of the right of the child to the highest attainable standard of health.[17] Thus formulated, States Parties can avoid family members being stigmatised as child abusers. However, there are those who argue that because of the damage to the female genitalia it ought to be regarded as a form of sexual

---

12 General Comment 16, 32 Session 1988. The General Comment continues, "The obligations imposed by this Article require the state to adopt legislative and other measures to give effect to the prohibition against such interferences and attacks as well as the protection of this right."

13 Amnesty International proposed that there ought to be a right of petition: *cf* Van Bueren, *The International Law on the Rights of the Child* (Nijhoff/Kluwer, 1995).

14 See *e.g.* comments by Nhlapo "International Protection of Human Rights and the Family: African Variations on a Common Theme" (1989) 3 *Intl Jo of Law and the Family* 1.

15 Van Bueren *op cit*, n. 13.

16 Korbin in Kempe and Helfer *op cit* n. 3, 22.

17 Art 24(3) in Van Bueren, *International Documents on Children* (Nijhoff/Kluwer, 1993).

abuse. Similar arguments rage around whether female circumcision is just that or mutilation, and whether it amounts to torture or cruel, inhuman and degrading treatment.

The right to health has traditionally been classified by states as a social right and as such states are only under a duty to implement it progressively. Hence although States Parties are obliged to take "all effective and appropriate measures" this is significantly weakened by the qualifying clause; "with a view to" abolishing such traditional practices. A more effective approach would be to place states under an immediate duty to prohibit such practices, but this would mean reclassifying female circumcision as a violation of a child's civil rights – either of privacy or as a form of torture, cruel, inhuman and degrading treatment. This is the attraction to some of classifying female circumcision as genital mutilation and conceptualising such mutilation as torture[18] – an approach adopted by the First Lady of Burkina Faso.[19] As a matter of international law such an approach is problematic both in terms of substance and strategy.

The definition of torture enshrined in the UN Convention on Torture and the Elimination of Cruel, Inhuman and Degrading Treatment or Punishment (1984), incorporates the notion of intentional infliction of severe mental or physical pain for:

> "such purposes as obtaining from him a confession, punishing him for an act he or a third person has committed or is suspected of having committed ... when such pain or suffering is inflicted by or at the instigation of or with the consent or acquiesence of a public official or other person acting in an official capacity ...".[20]

The definition may be criticised as being unjustifiably restrictive[21]; within that definition it is clearly impossible to counter female circumcision comprehensively.

Where girls are circumcised against their will, however insulting the classification may be to some communities, such circumcisions will clearly come within torture and other cruel, inhuman and degrading treatment and as such be subject to immediate prohibition as a fundamental violation of a civil right. Further, where a girl flees a country because it is the only way to avoid circumcision due to family and community pressure, the Conseil d'Etat has accepted as a matter of principle that she will be entitled to refugee status on the grounds that she has a well-founded fear of being persecuted for reasons of membership of a particular social group.[22] It is

---

18 Hosken, *The Epidemiology of Female Genital Mutilation* (1978). The term circumcision is also regarded as inappropriate as it describes only the removal of the hood of the clitoris and not the excision or infibulation of the clitoris which is also carried out.

19 Report of the UN Seminar on Traditional Practices effecting the Health of Women and Children, Annex 11, UN Doc E/CN.4/Sub.2/1991/48.

20 Art 1.

21 Charlesworth *et al*, "Feminist Approaches to International Law" (1991) 85 *Am Jo Intl Law* 613 at 628.

22 *Mademoiselle X.* Although Mlle X's application was rejected on the facts, the principle was accepted that women fearing persecution because of their refusal of circumcision are to be regarded as a "social group" within the meaning of the 1951 Convention.

also arguable that where such operations are conducted in hospitals run or licensed by the state, the relationship with the state is sufficient.[23] The World Health Organisation's policy is that female circumcision should "under no circumstances" be performed by health professionals or in health establishments.[24] This is akin to the international norms on medical ethics and such a comparison strengthens the analogy with torture. The majority of female circumcisions are however, not inflicted with such an intent, nor are they directly linked to the state as they are traditionally performed by private individuals and frequently with the consent of the girls. It is possible to seek to invalidate the consent by adopting a psychoanalytic approach and arguing that the child has internalised her culture but this has obvious dangers for those seeking to augment the autonomy of children. A stronger line is that the sanctions against not being circumcised, such as insult[25], or an inability to marry within the group and general rejection would nullify the necessary consent. As Mumma observes:

> "In a society where only those who have gone through the rite of passage have the right to know the secrets of that community and to be entrusted with various dignified duties, this is a serious sanction."[26]

One of the problems of international human rights law is that it has developed in an individualistic manner, paying little heed to the consequences of relationships which are particularly important for children. There are severe strategic disadvantages in ascribing the torture or the child sex abuse label as it may well close the ears of those to be persuaded. The language utilised does contribute to the degree of co-operation from those affected and therefore to its success or failure. One only had to witness the reaction of the Senegalese delegate to the Working Group on the Convention on the Rights of the Child when a translator working purely on her own initiative "translated" the word "traditional" into the French word for "barbaric".[27] Hence the practice is not classified as torture by the Inter-African Committee on Traditional Practices Affecting Women and Children who have set the goal of eradicating female circumcision by the year 2000.[28] Nor is it conceptualised as torture under the African Charter on the Rights and Welfare of the Child.[29]

To regard some female circumcisions as torture and others as traditional

---

23 See Byrne's criticism of the Committee against Torture's reaction to the report of Senegal in Byrne," The Committee Against Torture", in Alston (ed), *United Nations and Human Rights in United Nations and Human Rights* (Oxford University Press, 1992).

24 See *e.g.* the statement of the WHO representative in the Report on the Regional Seminar in Addis Abbab on Traditional Practices Affecting Women and Children, 1986.

25 "ekesagana" – an insult referring to uncircumcised girls among the Kisilii in Kenya: Mumma, *A Woman Beautiful in the Ways of the Child or an Abused Child,* Programme on International Rights of the Child, 1994. In Egypt a girl who is not circumcised is called "nigsa": Dorkenoo and Elworthy, *Female Genital Mutilation – A Proposal for Change* at 14.

26 Mumma *op cit,* n. 5 at 5.

27 The author represented Amnesty International at the UN during the drafting of the Convention on the Rights of the Child.

28 Hence falling within the goals of the Declaration of Alma Ata: see Van Bueren, n. 17.

29 Art 21(1)a, n. 17.

practices prejudicial to health does not produce a coherent global campaigning tool. A more productive line of argument may be to regard such circumcisions as breaches of privacy. The right to respect for privacy embraces notions of bodily integrity and such an approach is likely to be more acceptable to many states because it is less stigmatising than torture and child sexual abuse, while achieving the desired result of immediate eradication.[30] However, the issue of consent will again be relevant.

The real problem is not the labelling but the artificial distinctions in implementation. There are minimal resource implications attached to the first step in prohibiting female circumcision – the drafting and adoption of national legislation. Hence it is difficult to defend the approach of international human rights law that States Parties to the Convention on the Rights of the Child are only under a progressive as opposed to an immediate duty to prohibit. The resource implications are brought into being in the educative programmes which would accompany such legislation. However, rather than focusing on language, research ought to be undertaken amongst communities such as the Kikuyu and Akamba which have stopped or almost eradicated the practice. Such research would lead to practical strategies which have already been proven to work. Under the African Charter on the Rights and Welfare of the Child, legislation is expressly cited as an appropriate measure in relation to child marriage but not in relation to circumcision. The dispute over language diverts energy away from the need to campaign for effective social and educational measures.

Aside from the debates over whether female circumcision is a form of child sexual abuse, a cross-cultural conception of child sexual abuse has at least been achieved on an international and diplomatic level. As of 31 December 1993, 154 States Parties to the Convention on the Rights of the Child have not made any specific reservations in regard to child sexual abuse. The concept has been taken further by the Organisation of African Unity (OAU) in the African Charter on the Rights and Welfare of the Child, although this has yet to enter into force. The African Charter, which regardless of national ages of majority will be applicable to all those under 18 years of age, seeks to eliminate the possibility of child sexual abuse within marriage by establishing 18 as the minimum age for marriage.[31] To reinforce the prohibition, states will be obliged to make the registration of marriages compulsory and prohibit child betrothals. Although in Africa, as in many parts of the globe, some child marriages and betrothals are successful whilst others are abused, the OAU classifies *all* child marriages and betrothals as a harmful social or cultural practice affecting the "welfare, dignity, normal growth and development" of the child.[32]

Although the definition of child sexual abuse is a contentious issue, there does appear to be universal agreement at an international level as to the

---

30 Privacy being classified as a civil right.
31 Art 21(3).
32 Art 21.

desired approach to child sexual abuse. The principal method of protecting a child against sexual abuse is by supporting the family when it is in need. The original Canadian draft for Article 19 did not place sufficient emphasis on the importance of support for the family as the principal preventative measure, nor on preventative actions generally. An accepted amendment by the non-governmental organizations, places a duty on States Parties to establish social programmes for the prevention, identification, reporting, referral and investigation of abuse generally.[33] At the insistence of the non-governmental organizations, and in particular Defence for Children International, judicial involvement is only regarded as a protective measure to be resorted to "as appropriate". To emphasise this point judicial intervention appears last in the non-exhaustive list of preventative measures. Hence the approach for intra-familial sexual abuse is consistent with other forms of abuse – it is neither predominately punitive nor the responsibility of only one state agency. The Convention on the Rights of the Child regards it as consistent with the best interests of the child for there to be co-operation between health, law enforcement agencies and the judiciary. The African Charter, which is not yet in force, goes even further and specifically obliges future States Parties to establish "special monitoring units" to provide support both for the child and those who have care for the child.[34]

Where, however, States Parties to the Convention on the Rights of the Child lack the resources or knowledge concerning effective prevention programmes, they can request through the Committee on the Rights of the Child, technical advice and assistance, thus avoiding expending scarce resources reinventing the wheel.

The sexual exploitation of children

Although Kempe equates sexual exploitation with sexual abuse[35], and all forms of exploitation are intrinsically abusive, the distinguishing feature of sexual exploitation is that it generally involves notions of commercial gain[36]. Alone, a commercially available pornographic photograph of a child will amount to exploitation of the body, but not to its abuse. However, the commercial element – although generally present – is not a pre-condition. In contrast, child sexual abuse does not generally have a commercial element, and either occurs where there is some form of direct physical contact or fear of such contact.[37]

Historically, the international law on child sexual exploitation can be

---

33 Art 19(2).
34 Art 16(2). The Convention also provides for support for the child and for those who have care of the child but does not call for the establishment of specific monitoring units.
35 Kempe *op cit*, n. 3 at 198.
36 See *e.g.* Art 117(4) Juvenile Code, Bolivia, which refers to exploitation for lucrative purposes.
37 See *e.g.* the approach of the English courts in *R v Court* [1987] 1 All ER 120 at 122: "If there was no touching, then to constitute an indecent assault the victim must be shown to have been aware of the assault and of the circumstances of indecency."

traced to the League of Nations, and has developed from general international legal provisions prohibiting the exploitation of children and women. Both Declarations on the Rights of the Child (1924, 1959) provide that the child should be protected against every and any form of exploitation.[38] Neither expressly cite sexual exploitation but it is clearly included within such a broad prohibition. The International Covenant on Economic, Social and Cultural Rights (1966) also obliges States Parties to make "punishable by law" the employment of children in work harmful to their morals and health.[39] By implication this includes specific forms of "work" amounting to sexual exploitation, including prostitution and child pornography. Yet the sexual exploitation of children does not only occur in working environments, so the Covenant's potential to combat it is inherently limited.[40]

At the time the Covenant was drafted, the sexual exploitation of children occurred on a smaller and more localised scale. By the 1980s, the availability and rapidity of international transport had, in common with other violations, changed the nature of child sexual exploitation. Sexual exploitation is becoming more flagrant – particularly in a number of Asian states where the problems are linked to "sex tourism". The sale of children for sexual exploitation is also one of the reasons for the existence of networks engaged in the international trafficking of children involving cross-frontier abductions and disappearances. Child trafficking has reached such a scale that it has prompted responses from Interpol, including the establishment of a Standing Committee on Offences against Minors.[41]

These developments reveal the need for further international legislation. The provisions in the Convention on the Rights of the Child were drafted to provide a more comprehensive framework. In countering the sexual exploitation of children under the Convention, States Parties are obliged to take all national, bilateral and multilateral measures, thus expanding the punitive model of early enforcement of treaties. According to France and the Netherlands, the purpose of Article 34 of the Convention on the Rights of the Child is not to regulate the sexual life of children, but to combat the sexual exploitation of children "on the basis of concrete examples". The non-exhaustive examples are: the inducement or coercion of children into unlawful sexual activity[42], the exploitative use of children in prostitution or

---

38 See respectively Arts 4 and 9 in n. 17.

39 Art 10(3).

40 The delegations of Mexico, Senegal and Venezuela together with the ILO and the NGO's argued for a separate Art on child trafficking and sexual exploitation as the sale of children is broader than child sexual exploitation: see UN Doc E/CN.4/1987/25. Children may be subjected to trafficking for many reasons including economic exploitation and adoption, although the adoption may be a disguise for exploitation.

41 See the reports of the trafficking in children between the Lao Peoples Democratic Republic, Myanmar, China, Cambodia and Thailand reported at UN Doc E/CN.4/1993/SR.56. There have been calls in Germany, Switzerland and Scandinavia to extend their criminal jurisdiction to cover acts committed by their nationals against children abroad and see Early Day Motion 808, Children in Prostitution and Pornography, 1992.

42 Art 34(a).

other unlawful sexual practices[43], and the exploitative use of children in pornographic performances and materials.[44] As the sexual exploitation of children is often the consequence of prior breaches of the international rights of the child, the provisions should serve as a reinforcement of States Parties' duties towards children in other areas, particularly in the spheres of education and living standards.

The Convention also fills lacunae found in earlier treaties. Hence it places a duty on States Parties to prevent child pornography, an obligation which was omitted from the International Convention on the Suppression of the Circulation and Traffic in Obscene Publications (1923).

Norveson identifies three groups of children who are at particular risk from sexual exploitation: street children, the children of women who are themselves in prostitution and housemaids.[45] There are also specific additional factors relating to localised sexual exploitation, for example the presence of foreign military bases such as those sited in Angeles and Olongapo in the Philippines.[46] Hence the sexual exploitation of children often reflects state's underlying social and cultural patterns and values. It is not coincidental that Thailand only began countering the sexual exploitation of children as a reaction to the AIDS pandemic. Despite additional local factors, child prostitution is now a global phenomenon. The numbers are highest in Asia and Central and South America, but there are also reports of increases in Africa, North America and Europe.[47] In contrast child pornography is more widespread in industrialised states and increasingly in Eastern Europe. In 1977 the Special Rapporteur on Child Labour estimated that the trade in child pornography in the United States alone amounted to $500 million.[48]

Yet although Article 34 of the Convention on the Rights of the Child ought to prove valuable as it focuses attention on a problem which many would prefer to remain hidden and undiscussed, there are a number of unsatisfactory facets of the protection offered by the Convention. The first is the strange insertion of the concept of "unlawful" in Article 34(b) and (c). The "exploitative" use of children in prostitution and their "exploitative" use in pornographic performance and materials is prohibited. This generates the implication that the use of children in both pornography and prostitution could be other than exploitative.[49] In other words, individuals under the age of 18 who are legally permitted sexual

---

43 Art 34(b).

44 Art 34(c).

45 Norveson, "The Sexual Exploitation of Children in Developing Countries" in Redd Barn (ed), *Making Reality of Children's Rights* 1989. For a study of the situation in Europe see Breys, Report on the Sexual Exploitation of Children and Young Persons, Council of Europe 1987.

46 See Santos, "The Rights of Children to be Protected Against Sexual Exploitation" in Redd Barn (ed), *Making Reality of Children's Rights.* For a survey of the practical initiatives taken see International Catholic Child Bureau, The Sexual Exploitation of Children; Field Responses 1991.

47 For the figure see UN Doc E/CN/4/Sub 2/112 SR 7.

48 UN Doc E/CN/4/Sub 2/479 Rev 1.

49 Hence the Netherlands attempted unsuccessfully to delete the word "exploitative": see UN Doc E/CN 4/1987/25.

relations could become prostitutes, and children who are sufficiently mature would be free to consent to pornographic performances. Such an approach is not open to the relatively small number of states that are party to the Convention Concerning Minimum Age for Admission to Employment (1973), which establishes 18 as the minimum age for work "likely to jeopardise the health, safety or morals".[50]

Prostitution is defined by Ennew as the "enforced or voluntary hire or sale of sexuality by an individual to another individual for explicit material gain".[51] Unless one considers all children under the age of 18 who are prostitutes to be *de facto* exploited (an approach which has been adopted by the Spanish Penal Code[52]) the Convention appears to allow states to permit children who have reached the age of sexual emancipation to become prostitutes – as in some states sexual emancipation is reached at an earlier age than full majority. The word "unlawful" in Article 34, however, qualifies not only sexual activity but also prostitution. No cognisance appears to have been taken of the preamble to an earlier treaty, where prostitution was described as "incompatible with the dignity of the human person and endangers the welfare of the individual"[53] and hence by implication is equally descriptive of child prostitution. Nor did states appear to be aware of the provisions of an earlier treaty, in accordance with which states agreed to punish any person who "procures, entices, leads away for the purposes of prostitution another person even with the consent of that person."[54] Yet the parallels with hazardous work are even stronger in relation to child prostitution than with regard to pornography because of the direct and well-documented consequences to health. Nevertheless, because of the misplaced qualifying words, issues such as child consent to prostitution and pornography can be raised. This prompts the question of whether there is another approach to sexual exploitation besides relying solely on the provisions of the Convention on the Rights of the Child.

Outside the regime of the Convention on the Rights of the Child, the sexual exploitation of children raises two human rights issues. The first is whether specific forms of sexual exploitation of children, such as incarceration in brothels,[55] can be characterised as slavery, and if they can, what consequences does this have for combatting sexual exploitation? The many treaty provisions[56], together with the evidence of *opinio juris* and

---

50 Art 3 in n. 17.

51 Ennew, *Children in Especially Difficult Circumstance: The Sexual Exploitation of Children; Prostitution and Pornography* (Anti-Slavery Society, 1985).

52 Art 452 bis (b). It is a criminal offence for a person to provide the facilities or induce even where there is consent.

53 Preamble to Convention for the Suppression of the Traffic in Persons and of the Exploitation of the Prostitution of Others 1949 in n. 17.

54 Convention for the Traffic in Persons and of Exploitation of the Prostitution in Others 1949, n. 17.

55 Cited as an abuse in n. 47.

56 See *e.g.* Art 8 International Covenant on Civil and Political Rights 1966; Art 4 European Convention on Human Rights 1950 (although this does not expressly refer to the slave trade); Art 6 American Convention on Human Rights 1969; Art 5 African Charter on Human and Peoples Rights 1981. These provisions are in addition to the specific slavery treaties: Slavery Convention 1926; Protocol amending the Slavery Convention 1953; Supplementary Convention on the Abolition of Slavery, the Slave Trade and Institutions and Practices Similar to Slavery 1956.

general state practice, establishes that slavery[57], slavery-like practices and the slave trade are prohibited under international customary law. Sunga points both to their non-derogable status and to the consistency in the formulation of the prohibition and concludes that the international norms prohibiting slavery constitute *jus cogens*.[58] If the prohibition on slavery amounts to *jus cogens*, the argument that the prohibition on institutions and practices similar to slavery also amount to *jus cogens* is very compelling. This line of argument is supported by the Working Group on Contemporary Forms of Slavery. According to the Working Group, slavery in its various forms and practices constitutes a breach of *jus cogens* regardless of whether states are party to the relevant treaties.[59]

Separate from the issue of *jus cogens* is the question whether a state is only under a duty to eradicate progressively the sexual exploitation of children, or whether specific forms of child sexual exploitation – such as the non-consensual, forcing of children into prostitution – may amount to a fundamental violation of a child's civil rights requiring immediate eradication by the state. During the drafting of the Supplementary Slavery Convention[60], opinion was divided amongst the Ten Member Drafting Committee with the representative of the (then) USSR considering the words "progressively and" to weaken the Article and to be contrary to the principles of the UN Charter. His arguments were supported by Egypt. The representative of the United Kingdom argued that practices similar to slavery were rooted in the "traditions of many centuries in some parts of the world and that their immediate abolition would cause considerable disorganisation."[61] Although the United Kingdom's arguments succeeded and the progressive duty is enshrined in the Slavery Convention, it is arguable that states which are party to the International Covenant on Civil and Political Rights and to the American Convention on Human Rights[62] are now under a duty to eradicate immediately those specific instances of child sexual exploitation which amount to slavery or slavery-like practices.

Another approach which may place an immediate binding duty on a state to prevent and eradicate specific forms of child sexual exploitation is to argue that specific forms amount to degrading treatment. According to the European Commission of Human Rights, "[t]reatment or punishment of an individual may be said to be degrading if it grossly humiliates him before others or drives him to act against his will or conscience."[63] So according to

---

57 Art 1 Slavery Convention 1926 defines slavery as "the condition of a person over whom any or all of the powers attaching to the right of ownership has exercised".

58 Sunga, *Individual Responsibility in International Law for the Serious Human Rights Violations* (Nijhoff/Kluwer, 1992) at 92. See also *Barcelona Traction* ICJ Rep 1979 para 33. Weil criticises *jus cogens* because it forces states to accept "the supernormativity of rules they were perhaps not prepared to recognise as ordinary norms" in "Towards Relative Normativity in International Law" (1983) *Am Jo Intl Law* 77, 413 at 427.

59 UN Doc/E/CN 4/Sub 2/1993/30.

60 See Gutteridge "Supplementary Slavery Convention" 1956 *Intl and Comp Law Q* 6, 449.

61 *Ibid.*

62 This same approach arguably applies to States Parties to the European Convention on Human Rights and the African Charter on Human and Peoples Rights.

63 *The Greek Case Year book*, (1969) 12 186.

the characterisation of prostitution above, child prostitution would clearly fall within the concept of degrading treatment which a state has a duty to prevent. Child pornography is more problematic, as in considering whether a particular form of treatment is degrading, the presence of consent is a relevant factor.[64] Consent may deprive an act which would otherwise be degrading of that character.[65] There is,however, no absolute standard for the types of treatment which are regarded as degrading. Each treatment must be judged according to the circumstances of each individual case. One such circumstance is the age of the individual concerned.[66] Linked to the age of the individual are the circumstances under which any consent is given. As the UN Special Rapporteur on the Sale of Children, Child Prostitution and Child Pornography notes, children enter prostitution because of poverty, aggravated by family disintegration (including incest and domestic violence) and migration from rural to urban areas and from one country to another.[67] This analysis prompted Brazil to recommend the creation of rehabilitation centres for child victims of sexual exploitation.[68] In essence it is question of relative power, old over young and rich over poor, and arguably with tourism, the organized over the unorganized. Such factors must be weighed in the balance when considering the weight to be placed on the child's consent. As has been noted, despite the efforts of Amnesty International[69], the Convention on the Rights of the Child regrettably lacks an individual petitioning mechanism, but it still may be possible[70], under the International Covenant on Civil and Political Rights or the regional human rights treaties, to petition in respect of state inaction on specific forms of sexual exploitation of children which come within the category of degrading treatment.

Conclusion

Although the Convention on the Rights of the Child provides the opportunity for governments, inter-governmental and non-governmental organizations to offer technical advice and assistance in combatting child sexual abuse and exploitation, this alone is insufficient. Technical advice may be useful in such programmes assisting governments to draft legislation and establish social programmes, but are limited, as governments first have to acknowledge publicly that the country has a problem, something which

---

64 *X* v *Denmark*, (1983) 32 D & R 282.
65 Van Dijk and Van Hoof, *Theory and Practice of the European Convention on Human Rights*, (Kluwer, 1990) 229.
66 See the discussion of *Ireland* v *United Kingdom* in n. 13.
67 UN Doc E/CN 4/1992/55.
68 UN Doc E/CN 4/Sub/2/1993/30.
69 See n. 13 above.
70 Applying *Velasquez, op cit* n. 10 and *X and Y, op cit* n. 7 and providing there is sufficient nexus with the state concerned.

governments are not always willing to do. This is a particular problem with sexual exploitation. As the Council of Europe accepted, the extent and the nature of the problem are difficult to study because it is largely invisible.[71] Hence there are no reliable estimates of the figures involved and of the precise seriousness of the problem.[72] This ought not to deter however, and indeed the duties on states to prevent the sexual exploitation of children have been reinforced by the UN Programme of Action for the Prevention of the Sale of Children, Child Prostitution and Child Pornography.[73] The Programme incorporates a recommendation that the needs of children exposed to sexual exploitation ought to be taken into account in countries' development plans and assistance programmes.

The Commission on Human Rights has resolved to establish an open-ended inter-sessional working group to discuss:

> "guidelines for a possible draft optional protocol to the Convention on the Rights of the Child on the sale of children, child prostitution and child pornography as well as basic measures needed for their prevention and eradication."[74]

In general, in the post Convention on the Rights of the Child world, it is not that the standards protecting against sexual abuse and exploitation require revision, it is that child sexual abuse and exploitation require reconceptualising to enable more effective implementation. The two principle advantages of a human rights approach are, first, that it provides the campaigns of local indigenous groups with a much needed international legitimacy, and second, that it provides additional fora for action. Although the Convention on the Rights of the Child[75], in contrast to the Declaration of the Rights of the Child (1959)[76], places the best interests of the child as only "a" primary concern and not as "the" primary concern, in relation to child sexual abuse and exploitation there can be no question of other interests predominating.[77]

---

71 Council of Europe, "Sexual Exploitation, Pornography and Prostitution of and Trafficking in, Children and Young Adults" (1991) at 15. See also Recommendation No (91) 11, adopted by the Committee of Ministers.

72 Norway estimated that annually 1 m children are either "kidnapped, bought or in other ways forced to enter the sex market." The Norwegian delegate to the European Ministers of Justice did not offer any sources for this information, Council of Europe, "Pornography and Prostitution of, and Trafficking in Children and Young Women" (1988).

73 See Res 1990/67 adopted by the Commission on Human Rights entitled "Programme of Action for Prevention of Sale of Children, Child Prostitution and Child Pornography". On 1 Aug 1990 Vitit Muntarbhorn was appointed as Special Rapporteur.

74 Comm on Human Rights Res 1994/90.

75 Art 5.

76 Art 2.

77 In issues such as divorce the reasons for divorce may be other than in the best interests of the child but no parental or state considerations can enter the arena and be weighed against the sexual abuse and exploitation of children.

Acknowledgement

This paper is an expanded version of an article which first appeared in (1994) 2 *International Journal of Children's Rights* 45, and grateful acknowledgement is made to Martinus Nijhoff for permission to reproduce published material.

Chapter 20
Homemaker Services and the Law

Mika Oldham

Fellow of Jesus College and Lecturer in Law, University of Cambridge

Societal notions of the role of the family are of vital importance in shaping legal developments. Much of the present day debate about the future of the family reflects an increasing dissatisfaction with traditional ideologies and assumptions about the family and its role. This dissatisfaction challenges prevailing orthodoxies that romanticise "the family" as a "haven in a heartless world"[1], greet the rise of the "egalitarian" or "symmetrical"[2] family, classify modern families as "units of consumption"[3] and erect a barrier between the "public" and "private" spheres of life.[4] Many of these and similar orthodoxies and assumptions underlie the principles of family law as they are applied in England today. It is within this context that this paper proposes to examine the inconsistency with which homemaking services are treated in English law and to illustrate how emerging trends in other jurisdictions are beginning to reflect new shifts of perception and to suggest alternative approaches to legal problems posed by modern family living.

The law's treatment of homemaker services is of obvious importance to unmarried cohabitants, who cannot rely upon matrimonial property legislation on the breakdown of their relationships. However, the issue is also of major significance to the vast majority of women[5] whose employment market activities are prejudicially affected by social patterns of child-rearing and current divisions of paid and unpaid labour within families. In many ways we conceptualise "the family" as a single unit rather than as a group of

---

1   See, *e.g.*, Shorter, *The Making of the Modern Family* (Fontana, 1977) 272: "The nuclear family was a nest. Warm and sheltering, it kept the children secure from the pressure of the outside adult world, and gave the men an evening refuge from the icy blast of competition .... So everyone huddled happily within those secure walls, serene about the dinner table, united in the Sunday outing."

2   Shorter, *op cit* n. 1 above 278-280; Young and Willmott, *The Symmetrical Family* (Routledge and Kegan Paul, 1973) 275ff.

3   Galbraith, *Economics and the Public Purpose* (Houghton Mifflin, 1973), 33, 49.

4   Talcott Parsons, "The Social Structure of the Family", in Anshen (ed), *The Family: Its Function and Destiny* (Harper & Row, 1964): values such as ascription and particularism are necessary for the "private" sphere of family life but unacceptable and harmful in the "public" sphere of industrial society.

5   For the purposes of this paper it is assumed that the claimant is female, as the majority of homemakers are women. The same principles would, of course, apply to a male homemaker.

individuals, and from such a unitary perspective the division of paid and unpaid labour seems harmless, or even beneficial in that it promotes efficiency by specialisation. From a perspective which regards families as groups of individuals, however, the division of paid and unpaid labour takes on a different complexion. Here, the best interests of the unit clash with the best interests of certain individuals within the unit. From an individualist perspective the traditional division of paid and unpaid work both adversely affects the employment market prospects and achievements of homemakers, and, within the strong monetary ethos of modern cash economies, also exerts a strong effect on power relations between paid and unpaid workers.

In English law, non-financial contributions of domestic labour are recognised as being of value within certain limited areas. Thus, for example, in respect of married couples, there exists statutory recognition that value attaches to homemaker services in the provisions of the Matrimonial Causes Act 1973. Judges are instructed, in the exercise of their powers regarding property division on divorce, nullity, or judicial separation, to take into account factors including:

> "the contribution which each of the parties has made or is likely in the foreseeable future to make to the welfare of the family, including any contribution by looking after the home or caring for the family".[6]

Similarly, the caselaw on the Inheritance (Provision for Family and Dependants) Act 1975 illustrates that the rendering of domestic services can constitute "valuable consideration" for the purposes of that Act.[7] The 1975 Act differentiates between applications by spouses, who are categorised within section 1(1)(a), and applications by cohabitants, who can bring claims only if they fall within section 1(1)(e).[8] Judges have interpreted section 1(3) of the 1975 Act[9] in such a way as to deny relief where the domestic services are considered to be equivalent to the economic benefits received from the deceased.[10] The clear inference is that the rendering of domestic services can constitute "valuable consideration".

---

6   S 25(2)(f), as amended. See also Domestic Proceedings and Matrimonial Causes Act 1978, s 3(2)(f), but *cp.* the caselaw on the Fatal Accidents Act 1976, below.

7   Ss 1(1)(e), 1(3).

8   "[A]ny person ... who immediately before the death of the deceased was being maintained, either wholly or partly, by the deceased."

9   S 1(3) states that "For the purposes of subsection (1)(e) above, a person shall be treated as being maintained by the deceased, either wholly or partly, as the case may be, if the deceased, otherwise than for full valuable consideration, was making a substantial contribution in money or money's worth towards the reasonable needs of that person."

10 See, *e.g., In re Wilkinson, decd* [1978] Fam 22; *Jelley* v *Iliffe* [1981] Fam 128; *In re Beaumont, decd* [1980] Ch 444, and cases cited by Sachs, "Inheritance (Provision for Family and Dependants) Act 1975 – An Update" [1990] *Conv* 45. More recently, in *Bishop* v *Plumley* [1991] 1 WLR 582, the CA held that in balancing the contributions on each side, the "mutuality of the relationship" was to be taken into account. Butler-Sloss LJ at 587-588 felt that it could not have been the intention of Parliament that a claimant who gives the other partner "extra devoted care and attention, particularly when the partner is in poor health ..." should be in "a less advantageous position ... than one who may be less loving and give less attention to the partner."

On the other hand, activities such as child-raising or the rendering of domestic services are not, without more, accepted as trust-generating contributions[11], nor, very possibly, as sufficient consideration to support a contract at common law.[12] The inference here is either that such services are regarded as merely the "ordinary kind of work" to be expected of a woman and of no value[13], or that the non-claimant is entitled to receive the benefit of those services for nothing.

As the law currently stands the net effect of such inconsistencies is that if a cohabiting "homemaker" seeks a division of property while her partner is alive, her claim will be rejected because her domestic services are of no value, but if she seeks a share in the estate of her partner on his death, her claim may well be rejected precisely because her services *are* of value. It will be argued here that such inconsistencies should be rectified not by amending the 1975 Act[14], but by bringing the rest of the law into line with it – in short, by fully recognising the value of homemaker contributions in all areas of legal analysis.

The grave injustice that can result from a legal stance of non-recognition has been commented upon both by academics[15] and by the judiciary.[16]

---

11 *Gissing* v *Gissing* [1971] AC 886; *Burns* v *Burns* [1984] Ch 317; *Button* v *Button* [1968] 1 WLR 457 at 462 per Ld Denning MR; *Lloyds Bank plc* v *Rosset* [1991] 1 AC 107 per Ld Bridge at 132-133. See further, below.

12 *Horrocks* v *Forray* [1976] 1 WLR 230; below.

13 See, *e.g.*, the statement of Purchas LJ in *Lloyds Bank plc* v *Rosset* [1989] Ch 350 (CA) at 402: "before equity will intervene to protect the wife, her contributions must exceed that normally expected of a wife carrying out her normal matrimonial role." See also Freeman, "Towards a Critical Theory of Family Law" (1985) *CLP* 153 (commenting on *Grant* v *Edwards* [1986] Ch 638) at 154: "The message is clear: what women normally do, or are expected to do, has no economic value."

14 Arguments in favour either of amending the wording of the 1975 Act or of adopting an alternative construction of its present wording have been put forward by many writers, including Hand, "Family Provision: Are the Right People Receiving It?" (1980) 10 *Fam Law* 141; Naresh, "Dependants' Applications under the Inheritance (Provision for Family and Dependants) Act 1975" (1980) 96 *LQR* 534; Clark, "Deserving Mistresses Shunned?" (1978) 41 *MLR* 352; Pople, (1981) *JSWL* 364; *Cp.* Sherrin, "Disinheritance of a Spouse: A Comparative Study of the Law in the United Kingdom and the Republic of Ireland" (1980) 31 *NILQ* 21. See also the comments of Butler-Sloss LJ in *Bishop* v *Plumley* [1991] 1 WLR 582 at 587. The Law Commission have recommended that unmarried cohabitants be automatically eligible to apply under the 1975 Act: *Distribution on Intestacy*, Law Com No 187 (1990), Part IV.

15 See, *e.g.*, Bruch, "Property Rights of De Facto Spouses Including Thoughts on the Value of Homemakers' Services" (1976) 10 *Fam LQ* 101; Hodkinson, "Constructive Trusts: Palm Trees in the Commonwealth" [1983] *Conv* 420 at 423; Havighurst, "Services in the House – A Study of Contract Concepts in Domestic Relations" (1932) 41 *Yale Law Jo* 386; Glendon, "Patterns of Contemporary Legal Response to the Social Phenomenon of De Facto Marriage", in *Konflict und Ordnung: Festschrift Für Murad Ferid* (CH Beck, 1978) 491 at 509 n 48.

16 See, *e.g.*, the much cited words of Ld Simon of Glaisdale (in the context of spouses): "The cock bird can feather his nest precisely because he is not required to spend most of his time sitting on it": Sir J Simon, *With all my Worldly Goods* (Holdsworth Lecture, Birmingham, 1964) 14-15. In *Blanchford* v *Public Trustee* (unrep, Sup C of NSW, 10 Apr 1981, cited by NSW Law Reform Commission, *Report on De Facto Relationships*, LRC 36 (1983) at para 5.11), Wootten J stated that the case before him was "one of a significant number that come before the courts in which injustice results from the failure of the law to adapt to changing patterns of cohabitation." See also *Murray* v *Heggs* (1980) 6 Fam LR 781 per Powell J; *Pascoe* v *Turner* [1979] 1 WLR 431 at 438-439 per Cumming-Bruce LJ; *In re Evers' Trust* [1980] 1 WLR 1327 at 1329-1330 per Ormrod LJ; *Peter* v *Beblow* [1993] 1 SCR 980 at 993-994 per McLachlin J.

Current legal treatment of the rendering of domestic services is, however, but an extreme instance of a deeply embedded ideological bias which regards women's work in the home as secondary and subordinate to men's.[17] It becomes necessary, therefore, to examine the question of the status of homemaking in its wider contexts in order to arrive at a proper understanding of the problem and its possible solution. Studies carried out in recent years cast new light on old orthodoxies and challenge prevailing assessments of families, their functions, and their role within the larger economy.

The "invisibility" of homemaker services

A primary difficulty, and one that has served to obscure and perpetuate the present situation, is the problem of what can be termed the "invisibility" of homemaking.

There exist well-known sociological theories which trace the transformation of families from the basic units of social and economic production that they constituted in sixteenth and seventeenth century Europe to the modern "companionate"[18] families of post-industrial twentieth century societies. This transformation is usually described in terms of a "stripping" of family functions.[19] Industrialisation saw what is termed the "separation of home and workplace"[20], while industrial and post-industrial capitalism witnessed the relocation of functions previously undertaken by or within families in respect of welfare, education, and recreation. A result of this "stripping" of family functions is that sociologists describe modern families as more "privatised"[21], in the sense of more isolated, than they were in earlier societies. Thus homemaking can be described, first, as *geographically* "invisible", in that it is carried on in the intimate and relatively isolated zone of the household.

Second, homemaking can be described as *sociologically* "invisible" in that

---

17 See, *e.g.*, Matthews, *"Just a housewife": The Rise and Fall of Domesticity in America* (Oxford University Press, 1987); Finch, *Married to the Job* (George Allen & Unwin, 1983).

18 Burgess and Locke, *The Family: From Institution to Companionship* (American Book Co, 1945); Gavron, *The Captive Wife* (Penguin, 1968); Shorter, *op cit* n. 1 above. *Cp.* Fletcher, *The Family and Marriage in Britain* (Penguin, 1966) 86, who argues that the theory of the multi-purpose pre-industrial family is a fiction, since the harsh realities of life for the majority meant that most of the so-called functions such as welfare, education or recreation were largely neglected anyway.

19 Talcott Parsons and Bales, *Family Socialization and Interaction Process* (Free Press, 1955); Bilton *et al, Introductory Sociology*, 2nd ed (Macmillan, 1987) 260; Chodorow, *The Reproduction of Mothering: Psychoanalysis and the Sociology of Gender* (University of California Press, 1978).

20 Although the process had begun earlier than the late-eighteenth century: Bilton, *op cit* n. 19, 259. It is also true that all members of the family, including women and children, were at first employed in the factories and mines, and only gradually excluded: Harris, "Changing Conceptions of the Relation between Family and Societal Form in Western Society", in Scase (ed), *Industrial Society: Class, Cleavage and Control* (George Allen & Unwin, 1977) 86.

21 Ariès, *Centuries of Childhood* (Penguin, 1973) 385; Dailey, "Constitutional Privacy and the Just Family" (1992) 67 *Tulane Law Rev* 955, 964 *et seq.*

accepted theories that classify families as "units of consumption" and "stripped" of their functions have served to obscure important productive functions that families still fulfil.

Third, the rendering of homemaker services is *economically* "invisible". In conventional economic analysis, activities falling outside the market mainstream are considered peripheral to the economic system and not defined as "economic".[22] Homemakers are therefore traditionally classified as "inactive" in the economy[23]; their activities are not included in the gross domestic product "...even though they must add millions of hours to UK production of goods and services."[24]

Finally, and in line with the above, homemaking can be described as *legally* "invisible", partly as a hangover from the days when "...the law regarded husband and wife as one, and the husband as that one"[25], and partly because housework takes place in the "private" sphere of family life, "a domain into which the King's writ does not seek to run, and to which its officers do not seek to be admitted."[26] In an era when a regime of unity of property applied and a husband's right of consortium included a correlative legal duty on his wife to provide him with services[27], there was logic (if not justice) in a law that regarded homemaker contributions as incapable of generating a beneficial interest or of constituting valuable consideration. There is neither logic nor justice in a law that continues to apply the same restrictions well over 100 years after the introduction of a regime of separation of property[28] and in the face of express judicial recognition that the right of consortium is mutual.[29]

The law's approach to domestic contributions

In English law, as already noted, there exists statutory recognition that value attaches to homemaker contributions within certain limited

---

22 See, *e.g.*, Seccombe, "The Housewife and Her Labour Under Capitalism" (1974) 38 *New Left Rev* 3 at 11: "Domestic labour is unproductive in the economic sense"; Benería, "Conceptualizing the Labour Force: The Underestimation of Women's Economic Activities", in Pahl (ed), *On Work: Historical, Comparative and Theoretical Perspectives* (Basil Blackwell, 1988) 372 (using ILO methods of measurement of labour force participation to illustrate the underestimation of women's work in the household and in subsistence production generally) at 379.

23 Thus, *e.g.*, for Government statistics the definition of "economically inactive" includes homemakers: see (1993) *Social Trends 23*, 52, 53; *Labour Force Survey Quarterly Bulletin No 4*, June 1993, 23.

24 Kennedy, "The economy as a whole", in Artis (ed), *The UK Economy: A Manual of Applied Economics* (Weidenfeld & Nicolson, 11th ed, 1985) 1 at 8. See further. Benería, *loc cit* n. 22 above, at 373-374.

25 *Williams & Glyn's Bank* v *Boland* [1979] Ch 312 at 332 per Ld Denning MR. Austin, in his *Lectures on Jurisprudence*, described the doctrine of unity of husband and wife as "sheer imbecility": see Fuller, *Legal Fictions* (Stanford University Press, 1967) 33.

26 *Balfour* v *Balfour* [1919] 2 KB 571 at 579 per Atkin LJ. For a US equivalent, see *Trammell* v *West* 162 SE. 2d 353 (Ga, 1968) at 355.

27 *Re Cochrane* (1840) 8 Dowl 630 per Coleridge J.

28 Married Women's Property Act 1882.

29 *Place* v *Searle* [1932] 2 KB 497.

areas.[30] The position at common law is inconsistent. Thus, for example, there exists clear authority that in appropriate circumstances the rendering of domestic services can constitute sufficient "detriment" on which to base a claim in proprietary estoppel.[31] A claimant relying on estoppel, however, must also establish the further elements of representation or assurance[32] and reliance[33], and the expectation must relate to a specific asset, so that a promise of "financial security", even if acted upon, will not generate an estoppel equity.[34]

As regards constructive trusts, the approach is more restrictive. In English law, the constructive trust is a substantive institution whose component elements, common intention and change of position, must be proved in order to found a claim. Although common intention can be express or implied, courts are not willing to imply a common intention from the rendering of homemaking services, even though:

> "over a very substantial number of years [the claimant] may have worked just as hard as the man in maintaining the family, in the sense of keeping house, giving birth to and looking after and helping to bring up the children of the union".[35]

Except in extraordinary circumstances[36], the traditional approach of the courts has been to reject claims based on indirect or non-financial changes of position. In 1981 Lord Denning MR in *Hall* v *Hall*[37] had stated that

---

30 See, *e.g.*, Matrimonial Causes Act 1973; Domestic Proceedings & Matrimonial Causes Act 1978; Inheritance (Provision for Family and Dependants) Act 1975 and contrast the caselaw on the Fatal Accidents Act 1976, below: nn. 67-69.

31 As for example in *Greasley* v *Cooke* [1980] 1 WLR 1306 at 1311 per Ld Denning MR, at 1312-1313 per Waller LJ. See also *Maharaj* v *Chand* [1986] 1 AC 898 (PC) at 907, 908 per Sir Robin Cooke. *Cp. Hannaford* v *Selby* (1976) 239 *Est Gaz* 811 at 813; *Griffiths* v *Williams* (1978) 248 *Est Gaz* 947: merely paying money towards household expenses or running costs is not sufficient, as this is more readily seen as a contribution to the current living expenses of the family.

32 See *Taylors Fashions Ltd* v *Liverpool Victoria Trustees Co Ltd* [1982] QB 133 at 145 per Oliver J. In *Phillips* v *Phillips* [1993] 3 NZLR 159 at 169, Cooke P pointed out that the search for representation in estoppel suffers from the same "fictional quality" as the search for common intention in constructive trust doctrine (below).

33 In *Greasley* v *Cooke* [1980] 1 WLR 1306, Ld Denning MR at 1311 held that a presumption of reliance arose once a claimant had proved a statement "calculated to influence the judgment of a reasonable man". By contrast, in *Taylors Fashions Ltd* v *Liverpool Victoria Trustees Co Ltd* [1982] QB 133 at 156-157, Oliver J held that a heavy burden of proof of reliance fell on the claimant. See also *Coombes* v *Smith* [1987] 1 FLR 352 at 365-366.

34 *Layton* v *Martin* [1986] 2 FLR 227 at 238-239 per Scott J.

35 *Burns* v *Burns* [1984] Ch 317 at 345 per May LJ.

36 See, *e.g.*, *Cooke* v *Head* [1972] 1 WLR 518: Miss Cooke contributed nothing in cash towards the purchase, but did much heavy work, including using a sledgehammer to demolish old buildings, working a cement mixer, filling a wheelbarrow with rubble and helping with the painting. It is not clear that the outcome would be the same today. The case of *Eves* v *Eves* [1975] 1 WLR 1338, where similar labour was performed by Mrs Eves (as she called herself), can be explained on the alternative ground that Mr Eves, in telling Mrs Eves that as she was under 21 years of age the house could not be registered in joint names, had established the necessary common intention for a constructive trust. This was the analysis adopted by Ld Bridge in the Hse of Lds in *Lloyds Bank plc* v *Rosset* [1991] 1 AC 107; further at 133 Ld Bridge said that the efforts of Janet Eves "fell far short" of conduct which would by itself have supported a finding of common intention.

37 (1981) 3 FLR 379 at 381.

contributions in respect of keeping up the house, or looking after any children, could be taken into account, but this view was expressly criticised by Fox LJ in *Burns* v *Burns*[38] as unsupported by authority and inconsistent with principle, and by May LJ[39] as "wrong". In *Burns* v *Burns* May LJ held that the domestic endeavours of Mrs Burns were not trust-generating contributions because "the court is only entitled to look at financial contributions, or their real or substantial equivalent".[40]

More recent caselaw suggests a limited relaxation of the traditionally harsh treatment of constructive trust claims based on indirect or non-financial contributions. The House of Lords in *Lloyds Bank plc* v *Rosset*[41] approved, with qualifications, the approach adopted in the earlier cases of *Grant* v *Edwards*[42] and *Ungurian* v *Lesnoff*.[43] In *Ungurian* v *Lesnoff* Vinelott J, considering the effect of indirect or non-financial contributions, applied the distinction drawn in *Grant* v *Edwards* between cases where common intention has already been proved and cases where the contributions themselves are tendered as proof of common intention.[44] Where evidence of indirect or non-financial contributions is adduced in order to prove the existence of the common intention, courts are wary of accepting it, largely because of the dangers of circularity of argument.[45] On the other hand, where the relevant common intention has already been proved by some other evidence, courts will more readily[46] accept that later acts, even if indirect or non-financial, are a change of position undertaken in reliance on that common intention.[47]

Although welcome, the practical effect of these developments is limited, because it is only rarely that a homemaking claimant will be able to prove by extrinsic evidence the existence of the necessary common

---

38 [1984] Ch 317 at 331.
39 [1984] Ch 317 at 342. See also *Layton* v *Martin* [1986] 2 FLR 227 at 237-238 per Scott J; *Thomas* v *Fuller-Brown* [1988] 1 FLR 237 at 240-241, 246 per Slade LJ.
40 [1984] Ch 317 at 344. He added that it was "neither here nor there ... [that] the woman has spent so much of her time looking after the house, doing the cooking and bringing up the family." Waller LJ at 326 "reluctantly" agreed that "the law does not permit this court to impute a deemed intention" from the endeavours of Mrs Burns. Leave to appeal to the Hse of Lds was refused. More recently, see *Windeler* v *Whitehall* [1990] 2 FLR 505 at 514-515 per Millett J.
41 [1991] 1 AC 107.
42 [1986] Ch 638.
43 [1990] Ch 206; [1990] CLJ 25.
44 [1986] Ch 638 at 648-649 per Nourse LJ; at 652-653 per Mustill LJ; *Lloyds Bank plc* v *Rosset* [1991] 1 AC 107 at 132-133.
45 *Ungurian* v *Lesnoff* [1990] Ch 206 at 216-218, 222-224 per Vinelott J. See also *Grant* v *Edwards* [1986] Ch 638 at 652 per Mustill LJ; *Hammond* v *Mitchell* [1991] 1 WLR 1127 at 1129-1130, 1137-1138 per Waite J.
46 It seems, however, that the change of position must be of a "significant" nature: *Lloyds Bank plc* v *Rosset* [1991] 1 AC 107 at 132, below.
47 *Grant* v *Edwards* [1986] Ch 638 at 647-648 per Nourse LJ; at 652 per Mustill LJ; at 655 per Browne-Wilkinson V-C; *Ungurian* v *Lesnoff* [1990] Ch 206 at 216-218 per Vinelott J; *Lloyds Bank plc* v *Rosset* [1991] 1 AC 107 at 132; *Hammond* v *Mitchell* [1991] 1 WLR 1127 at 1137 per Waite J.

intention.[48] Absent such extrinsic evidence, the already restrictive approach of the courts is likely, if anything, to become even narrower. In *Lloyds Bank plc* v *Rosset*[49] Lord Bridge, although agreeing with the distinction drawn in *Grant* v *Edwards* and *Ungurian* v *Lesnoff*, held that on the facts before him the renovation work carried out by Mrs Rosset "could not possibly" justify the inference of a common intention.[50] He stated that:

> "... neither a common intention by spouses that a house is to be renovated as a 'joint venture' nor a common intention that the house is to be shared by parents and children as the family home throws any light on their intentions with respect to the beneficial ownership of the property."

Moreover, said Lord Bridge, in the absence of evidence of an express common intention, it was "extremely doubtful" whether anything less than direct monetary contributions to the purchase price would be sufficient.[51] The caselaw since *Lloyds Bank plc* v *Rosset* suggests that it will now be virtually impossible for a claimant to prove the necessary common intention by evidence of conduct.[52]

The position of the homemaker is similarly unsatisfactory if he or she wishes to base a claim in contract. On current authority it seems unlikely that an English court would hold that the rendering of domestic services within a personal relationship constitutes sufficient consideration to support a contract. In *Horrocks* v *Forray*[53], for instance, Megaw LJ suggested that, even if the plaintiff could show an intention to create legal relations, she would fail for absence of consideration.[54] In respect of relationships

---

48 In *Grant* v *Edwards* [1986] Ch 638, Nourse LJ at 647 described common intention as "the most difficult question" in constructive trust cases. Cases in which claims have failed for inability to prove common intention include *Gissing* v *Gissing* [1971] AC 886; *Burns* v *Burns* [1984] Ch 317; *Thomas* v *Fuller-Brown* [1988] 1 FLR 237; *Windeler* v *Whitehall* [1990] 2 FLR 505; *Lloyds Bank plc* v *Rosset* [1991] 1 AC 107. See Eekelaar, "A Woman's Place – A Conflict between Law and Social Values" [1987] *Conv* 93 at 95-99.

49 [1991] 1 AC 107 at 130-131.

50 The judge at first instance had found that Mrs Rosset had supervised building works and used "special skills" in decoration works. At [1991] 1 AC 107, 131, Ld Bridge said he felt her contributions "so trifling as to be almost *de minimis*"; moreover that the contributions would not have sufficed to raise a constructive trust even if there had been clear evidence of an express agreement.

51 [1991] 1 AC 107 at 132-133. The "direct contributions" could be made initially or by payment of mortgage instalments.

52 In *Hammond* v *Mitchell* [1991] 1 WLR 1127, Waite J at 1136-1138 found an express agreement in respect of a house in England, but could not draw any inference of common intention from the conduct of the parties in respect of a house in Spain; in *Ivin* v *Blake*, (unrep, CA) 25 May 1993 (Lexis tst), Glidewell LJ held that a daughter's claim to a beneficial interest in her mother's house failed because her contributions were indirect and non-financial and she had failed to prove by extrinsic evidence the necessary common intention; in *Barclays Bank plc* v *Khaira* [1993] 1 FLR 343 at 349, it was held that a pooling of earnings was not sufficient.

53 [1976] 1 WLR 230 at 239, 240 per Scarman LJ.

54 Although the case is possibly distinguishable from the "true" cohabitation situation in that the plaintiff had not been living with the deceased but in a house supplied by him: [1976] 1 WLR 230 at 232-233 per Megaw LJ. See also *Dale* v *Haggerty* [1979] Qd R 83 (claim failed for want of consideration). For examples of decisions where the rendering of domestic services was found to constitute sufficient consideration outside an ongoing domestic relationship, see *Ward* v *Byham* [1956] 1 WLR 496; *Binions* v *Evans* [1972] Ch 359.

outside marriage, there is the added risk that a court might decide that sexual relations formed part of the consideration and that therefore the contract was illegal and unenforceable.[55]

In contract doctrine the difficulties faced by the homemaking claimant are compounded by the presumption that there is no intention to create legal relations within domestic relationships.[56] Thus even if a court were to concede that value attached to homemaker contributions and that therefore such contributions could constitute consideration, the claimant would still have to rebut a presumption that her services were intended as a gift. And should both these hurdles be overcome, the claim may nevertheless fail if, as in the majority of cases, the major asset in dispute is the shared home and the agreement is not in signed writing. Since the enactment of section 2 of the Law of Property (Miscellaneous Provisions) Act 1989, contracts relating to the sale or other disposition of any interest in land must be in writing, incorporate all expressly agreed terms, and be signed by all parties. Non-compliance with section 2 renders the purported contract not merely unenforceable, but completely void.[57] The section does not, of course, affect the validity of oral contracts in respect of personalty rather than realty, nor would it apply to the creation of contractual licences, which are on present authority classified as personal rather than property rights.[58]

The economic value of housework[59]

Over the last two decades sociologists[60] and economists[61] have rejected as inaccurate and misleading the orthodox theories of the role of families in

---

55 *Fender* v *St John Mildmay* [1938] AC 1 at 42 per Ld Wright; *Diwell* v *Farnes* [1959] 2 All ER 379 at 381 per Ormerod LJ.
56 See, *e.g.*, *Balfour* v *Balfour* [1919] 2 KB 571 at 578 per Ld Atkin; *Jones* v *Padavatton* [1969] 1 WLR 328 at 332 per Danckwerts LJ; *Horrocks* v *Forray* [1976] 1 All ER 737 at 745 per Scarman LJ.
57 Subject to the possibility of rectification, which is specifically recognised in s 4 of the 1989 Act.
58 *Ashburn Anstalt* v *Arnold* [1989] Ch 1 at 12-13, 27-28 per Fox LJ (albeit *obiter*, since his ruling was based on the finding that the agreement in dispute comprised a lease rather than a licence).
59 It is perhaps ironic that the word "economy" is derived from the Greek for, and originally meant, "home management": see Mohr, "The Politics of the Family and the Family in Politics" (1978) I *Can J Fam L* 274 at 284. Lewenhak, *The Revaluation of Women's Work*, 2nd ed (Earthscan, 1992) 7, indicates that people have been pointing out the economic value of unpaid work in homes since at least 1921.
60 See, *e.g.*, Oakley, *The sociology of housework* (Martin Robertson, 1974); Fenstermaker (ed), *Women and Household Labour* (Sage, 1980); Rae, *Homemakers: the forgotten workers* (University of Chicago Press, 1981); Malos (ed), *The Politics of Housework* (Allison & Busby, 1982); Land, "Women: Supporters or Supported?", in Brown (ed), *The Structure of Disadvantage* (Heinemann, 1983); Delphy, *Close to Home* (Hutchinson, 1984) ch 5.
61 See, *e.g.*, Harrison, "The Political Economy of Housework" (1973) *Bulletin of the Conference of Socialist Economists* 35; Molyneux, "Beyond the Domestic Labour Debate" (1979) 116 *New Left Review* 3; Galbraith, *op cit* n. 3, 23; Matthews, *op cit* n. 17, 187. For a general economic analysis of family law, see Posner, *The Economics of Justice* (Harvard University Press, 1981) 184-192; Posner, *An Economic Analysis of Law* (Little, Brown, & Co, 3rd ed, 1986) ch 5.

modern society and in the wider economy. It is now generally accepted that to describe families as "non-productive" or "units of consumption"[62] is to ignore the important productive roles they play. More specifically, it is now widely recognised that housework contributes to the labour power of the wage earner by the production of use values necessary for the wage earner's subsistence.[63] Housework also plays an important part in the larger economy in the reproduction of labour – the tasks involved in the rearing and socialisation of the next generation of labour.[64] Until recently – and again largely because of unthinking acceptance of theories of the "stripping" of family functions – little attention has been paid to the important welfare functions[65] which are still carried on within families, in terms of care of the sick, elderly and disabled.

Interesting parallels can be drawn between earlier social and economic theories and the legal treatment of domestic services. Thus writers have pointed out that whether activities such as cooking, ironing, or cleaning are classified as "economic" or "non-economic" depends solely on whether they are carried out for market exchange or not.[66] In remarkably similar fashion, the law accepts, in the quantification of damages for accidental death or disablement, the cost of domestic services in the home where these are purchased on the market[67] or where the carer must give up outside (market) employment in order to look after the injured person[68], but refuses to accord any value to those same services where they are carried out by a homemaker-relative.[69]

---

62 For an economic analysis that, while recognising the importance of the problem of housework, nevertheless classifies the household as a unit of consumption, see Galbraith, *op cit* n. 3, 33, 49, and see the critical rejection of his view by Benería, *loc cit* n. 22, at 382.

63 Gough, *The Political Economy of the Welfare State* (Macmillan, 1985) 45-46; Harrison, *loc cit* n. 61; Molyneux, *loc cit* n. 61, at 8; Benería, *loc cit* n. 22, at 379-380.

64 Gough, *op cit* n. 63, 46; Berk, "Household production", and Brown and Preece, "Housework", in Eatwell *et al* (eds), *The New Palgrave – A Dictionary of Economics* (Macmillan, 1987) 676 and 678 respectively; Benería, *loc cit* n. 22, at 379-380; Molyneux, *loc cit* n. 61, at 8.

65 See Billup, "Caring for the carers in a laggard welfare state: Crises and alternatives (1988) 31 *Int Social Work* 23 at 27; Gough, *op cit* n. 63, 46-49 (welfare functions shared by and between state and family); Ungerson, "Women and Caring: Skills, Tasks, and Taboos", in Gamarnikow *et al* (eds), *The Public and the Private* (Heinemann, 1983); 62; Parker, "Who Cares? A Review of Empirical Evidence from Britain", in *On Work*, *op cit* n. 22, 496; Graham, "Women's Poverty and Caring", in Glendinning and Millar (eds), *Women and Poverty in Britain* (Wheatsheaf, 1987) 221.

66 Delphy, *op cit* n. 60, ch 4; Molyneux, *loc cit* n. 61, at 5; Benería, *loc cit* n. 22, at 374, 378-379.

67 See, *e.g.*, Fatal Accidents Act 1976, s 1, as substituted by Administration of Justice Act 1982, s 3(1); *Berry* v *Humm & Co* [1915] 1 KB 627 per Scrutton J at 631 (wife's domestic services); *Burgess* v *Florence Nightingale Hospital* [1955] 1 All ER 511; *Regan* v *Williamson* [1976] 1 WLR 305; *Spittle* v *Bunney* [1988] 1 WLR 847 (loss of mother's services). If the parties were not married, the court will take into account the fact that the claimant "had no enforceable right to financial support by the deceased as a result of their living together": Fatal Accidents Act 1976, s 3(4), as substituted by Administration of Justice Act 1982, s 3(1). See generally, Percy, *Charlesworth and Percy on Negligence*, 8th ed (Sweet & Maxwell, 1990) 1119-1167. For equivalent enactments in other jurisdictions, see Stang Dahl, *Women's Law: An Introduction to Feminist Jurisprudence* (Norwegian University Press, 1987) 98-99.

68 *Donnelly* v *Joyce* [1974] QB 454 (CA) per Megaw LJ; *Housecroft* v *Burnett* [1986] 1 All ER 332 at 343 per O'Connor LJ.

69 *Hay* v *Hughes* [1975] QB 790 (grandmother stepping in not taken into account); *Housecroft* v *Burnett* [1986] 1 All ER 332 at 343 per O'Connor LJ.

As well as re-evaluations of earlier theories about family functions, sociological studies of housework include detailed analyses of the tasks involved[70], studies devoted to evaluating the impact of technological developments on housework,[71] and demographic studies on the number of hours involved and participation of different family members in household tasks.[72] The empirical evidence obtained contradicts theories of lessening workloads and of new and "egalitarian" divisions of labour within households.[73]

Economic studies on housework[74] include re-evaluations of the place of domestic work in the economic system and in mainstream economic analysis[75], redefinitions of conventional official measurements of the labour force to include women's labour in their homes[76] and theories of valuation of domestic work.[77]

---

70 See Oakley, *op cit* n. 60; Oakley, *Housewife* (Penguin, 1976); Ungerson, *loc cit* n. 65, at 63 *et seq.*

71 See, *e.g.*, Schwartz Cowan, *More work for Mother: the ironies of household technology* (Basic Books, 1983); Eichler, "The Industrialization of Housework", in Lupri (ed), *The Changing Position of Women in Family and Society* (EJ Brill, 1983) 430; Hardyment, *From Mangle to Microwave: the mechanization of household work* (Polity Press, 1988).

72 Surveys on participation in household work are conducted by British Social Attitudes Surveys, Social and Community Planning Research. See (1990) *Social Trends* 20, Table 2.9 and 38-39. See also Kremer and Montgomery (eds), *Women's Working Lives* (Equal Opportunities Commission for Northern Ireland, HMSO, 1993) 15-41. For earlier demographic studies of this type see Ungerson, *loc cit* n. 65, at 71-74; Delphy, *op cit* n. 60, ch 5, and studies cited therein at 92 n. 1; Benería, *loc cit* n. 22, at 386-388. Oakley, *op cit* n. 60, estimated that the average number of hours per week spent on housework in 1971 was 77; other figures vary from 30 hours upwards.

73 See the statistics on participation in household tasks in (1990) *Social Trends* 20, 38-39, and Table 2.9; Kremer and Montgomery, *op cit* n. 72, 29-30, 38-39, 151-157. For earlier studies, see Oakley, *op cit* n. 60, 100-101; Eichler, *loc cit* n. 71, at 438.

74 For a general overview of the state of economic theory, see Brown and Preece, "Housework", and Berk, "Household production", in Eatwell *et al* (eds), *The New Palgrave – A Dictionary of Economics* (Macmillan, 1987) 679-680 and 675-678 respectively.

75 This is so of both Marxist and orthodox economists: see Benería, *loc cit* n. 22, at 380-381; Becker, *The Economic Approach to Human Behaviour* (University of Chicago Press, 1976); Fee, "Domestic labour: an analysis of housework and its relation to the production process" (1976) 8 *Review of Radical Political Economy* 1; Gronau, "Home Production – a forgotten industry" (1980) 62 *Review of Economics and Statistics* 408; Mackintosh, "Domestic Labour and the Household", in *On Work, op cit* n. 22, 392; Feiner and Roberts, "Hidden by the Invisible Hand: Neoclassical Economic Theory and the Textbook Treatment of Race and Gender" (1990) 4 *Gender & Society* 159 (new analyses of economic status of women should be incorporated into mainstream student textbooks).

76 Benería, *loc cit* n. 22, at 380 (who argues for a redefinition of labour force measurement concepts to include both use and exchange values. "Active labour should be defined in relation to its contribution to the production of goods and services for the satisfaction of human needs rather than, as at present, in relation to production for exchange.")

77 A summary of studies and their results is included in Quah, "Valuing family household production: a contingent evaluation approach" (1987) 19 *Appl Econ* 875 at 885-888 (arguing that valuation should be marginal, total, or net depending on whether the purpose is GNP accounting, matrimonial property settlements, or welfare and compensation issues respectively). For a discussion of some of the difficulties involved, see Molyneux, *loc cit* n. 61, at 10-11, 12; Peterson, "Problems in estimating the value of household services" (1978) 37 *Am Jo Econ and Sociol* 145; Quah, "Persistent problems in measuring household production (1986) 45 *Am Jo Econ and Sociol* 235.

Poverty and the homemaker

Since the role of domestic labour in producing the wage income is unrecognised, the income is regarded as belonging to the wage-earner alone. The force of this perception ensures the continuing dependence of the homemaker on the wage earner.[78] Studies indicate that the notion of the "family wage" is frequently more myth than reality[79]: empirical research confirms that, contrary to earlier presumptions, resources are not allocated or shared equally within families.[80]

Certain writers have argued that the solution lies in increased labour market participation by women. Thus Deech, for instance, argues in the context of unmarried cohabitation that:

> "women have had for a long time the choice of work or housewifery or both ... the sacrifice of a career is not a necessary precondition to cohabitation and it is not imposed."[81]

Unfortunately, however, the answer is not so simple. First, Deech's argument either ignores the fact that domestic services are of value, or else it tacitly assumes that the non-homemaking partner is entitled to receive for free the benefit of those services. Statistics show that even where both parties are working, the vast majority of housework is done by women.[82] Moreover, cases frequently come before the courts where both parties to the relationship are working, but where property has been bought in the name of one, with the other providing indirect contributions. If the facts cannot be brought within existing rubrics of property law, the non-titled party may be left the victim of considerable injustice, with no claim to a share in the family home.

Second, the argument clearly fails where families with children are involved. Quite apart from the absence of adequate day-care

---

78 Allan, "Property and Family Solidarity", in Hollowell (ed), *Property and Social Relations* (Heinemann, 1982) 165 at 176, 179.

79 See also Zaretsky, "Rethinking the Welfare State: Dependence, Economic Individualism and the Family", in Dickinson and Russell (eds), *Family, Economy and State* (Croom Helm, 1986) 85 at 101 *et seq*; Molyneux, *loc cit* n. 61, at 23; Land, "The family wage" (1980) *Fem Rev* 55. On arguments for a "housewife wage", see Stang Dahl, *op cit* n. 67, 111, and for counter-arguments, see Lewenhak, *op cit* n. 59, 12-15, 42-45.

80 Graham, *loc cit* n. 65, 221; Wilson, *Money in the Family: Financial Organisation and Women's Responsibility* (Avebury, 1987); Land, "Poverty and Gender: the Distribution of Resources within the Family", in Brown (ed), *op cit* n. 60, 49 (emphasising at 66-67 the connection between unequal distribution and the greater power of men); Pahl, "The Allocation of Money and the Structuring of Inequality within Marriage" (1983) 31 *Sociol Rev* No 2.

81 Deech, "The Case Against Legal Recognition of Cohabitation", in Eekelaar and Katz (eds), *Marriage and Cohabitation in Contemporary Societies: Areas of Legal, Social and Ethical Change* (Butterworths, 1980) 300 at 304. See also Zuckerman, "Formality and the Family – Reform and Status Quo" (1980) 96 *LQR* 248 at 276-277.

82 The SCPR statistics indicate, for example, that 77% of women prepared the evening meal, 72% did the cleaning, and 88% the washing and ironing: (1990) *Social Trends* 20, Table 2.9, and 38-39. See also Okin, *Justice, Gender and the Family* (Basic Books, 1989) 153ff; Kremer and Montgomery, *op cit* n. 72, 29-30.

facilities[83], research has shown that for the vast majority of women it is more economical to stay at home to look after the children until they reach school age.[84] Even after that time, labour market participation by working mothers is constrained: most full-time employers assume in various ways that "someone" is at home during at least part of the day to undertake primary responsibility for children.[85] Further factors may well be of relevance here: researchers have argued, for instance, that there is a clear correlation between the amount of time spent with children by parents and the ability of those children on starting school.[86] While not working, a housewife suffers a depreciation in employment market value of between 1% and 3% per annum depending on her level of educational achievement.[87] There is an obvious state interest in promoting the welfare of future citizens and the performance of the important social function of child-raising should not result in economic disadvantagement. Such reasoning has prompted some writers to suggest that a distinction should be drawn between "family property" cases on the one hand, and true "matrimonial or quasi-matrimonial" cases on the other, where childless couples separate.[88]

---

83 The UK has the third lowest level of publicly funded child care services in Europe; see Kremer and Montgomery, *op cit* n. 72, 166-167. A limited concession was made in the 1990 budget, in that child care facilities provided by employers ceased to be considered a benefit in kind and thus subject to tax. This leaves the anomaly that no tax relief is available on other public or private child care facilities. In 1986 Hilary Land found that the provision of day care places in local authority day nurseries, registered nurseries or with registered childminders, was sufficient to cover only 5.3% of children aged 4 or less: Land, "The Unwelcome Impact of Social Policies on Women in the Labour Market", (paper presented to the conference on Work and Politics, Harvard University Centre for European Studies.)

84 Niemi, "The Impact of Children on Female Earnings", in Kurian and Ghosh (eds), *Women in the Family and the Economy – an International Comparative Survey* (Greenwood, 1981). The study concludes that only for women with college and post-college education is it more economical to use day-care centres and return to work as soon as possible. The findings are confirmed by official statistics: employment market participation by mothers who fall within the "professional or employer/manager" category is much higher than that of mothers within other employment categories: (1993) *Social Trends* 23, Table 4.8 and 55-56.

85 *E.g.* the discrepancy between normal full-time working hours and school hours and holidays, and the high degree of mobility required by many higher level management positions. See further Okin, *op cit* n. 82, 155-156.

86 Leibowitz, "Home Investments in Children", in Schultz (ed), *Economics of the Family: Marriage, Children and Human Capital* (University of Chicago Press, 1974) 432. The more generally accepted view is that for healthy development infants need to forge warm, intimate and stable relationships, although not necessarily with their biological parents. The arguments are reviewed by Elliot, *The Family: Change or Continuity?* (Macmillan, 1986) 20-25.

87 See Artis (ed), *The UK Economy: A Manual of Applied Economics*, 11th ed (Weidenfeld & Nicolson, 1986) 301; Mincer and Polachek, "Family Investments in Human Capital: Earnings of Women", in *Economics of the Family, op cit* n. 86, 397; Skolnick, "The Social Contexts of Cohabitation" (1981) 29 *AJCL* 339 at 352; Okin, *op cit* n. 82, 155-156. For a more detailed analysis, see Joshi, "The Cost of Caring", in *Women and Poverty in Britain, op cit* n. 65, 112. For a recent American argument along similar lines, see Estin, "Maintenance, Alimony, and the Rehabilitation of Family Care" (1993) 71 *North Carolina LRev* 721 at 746.

88 Glendon, *The Transformation of Family Law: State, Law, and Family in the United States and Western Europe* (University of Chicago Press, 1989) 235; Glendon, *The New Family and the New Property* (Butterworths, 1981) 83; Glendon, "Family Law Reform in the 1980's" (1984) 44 *La L Rev* 1553 at 1558-1565; Davis, "The Marital Home: Equal or Equitable Distribution?" (1983) 50 *U Chicago L Rev* 1089; Oldham, "Is the Concept of Marital Property Outdated?" (1983-84) 22 *Jo Fam Law* 263.

Not only is women's work within the household unpaid and undervalued, but to a large extent their work in the market-place is also perceived as secondary to that of men.[89] Even where homemakers are in full-time employment, gender divisions in the labour market[90] ensure that the power their partners derive as "primary breadwinners" is preserved.[91] Because of their "dual role"[92], many women work in poorly-paid sectors of the employment market[93], in jobs for which they are overqualified[94], in part-time jobs[95], or as homeworkers.[96]

These factors have combined with ever-increasing patterns of family breakdown[97], unsatisfactory financial settlements and inadequate enforcement measures[98], to intensify the now well-known phenomenon

---

89   Allan, *loc cit* n. 78, at 177; Rapoport and Rapoport, *Dual Career Families Re-Examined* (Martin Robertson, 1976); Brannen and Moss, "Dual Earner Households: Women's Financial Contributions After the Birth of the First Child", in Brannen and Wilson (eds), *Give and Take in Families: Studies in Resource Distribution* (Allen & Unwin, 1987) 75 at 76-77, 87 *et seq.*

90   Despite formal equality, writers unanimously agree that there is a long way to go before actual equality is achieved: see Artis, *op cit* n. 87, 300-315; Walby (ed), *Gender segregation at work* (Open University Press, 1988); Coyle and Skinner (eds), *Women and work: positive action for change* (Macmillan, 1988) (studies of patterns of discrimination in various occupational fields and of the non-implementation of equal opportunities legislation).

91   Allan, *loc cit* n. 78, at 177; O'Donovan, *Sexual Divisions in Law* (Weidenfeld & Nicolson, 1985) 133; Okin, *op cit* n. 82, 156-159.

92   Articles which examine the relationship between women's work within the household and their paid work in the labour market include Joshi, "Gender inequality in the labour market and the domestic division of labour", in Nolan and Paine (eds), *Rethinking Socialist Economics: A New Agenda for Britain* (Polity Press, 1986) 258; Peterson, "Firm size, occupational segregation, and the effects of family status on women's wages" (1989) 68 *Social Forces* 397; Shelton and Firestone, "Household Labor Time and the Gender Gap in Earnings" (1989) 3 *Gender & Society* 105. See also Okin, *op cit* n. 82, ch 7.

93   Often in tasks that mirror the caring skills they practise at home: Bettio, *The Sexual Division of Labour: The Italian Case* (Clarendon Press, 1988) (study of sex-typing in occupations); Lonsdale, "Patterns of Paid Work", in *Women and Poverty in Britain*, *op cit* n. 65, 92 at 93, 94-95; Joshi, *loc cit* n. 92, at 258.

94   See Joshi, *op cit* n. 92, 258 at 261 and studies cited therein.

95   See Lonsdale, *loc cit* n. 93, 92 at 95, 103-105. The 1992 Labour Force Survey reported that only 6% of men, but 45% of women, were in part-time market employment (1993) *Social Trends* 23, Table 4.16 and p 59.

96   Allen and Wolkowitz, *Homeworking: Myths and Realities* (Macmillan Education, 1987) 85 describe homeworking as "a particularly appalling example of women's position in the labour market." Other studies include those of the Low Pay Unit, *The Hidden Army* (HMSO, 1979); Allen and Wolkowitz, "Homeworking and the Control of Women's Work", in Feminist Review (eds), *Waged Work* (Virago, 1986); Hope *et al*, "Homeworkers in North London", in Barker and Allen (eds), *Dependence and Exploitation in Work and Marriage* (Longman, 1976); Rae, *op cit* n. 60; Lonsdale, *loc cit* n. 93, at 106-109.

97   The divorce rate has doubled between 1971 and 1991: (1993) *Social Trends* 23, chart 2.11. It is estimated that if divorce rates continue at their present levels, 4 in 10 marriages will end in divorce: Haskey, "Current prospects for the proportion of marriages ending in divorce" (1989) *Population Trends* 55, 34.

98   See, *inter alia*, Maclean, "Households After Divorce: The Availability of Resources and their Impact on Children", in Brannen and Wilson (eds), *op cit* n. 89, 42; Maclean and Eekelaar, *Children and Divorce: Economic Factors* (Centre for Socio-Legal Studies, 1983); Davis *et al*, "Divorce: who supports the family?" (1983) 13 *Fam Law* 217; Morton, "Dividing the wealth, sharing the poverty: the (re)formation of 'family' in law in Ontario" (1988) 25 *CRSA* 254; Ullrich, "Equal but not equal – a feminist perspective on Family Law" (1986) 9 *Women's Studies Int Forum* 41 (New Zealand). It is to be hoped that the Child Support Act 1991 will have some impact on English trends.

that sociologists have labelled the "feminisation of poverty".[99] Recent and controversial government proposals to deal with the financial problems of one parent families have highlighted one of the most worrying aspects of this phenomenon: the number of children[100] who suffer as a direct consequence, both in terms of immediate deprivation and also by way of impaired future opportunity.[101]

The future: the "stripping" of the welfare state?

Political developments over the past few years suggest that the problems outlined above are likely in the future to become more acute. As regards paid employment, projections suggest that women are expected to make up the largest single group within the pool of new labour force entrants over the next five years.[102] Unfortunately, however, the majority of these women will take up jobs at the bottom end of the labour market hierarchy, since the vacancies will exist because of a shortage of young people, who have tended to be employed in lower-status occupations. The anticipated result is thus a polarisation in women's employment, with monetary and childcare incentives being offered only to those entering the top end of the labour market.[103]

As regards the problems of the homemaker, the outlook is particularly bleak. Current government cutbacks and policies of "community care" and "deinstitutionalisation" are effectively returning to families responsibility for welfare functions of which they were "stripped" with the setting up of the welfare state. With the closure of institutions such as large psychiatric

---

99 See generally Glendinning and Millar (eds), *Women and Poverty in Britain* (Wheatsheaf, 1987); Room, *"New Poverty" in the European Community* (Macmillan, 1990), esp at 83-97. As pointed out by Millar and Glendinning, the phenomenon is not new: "Towards the Defeminisation of Poverty", in *Women and Poverty, passim*, 261. Smith and Ward, "Women in the Labor Market and in the Family" (1989) 3 *Jo Econ Persp* 9, argue that the "feminisation of poverty" is a reflection of the growing instability of the American family rather than due to the wage gap. For recent judicial recognition that failure to recognise the value of homemaker services contributes to the phenomenon, see *Peter* v *Beblow* [1993] 1 SCR 980 (Sup Ct of Can) at 993-994 per McLachlin J.

100 Now estimated at 2.2 m, or 18% of all dependent children: Haskey, "Trends in the Numbers of One-Parent Families in Great Britain", (Spring 1993) *Population Trends* 71. There has been a substantial rise in the proportion of children living in lone parent families: in 1991 the percentage was more than double that of 1981: Murphy and Berrington, "Household Change in the 1980s: A Review" (1993) *Population Trends* 73, 18 at 19-20, 21, 25. For US statistics, see Okin, *op cit* n. 82, 160-162, 173.

101 For recent statistical evidence of the economic disadvantages suffered by lone parent families in terms of housing, income and employment, see Bridgwood and Savage, General Household Survey 1991 (OPCS, HMSO, 1993) 12-13. The 1991 GHS reported that 48% of lone mothers with dependent children had a gross weekly income under £100: General Household Survey 1991 (HMSO, 1993) 28 and Table 2.3.

102 Casey and McRae, "A More Polarised Labour Market?" (1990) 11.2 *Policy Studies* 31 at 34. See, in similar vein, (1993) *Social Trends* 23, 54-55.

103 Casey and McRae, *loc cit* n. 102, at 34-37; (1993) *Social Trends* 23, 55.

hospitals and homes for the elderly[104], a heavy burden of caring for some of the most vulnerable groups of society has begun – and will continue – to fall to adult female homemakers. For as pointed out by Parker[105]:

> "To talk about 'care by the community' or even 'family' care is to disguise the reality. In fact ... 'care by the community' almost always means care by family members with little support from others in 'the community'. Further, care by family members almost always means care by female members with little support from other relatives."

It is anticipated that present policies of "decentralization, deregulation and privatization"[106] will continue into the late 1990s[107], and concern over a new category of "carers" has emerged.[108]

Developments in other jurisdictions

Other common law jurisdictions have begun to modify their laws in an effort to alleviate the injustices that result from a stance of non-recognition.[109] In addition to statutory recognition that value attaches to homemaker contributions[110], recent developments in trust and contract law can be seen to facilitate the accommodation of homemakers' claims within a broader range of general legal doctrine.

---

104 The number of people over pensionable age is projected to rise by 50% between 2001 and 2031 to 14.4 m. By that year it is estimated that for every 100 of the population of working age, there will be 79 dependants (minors and elderly): *OPCS Monitor*, 23 Feb 1993, 5 Table 2; (1993) *Social Trends* 23, 15-16.

105 Parker, *loc cit* n. 65, at 508-509. See also Walker, "The meaning and social division of community care", in Walker (ed), *Community Care: The Family, the State and Social Policy* (Basil Blackwell, 1982), 13; Andrews and Jacobs, *Punishing the Poor: Poverty under Thatcher* (Macmillan, 1990) 50-73; Ungerson (ed), *Gender and Caring: Work and Welfare in Britain and Scandinavia* (Harvester Wheatsheaf, 1990).

106 See Lightman, "Welfare ideology, the market and the family" (1987) 30 *Int Social Work* 309.

107 See Government Response to the 6th Report from the Health Committee, *Community Care: The Way Forward* (Cm 2334, 1993); Allen, "Community Care: Rhetoric or Reality?" (1990) 11.2 *Policy Studies* 53.

108 It is estimated that in 1986 there were 1.3 m carers in this country, the value of whose work was put at between £5.1 and £7.3 b: Richardson *et al, A New Deal for Carers* (Kings Fund, 1989). See also Lewis, "'It All Really Starts in the Family ...': Community Care in the 1980s" (1989) 16 *Jo of Law and Soc* 83; Cecil *et al, Informal Welfare* (Gower, 1987); Lightman, *loc cit* n. 106; Lewis and Meredith, *Daughters who Care: Daughters Caring for Mothers at Home* (Routledge, 1988); Wright, *Left to Care Alone* (Gower, 1986); Billups, *loc cit* n. 65; Kremer and Montgomery, *op cit* n. 72, ch 9.

109 See, *e.g., Pettkus* v *Becker* (1981) 117 DLR (3d) 257 at 273 per Dickson J: "the judiciary is thus able to shape these malleable principles so as to accommodate the changing needs and mores of society, in order to achieve justice."

110 See, *e.g.*, Family Law Act 1975 (Australia), s 79(4)(b); De Facto Relationships Act 1984 (NSW), s 20(2); Cal Civ Code #4801 (a)(1)(B) (West Supp, 1992); Ohio Rev Code Ann #3105.18(e)(1)(m) (Anderson Sup, 1990).

Resulting and constructive trusts

Many courts in America have held that not only indirect financial contributions[111], but also contributions of domestic labour[112], can give rise to beneficial interests under resulting[113] or constructive trusts. More recently, and in spite of the reaction against Lord Denning's "new model" constructive trust[114], over the last decade or so courts in Canada, Australia and New Zealand have adopted forms of "remedial" constructive trust in place of the "orthodox" or substantive constructive trust.[115] The law in each of these jurisdictions is still in a state of flux, and problems remain to be resolved. Nevertheless there is in each case a clear divergence from the position in English law, where the constructive trust continues to be regarded as a substantive institution.

Canada: unjust enrichment

Since the decision of the Supreme Court of Canada in the case of *Pettkus* v *Becker*[116], it can now be said that the position in Canada closely resembles that which exists in the United States.[117] Effectively, Canadian law now accepts that the constructive trust is a remedial device which can be used in appropriate circumstances to prevent or rectify the unjust enrichment of one party to a relationship.[118]

In Canada a claim in unjust enrichment arises when there has been "an enrichment, a corresponding deprivation and the absence of any juristic reason for the enrichment".[119] The recent decision of the Supreme Court

---

111 *Edgar* v *Wagner* 572 P.2d 405 (Utah, 1978); *Beal* v *Beal* 577 P.2d 507 (Oregon, 1978) at 510 per Howell J.

112 *Marvin* v *Marvin* 557 P.2d 106 (Sup Ct of Cal, 1976) per Tobriner J at 119; *Beal* v *Beal* 557 P.2d 507 (Oregon, 1978). Earlier cases had held, as here, that indirect or non-financial contributions were insufficient: see, *e.g.*, *Vallera* v *Vallera* 134 P.2d 761 (Cal, 1943); *Keene* v *Keene* 371 P.2d 329 (Cal, 1962).

113 In some US states resulting trusts based on contributions to purchase monies have been abolished: Folberg and Buren, "Domestic Partnership: A Proposal for Dividing the Property of Unmarried Families" (1976) 12 *Williamette Law Jo* 453 at 470, n. 114.

114 See, *e.g.*, *Muschinski* v *Dodds* [1985] 62 ALR 429 at 452 per Deanne J and cases noted at n. 141, 159 below.

115 The terminology is unfortunate because confusing: inevitably any constructive trust claimant is seeking a "remedy". See Birks, "Proprietary Rights as Remedies", SPTL, Oxford, Dec 1993.

116 (1981) 117 DLR (3d) 257 (Sup Ct of Can); see also the judgment of Dickson J (Spence J and Laskin CJC concurring) in the earlier case of *Rathwell* v *Rathwell* (1978) 83 DLR (3d) 289 at 298; and, more recently, Trainor J in *Rosenfeldt* v *Olsen* (1985) 59 BCLR 193 at 211-215; *Sorochan* v *Sorochan* (1986) 29 DLR (4th) 1 at 4-12 per Dickson CJC. Earlier cases had treated the constructive trust as a substantive institution: see, *e.g.*, *Murdoch* v *Murdoch* [1975] 1 SCR 423, applying the *Gissing* formulation.

117 For the US, see, *e.g.*, *Omer* v *Omer* 523 P.2d 957 (1974): constructive trust imposed because defendant was unjustly enriched since he held sole title to property acquired through joint efforts.

118 *Pettkus* v *Becker* (1981) 117 DLR (3d) 257 (Sup Ct of Can) at 273 per Dickson J: unjust enrichment "lies at the heart of a constructive trust". Dickson J, with five justices concurring, based his decision on the concept of the constructive trust, while the other three rejected the constructive trust approach but agreed in the result by finding a resulting trust.

119 *Pettkus* v *Becker* (1981) 117 DLR (3d) 257 at 273-274 per Dickson J; *Sorochan* v *Sorochan* (1986) 29 DLR (4th) 1 (Sup Ct of Can) at 5 per Dickson CJC; *Everson* v *Rich* (1989) 53 DLR (4th) 470 at 473-474; *Rawluk* v *Rawluk* [1990] 1 SCR 70 at 85-86 per Cory J; *Peter* v *Beblow* [1993] 1 SCR 980 at 987, 989 per McLachlin J, at 1010 per Cory J.

of Canada in *Peter* v *Beblow*[120] confirms earlier rulings to the effect that homemaker contributions are sufficient to constitute the necessary "enrichment". In the words of McLachlin J[121]:

> "The notion that household and childcare services are not worthy of recognition by the court fails to recognize the fact that these services are of great value, not only to the family, but to the other spouse ... The notion, moreover, is a pernicious one that systematically devalues the contributions which women tend to make to the family economy."

Once enrichment has been established, a finding that the plaintiff has suffered a "corresponding deprivation" is, in the words of Cory J, "virtually automatic ... . Particularly in a matrimonial or long-term common law relationship it should, in the absence of cogent evidence to the contrary, be taken that the enrichment of one party will result in a deprivation of the other."[122]

The third element of the claim in unjust enrichment, "absence of any juristic reason for the enrichment", is fundamentally concerned with the "legitimate expectations" of the parties.[123] The requirement will be satisfied if there has been no gift, compromise, contract, or other legal obligation under which the services in question were rendered.[124] Moreover, and in stark contrast to the position in England[125], courts in Canada apply a presumption that homemaker contributions are to be compensated. Thus, for example, it was categorically stated in *Everson* v *Rich*[126] that:

> " ... no one should expect, in general, spousal services for free. They are given, in the absence of an indication to the contrary, with the expectation of something in return and should be received as such."

Once the claim in unjust enrichment is established, it falls to the court to determine the appropriate remedy, which can comprise monetary

---

120 [1993] 1 SCR 980.

121 [1993] 1 SCR 980 at 993. See also [1993] 1 SCR 980 at 1011-1012, 1014-1016 per Cory J; *Sorochan* v *Sorochan* (1986) 29 DLR (4th) 1 at 6 per Dickson CJC.

122 [1993] 1 SCR 980 at 1011-1013 per Cory J; at 989 per McLachlin J.

123 [1993] 1 SCR 980 at 990 per McLachlin J; at 1017 per Cory J. See also *Pettkus* v *Becker* (1981) 117 DLR (3d) 257 at 274, 275 per Dickson CJC; *Sorochan* v *Sorochan* (1986) 29 DLR (4th) 1 at 7, 10, 12 per Dickson CJC.

124 It has been held in several cases that, as between unmarried couples, there exists no general duty to perform work and services: *Peter* v *Beblow* [1993] 1 SCR 980 at 991 per McLachlin J; at 1018 per Cory J; *Sorochan* v *Sorochan* (1986) 29 DLR (4th) 1 at 7 per Dickson CJC; *Grant* v *Moore* (1993) 48 RFL (3d) 345 at 351 per Selbie J.

125 Compare, *e.g.*, *Grant* v *Edwards* [1986] Ch 638 at 657 per Browne-Wilkinson V-C: domestic contributions "may all be referable to the mutual love and affection of the parties and not specifically referable to the claimant's belief that she has an interest in the house".

126 (1988) 53 DLR (4th) 470 (Sask CA) at 474 per Sherstobitoff JA, citing with approval the commentary of Prof McLeod on *Herman* v *Smith* (1984) 42 RFL (2d) 154 (Alta QB). See also *Peter* v *Beblow* [1993] 1 SCR 980 at 1017, 1018 per Cory J; *Sorochan* v *Sorochan* (1986) 29 DLR (4th) 1 at 6 per Dickson CJC.

compensation[127] or the award of a beneficial interest under a constructive trust. The majority in *Peter* v *Beblow* held that a constructive trust should be imposed in circumstances where damages are inadequate and where there exists a sufficient nexus between the services rendered and the property in question.[128] In the family context the insufficiency of a monetary award usually lies in the fact that the claimant's efforts have given her a "special link" to the property[129], although the likelihood of a money judgment being satisfied can also be taken into account.[130] In determining whether the required nexus exists between the services and the property, the court is not limited to the claimant's contributions towards the acquisition of the asset. In *Sorochan* v *Sorochan*[131] Dickson CJC held that "a contribution relating to the preservation, maintenance or improvement" of property rather than a contribution to its acquisition would suffice for the award of a constructive trust.[132] Moreover, indirect financial contributions, such as the payment of expenses which the defendant would otherwise have to bear, are also sufficient.[133]

Such developments mean that legal doctrine in Canada now accords much more closely with the practicalities of modern-day living, where financial and non-financial burdens are allocated according to convenience

---

127 For examples of cases where monetary awards were made, see *Grant* v *Moore* (1993) 48 RFL (3d) 345 (BC Sup Ct); *Hartland* v *Reschke* (1993) 47 RFL (3d) (BC Sup Ct) at 373-376 per Hall J; *Marcon* v *Cicchelli* (1993) 47 RFL (3d) 403 (Ont); *Everson* v *Rich* (1989) 53 DLR (4th) 470 at 475 per Sherstobitoff JA; *Novick* v *Miller* (1989) 58 DLR (4th) 185 (Sask CA); *Sorochan* v *Sorochan* (1986) 29 DLR (4th) 1 at 7 per Dickson CJC (unjust enrichment remedied in part by award of beneficial interest under a constructive trust and in part by money award: at 12-13). See also the decision of the Sup Ct of Canada in *Rawluk* v *Rawluk* [1990] 1 SCR 70.

128 *Peter* v *Beblow* [1993] 1 SCR 980 at 996-997 per McLachlin J (La Forest, Sopinka and Iacobucci JJ concurring). *Cp.* Cory J, who at 1022 (L'Heureux-Dubé and Gonthier JJ concurring) held that no causal connection should be required in family (as opposed to commercial) cases. The majority view follows that expressed in earlier cases: see *e.g.*, *Pettkus* v *Becker* (1981) 117 DLR (3d) 257 at 277 per Dickson J; *Sorochan* v *Sorochan* (1986) 29 DLR (4th) 1 at 8, 10 per Dickson CJC; *Everson* v *Rich* (1989) 53 DLR (4th) 470 at 474-475 per Sherstobitoff JA. On a similar issue in English law, see *Midland Bank* v *Dobson* [1986] FLR 171.

129 [1993] 1 SCR 980 at 997 per McLachlin J. See also *Hartland* v *Reschke* (1993) 47 RFL (3d) 357 (Br Col Sup Ct) per Hall J (insufficient nexus so damages adequate); *Grant* v *Moore* (1993) 48 RFL (3d) 345 (Br Col Sup Ct) per Selbie J; *Archer* v *Cornfoot* (1990) 28 RFL (3d) 447 (Ont), affirmed (1991) 35 RFL (3d) 182 (Ont CA).

130 The respondent in *Peter* v *Beblow* was retired and unlikely to be able to pay any money judgment: [1993] 1 SCR 980 at 1007, 1024.

131 (1986) 29 DLR (4th) 1 at 8-10 per Dickson CJC. For a review of cases since *Sorochan*, see Farquhar, "Causal Connection in Constructive Trusts after *Sorochan* v *Sorochan*" (1989) 7 *Can J Fam L* 337.

132 See also *Peter* v *Beblow* [1993] 1 SCR 980 at 997-998 per McLachlin J, at 1010 per Cory J; *Reiss* v *Reiss* (1989) 22 RFL (2d) 152 (Sask); Farquhar, *loc cit* n. 131, at 339 n. 13. Compare the English position, stated by Slade LJ in *Thomas* v *Fuller-Brown* [1988] 1 FLR 237 at 240: "... the mere fact that A expends money or labour on B's property does not by itself entitle A to an interest in the property." See, in similar vein, Ld Upjohn in *Pettitt* v *Pettitt* [1970] AC 777 at 818.

133 In *Peter* v *Beblow* it was found that the appellant's contributions "saved the respondent the expense of hiring a housekeeper and someone to care for the children. As a result he was able to use the money which he had saved to purchase other property and to pay off the mortgage ..." [1993] 1 SCR 980 at 1024 per Cory J; at 1003 per McLachlin J. See also *Murray* v *Roty* (1983) 134 DLR (3d) 507 (Ont CA); *Pettkus* v *Becker* (1981) 117 DLR (3d) 257; at 277 per Dickson J (indirect contributions to be taken into account).

rather than in contemplation of acquiring precise beneficial interests in property. Further, as in *Peter* v *Beblow* itself[134], in appropriate circumstances the rendering of domestic services can give rise to a proprietary remedy by way of constructive trust.

There is some confusion in Canadian caselaw, and considerable disagreement amongst academics[135], as to precisely when the beneficial interest under the remedial constructive trust arises. The issue came directly before the Supreme Court of Canada in *Rawluk* v *Rawluk*[136], where Cory J, for a narrow majority, held that the interest crystallises not when judicially declared, but from the time when the unjust enrichment first occurred. The decision is controversial in its implications for third parties, who may already have had dealings in respect of the property and who had no way of discovering the existence of the constructive trust. Conceptually it is very difficult to reconcile the idea that the trust interest crystallises as the facts occur with the notion that the constructive trust is a remedy for unjust enrichment[137], to be awarded only when monetary compensation is inadequate and there exists a sufficient nexus between the contributions and the property.[138] For example, in the case of a claimant who makes no direct monetary contributions, but over 20 years[139] contributes services by way of housework, raising children, etc., at what point in time does the interest crystallise? Logically, this point in time cannot be before the required nexus or "special link" exists, yet such a condition would place third parties in the intolerable position of having to enquire not only as to the stability, duration, nature and quality of the relationship between titled and non-titled parties, but also as to the relationship of the non-titled party to the land. It seems that the view taken in *Peter* v *Beblow* by McLachlin J must be correct, and that there cannot be any trust interest before the court pronouncement.[140]

---

134 The appellant was awarded the entire interest in the house in question, on the basis that it was a proper share of "all the family assets": [1993] 1 SCR 980 at 100-1001 per McLachlin J. See also *Griffith* v *Anderson* (1992) 48 RFL (3d) 390 (BC CA); *Lawrence* v *Lindsey* (1982) 28 RFL (2d) 356; *Sorochan* v *Sorochan* (1986) 29 DLR (4th) 1; *Murray* v *Roty* (1983) 134 DLR (3d) 507 (Ont CA).

135 Fratcher, *Scott on Trusts*, 4th ed (Little Brown & Co, 1989), Vol V, #462.2, argues that the trust is in existence from the outset, with a discretion in the court as to whether it should be enforced. Bogert and Bogert, *The Law of Trusts and Trustees*, 2nd ed (West Publishing Co, 1979), #472, favour the view that the trust comes into existence only on an order being made, but that it has retrospective operation. See also McClean, "Constructive and Resulting Trusts – Unjust Enrichment in a Common Law Relationship – *Pettkus* v *Becker*" (1982) 16 *UBC L Rev* 155 at 174; Paciocco, "The Remedial Constructive Trust: A Principled Basis for Priorities over Creditors" (1989) 68 *Can Bar Rev* 315 at 316.

136 [1990] 1 SCR 70 at 91-92 per Cory J, Dickson CJ, Wilson and L'Heureux-Dubé JJ concurring. McLachlin J for the minority (La Forest and Sopinka JJ concurring), disagreed, stating at 103 "When the court declares a constructive trust, *at that point* the beneficiary obtains an interest in the property subject to the trust. That property interest, it appears, may be taken as extending back to the date when the trust was 'earned' or perfected" (emphasis added).

137 See Waters, "The Remedial Constructive Trust", SPTL, Oxford, Dec 1993, at 33.

138 See *Peter* v *Beblow* [1993] 1 SCR 980 at 996-997 per McLachlin J.

139 Cases frequently involve relationships of very long standing: see, *e.g.*, *Sorochan* v *Sorochan* (1986) 29 DLR (4th) 1 (42 years).

140 See n. 134 above.

A possible solution to this problem might lie in the adoption of Professor Waters' suggestion, that:

> "Canadian courts should routinely state in the order the date from which the judicially-created property interest is to run. If the order is to be retrospective to any earlier date and thereby have any degree of retroactive operation, then, reasons having been given for this, the court order should state against whom the proprietary order is to operate."[141]

Australia: unconscionability

Australian caselaw reveals an emphatic rejection of Lord Denning's approach to the constructive trust[142], but the law of constructive trusts has nevertheless taken a different direction to that which prevails in England. In *Baumgartner* v *Baumgartner*[143] the High Court of Australia abandoned the need to look for common intention and adopted instead a broad and flexible approach which regards the constructive trust as a remedy[144] imposed in order to prevent unconscionable conduct.[145] As a remedial device, the constructive trust can be imposed "regardless of actual or presumed agreement or intention".[146]

Both indirect[147] and non-financial contributions can be taken into account[148], although as yet there is uncertainty about the precise extent to which courts will recognise homemaker contributions. In *Baumgartner* itself, in assessing the respective contributions of the parties, the High Court of Australia added the sum of $3,000 to the respondent's total as representing the sum which she would have earned during the three month period she remained at home giving birth to and looking after the son of the

---

141 See Waters, *loc cit* n. 137, 32-34. Both Cory and McLachlin JJ cited with apparent approval a passage from a judgment of Ld Denning to support the suggestion that "the interest may arise at the time of declaration or from the outset, as the case may require": [1993] 1 SCR 70 at 92, 103. See also (Ont C Appeal) (1987) 10 RFL (3d) 113.

142 *Baumgartner* v *Baumgartner* (1987) 62 ALJR 29 at 36 per Toohey J, at 33-34 per Mason CJ, Wilson and Deanne JJ; *Muschinski* v *Dodds* (1986) 60 ALJR 52 at 65-66 per Deane J.

143 (1987) 62 ALJR 29. No common intention could be inferred from the facts, and under orthodox constructive trust principles the claim would have failed.

144 *Allen* v *Snyder* [1977] 2 NSWLR 685; *Baumgartner* v *Baumgartner* (1987) 62 ALJR 29 at 33 per Mason CJ, Wilson and Deane JJ, at 35 per Toohey J; *Muschinski* v *Dodds* (1986) 60 ALJR 52 at 64, 65-66 per Deane J; *Lipman* v *Lipman* (1989) 13 Fam LR 1 (NSW Sup Ct) per Powell J.

145 (1987) 62 ALJR 29 at 33 per Mason CJ, Wilson and Deane JJ: "the foundation for the imposition of a constructive trust ... is that a refusal to recognise the existence of the equitable interest amounts to unconscionable conduct and that the trust is imposed as a remedy to circumvent that unconscionable conduct."

146 *Muschinski* v *Dodds* (1986) 60 ALJR 52 at 64, 66 per Deane J; *Baumgartner* v *Baumgartner* (1987) 62 ALJR 29 at 34 per Mason CJ, Wilson and Deane JJ, at 35 per Toohey J.

147 *Hibberson* v *George* (1989) DFC 95-064 (NSW CA): money spent on home and family but no contribution towards acquisition of house – held to give rise to equitable interest under constructive trust.

148 *Baumgartner* v *Baumgartner* (1987) 62 ALJR 29 at 37 per Gaudron J; *Hibberson* v *George* (1989) DFC 95-064 at 75,763-4 per Mahoney JA. For a review of later caselaw, including a discussion of problems in respect of homemaker contributions, see Neave, "The New Unconscionability Principle: Property Disputes Between De Facto Partners" (1991) 5 AJFL 185.

relationship[149], but failed to accord any value to her domestic contributions while she was in full-time employment. Later cases apply an even more restrictive approach, causing several writers to comment that courts are as yet unwilling to give full rein to the principles expounded in *Baumgartner*.[150] Decisions suggest in particular that many judges are unwilling to find in favour of claimants who rely solely on the rendering of domestic contributions, and limit relief to cases involving financial as well as non-financial contributions.[151] It seems likely that a further decision of the High Court will be required.

The beneficial interest under the Australian constructive trust does not crystallise until the time of the court decision. It was even implied in one case that the court might postpone the creation of the right until a *later* date in order to protect third parties.[152] This crystallisation of the equitable interest on or after the date of the court award means that third parties who have earlier acquired some right in the disputed property will not be affected[153] – unless, of course, the circumstances are such that some sort of personal liability[154] is imposed. Monetary awards rather than aliquot shares can be awarded in appropriate circumstances.[155]

New Zealand: reasonable expectations

Parallel developments to those that have occurred in Canada and Australia can be found in the recent caselaw of New Zealand. The liberalisation of constructive trust doctrine hinted at in cases such as *Hayward* v *Giordani*[156], *Pasi* v *Kamana*[157] and *Oliver* v *Bradley*[158] suggested that Lord Denning's "new model" constructive trust might be adopted in New Zealand. However, such an approach was firmly rejected in 1989 in *Gillies* v *Keogh*.[159] Instead,

---

149 (1987) 62 ALJR 29 at 31, 34 per Mason CJ, Wilson and Deane JJ; at 37, 38 per Gaudron J.
150 See Bryan, "The Conscience of Equity in Australia" (1990) 106 *LQR* 25. Bryan discusses only two cases: *Arthur* v *Public Trustee* (1988) 90 FLR 203 (Northern Territory CA) (absence of any financial contributions emphasised by the court); and *Hibberson* v *George* (1988) 12 Fam LR 735, from which an appeal was later allowed: (1989) DFC 95-064 (NSW CA). In *Baumgartner* itself, Toohey J stated that the task now before the Australian courts is "to continue sharpening the edges of the criteria which must be satisfied before the claimant can obtain constructive trust relief": (1987) ALJR 29 at 36, citing with approval from a paper given by Waters, "Where is Equity Going? Remedying Unconscionable Conduct" (University of Western Australia, 1987).
151 See Neave, *loc cit* n. 148, 185; Bailey-Harris, "Property Disputes Between De Facto Couples: Is Statute the Best Solution?" (1991) 5 *AJFL* 221 at 225-226, 235-236, 239.
152 *Muschinski* v *Dodds* (1986) 60 ALJR 52 at 65 per Deane J: "In particular, where competing common law or equitable claims are or may be involved, a declaration of constructive trust by way of remedy can properly be so framed that the consequences of its imposition are operative only from the date of judgment or formal court order or from some other specified date."
153 *Muschinski* v *Dodds* (1986) 60 ALJR 52 at 65, 69 per Deane J. See also *Re Osborn* (1989) 91 ALR 135.
154 See Hayton, "Developing the Law of Trusts for the Twenty-First Century" (1990) 106 *LQR* 87 at 96.
155 *Baumgartner* v *Baumgartner* (1987) 62 ALJR 29; *Muschinski* v *Dodds* (1986) 60 ALJR 52 at 67 per Deane J; *Hibberson* v *George* (1989) DFC 95-064; *Lipman* v *Lipman* (1989) DFC 95-068.
156 [1983] NZLR 140 at 148 per Cooke J; at 153 per McMullin J.
157 [1986] 1 NZLR 603 at 605 per Cooke P; at 607 per McMullin J.
158 [1987] 1 NZLR 586.
159 [1989] 2 NZLR 327 at 343-344 per Richardson J. See also *Phillips* v *Phillips* [1993] 3 NZLR 159 at 168 per Cooke P.

another version of the remedial constructive trust is developing[160] – with the emphasis here on the "reasonable expectations" of the parties involved.[161] In assessing these "reasonable expectations", the factors to be taken into account include (1) the degree of sacrifice by the claimant[162]; (2) the broadly measurable contributions of the claimant by comparison with the value of the broadly measurable benefits received[163]; and (3) any contrary stipulation or agreement.[164]

As with the Canadian and Australian models, contributions in respect of the New Zealand constructive trust can be indirect or non-financial. The rendering of domestic services is sufficient: in *Keogh* Cooke P cited with approval the passage from the Canadian case of *Everson* v *Rich*[165] to the effect that no one should expect spousal services for free.[166] Richardson J in his judgment held that there should be no presumption that a contribution of a monetary nature is of greater value than a contribution of a non-monetary nature.[167] Further, and again following the lead taken in Canada and Australia, the judges in *Keogh* anticipated the possibility of a monetary rather than a proprietary award in suitable cases.[168]

Unlike its Canadian counterpart, it seems that the New Zealand remedial constructive trust requires no causal link between the contributions and the property.[169] Moreover, whatever type of contribution is relied upon and whether the court awards proprietary or monetary relief, the "reasonable expectation" must relate to the acquisition of a beneficial interest in property.[170]

---

160 Cooke P at [1989] 2 NZLR 327, 330, described the case as "a stage in the evolution of the New Zealand law of constructive trusts and the like."

161 "Whatever legal label or rubric cases in this field are placed under, reasonable expectations in the light of the conduct of the parties are at the heart of the matter": [1989] 2 NZLR 327 at 331 per Cooke P; at 352 per Bisson J. See also the formulation of the test in *Cossey* v *Bach* [1992] 3 NZLR 612 at 626 per Fisher J.

162 Including the length of the union, and whether other opportunities were foregone: [1989] 2 NZLR 327 at 334 per Cooke P.

163 *Cossey* v *Bach* [1992] 3 NZLR 612 at 631, 632 per Fisher J.

164 *Gillies* v *Keogh* [1989] 2 NZLR 327 at 334 per Cooke P. On the facts of *Keogh*, the CA held that because the appellant made it clear to the respondent at all times that the house was hers and hers alone, the respondent could not have reasonably understood that he was acquiring any interest. His claim therefore failed. See also *Cossey* v *Bach* [1992] 3 NZLR 612 at 627-629, 631-632 per Fisher J; *Daly* v *Gilbert* [1993] 3 NZLR 731 at 737 per Hammond J. *Cp. Gibb* v *MacDonnell* [1992] 3 NZLR 475, below.

165 (1989) 53 DLR (4th) 470 at 472 per Sherstobitoff JA.

166 [1989] 2 NZLR 327 at 332. See also Richardson J at 346; *Cossey* v *Bach* [1992] 3 NZLR 612 at 632.

167 At 346 per Richardson J – using very similar wording to that contained in s18(1) of the New Zealand Matrimonial Property Act 1976 in respect of contributions to the matrimonial partnership.

168 [1989] 2 NZLR 327 at 335; *Cossey* v *Bach* [1992] 3 NZLR 612 at 631. For examples of monetary awards, see *Terry John Ireland* v *Lorraine June Hepurn* (Palmerston North HC 19, April 1991, CP 221/89) (award of $6,000), and commentary by Francis, [1991] *NZLJ* 223; *Nash* v *Nash* (Auckland, CP 2400/8, 3 Sept 1992); *D* v *A* (1992) 9 FRNZ 43. For proprietary awards, see *Cossey* v *Bach* [1992] 3 NZLR 612.

169 *Cossey* v *Bach* [1992] 3 NZLR 612 at 630-631 per Fisher J.

170 *Pasi* v *Kamana* [1986] 1 NZLR 603 at 605 per Cooke P; *Cossey* v *Bach* [1992] 3 NZLR 612 at 626, 632 per Fisher J, although he also held that a rebuttable presumption of reasonable expectation would apply in cases of "stable and enduring" *de facto* relationships.

There are indications, both in *Keogh*[171] and in later caselaw, of considerable anxiety that these new developments be kept within manageable bounds. In particular, many judges feel that the remedial constructive trust should be confined in application to cases involving *de facto* relationships and that the doctrine is inappropriate in a commercial context.[172] Two recent developments nevertheless suggest that, at least within the domestic context, the same reluctance to broaden the scope of the doctrine does not apply. First, it was held in *Gibb* v *MacDonnell*[173] that a reasonable expectation as to a possessory (as opposed to a proprietary)[174] interest gave rise to a restitutionary remedy in equitable damages. Second, in the recent case of *Daly* v *Gilbert*[175], despite an express finding that there had been no reasonable expectation as to either a proprietary or a possessory interest, Hammond J nevertheless granted a monetary award based in part on *quantum meruit* and in part on unjust enrichment.[176] He was, moreover, ready to contemplate the possible eventual acceptance in New Zealand of a general principle of unjust enrichment.[177]

The New Zealand remedial constructive trust is still in the early stages of its development, but already nevertheless represents a definite and deliberate shift away from the strictures and artificialities of the orthodox constructive trust. Although certain inconsistencies and problems remain to be resolved[178],

---

171 Thus at [1989] 2 NZLR 327, 331 Cooke P was at pains to point out that although the question of third party rights did not call for consideration on the facts of the case, nevertheless "certainly a third party dealing without notice, in good faith and for value cannot be affected by a *de facto* partner's interest." See also Casey J at 348-349.

172 *Gillies* v *Keogh* [1989] 2 NZLR 327 at 333 per Cooke P, at 348-349 per Casey J; *Partridge* v *Moller* (1990) 6 FRNZ 147; *Marshall Futures Ltd* v *Marshall* [1992] 1 NZLR 316 at 325-326 per Tipping J, criticising *Powell* v *Thompson* [1991] 1 NZLR 597 (Thomas J applied the doctrine in a commercial context). *Cp.* the opinion of McLachlin J in Sup C of Canada in *Peter* v *Beblow* [1993] 1 SCR 980 at 996-997 that "clarity and doctrinal integrity" require that no distinction be drawn between commercial and family cases.

173 [1992] 3 NZLR 475.

174 The defendant had at all times made it clear to the plaintiff that the house was purchased in her sole name to ensure that her own proprietary interest was preserved and so that she could protect the interests of her children by a previous marriage. Reasonable expectation as to possessory interest was implied from conduct: at 480.

175 [1993] 3 NZLR 731.

176 At 740-741. The *quantum meruit* award was in respect of services and materials contributed to the construction of a house which the plaintiff admitted was intended to belong to the defendant alone; the unjust enrichment award concerned the sum of $7,000 that the plaintiff paid towards the purchase of a car five days before the couple separated. To determine whether the enrichment was unjust, Hammond J applied Birks' tests of "free choice" and "incontrovertible benefit".

177 [1993] 3 NZLR 731 at 739, 740. He acknowledged, at 739, that many lawyers react with "instant alarm" to any such suggestion. In *Gillies* v *Keogh* [1989] 2 NZLR 327, Casey J at 348-349 admitted that he had "reservations about the extension beyond this area of a concept of unconscionability based on the frustration of the parties' reasonable expectations, or on unjust enrichment".

178 *E.g.*, there are conflicting comments on the level of contribution required: in *Keogh*, Cooke P stated at [1989] 2 NZLR 327, 334 that "Contributions to household expenses, or to maintenance, repairs or additions, may amount to no more than fair payment for board and lodging and the advantages of a home for the time being. More than that is commonly needed to justify an award." In *Cossey* v *Bach* [1992] 3 NZLR 612, Fisher J at 631, 632, held that "even intangible contributions of little measurable value" could qualify. See also *Terry John Ireland* v *Lorraine June Hepurn* (Palmerston North, HC, 19 Apr 1991, CP 221/89), [1991] NZLR 223.

this shift has resulted in a doctrine which much more closely accommodates the diverse living patterns of modern society in general[179], and the needs of the homemaking claimant in particular.

Quantifying the remedy

Within as well as between jurisdictions, there exists a lack of consensus as to how to quantify awards to home-making claimants. There seems to be general agreement that the size of any award, whether monetary or proprietary, should reflect the contributions of the claimant while making allowance for the compensating benefits received.[180] In addition, most judges feel that a broad approach is to be preferred to one that requires a detailed scrutiny of every benefit conferred and received.[181] Beyond these basic points, however, approaches range from calculating the award on the basis of the minimum wage of a domestic cleaner or housekeeper[182], to a division of assets by analogy with that which occurs on the dissolution of a partnership.[183]

The judges in *Peter* v *Beblow*[184] discussed the issue of quantification in terms of a choice between the "value received" and the "value survived" approaches. "Value received" is determined by assessing the value of the services rendered by the claimant[185], often by reference to what a housekeeper would have been paid after a deduction for board and lodging.[186] "Value survived" is calculated by determining what portion of the property is attributable to the claimant's efforts.[187] To equate homemaker contributions with those of a paid domestic is to relegate the homemaker to the status of servant. Such an approach devalues and misrepresents the contributions and role of the homemaker[188], and ignores

---

179 In *Phillips* v *Phillips* [1993] 3 NZLR 159 at 170, Cooke P commented that the "reasonable expectations" test "appears to be working reasonably well". See, in similar vein, *Gillies* v *Keogh* [1989] 2 NZLR 327 at 352 per Bisson J.

180 *Pettkus* v *Becker* (1981) 117 DLR (3d) 257 at 277 per Dickson J; *Peter* v *Beblow* [1993] 1 SCR 890 at 998-999 per McLachlin J; *Cossey* v *Bach* [1992] 3 NZLR 612 at 631 per Fisher J; *Grant* v *Moore* (1993) 48 RFL (3d) 345 (Br Col Sup Ct) at 352 per Selbie J.

181 *Gibb* v *MacDonnell* [1992] 3 NZLR 475 at 481 per Anderson J; *Griffith* v *Anderson* (1993) 48 RFL (3d) 390 (Br Col CA) at 391 per Hinkson JA; *Peter* v *Beblow* [1993] 1 SCR 980 at 1000 per McLachlin J, at 1014, 1016 per Cory J. See also Parkinson, "Beyond *Pettkus* v *Becker*: Quantifying Relief for Unjust Enrichment" (1993) 43 *UTLJ* 217.

182 *Herman* v *Smith* (1984) 42 RFL (2d) 154 (Alta QB).

183 *Baumgartner* v *Baumgartner* (1987) 62 ALJR 29. Such an approach was rejected as inappropriate on the facts of *Phillips* v *Phillips* [1993] 3 NZLR 159 at 170 by Cooke P. In *Peter* v *Beblow* [1993] 1 SCR 980, McLachlin J at 1001 talks of the "joint family venture".

184 [1993] 1 SCR 980 at 998-999 per McLachlin J, at 1025-1026 per Cory J. See also Parkinson, *loc cit* n. 181, 217 at 228-230.

185 [1993] 1 SCR 980 at 998 per McLachlin J.

186 See, *e.g.*, *Herman* v *Smith* (1984) 42 RFL (2d) 154 (Alta QB). In *Cossey* v *Bach* [1992] 3 NZLR 612, Fisher J at 631 said that where a monetary award is made, "the interesting but unobjectable result is that proceedings of this type could sometimes seem to have much in common with the claims to net wages for housekeeping after allowance for board and lodging." See also Parkinson, *loc cit* n. 181, 217 at 228-230.

187 [1993] 1 SCR 980 at 998-999 per McLachlin J.

188 This fact was recognised by the NSW CA in *Black* v *Black* (1991) 15 Fam LR 109 at 114 (case decided under the New South Wales De Facto Relationships Act 1984).

the real cost of such services in terms of employment market sacrifice and impaired future earning capacity. Although in *Peter* v *Beblow* both Cory and McLachlin JJ expressed a preference for the "value survived" approach in that it more closely reflects the expectations of the parties[189], both unfortunately were of the opinion that the "value received" approach was appropriate in calculating monetary awards. It is difficult to reconcile such an attitude with the need, expressly acknowledged by Cory J, to take into account both opportunity cost to the homemaker and the enhanced "income, earning capacity and the ability to acquire assets" of the non-homemaker.[190]

There are suggestions in some judgments that awards are deliberately kept below certain standards for policy reasons. Thus the New Zealand caselaw includes several comments that justify on policy grounds the fact that awards made under the "reasonable expectation" test are lower in value than equivalent awards made under the matrimonial property legislation.[191] Even if it were possible to justify a deliberate policy of making lower awards to unmarried claimants than to their married counterparts, such an attitude is illogical. The judgment that penalises the unmarried female homemaker necessarily and inevitably also has the effect of rewarding the unmarried male.

Resulting and constructive trusts – conclusions

From the foregoing discussion it becomes apparent that English constructive trust principles are far less capable of dealing adequately with the problems of the homemaking claimant than are their newly developed counterparts in other common law jurisdictions. In essence, and in spite of various difficulties that remain to be resolved, the "remedial" constructive trust can be seen in the present context to have three important advantages over current English doctrine.

Abandonment of the search for "common intention"

The remedial constructive trust, based as it is on broad and fluid equitable principles, has the advantage that judges no longer need to rely on the traditional juristic basis of the constructive trust – common intention. Judges in all common law jurisdictions have criticised the difficulties and artificiality of endeavouring to "glean phantom

---

189 [1993] 1 SCR 980 at 999 per McLachlin J; at 1025-1026 per Cory J.

190 [1993] 1 SCR 980 at 1015, 1016. See also *Gillies* v *Keogh* [1989] 2 NZLR 327 at 333 per Cooke P. Opportunity cost to the homemaker was an element in the calculation in *Baumgartner*, n. 149 above and text.

191 *Daly* v *Gilbert* [1992] 3 NZLR 731 at 736 per Hammond J; *D* v *A* (1992) 9 FRNZ 43 per Doogue J. In *Phillips* v *Phillips* [1993] 3 NZLR 159, Cooke P at 171 said that a "particularly meritorious" claim would be needed to justify division of assets as in divorce. *Cp. Black* v *Black* (1991) 15 Fam LR 109 at 114, where the NSW CA expressly rejected the idea that the homemaker contributions of a *de facto* partner were in some way inferior to those of a spouse.

intent"[192] about beneficial entitlement from the conduct of people who at the relevant time almost certainly did not turn their minds to the question at all. The initial investigation as to common intention that a judge must make in determining a claim based on orthodox constructive trust doctrine[193] means, as Waite J said in *Hammond* v *Mitchell*:

> "that the tenderest exchanges of a common law courtship may assume an unforeseen significance many years later when they are brought under equity's microscope and subjected to an analysis under which many thousands of pounds of value may be liable to turn on fine questions as to whether the relevant words were spoken in earnest or in dalliance and with or without representational intent."[194]

Recognition of indirect or non-financial contributions

The second advantage that the remedial constructive trust has over the orthodox constructive trust is its ability – whether based on unjust enrichment, unconscionability or reasonable expectations – to recognise the value of indirect or non-financial contributions. As a parallel but equally important development, the jurisdictions concerned have jettisoned the presumption which still prevails in English law that domestic services are rendered gratuitously. The net effect is that in appropriate situations judges are able to grant relief – in the form of either proprietary or monetary awards – to homemaking partners.

By comparison, and despite the limited change of attitude in cases such as *Grant* v *Edwards*[195] and *Ungurian* v *Lesnoff*[196], English courts have remained extremely restrictive in their approach. Unless there exists extrinsic evidence of common intention, they adhere to the view that the rendering of domestic services is the "ordinary kind of work" to be expected of a woman, and incapable of generating any interest under a trust. In the words of one writer, "A woman's place is often still in the home, but if she stays there, she will acquire no interest in it".[197]

---

192 *Pettkus* v *Becker* (1981) 117 DLR (3d) 257 at 270 per Dickson J. For English examples, see *Pettitt* v *Pettitt* [1970] AC 777 at 799-800 per Ld Morris; *Gissing* v *Gissing* [1971] AC 886 at 906 per Ld Diplock; *Bernard* v *Josephs* [1982] Ch 391 at 404 per Griffiths LJ; *Burns* v *Burns* [1984] Ch 317 at 323-324 per Waller LJ; *Grant* v *Edwards* [1986] Ch 638 at 647 per Nourse LJ; *Lloyds Banks plc* v *Rosset* [1991] 1 AC 107 at 127-128 per Ld Bridge; *Hammond* v *Mitchell* [1991] 1 WLR 1127 at 1129-1130 per Waite J. See also (NZ) *Philips* v *Phillips* [1993] 3 NZLR 159 at 169 per Cooke P; *Cossey* v *Bach* [1992] 3 NZLR 612 at 627, 628 per Fisher J; *Stokes* v *Brown* [1978] NZ Rec Law 52 at 53 per Casey J; *Hayward* v *Giordani* [1983] NZLR 140 at 143 per McMullin J; *Gillies* v *Keogh* [1989] 2 NZLR 327 at 343 per Richardson J, at 348 per Casey J; (Can) *Rathwell* v *Rathwell* (1978) 83 DLR (3d) 289 per Dickson J; *Rawluk* v *Rawluk* [1990] 1 SCR 70 at 84 per Cory J.
193 *Lloyds Bank plc* v *Rosset* [1991] 1 AC 107 at 132 per Ld Bridge.
194 [1991] 1 WLR 1127 at 1139.
195 [1986] Ch 638.
196 [1990] 1 Ch 206.
197 Eekelaar, *loc cit* n. 48, at 94 (commenting on *Grant* v *Edwards* [1986] Ch 638).

Third party protection

The third advantage of the remedial constructive trust is the fact that, with the possible exception of the Canadian model, the right created under the trust does not arise until the time of, or possibly even after, the court award.[198] The later crystallisation of the trust-based right means that third party interests are better protected and that courts in consequence will not be wary of granting claimants relief because of possible detrimental effects on innocent creditors.[199]

In *Stokes* v *Anderson*[200], Nourse LJ in the Court of Appeal said that it was possible that the House of Lords would one day decide to solve the problems presented in the English caselaw by following the recent trend in other Commonwealth jurisdictions. If the decision in *Lloyds Bank plc* v *Rosset*[201] is any reliable indicator of the current opinions of the Law Lords, the comment of Nourse LJ is, regrettably, optimistic.[202] Overall, and in sharp contrast with England, the judiciaries of other common law countries have recognised the need to liberate the constructive trust from its "temporarily paralysed"[203] state, and have been willing to develop equitable doctrines in order to achieve social justice.[204] Cooke P in the New Zealand case of *Gillies* v *Keogh*[205] said that he was of the opinion that English law was "not out of line" with the rest of the Commonwealth. As the foregoing analysis illustrates, his comment was, with respect, incorrect.

Contract:

As with trust law, developments in other jurisdictions in contract doctrine have resulted in a greater ability to accommodate the needs of the homemaker. Thus, for instance, in American jurisdictions there existed for many years a "presumption of gift", whereby the rendering of household services within a "domestic relationship" was regarded as presumptively gratuitous.[206] As early as 1932 one American writer remarked on the

---

198 Under orthodox constructive trust doctrine, the court gives retrospective recognition to informal rights that have been created at an earlier point in time.

199 In *Midland Bank plc* v *Dobson* [1986] FLR 171, Fox LJ at 174 stated that courts should be cautious about accepting evidence of common intention when the assertion of a beneficial interest would defeat the claim of a creditor. In *Peter* v *Beblow* [1993] 1 SCR 980 at 1022-1023, Cory J was of the opinion that a proprietary remedy should not be imposed where the rights of *bona fide* third parties would be affected.

200 (1991) 1 FLR 391 at 399.

201 [1991] 1 AC 107.

202 See also the comment of May LJ in *Burns* v *Burns* [1984] Ch 317 at 333 to the effect that "the courts should be slow to attempt in effect to legislate themselves."

203 Wade, "Discretionary Property Scheme for De Facto Spouses – the Experiment in New South Wales" (1987) 2 *AJFL* 75 at 77.

204 *Gillies* v *Keogh* [1989] 2 NZLR 327 at 340 per Richardson J; *Pettkus* v *Becker* (1981) 117 DLR (3d) 257 at 273 per Dickson J.

205 *Gillies* v *Keogh* [1989] 2 NZLR 327 at 333.

206 See, *e.g.*, *Franklin* v *Northrup* 215 P.494 at 499 (Oreg, 1923); *Hill* v *Estate of Westbrook* 247 P.2d 19 at 21 (Cal, 1952); *York* v *Place* 544 P.2d 572 (Sup C of Oreg, 1975); *Keene* v *Keene* 371 P.2d 329 at 326 (Cal, 1962); *In re Gordon's Estate* 168 NE.2d 239 at 240-241 per Van Voorhis J (NY, 1960).

willingness of the courts to find this presumption rebutted in order to do justice to the merits of a case.[207] In later cases courts were to reject the presumption outright[208], thereby facilitating the successful resolution of cohabitation and other domestic relationship cases based on agreements between the parties.[209]

As regards sufficiency of consideration, early American cases show that most jurisdictions were reluctant to regard homemaking services as sufficient consideration to support a contract.[210] However, following both judicial[211] and academic[212] criticism, the Supreme Court of California in *Marvin* v *Marvin*[213] emphatically disapproved such decisions as exhibiting a "schizophrenic inconsistency".[214] The Supreme Court's approach has now been followed by the majority of states, even those disagreeing with the *Marvin* attitude to implied contracts.[215]

Similar trends towards facilitating the accommodation of homemaker contributions within contract doctrine are evident in Canadian caselaw. Thus, for example, in *Chrispen* v *Topham*[216], an unmarried cohabitant successfully claimed compensation for the value of household services which were rendered yet not included within the terms of an express cohabitation contract. In cases involving unmarried claimants, different jurisdictions have solved the problem of illegality of consideration by a variety of means, including severance[217], judicial acceptance of changing

---

207 Havighurst, *loc cit* n. 15, 393.

208 See, *e.g.*, *Morone* v *Morone* 407 NE.2d 438 (NY, 1980) at 441 per Meyer J (although refusing to apply the same reasoning to implied as well as express agreements).

209 Cf., however, *Roznowski* v *Bozyk* 251 NW.2d 606 (Mich, 1977), where the presumption was applied.

210 *Vallera* v *Vallera* 134 P.2d 761 (Cal, 1943); *Keene* v *Keene* 371 P.2d 329 (Cal, 1962).

211 In *Vallera* v *Vallera* 134 P.2d 761 (Cal, 1943) at 764, Curtis J, dissenting, stated: "Unless it can be argued that a woman's services as cook, housekeeper and homemaker are valueless, it would seem logical that if, when she contributes money to the purchase of property her interest will be protected, then when she contributes her services in the home, her interest in the property accumulated should be protected." See also *In re Estate of Atherley* 119 Cal Rptr 41 (1975) at 48 n. 11.

212 See, *e.g.*, articles cited in n. 15 above.

213 557 P.2d 106 (1976). Even though on the facts the plaintiff did not succeed in her substantial claims, the case has been a landmark in the development of this area of the law.

214 At 118 per Tobriner J.

215 *Morone* v *Morone* 407 NE.2d 438 (NY, 1980) at 441; *Tapley* v *Tapley* 449 A.2d 1217 (NH, 1982); *Cook* v *Cook* 691 P.2d 664 (Sup Ct of Ariz, 1984); *Caroll* v *Lee* Sup Ct of Arizona, Slip Opinion, Jan 6, 1986 (Lexis tst) – Vice Ch J Gordon: but here it was emphasised that the property in question was in joint names, suggesting that the court might not find such services sufficient where title was in the name of one party alone. *Cp. Glidewell* v *Glidewell* 790 S.W. 2d 925 (KY App, 1990) at 927: the court refused to allow the performance of domestic and household work to generate any rights in favour of a female cohabitant.

216 (1986) 28 DLR (4th) 754 at 760-761 per Kindred J (the parole evidence rule was used). *Cp. Lazarenko* v *Borowsky* [1966] SCR 556 (appellant's claim in contract failed for lack of intention to create legal relations).

217 See, *e.g.*, *Marvin* v *Marvin* 557 P. 2d 106 (Sup Ct Cal, 1976) at 114 per Tobriner J; *Stevens* v *Muse* 562 So. 2d 852 (Fla App 1990); *Shold* v *Goro* 449 N.W. 2d 372 (Iowa, 1989) at 373, 480 N.W. 2d 892 (Iowa, 1992).

public policy[218], or statutory reform.[219] In addition, legislation in many jurisdictions permits or even encourages parties to personal relationships, whether married or unmarried, to enter into contracts, and statutory provisions provide that homemaker services can constitute valuable consideration or that such agreements are enforceable "without consideration".[220]

The problem of housework: conclusions

From the above discussion it becomes apparent that many of the problems surrounding families and family life in present-day society are either caused by, or related to, traditional cultural, ideological and legal biases that regard homemaking as of little or no value.

There is clearly a need to enhance the viability of market employment for women. Suggestions aimed at achieving this objective have included increased efforts towards full implementation of equal opportunities legislation[221], better provision of public or publicly-subsidised child care facilities[222], greater flexibility as to working hours[223], job-sharing by both parents[224] and the encouragement of participation in child care and other household tasks by fathers.[225]

It is unrealistic, however – particularly in light of current Government policies – to imagine that large numbers of women will not continue to remain full-time homemakers, or that primary responsibility for child-rearing, homemaking and other caring tasks will not continue to devolve upon women.[226] It becomes essential, therefore, to implement policies that will accord to homemakers a proper recognition of the value of their work and increase their financial security.[227] Implementation involves not only

---

218 See, *e.g.*, *Latham* v *Latham* 547 P. 2d 114 (Sup Ct Or, 1976); *Andrews* v *Parker* [1973] Qd. R. 93 at 104 per Stable J; *Seidler* v *Schalhofer* [1980] 2 NSWLR 80 at 97, 99, 102-103 per Hutley JA.

219 See, *e.g.*, De Facto Relationships Act 1984 (NSW), s 45(1); Family Law Act 1986 (Ont), s 53; Minn Stat 513.075-076 (1984).

220 See, *e.g.*, Uniform Premarital Agreements Act, s 2 (Uniform Laws Annotated, Vol 9A, Matrimonial, Family and Health Laws, West Publishing Co., Minn.)

221 Coyle and Skinner (eds), *op cit* n. 90; Rhode, *Gender Justice* (Harvard University Press, 1989), 183 *et seq.*

222 Casey and McRae, *loc cit* n. 102, 31 at 38; Lonsdale, *loc cit* n. 93, 92 at 109-111; Millar and Glendinning, *op cit* n. 65, at 265-267. For an interesting discussion of how the problem was tackled in Norway, see Leira, "Time for Work, Time for Care: Childcare Strategies in a Norwegian Setting", in Brannen and Wilson (eds), *op cit* n. 89, 175.

223 Falkenberg and Monachello, "Can organisations respond to the role overload in dual-earner families?" (1989) 8(6) *Jo Manag Devel* 17; Casey and McRae, *loc cit* n. 102, 31 at 38-39; Phillips, *Hidden Hands* (Pluto Press, 1983), 56-57.

224 Joshi, *loc cit* n. 92, 258 at 261 (arguing that higher joint life-time earnings might be achieved by both partners working part-time than by the conventional sex specialisation of labour).

225 Coltrane, "Household labor and the routine production of gender" (1989) 36 *Social Problems* 473; Joshi, *loc cit* n. 92, at 261, 264-265.

226 In similar vein, see Ungerson, *loc cit* n. 65, at 63.

227 Stang Dahl, *op cit* n. 67, 90, states that "a minimum amount of one's own money is a minimum welfare requirement in a money world". It has even been suggested that women with no independent resources are at greater risk of domestic violence: Walby, "Women's Unemployment, Patriarchy and Capitalism", in Sawyer and Schott (eds), *Socialist Economic Review 1983* (Merlin Press, 1983) 99; Okin, *op cit* n. 82, 152.

the reappraisal of those areas of English law which currently deny recognition to the value of homemaker contributions, but also a reassessment of the weight given to such contributions within statutory criteria. This type of reassessment is beginning to take place in certain American jurisdictions, where courts are now instructed to take into account a spouse's "impaired present or future earning capacity" or "lost income production capacity" when assessing property reallocation.[228] Such measures should go some way towards improving the status of housework and the self-esteem[229] of homemakers, and may perhaps also constitute a step towards achieving a real, as opposed to merely formal, equality between homemaking and non-homemaking partners.[230] Legal recognition would impact on out-of-court activity[231] and, because of law's "constitutive" function[232], could also promote the reshaping of wider social perceptions of the nature and value of homemaker contributions.

---

228 Cal Civ Code # 481(a)(1)(b) (West Supp, 1992); Ohio Rev Code Ann #3105.18(e)(1)(m) (Anderson Supp, 1990). See further, Estin, *loc cit* n. 87, 721 at 749ff; and see also (Australia) Family Law Act 1975, ss 75(2)(j), (k), 79(4)(d).

229 The importance of the human dignity aspect of the problem has been emphasised by several writers: see *e.g.*, Loutfi, "Development with women: Action, not alibis" (1987) 126 *Int Lab Rev* 111; Stang Dahl, *op cit* n. 67, 90; Benería, *loc cit* n. 22, 384-385, 388.

230 Waldron argues that "having something to fall back on if an attachment fails may be a *condition* of being able to identify intensely with one's attachments, rather than something which derogates from that intensity": Waldron, "When Justice Replaces Affection: The Need for Rights" (1988) 11 *Harv Jo Law and Pub Po* 625.

231 See Mnookin and Kornhauser, "Bargaining in the Shadow of the Law: the case of Divorce" (1979) 88 *Yale Law Jo* 950; Ingleby, "Rhetoric and Reality: Regulation of Out-of-Court Activity in Matrimonial Proceedings [1989] *OJLS* 230.

232 Glendon, *Abortion and Divorce in Western Law: American Failures, European Challenges* (Harvard University Press, 1987), 8-9: "Law is constitutive when legal language and legal concepts begin to affect ordinary language and to influence the manner in which we perceive reality."

Chapter 21

The Property Rights of Cohabitees – is Statutory Reform the Answer?

Patrick Parkinson
Associate Professor of Law, University of Sydney, Australia

The need for reform

There has been a great deal written about the property rights of cohabitees in the last 20 years, and a variety of approaches have been taken by courts in the major common law jurisdictions. In England, *Gissing* v *Gissing*[1] seems to have given rise to a number of different interpretations over the years, with sometimes the emphasis being upon the parties' direct and "indirect" contributions to the purchase price, and more recently, with a focus upon representations and reliance, combined with a more restrictive attitude to the implication of intentions by reason of financial contributions.

Other Commonwealth countries, which initially followed the House of Lords in *Gissing* with variants of the common intention trust[2], have since developed different doctrines, based upon a wider range of the parties' contributions. In Canada, the Supreme Court in *Pettkus* v *Becker*[3] drew upon restitution law to develop a broad principle of "unjust enrichment", while in Australia, the High Court held that a constructive trust may arise where one party seeks to retain the benefits of a joint endeavour in circumstances which make it unconscionable to do so.[4]

These various doctrines have been extensively criticised in the academic and professional literature. Sometimes the criticisms have been made that the various doctrines lack consistency with established principles of the law

---

1   [1971] AC 886.
2   In Canada, the common intention trust was treated as a species of resulting trust: see *Rathwell* v *Rathwell* (1978) 83 DLR (3d) 289. In Australia, the NSW Court of Appeal held in *Allen* v *Snyder* [1977] 2 NSWLR 685 that the courts would give effect to the "common intention" as a form of express trust, enforced, in the case of land, despite the absence of writing in order to prevent fraud: *cf Bannister* v *Bannister* [1948] 1 All ER 133.
3   (1980) 117 DLR (3d) 257.
4   *Muschinski* v *Dodds* (1985) 160 CLR 583; *Baumgartner* v *Baumgartner* (1987) 164 CLR 137. For the development of the unconscionability principle in Australian law, see P Parkinson, "Doing Equity Between De Facto Spouses: From Calverley v Green to Baumgartner" (1988) 11 *Adelaide LR* 370.

of trusts or restitution.[5] More commonly, the criticism has been made that the various doctrines are too narrow in approach to encompass all the circumstances in which it is appropriate to confer equitable proprietary rights on a cohabitee. In particular, it has often been pointed out in relation to English law, that an intention to share property beneficially is difficult to prove, involving as it does a search for the "fugitive common intention"[6], while the contributions which might give rise to an implication of such an intention must be of a financial nature. Homemaker contributions are not sufficient.[7] Indeed, Lord Bridge indicated in *Lloyds Bank* v *Rosset*[8], that in the absence of evidence of expressed intention, only direct contributions by payment of mortgage instalments is likely to suffice to indicate a common intention.

If the problem of homemaker contributions is most acute in English law, it has also been a difficulty in Canada and Australia. In Canada, some provincial courts were unwilling to find an unjust enrichment where a woman's claim was based on homemaking, since, it was argued, her contributions to the welfare of the family were already compensated by the benefits conferred on her by way of accommodation and other support.[9] Only in 1993, did the Supreme Court of Canada resolve the conflict between the authorities in different provinces by making it clear that homemaker contributions alone could be the basis of a claim of unjust enrichment.[10] In Australia, the *Baumgartner* doctrine of unconscionability found its origin in an analogy with the breakdown of a commercial partnership or joint venture[11], and the courts have found difficulty in extending it to cases where the contribution relied on is of a non-financial nature.[12] In Australia, as in England, women who cannot show a significant monetary contribution to the household budget must demonstrate detrimental reliance on a common intention, or on the representations of the defendant.[13]

It is surprising, given the extent of the dissatisfaction with the existing law

5   *E.g.*, Meagher and Gummow, *Jacob's Law of Trusts in Australia* 5th ed (Law Book Co, 1986) ch 16, "Implied Trusts"; Gardner, "Rethinking Family Property" (1993) 109 *LQR* 263.

6   *Op cit* n. 3 at 269, Dickson J.

7   As Eekelaar has said: "A woman's place is often still in the home, but if she stays there, she will acquire no interest in it". "A Woman's Place – A Conflict Between Law and Social Values" (1987) *Conv.* 93 at 94.

8   [1991] 1 AC 107.

9   *E.g.*, *Connors* v *Connors* (1986) 1 RFL (3d) 94 (Newf SC); *Jourdrey* v *Gavel Estate* (1988) 29 ETR 233 (NS Co Ct); *Stanish* v *Parasz* (1989) 25 ETR 227 (Man. QB); *Peter* v *Beblow* (1990) 29 RFL (3d) 268 (BCCA). Other provincial courts allowed claims based upon household services. The Saskatchewan Court of Appeal commented in *Everson* v *Rich* (1988) 53 DLR (4th) 470 at 474, that no one should expect spousal services for free. See also *Herman* v *Smith* (1984) 42 RFL (2d) 154.

10   *Peter* v *Beblow* (1993) 44 RFL (3d) 329.

11   See the reasoning of Deane J in *Muschinski* v *Dodds* (n. 4, above).

12   For a review of the caselaw see Neave, "The New Unconscionability Principle: Property Disputes Between De Facto Partners" (1991) 5 *Aus J Fam Law* 185. In *Miller* v *Sutherland* (1991) 14 Fam LR 416 (NSW SC), contributions of labour in renovating the defendant's house were deemed sufficient.

13   *Green* v *Green* (1989) 17 NSWLR 343.

expressed by many judges and commentators, that there has not been more legislative activity concerning the property rights of cohabitees. It is the one major area of family law which was not until recently even the subject of a referral to the Law Commission in England, although limited statutory reform has recently been proposed by the Scottish Law Commission.[14] The tendency among academic commentators has been to examine ways in which existing equitable doctrines, or the law of contract, might be developed to deal more appropriately with such cases. There has been scant recognition that the variety of doctrines available may together be inadequate to deal with the situations to which intimate relationships give rise. Further, discussion has taken place almost entirely with reference to the rights of the adults involved in the relationship. The housing and other financial needs of any children born to the relationship seem to have been forgotten in the debates.

In Australia, however, four jurisdictions have enacted legislation which is unique in the world.[15] The first was New South Wales, which in 1984 enacted the De Facto Relationships Act, following a report of the NSW Law Reform Commission.[16] This Act gives to the courts powers of equitable distribution in relation to the property of the parties, confers limited maintenance rights, and has other provisions concerning the enforceability of private agreements. In 1987, Victoria amended its Property Law Act 1958 to confer discretionary powers on the courts in relation to real property[17], while in 1991, the Northern Territory enacted legislation in similar terms to that in NSW.[18] In these three jurisdictions, equitable doctrines continue to have a place (indeed they are preserved by the legislation) but they are generally only invoked in circumstances where the legislation does not apply[19], for example, between relatives or couples in a homosexual relationship. In 1994, the Australian Capital Territory enacted the Domestic Relationships Act which applies similar principles to all sorts of domestic relationship. It is the NSW De Facto Relationships Act 1984 which will be discussed here, since this has provided a model for the other jurisdictions, and the cases decided under this legislation have provided the major source of guidance for the other jurisdictions.

---

14 Scottish Law Commission Report no 135, *Report on Family Law* (HMSO, 1992) para 16.23 (see also n. 50).

15 The Australian legislation is unique because it divides the property of the parties in a cohabiting relationship. In some Canadian jurisdictions, maintenance may be awarded, while in other jurisdictions, including Scotland, marriage may be proven by habit and repute. For a survey, see Scottish Law Commission, Discussion Paper no 86, *The Effects of Cohabitation in Private Law* (HMSO, 1990).

16 NSW Law Reform Commission, *De Facto Relationships* (Govt Printer, 1983).

17 Property Law (Amendment) Act 1987 (Vic).

18 De Facto Relationships Act 1991 (NT).

19 There have been cases, especially some of the early decisions in NSW, where the court has declared the equitable interests of the parties – in accordance with the law of resulting and constructive trusts – before going on to determine whether further adjustment is warranted under the statutory provisions. This probably reflects a certain judicial discomfort with the statutory alteration powers in the early years of the Act's operation.

The De Facto Relationships Act 1984 (NSW)

The De Facto Relationships Act gives to the Supreme Court (and within limited parameters, to magistrates' courts) a power to effect an adjustment of the interests of the partners in any of the property they own as it considers just and equitable to do so. A *de facto* relationship is defined by reference to the paradigm of marriage. Section 3 provides:

> "'De facto relationship' means the relationship between de facto partners, being the relationship of living or having lived together as husband and wife on a bona fide domestic basis although not married to each other."

The jurisdiction to adjust property rights depends on evidence that the parties have lived together for at least two years, or that there is a child of the parties to the application. There is a residual power to allow an application if the applicant has made substantial contributions which would otherwise go uncompensated, or if he or she has care and control of a child of the respondent.[20]

The central section of the Act is section 20(1) which provides:

> "In an application by a de facto partner for an order under this Part to adjust interests with respect to the property of the de facto partners or either of them, a court may make such order adjusting the interests of the partners in the property as to it seems just and equitable having regard to
> (a) the financial and non-financial contributions made directly or indirectly by or on behalf of the de facto partners to the acquisition, conservation or improvement of any of the property of the partners or either of them or to the financial resources of the partners or either of them; and
> (b) the contributions, including any contributions made in the capacity of homemaker or parent, made by either of the de facto partners to the welfare of the other de facto partner or to the welfare of the family constituted by the partners and one or more of the following, namely:-
> (i) a child of the partners;
> (ii) a child accepted by the partners or either of them into the household of the partners, whether or not the child is a child of either of the partners.

The section requires the court to make an assessment of all the contributions of the parties to the property and financial resources of each of them, and then to adjust their property rights accordingly. "Property" is broadly defined so as to include all choses in action including a cause of action for personal injury. It also includes debts.[21] All the property of the parties, howsoever and whensoever acquired, is, in principle, available for distribution. This includes both assets acquired before the relationship

---

20 De Facto Relationships Act 1984 (NSW) s 17.
21 S 3 defines property as follows: "'Property', in relation to de facto partners or either of them, includes real and personal property and any estate or interest (whether a present, future or contingent estate or interest) in real or personal property, and money, and any debt, and any cause of action for damages (including damages for personal injury) and any other chose in action, and any right with respect to property."

began, and assets acquired following separation. The De Facto Relationships *Act* therefore does not specify a model based on the partnership of acquests. It is not confined to distribution of the property of the parties which has been accumulated in the course of the relationship, although an award has to be justified on the basis of a broad assessment of the parties' contributions.

The term "financial resources" encompasses many sources of wealth which do not give vested proprietary rights[22], such as an interest as a beneficiary under a discretionary trust, or an entitlement in a pension scheme. Interests which are not proprietary in nature cannot, of course, be transferred from one party to another, but a contribution by one *de facto* partner to the acquisition by the other of a financial resource such as a pension entitlement, may be taken into account in the allocation of the property of the parties.

The advantages and difficulties of the statutory scheme in NSW may be seen by contrasting the position at common law in the various Commonwealth jurisdictions. Although an equitable claim might be made in respect of any property which is capable of being held on trust or which may be transferred by an order of the court, in practice, equitable claims tend to be successful only with respect to the home in which the parties lived. This is particularly the case in English law. Where there are other assets, it may be difficult to prove a common intention in respect of all the assets of the parties. In *Hammond* v *Mitchell*[23], for example, a variety of assets had been built up in the course of a twelve-year cohabiting relationship, but the female applicant succeeded only in gaining a half share of the bungalow in which the parties had lived.

A further advantage of the NSW legislation is that, unlike the position in English law, there is no necessity to show a nexus between the contributions made and particular property. Therefore, it is easier to gain appropriate recognition for homemaker contributions. The NSW law specifically includes contributions to the welfare of the other partner and any children living with them, as relevant contributions under the Act.

A further point of difference between the NSW statute and English law, is that there is no reference in the Act to the parties' intentions. Indeed, they are irrelevant. This absolves the court from an enquiry into whether an intention was "common", or whether an intention should be inferred from contributions. However, it is by no means clear that the parties' intentions should be irrelevant. For example, in the leading New Zealand decision of

---

22 S 3 defines financial resources as including: "(a) a prospective claim or entitlement in respect of a scheme, fund or arrangement under which superannuation, retirement or similar benefits are provided; (b) property which, pursuant to the provisions of a discretionary trust, may become vested in or used or applied in or towards the purposes of the de facto partners or either of them; (c) property, the alienation or disposition of which is wholly or partly under the control of the de facto partners or either of them and which is lawfully capable of being used or applied by or on behalf of the de facto partners or either or them in or towards their or his or her own purposes; and (d) any other valuable benefit".

23 [1991] 1 WLR 1127; (1992) 1 FLR 229.

Gillies v *Keogh*[24], relief was denied to a male plaintiff who lived with the defendant for three years because the woman concerned made it clear from the inception of the relationship that she did not intend to share her financial capital, and financed the purchase of a home mainly from her own resources and borrowings. Cooke P argued in this case that underlying the approaches to equitable relief in Australia, Canada, England and New Zealand was the fulfillment of the parties' "reasonable expectations". In relation to this case, he said:

> "Although a party to such a partnership may have contributed by services or money to augment the assets owned in law by the other, or there may have been a pooling of resources and efforts, I think that a claimant cannot succeed if a reasonable person in his or her shoes would have understood that throughout the relationship, the other party had positively declined to acquiesce in any property sharing or other right."

Sir Robin Cooke's position is a defensible one. The fact that both parties have contributed to the household budget should not in itself be sufficient to indicate that a house, which is paid for essentially by just one of them, should be held subject to a constructive trust. The result in *Gillies* v *Keogh* would almost certainly have been different if the case had been brought under the NSW legislation. If parties want to ensure that they retain separate ownership of their property, they would be well advised to enter into a cohabitation contract, which is, in principle, enforceable under the De Facto Relationships Act.[25]

A further difficulty with the NSW legislation is that once eligibility for statutory relief depends upon fixed criteria, there will be numerous cases in which that eligibility is in doubt, and the court's time is of necessity taken up in deciding issues which, in applying equitable principles, would be irrelevant. There are ongoing issues concerning the definition of a *de facto* relationship. Would the equivalent of an "open marriage" come within the definition of a *de facto* relationship? What if the parties only lived together at the weekends because of the work commitments of one of them? What if the man lived for part of the week with one or more other women in different households?[26] Does cohabitation which is continually punctuated by periods of separation and then reconciliation come within the statutory definition if the couple do not at any time live together for a continuous period of two years? Many of these questions have been asked, and have had to be answered, in the few years since the Act commenced.

---

24 (1989) 2 NZLR 327.
25 A cohabitation agreement entered into with independent legal advice will only be subject to variation if the circumstances of the parties have so changed that it would lead to serious injustice if the agreement was enforced: De Facto Relationships Act 1984, ss 44-50.
26 This occurred in *Green* v *Green* (n. 13 above). In this case, Mr Green lived for a number of years in three different households with his wife and two other women, and his various children by them. None of the women were aware of the existence of the others until shortly before Mr Green's death. The NSW Court of Appeal decided the case in accordance with the principles in *Grant* v *Edwards* [1986] Ch 638.

Despite these difficulties with the De Facto Relationships Act, it is clear that for plaintiffs, there are great benefits in making applications under the legislation. All the property of the parties is considered, a wider range of contributions is taken into account, and in particular, the court may make an award on the basis of the homemaker contributions of an applicant.

The central question, however, is how the court's discretion should be exercised, and in particular, how far the court should be influenced by the analogy of statutory relief in the case of the breakdown of a marriage. This has proved to be the most controversial issue in the caselaw on the Act since its inception.

Interpreting the De Facto Relationships Act

The Analogy with the Family Law Act

In drafting section 20 of the De Facto Relationships Act 1984, the Family Law Act 1975 (Cth)[27] (which applies to married couples) clearly provided a model. There are numerous similarities. The De Facto Relationships Act mirrors the Family Law Act in making all the property of the parties available for distribution, however it was acquired. It also mirrors the Family Law Act in focusing attention on the parties' contributions not only to the property of each of them, but contributions made to the welfare of the family. There are differences in the wording of the De Facto Relationships Act and the Family Law Act, but in practice, there is little difference in the range of contributions which the court is required to take into account under each Act.

There is, however, a fundamental difference between the two Acts: under the De Facto Relationships Act, the future needs of the parties, and of any children, are irrelevant to the property adjustment process. By contrast, under the Family Law Act, there is a two-stage process.[28] First, the court considers the variety of contributions of each of the parties, including "homemaker" contributions. Typically, a couple who have built up their assets together over a number of years are likely to be considered to have contributed equally to the property, although there is no legal presumption to this effect.[29] At the contribution stage, initial percentages of the total wealth of the parties are allocated, and then a further adjustment is

---

27 The Family Law Act 1975 is a federal law. The Commonwealth has exclusive legislative authority concerning marriage and divorce, but has no right to legislate about the property rights of cohabitees. Cases are heard in the Family Court of Australia, a federal court, which may also occasionally hear cases under the De Facto Relationships Act. Normally, however, cases brought under the state *de facto* relationships legislation are heard in state courts.

28 *Lee Steere and Lee Steere* [1985] FLC 91-626.

29 *Mallet* v *Mallet* (1984) 156 CLR 605. Usually, an equal sharing on the basis of contribution would not occur if one party had brought in significant assets to the marriage at its inception, or had inherited substantial property, or had been engaged in entrepreneurial activity which generated significant wealth.

considered to take account of the parties' future needs. Where there is only a moderate amount of property, the custodial parent will often get a substantial adjustment in his or her favour.

Under the Family Law Act, lump sum or periodic spousal maintenance may be awarded in addition to the amount awarded as a property settlement. There is a power to award maintenance in favour of a former *de facto* partner under the De Facto Relationships Act also, but only in more limited circumstances.[30]

These grounds of similarity and distinction between the De Facto Relationships Act and the Family Law Act reflect the intentions of the NSW Law Reform Commission in recommending the enactment of the legislation. The Commission said that it was:

> "influenced by the adjustive jurisdiction of the Family Court. This model ... is suitable for the resolution of financial disputes between de facto partners. We take this view because in general the financial arrangements, or the variety of financial arrangements, made by de facto partners appear to be similar to the arrangements, or variety of arrangements, made by married couples."[31]

However, it did not consider that de facto relationships and marriages should be equated in every respect, and recommended that future needs should be considered, if at all, only through the award of maintenance.

The Partnership Approach and the Restitutionary Approach

The question which faced the Supreme Court of New South Wales in interpreting the De Facto Relationships Act, was how far the analogy with marriage should be taken. Implicit in the approach which the Family Court of Australia has taken in regard to married couples is the idea of marriage as a social and economic partnership, in which the husband and wife may well make quite different contributions to the welfare, happiness and financial support of the family unit, while both contribute equally in their respective spheres. The question has arisen whether the court should adopt the caselaw of the Family Law Act on the assessment of contributions, or whether a more limited approach is justified. Should cohabitees be treated as being engaged in a social and economic partnership for the duration of their cohabitation – justifying, in principle, an equal division of their joint acquests – or should the court assume a more arms' length economic relationship between the parties, in which case the court's role is confined to ensuring that the contributions each party has made both financially and otherwise, have been properly compensated? The first approach, which prevails under the Family Law Act, could be deemed the partnership model. The second approach could be called the restitutionary model.

---

30 S 27 provides that maintenance may be awarded if the applicant cannot provide his or her own support and has care of a child under 12 (or if handicapped, under 16) or [her] earning capacity has been adversely affected by the circumstance of the relationship and an order for maintenance would increase this by allowing [her] to undertake further training or education.

31 *Op cit*, n. 16, 150.

Under the Family Law Act, the parties are treated as having together acquired property during the course of the marriage (and any period of cohabitation which preceded it). The court proceeds on the basis that it is *their* property, and the state of the legal title is irrelevant except in so much as it may demonstrate an inequality of contribution between them. The difference between this and the restitutionary model may be illustrated by examining the treatment of property brought into the relationship at its inception. Under the Family Law Act, if the husband brought a house into the marriage, he would be credited with having made a major financial contribution, but this could be offset, to some extent, by the homemaker contribution of the wife, and other contributions which she has made in the course of the marriage. In cases where the husband brings significant wealth into the marriage, for example, a business or family farm, this justifies an unequal division of the "partnership assets", but when a marriage lasts for more than four or five years, and there are children, it is unusual for women to receive less than about 20% of the property on the basis of contribution, with further adjustments being made for her future needs.[32]

The restitutionary approach takes as its starting point the existing legal title, and considers whether the contributions of the other party to the acquisition, maintenance and improvement of that property, or his or her home-making role generally, justifies an alteration of that legal title in favour of the other partner. On this approach, if one party owned a house before the cohabitation began, the starting point would be that the house should remain the property of him or her, and the question for the court would be whether the other party's contributions, broadly assessed, have been inadequately compensated in the present state of the legal title of the property which is owned between them.

Very similar issues of approach have arisen concerning the law of unjust enrichment in Canada. Under these principles of unjust enrichment, the court is required to ask whether the defendant has been enriched by the contributions of the plaintiff, whether there has been a corresponding deprivation of the plaintiff, and whether there was a juristic reason for the enrichment. The difficulty in applying these principles to cohabitees is that typically they confer benefits on each other. One may do the majority of the housework and contribute to the finances of the household, while the other, who also earned during the relationship and paid for various expenses in the household, already owned the house when the relationship began. When should those contributions of the plaintiff give rise to a share of the property? If the major increase in its value is attributable to inflation rather than to the financial input of the parties, what justifies a sharing of those inflationary increases? If a plaintiff bases his claim on his

---

32 *e.g., Lee Steere and Lee Steere* (n. 28 above), in which the husband inherited a farm worth over $600,000. The marriage lasted 8 years and they had three children. She was awarded a 20% share on the basis of contribution and a further 5%, as well as child maintenance, to account for her future needs, and those of the children. This was considerably in excess of her needs in terms of purchasing another house.

contributions in renovating a home or building an extension, how should those contributions be characterised and valued? Are they contributions to a social and economic partnership which would justify an award of a percentage share of the property, or should his recompense be the reasonable value of his services less the value of the benefits he has received? Although the matter of quantification has been considered by the Supreme Court of Canada in relation to the value to be attributed to housework, no clear answers have emerged.[33] In the lower courts, while some awards to cohabitees reflect the analogy of marriage, in other cases, a narrower compensatory approach has prevailed.[34]

The Early Case Law on the De Facto Relationships Act

The early case law on the De Facto Relationships Act indicated a restitutionary approach. In *D* v *McA*,[35] Powell J laid down a four-stage analysis. He said that the court:

> "... should proceed, first, to identify, and value, the assets of the parties; second, to determine whether any, and if so, what contributions of the type contemplated by s 20(1)(a),(b) have been made by each partner; third, to determine whether, in the circumstances, the contributions of the applicant have already been sufficiently recognised and compensated for; and finally, to determine what order is called for in order that the applicant's contributions be sufficiently recognised and compensated for."

The four-stage approach became the standard method of analysis in the ensuing years. It was justified by the judges in terms of the difference between marriages and *de facto* relationships. Indeed, one judge emphasised explicitly the contrast between the lifelong commitment of marriage and the situation in many cohabiting relationships, in which one or both parties make a conscious choice not to commit themselves in the way which marriage involves.[36] The result of this approach was that awards, at least in cases where the couple did not have children, tended to be relatively low. Courts were willing to make higher awards where there were

---

33 The Supreme Court in *Peter* v *Beblow* (n. 10 above) expressed a preference for the "value surviving" approach to quantifying relief, rather than the "value received" (*quantum meruit*) approach. However, the Court gave little guidance about how to quantify the value surviving from a person's contribution. The Court was vague about how household work could create value surviving in the property, and it largely ignored the benefits which the plaintiff had received herself during the period of cohabitation. It upheld the trial judge's award of the entire value in the home in which the parties had lived, without explaining why the woman's contribution was so great that it should extinguish the man's financial contributions to the acquisition of that home. The trial judge's award had been based upon the value of the household services.

34 For a full discussion, see Parkinson, "Beyond *Pettkus* v *Becker*: Quantifying Relief for Unjust Enrichment" (1993) 43 *Univ of Toronto LJ* 217. For a striking example of the partnership approach as applied to an engaged couple, see *Rabichuk* v *Cartwright* (1990) 26 RFL (3d) 206 (BCSC).

35 (1987) 11 Fam LR 214.

36 *Wilcock* v *Sain* (1986) 11 Fam LR 302.

children and one of the parties was involved on a full-time basis with their care.

An example of the restitutionary analysis is the decision, at first instance, of the court in *Dwyer* v *Kaljo*.[37] The parties lived together for six and a half years. There was a considerable difference in age between them. They met when she was 20 and he was 45. They had no children, but in the course of their relationship, she did look after his teenage son from a previous marriage. She was also his constant companion and social secretary, and supervised the household. They had a full-time housekeeper. At the time of the hearing, his assets were valued at over $11 million. She sought an award of $400,000. The trial judge, noting all the plaintiff's various contributions in the course of their relationship, applied stage three of the *D* v *McA* test, and asked whether she had been adequately compensated already. He observed that she had enjoyed a luxurious lifestyle, had received numerous expensive gifts and had travelled with Mr Kaljo on overseas' holidays. Nonetheless, he saw it as appropriate to make an award of $50,000. This figure was, to a limited extent, based upon what a housekeeper, performing the services of the plaintiff, might have received after tax, minus the monetary gifts she retained on the breakdown of the relationship; however the judge recognised that neither her contributions, nor their relationship, could be reduced to such a primitive accounting of the credits and debits on a balance sheet.

Applying the marriage analogy: the intervention of the Court of Appeal

The four-stage approach, or at least the restitutionary model which it implied, was effectively overruled by a decision of the NSW Court of Appeal, *Black* v *Black*.[38] In this case the parties lived together for eleven years and had two children. The woman ceased remunerative employment when the first child was born, and from that time until the breakdown of the relationship was a full-time homemaker. They lived in a house belonging to Mr Black. The Court of Appeal in this case accepted the view, advanced in the early cases on the De Facto Relationships Act, that it was inappropriate to apply the approach taken by the Family Court under the Family Law Act uncritically. However, the Family Law Act decisions could be of assistance concerning aspects which were broadly common to both Acts. The court gave, as an obvious example of this, the evaluation of the contribution of a homemaker or parent. It also rejected any notion that "a de facto partner should be regarded as in some way inferior to a spouse",[39] or that her homemaker contributions should be evaluated as less worthy of compensation than those of a married woman. Finally, they said that the commercial value of domestic services cannot be equated with the contribution of a homemaker and parent. A homemaker's contribution to

---

37 (1987) 11 Fam LR 785.
38 (1991) 15 Fam LR 109.
39 *Ibid* at 114.

the family unit will usually be much greater than the value of domestic services. The result in this case stands comparison with how the contributions of the parties might have been assessed under the Family Law Act, although had she been married, Mrs Black could have expected a substantial additional sum to take account of her future needs as a custodial parent.

The effects of this change of view were seen a few months later in the appeal from the trial judge in *Dwyer* v *Kaljo*.[40] This appeal was heard five years after the decision at first instance. The reasons for this delay are not recorded. The Court of Appeal, by a majority, increased Ms Dwyer's award from $50,000 to $400,000 (the amount which she had sought), and hinted that they would have been prepared to award a higher sum, if she had asked for it in her application.[41] The majority said that a claim under the De Facto Relationships Act is not in the nature of a *quantum meruit* claim for the reasonable value of the appellant's services, and nor was the rate of wages ordinarily paid to housekeepers an appropriate starting point. Furthermore, they said that while the Act may be used to secure adequate compensation for an applicant, it did not follow that the section was limited to compensatory orders. The court's power under the section is to make an order which is "just and equitable". They considered, by analogy, three forms of quantifying damages, and stated that the Act allows the court to remedy any injustice which would be suffered by the applicant as a result of her reasonable reliance on the relationship (the reliance interest), or his or her reasonable expectations from the relationship (the expectation interest), or the value of benefits conferred on the defendant (the restitution interest). Her reliance – by giving the "best years of her life" to the relationship – and her expectations resulting from the lifestyle they had enjoyed in the course of the relationship, justified the amount sought.

The dissenting judge adopted the restitutionary reasoning of the earlier cases. While he would not have interfered with the discretion of the trial judge, he indicated that he might not have awarded Ms Dwyer any compensation at all. There was no reason to suppose that the plaintiff contributed to the defendant more than the defendant contributed to the plaintiff. They each contributed to the welfare of the other, and received from the relationship the mutual companionship and other benefits for which they had entered it.[42]

The division between the majority and dissent in *Dwyer* v *Kaljo* reflects the arguments concerning the legal recognition of cohabitation which have been rehearsed in the academic literature.[43] For those who take the view that the award should be merely restitutionary in nature, there are pertinent questions which might be asked of the majority in *Dwyer* v *Kaljo*.

---

40 (1992) 15 Fam LR 645.
41 *Ibid*, Handley JA at 660.
42 *Ibid*, Mahoney JA at 654.
43 *E.g.*, the arguments for and against the equivalent treatment of cohabitees in Freeman and Lyon, *Cohabitation Without Marriage* (Gower, 1983) chs 6 and 7.

Had Ms Dwyer been only a girlfriend for that six year period, would she have been entitled to compensation? If not, why is it that cohabitation makes a difference? Had she suffered detrimental reliance upon the security of the relationship? If so, what detriment? Certainly, Mr Kaljo had never promised marriage. Had she given him the best years of her life? The majority's notion that the years between 22 and 29 are the best years of a woman's life is an interesting value judgement. In choosing to live those years with him, had she made a decision which required him to compensate her? Does a luxurious standard of living in the course of a cohabiting relationship mean that compensation should be paid to ensure that, for the one left without resources on its termination, a reasonably high standard of living remains possible in the years to come? In the approach taken by the majority of the court in *Dwyer* v *Kaljo*, there is at least the faint echo of that promise which has, for centuries, been made in the course of wedding ceremonies: "With all my worldly goods, I thee endow." As a result of this case, an entitlement to some of the wealth of another seems to flow, without more, from the fact of cohabitation with that person.

Thus a shift appears to be occurring in the NSW caselaw – from a narrow restitutionary approach in which the goal of the Act is seen to be to compensate for contributions which have not been sufficiently recompensed in the course of the relationship, to a situation in which the analogy of the marriage partnership, with the sharing of resources which this implies, is guiding the courts in their application of the legislation. The question remains whether this is appropriate, and if so, is the analogy of marriage in assessing contributions a suitable one for all cohabiting relationships, or only some?

Confronting the issues of policy

The equity of property adjustment laws

The difficulty which the NSW courts have had to confront, and which is reflected in this caselaw, is why it is that courts should make transfers of property between men and women on the breakdown of their cohabiting relationships? Why, for that matter, do courts make property transfers between husbands and wives under statutes such as the Matrimonial Causes Act 1973 in England, or the Family Law Act in Australia?

To these questions, equity jurisprudence has developed some partial answers. Taking the caselaw of the various Commonwealth jurisdictions, the reasons which have been given are essentially that the intentions of the parties are sometimes not reflected in the legal title to property, that the parties' contributions, particularly where they pool their resources in the purchase of property, are often not adequately reflected in the legal title, and that if equity did not intervene, plaintiffs would suffer loss through their reasonable reliance upon promises or representations made by the other.

These reasons, focusing on intentions, contributions and detrimental reliance, justify equitable or statutory modification of legal title on the breakdown of cohabiting relationships as much as they do when couples divorce. Yet the equity caselaw has thus far failed to address the most important reasons why statutory adjustment powers are necessary. These are, first, the detriment which many women suffer by relying upon the security of the relationship to withdraw from the full-time workforce and care for children. Second, where there are children, their needs for housing and financial provision. In short, while the equity jurisprudence is commendable in seeking to identify with some precision the "equity" which requires judicial intervention, its great defect is its failure to address adequately the implications of parenthood for the property rights of cohabitees.

The cost of caring

Parenthood tends to have a serious adverse impact on the earning capacity of the parent who acts as the primary caretaker, and this is usually still the woman in modern society. Despite the growth in the numbers of women in the workforce, the provision of paid maternity leave and the increasing availability of child care, it remains a common pattern for women to withdraw from the workforce entirely for the first few years after children are born, and return to work, often part-time, when the youngest child enters school. Indeed, although women's participation in the paid workforce in Britain has doubled since the 1920s, all of the increase in women's participation since World War II has been in part-time jobs.[44] Thus it remains the case as it was forty years ago, that women subordinate their earning potential to the needs of their families. They are, however, more likely to return to part-time work when their children are young, than was the case earlier this century.

Even where women work full-time, it is clear that their family responsibilities affect the jobs which they take. The primary caretaker's need for a job to have convenient hours and to be located close to home restricts her choice of employment and career mobility. This is at least a partial explanation for the concentration of women in a few, mainly low-paid, occupations in which they outnumber men. There is evidence that a substantial minority of women return to the workforce in a job which carries a lower status than the job which they held before child-bearing.[45] This is especially likely to be the case where the skills acquired in the workforce before childbirth were specific to that place of employment. Joshi and

---

44 Joshi, "The Changing Form of Women's Economic Dependency" in Joshi (ed) *The Changing Population of Britain* (Blackwell, 1989) 157.

45 The 1980 Women and Employment Survey found that 37% of mothers returning to work after their first birth returned to a lower status occupation: Martin and Roberts, *Women and Employment: A Lifetime Perspective*, (HMSO, 1984).

Newell found that while professional people such as teachers were relatively immune from job-downgrading, the greatest downward mobility was experienced among those such as better-paid office workers, whose skill and experience were most likely to be valued by the particular institution or business in which they had been employed.[46] Such experience, because it is not portable, is usually lost to the woman with her withdrawal from the workforce following the birth of her first child.

Interruptions in workforce participation, and taking part-time employment, both have a negative impact on women's career advancement and earning potential. Career advancement often correlates with the accumulation of experience and seniority within a place of employment. Thus continuous workforce participation not only brings in income for the present but enhances earning capacity for the future. Part-time work also has the effect of reducing earnings by comparison with employees doing identical work on a full-time basis. Studies have estimated this part-time effect as reducing earnings by an average of about 10%.[47]

Together, lost employment experience, job-downgrading, taking part-time employment – or full-time employment which is compatible with the demands of child-rearing – constitute the costs of caring for those who subordinate their earning capacity to their role as the primary caretaker of the children within the family unit. These may be characterised as opportunity costs: the costs of those opportunities which have been forgone for the sake of the child-rearing role. As long as the family unit subsists, those economic sacrifices are shared. The household income of the family is lower than it would have been had the couple not had children. However, on separation, one partner leaves with his earning capacity intact while the other's earning capacity is not only hindered for as long as the children continue to live with her and remain dependent upon her, but is impaired in the long term by the effects on her earning capacity of her years of withdrawal from the workforce, or occupation in jobs which are most compatible with her child-rearing responsibilities.

It is primarily these factors which explain women's downward slide into poverty on divorce,[48] a poverty in which the children share as long as they continue to live with her. It is proper for statutory regimes, in adjusting the financial interests of the parties on divorce, to give primacy to the needs of the children and to weight the property distribution in favour of those – usually women – whose earning capacity has been adversely affected by

---

46 Joshi and Newell, "Job Downgrading After Child-Bearing" in Uncles (ed), *Longitudinal Data Analysis; Methods and Applications*, London Papers in Regional Science 18, 89 (Pion, 1988).

47 Joshi, "The Cost of Caring" in Glendinning and Millar (eds) *Women and Poverty in Britain* (Wheatsheaf, 1987) 112.

48 This effect of divorce on women's economic position has been observed in numerous studies *e.g.* McDonald (ed) *Settling Up* (Prentice Hall and Australian Institute of Family Studies, 1986); Funder *et al* Weston, *Settling Down* (Australian Institute of Family Studies, 1993); Eekelaar and Maclean, *Maintenance After Divorce* (Clarendon, 1986); Hoffman and Duncan, "What are the Economic Consequences of Divorce?" (1988) 25 *Demography* 641; McLindon, "Separate but Unequal: The Economic Disaster of Divorce for Women and Children" (1987) 21 *Fam LQ* 351. See also Oldham, pp 107-122, *supra.*

family responsibilities, and whose freedom to take employment commensurate with their qualifications and ability is affected by their ongoing child-rearing commitments.

The cost of caring is likely to be the same whether or not the parents went through a ceremony of marriage. It is this reliance interest of those who, trusting in the security of their relationship, take the risk of interrupting or reducing their workforce participation which needs to be protected by the courts on the breakdown of that relationship.

In the light of this, the defects of both the existing equitable principles and the statutory regimes for cohabitees in Australia, may be more clearly seen. Equitable doctrines which require proof of a sharing intent, or reliance upon specific representations concerning interests in property, are not themselves sufficient to meet the justice of the case when women sacrifice their earning potential for the sake of child-rearing without their property rights being discussed. Doctrines based upon proper recognition of the parties' financial contributions are appropriate as far as they go, but do not assist people whose moral claim arises because they sacrificed their capacity to make financial contributions for the sake of the family. There are no equitable doctrines which properly protect the reliance interest of people in the absence of a representation concerning property rights, and the De Facto Relationships Act, by endeavouring to award homemaker "contributions", approaches the problem in an oblique manner. So too does the Canadian law of unjust enrichment. The added dimension which is necessary to make sense of the law is that which is emerging in the NSW caselaw, that the parties have engaged in an economic and social partnership, a sharing of lives, property and incomes, in which they have made contributions of different kinds for the benefit of the partnership. In such cases, it is the role of the courts to divide the assets of the partnership perhaps equally, perhaps not, but in a way which truly reflects the opportunity costs which have been incurred as a result of their role division.

It is the weakness of the unjust enrichment caselaw in Canada that this concept of a partnership of lives, property and incomes, is not clearly articulated.[49] There is a similar weakness in the De Facto Relationships Act, and perhaps, in the proposals of the Scottish Law Commission.[50] The unjust

---

49 See Parkinson, *op cit* n. 34.

50 The proposals of the Scottish Law Commission (*op cit* n. 14) may also suffer from the difficulty of how far to apply the analogy of marital partnership in quantifying relief. The Commission recommends that fair account should be taken of any economic advantage derived by either party from contributions by the other, and of any economic disadvantage suffered by either party in the interests of the other party or of any child of the family. This is based upon one of the principles for relief in relation to married couples in the Family Law (Scotland) Act 1985, s 9. The question to which this gives rise in quantifying relief for a former cohabitee, is to what extent the benefits conferred, and detriments incurred, by the plaintiff have been offset by the benefits conferred by the defendant in the course of the relationship. If they are treated as economic partners, then the court might intervene where one is left much better off than the other when the relationship breaks down. However, this involves, to some extent, an analogy with marriage which the Law Commission appeared to reject, and the discussion accompanying its recommendation suggests that it had in mind a narrower, restitutionary, approach.

enrichment caselaw and the Australian statutes suffer also from the defect that they fail to distinguish between cases where this sort of partnership has occurred – together with the reliance interest of sacrifices incurred in child-rearing – and those situations where the equity of the case demands nothing more than the restitution of money or property contributed, or services rendered, which, without the court's intervention, would leave the defendant with an unjust enrichment. In the De Facto Relationships Act, one set of principles, based upon the reward of contributions, is proffered to meet quite a variety of different moral claims. In short, the Act suffers from the weakness that it fails to distinguish cases in which the analogy with marriage is appropriate, and those where it is not.

Reforming the law: towards a new law of family property

In modern family law, marriage as a legal status is declining in significance. For the purposes of the law concerned with domestic violence, social security, housing entitlements and testator's family maintenance legislation, to name just a few areas, many jurisdictions do not distinguish significantly between married couples and cohabitees. The consequences for children of illegitimacy have largely, or entirely disappeared. By contrast, the legal significance of parenthood continues to increase. This is reflected in the British Child Support Act 1991, which includes a maintenance component for the child's custodial parent in its calculation of the other parent's child support obligations, without distinguishing between formerly married and unmarried parents. Indeed, the component for the child's carer is typically the largest component which goes to make up the maintenance requirement of a child. "Spousal" maintenance is now payable in Britain by *de facto*, as well as *de iure* spouses.

In the light of this, the question must be asked whether there is any reason for distinguishing between married and *de facto* parents in the allocation of property.[51] If it is parenthood which markedly diminishes the capacity for economic self-sufficiency of so many women, and if children's needs for housing and financial security are the same whether or not their parents were married, is there any reason why the law should not treat all parents according to the same principles in the division of the property? The principles contained in the financial provision sections of the Matrimonial Causes Act 1973, provide a useful basis for a law of financial provision which could be applied to all parents following the breakdown of their cohabiting relationship. The principles of that Act would better meet the justice of many cases if the courts were required also to consider whether the earning capacity of either party has been adversely affected by withdrawal from, or

---

51 See also Oldham, "Is the Concept of Marital Property Outdated?" [1983-84] 22 *Jo Fam Law* 263. Oldham argues that "marital" property rights ought to be triggered not by the ceremony of marriage, but by either five years' cohabitation or parenthood.

reduction in the extent of, workforce participation in the interests of the other party or of any child of the family. The numbers of people involved are considerable. There were 766,000 births in 1991, of which 30% were outside wedlock, and of these, half the parents lived at the same address.[52] While some of these parents will go on to marry, others will break up their cohabiting relationship without marrying. Reform of the law, even if it were limited to cohabiting parents, would affect a large number of parents and children.

There is less reason for statutory reform in the case of cohabitees without children. At least in Australia and Canada, doctrines have emerged which provide relief where the financial contributions of one of the parties are not adequately reflected in the legal title. Existing equitable principles already endeavour to give effect to the parties' sharing intentions – where appropriate – if these have been expressed. There are considerable evidential problems but these would remain even if statute recognised the parties' sharing intentions as sufficient grounds for relief. It is in cases where there has been detrimental reliance that equity may still be inadequate. There are, no doubt, situations where there has been detrimental reliance on the security of the relationship without a specific provable representation of an interest in property (which is necessary to give rise to a constructive trust or proprietary estoppel). This is most likely to occur where a woman has remained out of the workforce, or has worked part-time, while caring for the children of her partner by a previous relationship. It is possible that women may suffer economic detriment even where neither of them has children. There is evidence that while married women are as likely as single women to be in employment, they are more likely to be doing part-time work.[53] This may also be true of cohabitees. Career sacrifices may also occur where one partner leaves employment in order to move to another city or country as a consequence of the other partner's change of employment.

Thus even where there are not children born to the relationship, there may be a need for statutory relief. Yet how should such a statute be framed? Cohabitees are not a homogenous group. Furthermore, it is clear from the history of the interpretation of the NSW Act, and from the law of unjust enrichment in Canada, that an approach based upon an assessment of the parties' "contributions" alone is too full of ambiguity to be satisfactory. It fails to guide the courts as to how those contributions should be characterised, assessed and valued.

A comprehensive reform of family property law could involve a single set of principles being devised for married couples and those who cohabit for a certain length of time. The central factor in distinguishing between different relationships, and different sorts of moral claim, could be – rather than marriage – parenthood. The law should equalise the position of

---

52   (1993) *Social Trends* 23 (HMSO, 1993) charts 2.20-2.22.
53   Joshi *op cit* n. 47.

married and unmarried (but formerly cohabiting) parents for the purposes of financial provision, while granting the court the power to adjust the property rights of couples without children where they have pooled their resources in the course of the relationship, and where its breakdown would otherwise leave the defendant with an unjust enrichment, or where the plaintiff's earning capacity has been adversely affected by the circumstances of the relationship.

It is questionable whether such a reform would undermine the primacy of marriage. It might merely return the law closer to the position it occupied before Lord Hardwicke's Act 1753, in which a ceremony of marriage was not essential for the recognition of marital status. Such a reform would, however, have the important effect of ensuring that the courts have the same power to adjust the property rights of parents whether they cohabited within or outside marriage, and so reduce the harm which may be caused to children by economic deprivation following the breakdown of their parents' relationship.

Index